Crime and Justice

Crime and Justice

An Annual Review of Research

Edited by Norval Morris and Michael Tonry

VOLUME **2**

The University of Chicago Press, Chicago and London

The University of Chicago Press, Chicago 60637
The University of Chicago Press, Ltd., London

ISSN: 0192-3234
ISBN: 0-226-53957-1

This volume was prepared under Grant Number 79NIAX0048
awarded to The University of Maryland by the National
Institute of Law Enforcement and Criminal Justice, Law
Enforcement Assistance Administration, U.S. Department
of Justice, under the Omnibus Crime Control and Safe
Streets Act of 1968 as amended. Points of view or
opinions expressed in this volume are those of the
editors or authors and do not necessarily represent the
official position or policies of the U.S. Department of
Justice.

Contents

Introduction

One immodest aim of this series is to mount a sustained attack on the walls of disciplinary division that impede the acquisition of knowledge about crime, its prevention, and its treatment. The criminological journals present largely the work of sociologists, criminologists and, recently, teachers of "criminal justice." The writing of psychologists, political scientists, and economists less often appears; the work of lawyers occasionally; and that of writers from other disciplines rarely. *Crime and Justice* will draw from the traditional core disciplines but will also seek contributions from disciplines and on topics less fashionable in the criminological literature. This volume contains four such essays, two on historical research, one on biology and crime, and one on comparative criminal procedure.

The first two essays in this volume, by Roger Lane and Douglas Hay, summarize recent work by historians on the criminal law and its institutions. Both essays bring together bodies of research and writing that are growing rapidly and that have, in the main, come into being in the last fifteen years. Roger Lane's essay traces the early development of professional policing in the United States and recounts the evolution of a widely held view that violent crime rates declined during much of the nineteenth century. Douglas Hay's essay on eighteenth- and nineteenth-century England describes major changes in the institutions of the English criminal law between 1700 and 1900 and surveys work by social historians that seeks to explain those changes. The historians on both sides of the Atlantic are making important contributions to understanding the origins and patterns of our institutions for crime control; and the contrasts between the development of comparable institutions in the United States and in England are particularly revealing. These historical perspectives have too little currency among criminologists.

The subjects discussed in "Biology and Crime" by Sarnoff Mednick and Jan Volavka are not new. However, much of the writing on biology and crime appears in journals that tend to be housed in medical and other specialized libraries. The literature, while extensive, is detailed and scattered, and is not well known to nonspecialists. The essay published in this volume manages to present, in a form comprehensible to those of us untutored in biological research, the findings of psychophysiological, neurophysiological, electroencephalographic, and pharmacological research on the relations between physiology and antisocial behavior. The longitudinal research on the criminality of families, twins, and adoptees stretches these findings across the generations. The relations among genes, body chemistry, the environment, and crime pose questions that many would rather not confront. This essay takes a modest approach: it hypothesizes that biology plays *some* role in antisocial behavior and assesses each of the major literatures reviewed in terms of whether its findings should cause us to reject the hypothesis. None does.

Thomas Weigend's essay on French and West German criminal procedure contributes to an ongoing debate among lawyers and comparativists about the workings of criminal justice institutions in those countries. Some European systems are said to be both more just and more efficient than are American institutions: independent magistrates supervise investigations and control the police; professional prosecutors possess relatively little discretion over case processing; and plea bargaining doesn't exist. In response, critics have suggested that the differences between the two systems have been exaggerated, that they are formal rather than substantive, and that we do not have a great deal to learn from French and West German practice.

Weigend describes both the formal organization of the French and West German systems, and the findings of empirical research. He concludes that, as in America, the police control criminal investigation and the prosecutor possesses substantial autonomy over the conduct of criminal prosecutions. However, critically, he concludes that American plea bargaining has no analogue in France or West Germany.

The remaining essays treat topics that are more familiar to readers of the criminological journals. Three review major research subjects: criminal juries, deterrence, and criminal careers. One is a critique of Marxist criminology and one an assessment of the impact of prisoners' rights litigation.

So much for the menu. The meal you will judge for yourself.

Norval Morris

Michael Tonry

Roger Lane

Urban Police and Crime in Nineteenth-Century America

A B S T R A C T

Interest in the history of police and crime has been strong over
the past half generation. From the traditional historians' point of
view, the resulting scholarship has grown not only in amount but
in "sophistication," as sociologists and political scientists have
contributed not only their work but often their methods and
approaches. This development, however, seems to present
problems as well as advantages.

The history of police, as first outlined in rather traditional case
studies of nineteenth-century Boston and New York, has clearly
benefited from the myriad of subsequent approaches. The original
accounts have been not so much challenged, with few exceptions,
as enriched by later ones which stress points that had been at
least relatively slighted: cross-national comparisons with London,
the search for legitimacy, class conflict, social control, battles
over social values. Most disagreements appear to be matters of
emphasis, the result of differing angles of approach, or perhaps of
the differing times and places studied.

With the history of "criminality," however, consensus breaks
down. Traditional historical methods have yielded a reasonably
coherent, nonquantitative picture of professional crime and vice
in the previous century. But the attempt to measure the incidence
of most ordinary common law offenses against persons and
property, often using the "hard" methods of the quantitative social
sciences, has resulted in much disagreement not only about
methods but about values. While there is some hope that a
scholarly consensus may soon emerge about the rate and direction
of ordinary crime in both England and the U.S. (down through

Roger Lane is Professor of History, Haverford College.

I

most of the nineteenth century, up from about World War II), there are other profound issues which seem beyond the reach of "social science." The issue of how properly to define "crime," the degree to which "deviance" is social or individual in origin, the degree to which authority may shape or contain behavior— all of these, as yet, seem immune to empirical demonstration.

By the standards of a discipline professionally concerned with time and change, the historical study of cops and crooks is very recent, and yet evolving rapidly. Fifteen years ago virtually nothing had been written; today there are all the signs of a scholarly coming of age. For those tilling these adjoining academic subfields, the onset of maturity has been marked by such welcome signs as increasing attention, increasing production, and increasing sophistication. But it has also brought an increasing awareness of stubbornly persistent problems.

One sign of scholarly maturity, certainly, is the establishment of a specialized journal, *Crime and Justice: An Historical Review*, which began publication in the spring of 1980. A second is official or government attention, as manifested by the Symposium on History and Crime sponsored the preceding fall by the National Institute of Law Enforcement and Criminal Justice. A third is the appearance of assessments such as this one; each new book in the field now surveys the state of the art, and independent pieces have recently been contributed by James A. Inciardi, Alan A. Block, and Lyle A. Hallowell (1977), and in more sophisticated fashion by Michael Hindus (1979), Eric Monkkonen (1979b), and Ted Robert Gurr (1979).

Increasing sophistication, for historians, has been in recent years synonymous with increasing awareness and use of the methods and findings of the other and "harder" social sciences. In the late 1960s and early 1970s this simply meant that historians of police, for example, became familiar with contemporary studies in the same field, notably those by Michael Banton (1964), Jerome Skolnick (1966), William Westley (1970) and James Q. Wilson (1968). By the middle 1970s this awareness had extended not only to include such specifically criminological concerns and issues as labeling theory, and in such obvious directions as quantification, but to the use of social science concepts, definitions, and methods whenever it seemed appropriate. Several historical studies, or at least studies with an historical dimension, have been written by sociologists and political scientists.[1]

For nonhistorians, all of this interdisciplinary activity may be useful in at least two ways. It is one of the oldest and most valued functions of history simply to provide perspective, to separate deeply rooted phenomena from new ones, or to demonstrate, for example, that what is was not always so, and thus need not always be so. This is a function most consciously served by a book such as James Richardson's *Urban Police in the United States* (1974), a survey well designed to provide students of the justice system with some historical understanding of problems ranging from vice control to the abuse of force. Whether as raw material or as filtered through a professional's analysis, history may serve also as a body of data which criminologists, much like econometricians, may employ for a kind of retrospective testing of current hypotheses. This function, in particular, has considerable unrealized potential, if only because it has been so rarely recognized (Pepinsky 1978). Traditional historians may take an almost malicious delight in its negative application, demonstrating that much modern theory does not work when applied to the past.

But it must be noted that the bridge between history and the other social sciences has been traveled, so far, largely in one direction only, and that the traffic has been limited in nature. Public policy makers will find that we historians have rarely addressed their concerns directly, while social scientists may note that we have often used their concepts and methods awkwardly, without generating any useful ones in return. While any traffic at all must be regarded as an advance, since almost none existed only half a generation ago, there is obviously much room for improvement. The survey which follows, in indicating where we have been,

[1] Both the most ambitiously cross-cultural and the most ambitiously longitudinal studies in the study of criminality have been contributed by a political scientist, Ted Robert Gurr, the first in collaboration with Peter N. Grabowsky and Richard C. Hula (1977), the second on his own (1979). While both seem flawed by an uncritical attitude toward published official sources and secondary studies, the achievement remains impressive.

may give some clues as to where we are going and the obstacles we are encountering.

The survey deals with studies of nineteenth-century urban police and crime simply because most historical research has been concentrated in these areas. Modern police departments date only from about 1830; so do most of the usual records of criminal activity, especially those which can be used for quantitative analysis. For heuristic purposes, I have artificially divided this survey into three overlapping parts. The first is a simple description of the origin and development of police, and the second an account of various issues concerning their governance and purpose. The third surveys our current understanding of the nature, level, and direction of nineteenth-century criminality. As there is, for reasons which will be noted, no full consensus concerning the central issues involved, the viewpoint is necessarily personal, perhaps even idiosyncratic. But I think that most other observers would note the irony that as the level of technical or conceptual sophistication tends to rise between section I and section III, so does the level of controversy and disagreement.

I. Police History: A Synthesis

Writing the history of the antecedents, activities, and development of urban police in America has been facilitated by the simple fact that institutional history is an ancient form. And the first scholarly histories, my own *Policing the City: Boston, 1822–1885* (1967), and James Richardson's *The New York Police: Colonial Times to 1901* (1970), while they opened up entirely new subjects for study, were based on the kinds of evidence—the appropriate bureaucratic reports, newspapers, biographies—with which historians have always been familiar. Both these early studies were conceived and largely executed before the events of the 1960s made the study of cops a minor academic subindustry, and neither was much inspired by current events, or informed by current or prior work in other disciplines. It is perhaps a sort of tribute to the traditional historian's rather haphazardly inductive method that both independently identified substantially the same themes and issues. A partial list would include: the origins of full-time salaried police out of a variety of antecedents; the role of riot in precipitating changes; the origins of official responsibility for detective work; the symbiotic relation between police detectives and the underworld; the role of police in local politics; the continuing controversy over enforcement of the vice laws; the appeal of the London and military models for American reformers—and their lack of appeal for American politicians; the class and ethnic origins of policemen; the changing variety of their duties and deployment; structural reform and bureaucratization.

While some of these subject categories have been transcended by later and—by the standards of other disciplines—more sophisticated work, most have served as a kind of topical agenda, as later scholars have enlarged upon or modified the original findings about Boston and New York. It is possible, as a result, to draw a composite sketch of police development, using many studies without doing substantial violence to any.[2]

Well into the nineteenth century, despite much morally and economically ambitious legislation at the state level, American local governments had very limited powers of administration. Enforcement of criminal law, in particular, was largely the responsibility either of the community as a whole or of the individual victim of some offense, rather than something delegated to specialized agents of the state. Towns and cities encouraged individual initiative by offering rewards for the capture of badly wanted felons; groups of citizens might be called to form a posse to chase offenders or break up disorderly crowds; citizens went to court in person to swear out warrants against those who had injured them.

Some officials did deal directly with criminal law enforcement, but only as one of a number of duties. Centuries of legal independence and physical distance from the original British prototypes had created much variety among the policing arrangements of early nineteenth-century cities. Still, some combination of

2 In addition to Lane and Richardson, the following sketch draws especially upon the comprehensive work of Eric Monkkonen (forthcoming) and Samuel Walker (1977), as well as that of Wilbur R. Miller (1977), David R. Johnson (1979), and many of the others whose work is described below in section II.

watchmen and constables, sheriffs and marshals, elected or appointed, paid by salary or by fee, operated in every major town or city. The watch, in smaller places detailed only under the threat of war (or slave insurrection in the South), patrolled some sections at night, calling the hours, tending the street lamps, watching for fires, and (in theory) breaking up fights, answering disturbance calls, and arresting "suspicious persons." They reported typically to a head constable, one of a body of men who, like sheriffs on the county level, were primarily servants of the courts, doing civil as well as criminal business, the latter largely by aiding aggrieved citizens to make arrests once warrants had been secured. Most of what was considered the "police" function —and the word itself was then very nearly synonymous with "local administration"—was carried on by interested private parties, marshals, and inspectors, who examined health hazards and otherwise enforced compliance with a range of local ordinances.

However inefficient these arrangements—and the derelictions of the watch, in particular, were a standing joke—they had the enormous advantage of economy, in that the cost of administration fell largely upon those immediately interested, the complainants or victims who paid the fees. Their typically "reactive" nature, too, obviated the fears of executive tyranny which had dominated Anglo-American political thought since the seventeenth century.

The twin fears of governmental expense and power were equally evident on the other side of the Atlantic, in Great Britain itself. But there, after years of agitation, Home Secretary Robert Peel in 1829 was able for a variety of reasons to secure the establishment of a Metropolitan Police for London, the first in the English-speaking world. And with this precedent somewhat loosely in mind, the municipal authorities in Boston, New York, Philadelphia, and other major eastern cities in the United States all took parallel steps, over the next three decades, to strengthen their police.

In America, during this critically turbulent period, the precipitating issue in most cases was riot. Pauline Maier (1970) has shown that, during the pre-Revolutionary era, mob activity up to and including armed riot was frequently tolerated by governments either weak or wise enough to recognize that, in a period in which formal government was often unresponsive to local needs, it was foolish to defy deep-rooted community resistance to unpopular official action. Under the Republic, however, those who controlled local government were unwilling to admit the legitimacy of direct action. And during the long generation between the early 1830s and the Civil War, mob activity was in any case directed not against a few cowed representatives of a distant crown but against rival groups of private citizens, some of whom had the capacity to fight back and did.

Several elements combined to make this period the most riotous in our history.[3] The painful transition from a local to a national marketing system, the changes associated with the early Industrial Revolution, squeezed some workmen out of the urban economy and brought the boom and bust cycle to all of them. All the eastern cities swelled dramatically with mutually hostile immigrants from Ireland, Germany, and native hinterlands, just as national tensions over what would become the Civil War exacerbated tensions with and among the free black population. Rival groups other than the blacks could often count on support from youth gangs or volunteer firemen, all of them organized along parallel ethnic, political, and territorial lines, and all eternally battle-ready in the absence of any form of recreation other than drinking or fighting (Laurie 1973). The authorities were no better equipped than in the previous century to deal with mob violence. Neither elderly watchmen nor elected writ-servers offered much help, once the blood was up. As population grew, it was no longer possible for a charismatic mayor or alderman to step in and organize a posse among responsible citizens. The state militia, like the army in Great Britain, was the weapon of

---

[3] The study of riot, pioneered by George Rudé's analysis of France and England in the eighteenth and nineteenth centuries (1964), was boosted enormously by the ghetto riots of the 1960s. Most historians, following Rudé, have stressed the relatively limited, purposeful goals of Jacksonian and other rioters once thought wholly mindless. The literature is enormous; among the leading studies are Adrian Cook's (1974) of the great New York draft riots of 1863, the culmination of three decades of unrest and the bloodiest in our history, and Michael Feldberg's of the archetypal Philadelphia disturbances of 1844 (1975).

last resort. But militia companies themselves were often organized along the same divisive lines which inflamed the rioters, and it was both cumbersome and politically embarrassing for local leadership to call in outside aid. What was needed, the city fathers were apt to conclude, was a body of men answerable to themselves alone.

Following three major riots in four years, Boston commissioned a small group of such police in 1838; political jealousies and traditional fears held up New Yorkers until 1844; Philadelphia, perhaps the most riot-torn of all, had to restructure its local government entirely in order to create a single consolidated force in 1854. But in most cases the new police did serve the purpose intended, generally proving their ability to obey orders and deal effectively with hostile crowds of pro- and antislavery men, Irishmen and natives, whatever their own political views or ethnic affiliations. If they were not always successful—in protecting abolitionist meetings, for example—the failure was traceable not to a lack of means but to a lack of will on the part of local authorities hesitant to aid politically unpopular groups. But in Boston and, especially, New York, courageous efforts in the great anti-draft riots in the Civil War summer of '63 were proof of policemen's ability to transcend their private beliefs on behalf of those who paid their wages. And with the ending of the war and the passage of riot as a normal form of political expression, the fear of conflict between personal inclination and public duty was ended also.

In any case, if riot was often the precipitating cause for the creation of police, it had never been the only one. Whether over the course of fifteen years, as in Boston, or immediately upon their creation, as in Philadelphia, the new men displaced the old night watch and largely confined the constabulary to the service of civil writs. Meanwhile, citizens and city fathers alike found that a regular force of patrolmen answering to a central office and on duty round the clock was a conveniently flexible instrument of administration. The men on the beat gave directions, unsnarled traffic, returned lost children, aided victims of sudden accident, escorted drunks either to the station house or home.

The chief often inherited the older functions of watchmen and marshals, remaining responsible in Boston for public health until 1853, and in New York for street cleaning until 1881. Newer functions without obvious place elsewhere in city administration, such as the maintenance of weather records, also gravitated to the police. Homeless drifters, in the late 1850s, were given nightly lodging in the station houses; by the 1870s in the bigger cities, tens of thousands annually were put up in this fashion. In hard times, policemen sometimes ran soup kitchens for the hungry. It seemed natural, too, to assign the oversight and sometimes issuance of a variety of municipal licenses—for hackney drivers, pawnbrokers, and, most important, liquor dealers—to the "eyes and ears" of the city.

It was the group of issues surrounding liquor sales which came to dominate the politics of policing. Much recent political history has stressed the importance of ethnocultural differences in determining the party preferences of nineteenth-century voters.[4] Such divisions often found symbolic expression in battles over enforcement of moral codes. And for politicians the results of these battles had real as well as symbolic consequences. The sale of alcohol was associated with a host of other popular recreations and vices, from roller-skating and prize-fighting to prostitution and gambling, and the right to grant or deny such sale was measured in dollars as well as other forms of power. Shifting coalitions of Catholics and Protestants, Irishmen, natives, and Germans, Republicans and Democrats, state legislators and city councilmen, enacted a variety of policies ranging from absolute prohibition to nearly free license. But ultimate responsibility came always to rest on the police, who might enforce these regulations strictly, selectively, or not at all. The inevitable results—shakedown and shakeup, cyclical waves of protest—made this aspect of police work a matter of chronic tension.

Parallel problems marked the emergence of another function, criminal detection. The business of "thief taking" had never been fully a public responsibility, in Anglo-American tradition, except

4 On the ethnocultural approach to political history, see Bogue, Clubb, and Flanigan (1977).

for the occasional offer of reward from the treasury. While constables and other peace officers had certain obvious advantages in collecting these rewards, their legal standing was little different from that of any interested amateur or bounty-hunter. And in cases involving the return of stolen goods, or the finding of an unknown felon, as distinct from the arrest of a suspect named by the victim, it was customary for these experts to hire themselves out to the injured party. Problems arose, however, when such private arrangements were partially transformed into public services.

The first American detective bureau was set up as part of the Boston police department in 1846, a step followed shortly in nearly every other major city. But private competitors continued at work, and police detectives themselves found it hard to walk the line between public duty and private enterprise. In an era before technological aids of any kind, with criminal informants not the main but the sole available resource, an intimate familiarity with or even background in the underworld of professional thieves was often the only qualification for success. The need to protect informants and, when substantial sums were involved, the temptation to arrange illegal deals, sometimes at the expense of the victims, were more compelling motives than the duty to prosecute as the law required. Detective work, then, like vice control, involved law enforcers with law breakers in a complicated tangle of relationships as much mutually supportive as hostile. Once government and citizens came to expect and then demand that thief catching was public business, and so long as it took a thief to catch another, there was no way out of recurrent scandal and turnover.

Many groups outside of the force never accepted this situation, however. Elite reformers, in particular, repeatedly called up a somewhat idealized vision of the prototype, the London Metropolitan Police. This was understood as a strictly disciplined, indeed semimilitary body whose major responsibility was to prevent disorder and "enforce the law" almost mechanically and without favor.

Some elements of the "London model" had been incorporated

in American police systems from their origins, and others continued to appeal to politicians in power. It was stressed from the beginning that full-time police on patrol would have a "preventive" effect. While there were differences as to what they were supposed to prevent, and how, it was clear that they were to be more "proactive," less purely reactive, than their predecessors. And if this more aggressive activity were to serve useful public or political purposes, from staving off riot to closing (or taking assessments from) saloons, the men would have to be responsive to direction, as in the military.

There was little resistance to some aspects of the progressive militarization of the police. Supervisory officers easily adopted such titles as captain and lieutenant. Given the original importance of mass collective action, as in riot duty, and the prestige attaching to the military during the Civil War, the occasional adoption of such devices as morning roll call and training in parade drill seemed equally natural. Surprisingly little attention or controversy accompanied the official issuance of firearms, although this represented a major break with the British tradition. A host of historical circumstances, symbolized and reinforced by the Second Amendment to the Constitution, had maintained and even extended the colonial gun culture (Kennett and Anderson 1975). Many patrolmen had begun to carry pocket revolvers soon after they became common among sporting men and young toughs in the 1850s, so that the adoption of an official policy ten or fifteen years later only legitimized a long-accepted practice. But the most significant step in the attempt to impose a quasi-military discipline, the adoption of blue uniforms, was bitterly resisted.

The first move to uniform the police, in New York in 1853, was greeted with mass protests, resignations, and a number of civil suits following dismissals for insubordination. The same pattern, in some form, was repeated elsewhere through the decade. Some supporters appealed to traditional democratic objections to the wearing of "livery" and fancy foreign innovations in general. Underlying these symbolic objections were very real ones for the men themselves; a cop in uniform was easily spotted not only by citizens looking for help but by street toughs looking for trouble and, most important, by "roundsmen" trying to assure that he was walking the beat and not whiling the time in the comfort of a billiard hall or saloon.

Beyond the instrumental need for a measure of discipline on the force, however, American politicians were generally united in opposition to the deeper implications of adopting the London model in its entirety. The Metropolitan police commissioners were answerable not to the London authorities but to the home secretary; their men were deliberately chosen from outside of the city, and to preserve "impartiality" were encouraged to remain socially and residentially segregated from the citizens they dealt with. Nothing could be more alien to American political culture. Local police in the United States were supposed, like other municipal employees, to be politically active residents and voters. No political faction wanted independent or impartial law enforcement; the real issue was simply which one, and at which level, would direct the force. Ward leaders, as in New York, attempted to maintain control over precinct captains in their districts. But the same opportunities for power and profit tempted upstate politicians as well, and the police of Boston and New York as well as those of several other cities in the nineteenth century all fell for a time under state control. If a one-sided partisanship proved intolerable to the minority party, the solution generally adopted, as in many other municipal departments, was not nonpartisan but bipartisan rule in the form of a board of commissioners representing both major political organizations.

At the beat level, however, supervision from outside or above was in any case limited by the nature of the job as well as the job holders. While telegraph lines linked district stations to headquarters in the 1850s, call boxes on the beat were not generally introduced until late in the nineteenth century, and radio and motorized communications lay well in the future. Though called together on a number of ceremonial occasions and, decreasingly, during riot duty, policemen spent most of their time acting not in groups, or under specified orders, but alone and on their own initiative.

Nineteenth-century policemen were well paid but hardly well trained. With yearly if not daily wages comparing favorably with those for skilled labor, men from even the best blue-collar jobs could be tempted into police work. With some exceptions, however, chronic scandal and political vicissitudes created a high turnover. Little experience was accumulated and very little formally codified. New men were sent out on patrol with no training and few instructions beyond those contained in their cumbersome and largely irrelevant rulebooks. Left thus to themselves, they had to develop their own strategies for coping with life in the streets.

Relatively little can be learned, historically, about ordinary patrol work or routine interactions with the public. It is simple, in contrast, to document such highly charged matters as changing enforcement of the vice laws. The nineteenth-century judiciary, often unsympathetic to moral reformers, imbued with common law notions about the sanctity of property and armed with the Fourth Amendment to the Constitution, made it quite clear how and when vice raids and liquor seizures should be carried out. But the arrest of persons, in law, depended then as now upon matters of difficult definition: "undue force" and "reasonable suspicion." It is hard to tell just how individuals and departments reacted to the variety of characters and situations they encountered on the streets.

Following the Civil War, however, and the period of innovation and experiment led by the major eastern cities, the outlines of formal departmental development are relatively easy to trace. New and smaller cities across the country adopted full-time uniformed police forces, as Eric Monkkonen (forthcoming) has shown, not in reaction to any specific precipitant but almost automatically as a function of rank order in size. And in contrast to the variety of arrangements which had characterized the early nineteenth century, the tendency by its end was toward convergence, a similarity of purpose and function symbolized by the nearly universal adoption of uniform blue. Older departments abandoned such duties as the care of streets, lights, and sewers to more specialized agencies, and new ones never had to deal with them at all. Such charitable activities as the maintenance of soup kitchens and the provision of nightly lodging for the homeless were also surrendered. Since very few policemen ever followed their careers in more than one city, the means of communication between cities remain obscure. But police departments had long exchanged information about wanted criminals; communication was furthered by the first national police convention, held in 1871, followed in the late 1890s by the establishment of the International Association of Chiefs of Police.

By that time the formal responsibilities of American police systems had been largely standardized along lines still familiar. While continuing to deal with a variety of citizens' complaints and requests, police were charged chiefly with maintaining patrol, enforcing certain sections of the criminal law, providing detective service, and regulating traffic. The existence of thousands of separate jurisdictions was rarely reflected in innovation but only in differences in size, efficiency, and such politically sensitive matters as job security and vice control.

II. Police History: Issues and Questions

Most historians of nineteenth-century crime and policing would probably agree that the sketch given above, based on the framework supplied by the Lane (1967) and Richardson (1970) studies and elaborated by much other work, is basically accurate. Like the original studies, however, it is largely a political or administrative account, and there are a number of other possible approaches—social, statistical, and comparative—to the study of police. While relatively little work has challenged these studies directly, much has gone beyond them, exploring issues which had been merely sketched or even overlooked. Most of the later studies deal with the related issues of governance and of "social control," somewhat loosely defined. The issues are as important as the viewpoints are, at least apparently, in conflict.

The older studies provided only implicit answers to the question, Who controlled the police? To the extent that the force did not simply grow, like Topsy, in response to its own developing needs and experience, it was directed by state and local politicians. These nineteenth-century politicians were never a wholly homogeneous group. At the beginning of the period the city's social and economic elite was often directly involved in government. Continued growth and foreign immigration, however, forced members of that elite to share or surrender power to organized professionals drawn from the lower-middle and even lower classes. Few of these politicians, whatever their backgrounds, had ideological interests of their own, as distinct from personal or organizational concern with power and profit. Their attitudes, as a result, and those of the police they directed, were ultimately shaped by the expectations of the people who elected them. Thus with the notable exception of vice control, and certain obviously partisan functions such as poll watching, the police were supposed to operate in a fashion which would not offend any substantial number of constituents. Many functions were a matter of sheer administrative convenience; few denied the need for riot control, at the beginning, and it was assumed that most citizens welcomed a visible effort to combat crime and disorder.

Such a "consensus" view was and is obviously unsatisfactory to those searching for more profound answers about governance. The question of who controlled the police has wide ramifications, after all, if viewed as a subset to the question of who controlled the city, or the society, or institutional development in general. Among historians and other social scientists, such questions evoke at least some consideration of social class, and class conflict—and so they have with the issue of police.

The view that urban police were created by a dominant bourgeois elite to serve as "an instrument of ruling class domination," largely by suppressing working class unrest, has been championed most strongly by Sidney L. Harring (Harring and McMullin 1975; Harring 1979). The documentation for this argument has been drawn or extrapolated from the experience of the city of Buffalo in the later nineteenth century. Its dialectical opposite has been asserted by a sociologist, Bruce Johnson, whose provocative article "Taking Care of Labor: The Police in American Politics" (1976) argues instead that urban cops have served an important function as representatives of the "white working class community"; "Many of their activities have served and do serve to define or extend the (modest) social privileges of this class." Neither the "working class" thesis nor its "anti-working class" antithesis has found much support among historians, however. Although neither Johnson nor Harring has written extensively, the objection is not lack of documentation—it would easily be possible to multiply their examples—but rather that they have overgeneralized from insights or evidence limited in time or place.

Harring's insistence upon understanding the police as instruments in the repression of the industrial working class—and in dealing with the harassment of tramps, for example, he insists upon "working class" rather than "criminal class" or "lower class" more generally—clearly does not apply to the origins of American police in preindustrial eastern cities. Buffalo's force was founded in 1866, and local police were indeed used, after the Civil War, to suppress strikes and discourage "undesirables" in many jurisdictions. These were typically mill towns or smallish industrial cities, however, with relatively simple social structures. In Boston, the official use of police in labor disputes was forbidden by politically sensitive local councilmen; in New York and elsewhere, their use was not automatic but governed by such considerations as the number, appeal, and ethnic composition of the strikers, as judged by the dominant political organization.

There were in fact a variety of other alternatives open to capitalists and other bourgeois. Frank Morn (1975), filling a substantial gap in previous histories, has shown how private watchmen, often officially deputized as "special police," were used to patrol the central business district downtown. In Chicago, during the 1850s, serious thought was given to the possibility of relying upon these mercenaries alone, eliminating the publicly paid police with all of their attendant problems and complications. After the Civil War, too, small armies of railroad cops, for example, protected the special interests of the great roads. And as Bruce Johnson points out (1976), the Pinkertons and others were available for emergency strike-duty as well as to guard against vandalism and theft. As the Pinkertons became notorious, in some districts, or simply as state politics allowed, state police were organized to serve parallel functions. Only Massachusetts possessed such a force in the nineteenth century, but a number of other states, notably Pennsylvania, followed just before World War I. And it is significant that these "cossacks," as they were known to labor leaders, were supposed to live in isolated "barracks," free of the local pressures and community sentiment which made urban police seem "unreliable" to capitalist employers. Given these and other shifts in responsibility, Robert Liebman and Michael Polen (1978) have concluded, sensibly, that it might be fruitful to think of both law enforcement and the protection of property as police functions which were assumed at different times by private, local, state, and federal agents, as political conditions allowed—or demanded.

From any perspective, however, to conclude that nineteenth-century "capital" could not rely upon local police is not to conclude that "labor" could. Bruce Johnson's argument that the police formed a useful alliance with the working class seems an example of reading the present back into the past. For the past decade and a half the cop has been a favorite symbol, and "law and order" a favorite issue, among "white ethnics" who perceive themselves threatened by black neighbors in urban working class districts. But the symbolism results from the fact that black-white divisions have recently obliterated older ones. In the nineteenth century, the term "white ethnic" would have been incomprehensible for the same reason that a truly united labor movement would have been inconceivable. In a world in which differences in national origin and religion remained too vivid to allow any sense of class unity, the fact that cops were typically recruited from among white workingmen did not insure that they represented the interests of their "class."

A more sophisticated approach to the issue of class and the police has been taken by Wilbur Miller's study of *Cops and Bobbies* (1977). Not only the first comparative study, the book contains the best scholarly account of the development of the London police—its only competitor being the heavily legal and political and often turgid account contained in Sir Leon Radzinowicz's massive study of criminal law and administration (1948–68). And as the British, in the age of Chartism, were far more frank in discussing matters of class than their American counterparts in the age of Jackson, the issue becomes inescapably prominent.

Like all the historians who have published in the 1970s, Miller is thoroughly conversant with modern sociological studies of police. But his organizing principle is supplied by Max Weber himself: the issue of "legitimation," the process by which authority wins acceptance from the governed. It is this, he finds, which explains the often noted differences between the police in London and those in New York (and, by extension, in America generally).

The central paradox is that the highly undemocratic London Metropolitan Police, founded in 1829 by the last of the pre-reformed parliaments, was much less tolerant of abusive brutality—largely directed against the "lower orders"—than were their counterparts in democratic New York. The explanation offered is that in England the governing elite was so small and so conscious of its own vulnerability vis-à-vis the "Other Nation" that it was careful to insist that the police were merely impersonal and neutral agents of "The Law." In all encounters with subjects, as a corollary, individual officers were forcefully enjoined to patience and politesse. The rulebook in New York contained parallel injunctions—but the rules were often honored only in the breach. New York's politicians, in contrast to those in Britain, feared a "dangerous class" composed not of a majority of their fellow citizens but of a minority—albeit a large one—comprising much of the immigrant population as well as the more disorderly natives. Always recognized as partial agents of the party in power, New York's cops never won the respect eventually accorded Her Majesty's representatives in London. The fiercely partisan nature of American politics in the 1840s precluded any realistic attempt to appeal to "neutral" law enforcement, and those who founded the police, all of them potential "outs," were careful not to grant unchecked powers of enforcement. But there was a pervasive fear of violent behavior in the streets—New York, Miller argues, was a rougher town than London. And this fear helped prompt politicians, judges, and the middle classes generally to encourage cops, in the absence of such ex officio authority, to use extralegal personal authority, muscle and hickory, in putting down the poor, the criminal, and the riotous.

A great deal of historical attention has been devoted in recent years to those nineteenth-century institutions used, scholars have argued, as instruments of "social control," through which an elite hoped to curb dangerous tendencies in the "dangerous classes."[5] The relevant literature is too great even to survey here, but much police history, including Miller's, may obviously be considered from this perspective. Two of the most explicit studies are those by John Schneider (1978), and more comprehensively by Eric Monkkonen in *Hands Up: American Policing, 1860–1920* (forthcoming).

Schneider's account of the origins and early development of the department in Detroit is concerned especially with the physical and social geography of the city. He finds that the force was designed especially to deal with the progressively intrusive presence of a "bachelor subculture." The transient young men who populated the fears of the city's more settled residents formed an economically useful labor pool, but were also thought to represent a threat to established values, as their habitat, down by the river, was also the scene of much of the city's vice, robbery, and violence generally.

Monkkonen, although less concerned with origins, would agree that the police all over the United States were founded as instruments of "social control," but never operated simply as agents of oppression. Indeed, they became agents of "class control" in humane as well as punitive fashion. Even the humblest residents turned to the police for various services best symbolized by help in finding lost children, while transients took shelter in the station houses on cold nights. And it was often the cops themselves, seeking a vaguely "professional" upgrading of their own status, who rebelled against these untidy and unwelcome functions. Late in

[5] For a balanced critique of some of the major studies which deal with the "social control" issue see William A. Muraskin's evaluation (1976).

the century, in a move anticipating the current emphasis, they turned increasingly to the narrower business of law enforcement and crime control.

Those studies which emphasize political battles for control of police usually agree with Schneider and Monkkonen in stressing the cultural rather than the directly economic dimensions of class conflict. Such studies include several still unpublished, such as theses by Allan E. Levett (1975), and Maximillan Reichard (1975). The most notable published work in this category is Robert M. Fogelson's *Big-City Police* (1977), a survey of reform efforts which, although largely confined to the twentieth century, begins with a description of the situation at the end of the nineteenth. For Fogelson the battle for control of the police was simply the symbolic focus of a wider conflict between an entrenched native elite and a largely immigrant majority in the nation's great cities. The points at issue included differences over the nature of public and private morality, the nature of social mobility, and the proper locus of political power. Fogelson in effect defines the police in terms of those who were most critical of them, the often moralistic reformers of the Progressive Era and after. The answer to the question, Who controlled the police? is simply, as in the older studies, local politicians. But in contrast to both Monkkonen and Schneider, Fogelson conceives these politicians as primarily representing the immigrant lower and lower-middle classes—a development which Lane (1967) and Richardson (1970) would find typical of the late but not the early nineteenth century. Ward leaders insisted above all upon the right to appoint police captains in their districts, and used the force to preserve their own decentralized power base, to provide employment and an avenue of upward mobility for their supporters, and to regulate liquor, vice, and gambling interests, protecting them from competition and outside interference. This view seems flawed in many respects. It overlooks the fact that the police originated in an era during which urban politics was still largely dominated by a local elite rather than by representatives of the lower classes, and ignores the many and at least partially successful efforts at vice control which antedated the Progressive Era.

It tends further to confound all ethnic groups together, the relaxed and the puritan, the Catholic and the socialist, as well as identifying "ethnicity" too often with "class." But despite these faults it does rather starkly describe many of the political realities of the Gaslight Era.

Fogelson's book has the virtue, too, of showing—as do all scholars with the exception perhaps of Sidney Harring—that the police were never fully "controlled" from outside or above. In practice the generally decentralized governments of the nineteenth-century city were incapable of enforcing real direction along a hierarchical chain of command, as in the London or military models. And whether explicitly or implicitly—through the use of such passive locutions as "the force grew," or "the police developed"—scholars generally agree that in most cases the men themselves were largely responsible for shaping their own development and traditions. Some of the twentieth-century drive toward self-conscious independence was already evident by the late nineteenth. First Jerald E. Levine (1971), and then more notably Samuel Walker (1977), and John F. Maniha (1973), in what are respectively the most comprehensive and tightly argued studies in the field, have traced early efforts at civil service, at unionization, and at what later police reformers—although not scholars—would call "professionalization." But before such efforts, even before any substantial degree of job security or continuity had been won, some sort of police subculture was developing.

Much of the best work about contemporary cops assumes or describes such a subculture, one which underlies a high degree of internal autonomy. Among historians, David R. Johnson (1979) has been most concerned with its origins. His study, with materials largely but not exclusively drawn from Philadelphia and Chicago, is concerned especially with the response to the "crime prevention" function. From their beginnings, police on patrol were supposed to help protect citizens from assault and theft, as well as to combat vice in the form of drunkenness, gambling, and prostitution. Given only the vaguest of formal instructions from superiors, however, they had to develop their own means of implementing this impossible mission, a task complicated by a variety of legal and social restraints on their behavior. In dealing with real or putative "troublemakers," or "suspicious persons," patrolmen quickly learned to concentrate on those low-status groups—the young, the idle poor, the intemperate—which excited the least general sympathy and the most distrust. The principal tactic in newly formed departments in particular was to make large numbers of arrests for such minor offenses as drunkenness or disorderly conduct. The tabulation of such arrests, or body count, was also a convenient way of measuring effort in doing a job which in reality defied precise evaluation. It was quickly discovered, too, that in making such arrests, or indeed any arrests, a personal or departmental reputation for toughness, even for carrying and using weapons, was a decided asset. Superiors, then, often ignored the rulebook in refusing to discipline cops who used their clubs routinely—except upon respectable complainants. The men themselves justified brutality in terms of the dangers of their working environment. Discretion was learned rather in dealing with the world of vice—a world close to and thoroughly entangled with their own—whose entrepreneurs bribed, voted for, protested against, and socialized with police and politicians both. The law, taken literally, was no better as a practical guide in dealing with vice than the rule book in dealing with the street. The result was that the men developed their own code, one which emphasized personal toughness, tolerance of "deviant" behavior, and a spirit of emotional cohesion and mutual support born out of shared experience.

David Johnson's book stands alone in one highly significant respect. Most scholars would assent to its specific findings. Indeed, the whole question of who controlled the police and to what end has generated evidence which, while emphasizing rather different aspects and approaches, is in large degree compatible. Disputes have centered around accusations of overgeneralization, oversimplification, neglect, or omission rather than outright error. It may at least be argued that differences of interpretation have resulted typically from concentration on some short segment of an experience that stretched over several generations and countless jurisdictions. Thus even those farthest from consensus (and from each other), such as Sidney Harring and Bruce Johnson, may have something to say about Buffalo in the 1890s or Philadelphia in the 1960s. Similarly, if Robert Fogelson and John Schneider and I have differed in approach or emphasis, at least some of this is explicable in terms of the fact that New York in the 1890s, Detroit in the 1860s, and Boston in the 1820s were all rather different places. What makes David Johnson's approach unique is simply that he is the only historian of nineteenth-century development who has chosen to focus predominantly on that function which has come to dominate most thought about police work: the control of crime.

III. Criminals and Criminality: Problems and Promises
Questions about criminal behavior in the nineteenth century are far more complicated than any of the issues touched upon so far. A number of scholars, including several from Great Britain, have treated nineteenth-century crime as a subject in its own right. Moreover, if few have stressed it, all but the most specialized studies of the police, as described above, have devoted at least some attention to crime, and ventured some opinions about its nature and extent. The range of relevant scholarship, as a result, is far greater than with the police; some of it is rather naive while some, by the standards usual to historians, is sophisticated both methodologically and conceptually. There is agreement about some aspects of criminal behavior in the previous century, notably about the professional underworld, but much more remains in dispute despite or even because of the best of efforts. The one common point of approach is that most scholars have at least tried to assess the impact of various social institutions or developments, from professional policing to the Industrial Revolution, upon the shape and trend of urban criminal disorder. But the conclusions so far have varied widely, a condition significantly compounded by differences in definition and method. There is some hope, yet, that the newest work in the field may find general acceptance, and that better communication may dispel some of the current confusion. But much may continue to defy a scholarly solution.

The study of the underworld has proceeded along relatively untroubled lines perhaps because it presents few problems of viewpoint or method. Whatever their private views about drinking, gambling, and sexuality, modern historians are not unsympathetic either to those who sold "vice" or to those who bought it. Without much concern for distinctions between the illegal, the deviant, and the immoral, they have simply described these matters as the economists have come to do, as they would other and more fully licit enterprises. The general framework first supplied by Oscar Handlin in *The Uprooted* (1951) has never really been challenged. Since then it has been somewhat overemphasized by Daniel Bell (1960), elaborated in a series of articles by Mark Haller and others (Haller 1971a; Haller and Alviti 1977), and most recently publicized by Robert Fogelson (1977). Whether or not boxing, say, or liquor dealing, or gambling are legal at any given time, the worlds of entertainment, sports, and politics, of the saloon and the bookmaker, are and have been inextricably intertwined. Among urban youngsters physical prowess, street smarts, the ability to command a gang of one's fellows at the polls, on the field, or at the construction site were all interchangeable assets in the American game of success. Politics, the rackets, the labor movement were and are traditional avenues of upward mobility, just as drink and sport were traditional recreations among the poor and especially the immigrant. If there is any hint of indignation in a few accounts, notably Fogelson's, it is generally reserved for the established elite, the natives or reformers who would impose "middle class values" on the unwilling, blocking the route to power as well as stifling expressions of lifestyle or culture.

The sources used in describing the underworld, too, present no apparent difficulty except that, in common with most others, they become progressively less common as one moves back in time. "Penny" papers, which first exploited popular fascination with the underworld, date only from the late 1830s and 1840s, followed in a few years by mass circulation magazines. The police and police reports date not quite coincidentally from the same period. Legislative investigations awaited the formation of

the police, and autobiographies of cops and crooks awaited the
necessary public appetite for their stories. The major historians
of underworld activity, Haller and Humbert Nelli (1976), have
concentrated largely on the twentieth century, although their
accounts do stretch back into the late nineteenth. For the rest,
no one has supplied as much richness of detail as David Johnson
(1979).

Johnson is especially good at describing prostitution and gambling as business enterprises. Neither was a simple one. Each operated differently in different areas of the city, with prices and
institutions appropriate for each of the classes they catered to.
And if prostitution is "the world's oldest profession," gambling
has evolved continually. Johnson gives a richly complex account
of changing games and systems, ethnic differences, and the origins of such now familiar institutions as the policy racket and
parimutuel betting.

Professional thievery is not so easily fitted as vice into an interpretation which stresses popular urban values and ethnic social
mobility. But the relevant sources are similar, and as thieves
clearly inhabited the same underworld as gamblers, saloonkeep-
ers, and detectives, historians have described them in the same
dispassionate terms. Full-time urban thieves, as described in my
own police history (1967), seem originally to have grown out
of the British underworld. The matter of origins is naturally
obscure—David Johnson's account is the fullest—but by the 1840s
or '50s professional thievery had clearly matured in patterns
which were recognizably those of Edwin Sutherland's famous
"Chic" Conwell, in the 1930s (Sutherland 1937), or indeed of
the hard-core pros described more recently by Charles E. Silberman (1978). Highly skilled specialists in theory—not only con
men and fences, pickpockets and forgers, but several varieties of
burglar, each distinguished by characteristic methods and targets
—they were not quite so choosy in practice. While certain spe-
cialties came and went with technological advance and social
change, the loose fraternity of thieves remained marked by common associations, habits, and habitats. The nineteenth century
may have been their heyday—a period of relatively primitive pro-

tective systems, and widespread if never fully trustworthy police "cooperation." Partly because, like their British cousins, they generally sought to operate through craft and wit rather than violence, the popular press tended to glamorize as much as condemn them. And historians have followed social observers ever since Lincoln Steffens in agreeing that, as with vice, the police in big cities did not so much attempt to suppress as to regulate professional theft, protecting favored sources, confining depredations to acceptable locations and perhaps acceptable victims. But their mutual relations were tense, rarely lasting, and the estimate for the late nineteenth century is identical to that for the late twentieth: professional thieves could expect to spend a third to a half of their lives behind bars.[6]

For historians of crime the real difficulties arise then not with the relatively rational and well-recorded activities of the entrepreneurial underworld, but with the behavior, at once more and less routine, of amateur criminals, acts of desperation and violence, disorderly conduct, petty theft, arson, assault and murder. The questions asked about this have been far more ambitious than those concerning the underworld. Historians have sought not only to describe but to measure the level of criminal behavior, to determine whether it was rising or falling with time and why. These questions in turn have been sometimes aided but always complicated by the methods and approaches of other social sciences. Whether historians have consciously so labeled them or not, they have always been aware at some level of the issues raised by labeling theorists in their continued efforts, complicated by problems of viewpoint as well as of verification, to distinguish "real" from "official" rates of crime, the "serious" from the "trivial," those produced by criminals and those produced by the machinery of criminal justice.

My own thinking about these issues has gone through several reformulations as the result of criticism, reflection, and the impact of new work. And if I may be forgiven the personal in-

---

[6] The same estimate is given in Charles E. Silberman (1978, p. 78) for modern professionals, and by myself (1967, pp. 141, 274) for those of the nineteenth century.

dulgence, an account of this process may serve as a convenient framework, the only one I have, through which to view the untidy and contentious evolution of the field as a whole.

Many historians of police have begun with the assumption that the creation of the force was at least in part a response to "rising crime rates" that were a natural concomitant to urban growth. The assumption seemed reinforced by many of the sources, often local authorities urging a strengthening of patrol. In the 1960s, when the alternative popular explanations seemed dangerously racist, this was a good, "neutral" way of looking at the contemporary situation. Its academic credentials were ancient, going back as they did to the founders of sociology, with their concern for the dislocating effects of the passage from gemeinschaft to gesellschaft, a view strongly reinforced in this country by Robert E. Park, Ernest Burgess, and their followers in the Chicago school (Lane 1974).

Intensive research on a century of urban growth in Boston, however, suggested that the metropolis of the late nineteenth century was a less violent and disorderly place than the small commercial city of the 1840s, and that continual pressure to expand the police was the product not of any absolute need but of changing standards, a lowered threshold of tolerance for what constituted acceptable behavior. An article which attempted to demonstrate this through a survey of criminal statistics, the first by a historian, appeared in the winter of 1968 (Lane 1968). Its argument, which partially parallels much criminological work in labeling theory, is that rising aggregate statistics for the commonwealth of Massachusetts may be radically misleading guides to "real" behavior. The increase over much of the nineteenth century was due wholly to "public order" offenses, notably drunkenness. "Real" criminal activity, defined as the commission of offenses against persons and property, was decreasing, certainly from the Civil War to the end of the century, possibly—the records are ambiguous—from the beginning of the first of the several statistical sets I used, which dated from 1835. Since the commonwealth was meanwhile urbanizing rapidly—only 19 percent of its population reportedly lived in urban areas in 1835, fully 79 percent in 1900—the conclusion was that "real" crime did not increase with urban growth. Quite the contrary: the regularity, cooperation, and interdependence demanded by life and especially work in the city literally "civilized" its inhabitants. The progressive increase in "order" offenses reflected this as well as did the decrease in "real" ones. With less "real" crime to contend with, increasing numbers of police concentrated on enforcing higher standards of public behavior, and rising arrests for drunkenness indicated an actual decrease in its occurrence.

This article, since widely reprinted, is in various ways flawed internally. The statistics for the pre–Civil War era are ambiguous, as noted. Even apart from criticism that might obviously be leveled by more rigorous labeling theorists, the distinction between "real" crime and "public order offenses" is unreliable: the most common of "real" crimes of violence, simple assault, may often have been a synonym for drunk and disorderly conduct. As Michael Hindus has properly pointed out (1979), it is further an "ecological fallacy" to conclude anything about individual cities from trends in the state as a whole. While in practice the correlation between urbanization, industrialization, and a drop in "serious" crime seems strong, in logic there may be no direct causal connection.

At the time, however, in the absence of any contrary argument or indeed relevant evidence from other scholars in this country, it seemed logical to refine the hypothesis about the connection between disorderly behavior and economic change by looking at the effects of the first Industrial Revolution, the one experienced in Great Britain. There was then, apart from such traditional descriptive books as Kellow Chesney's (1970), only one specialized study of English crime in the nineteenth century, the important but deliberately nonstatistical book by J. J. Tobias (1967). But a number of scholars had done relevant work as part of wider social and economic histories (Lane 1974). And for none of them, it turned out, did our own conventional wisdom apply. If "crime" be defined more precisely as individually disruptive or disorderly behavior, ranging from drunken rowdiness through assault to murder (excluding collective action or calculated offenses), then British scholars, whatever their other differences, were united in agreeing that the preindustrial population of the early eighteenth century was far more criminal than the largely urbanized, more fully industrialized population of the late nineteenth. The change—whether framed in terms of Marx, or of Weber, or without theoretical basis at all—was, all perceived, connected with the changing economy. It was accomplished by some combination of factory or other economic discipline, fuller employment, and a variety of social control measures from temperance campaigns and increased schooling through the introduction of police. First in the factory towns, then in agricultural districts dominated increasingly by rational entrepreneurs, lastly in the great commercial (nonindustrial) metropolis of London, a nation once famed for its boozy rowdiness at public hangings acquired a stereotype involving roses, tea, and understatement.

The process through which this transformation occurred seems so fundamental, the article concluded, that it must have been operating in nineteenth-century America as well. But a number of national differences appear to have hidden it from our social scientists, including our relative ignorance of preindustrial levels of disorder, the traditional suspicion of social theory which has marked our historiography, an even stronger traditional anti-urban bias, given strong academic sanction by the Chicago sociologists, and the sheer complexity of our social and economic development, in which any given ethnic group or region might be new or old, settled or unsettled.

By the time I published this analysis in 1974, however, a number of studies had appeared or were in process, many of them quantitative and far more sophisticated than any previous.

Perhaps the best of the full-length monographs is Eric Monkkonen's *The Dangerous Class: Crime and Poverty in Columbus, Ohio, 1860–1885* (1975). Monkkonen uses those named in a series of Franklin County criminal indictments as representative of "criminals" in general; the obvious problems in this approach, together with a number in the data intended to link population and industrial growth to the indices of crime and poverty, limit the usefulness of some but by no means all of his conclusions. With respect to the hypothesis outlined above he finds no evidence for any "civilizing process" over time, although rural indictees slightly outnumbered urban ones and were more inclined to impulsive and less to guileful offenses. There is also no evidence, as illustrated by low rates of recidivism, for the existence of a truly professional criminal "class"—although perhaps only because Columbus was a relatively small city. And among a number of other findings that are important, provocative, or both, Monkkonen points out that there was virtually no measurable difference between those indicted for criminal offenses and the general population. This truly remarkable result has been partially or indirectly confirmed by Harvey Graff (1977), who has demolished the old Victorian argument that criminals were distinguished by levels of illiteracy which forced them into the paths of error.

For purposes of truly long-term comparison, the need for some comprehensive study of criminality in the eighteenth century has unfortunately not been filled by Douglas Greenberg's potentially promising monograph on colonial New York (1976). Greenberg makes a number of interesting points in the course of analyzing all of the surviving criminal records of New York between 1691 and 1775. The total he works with, over five thousand cases, is large enough to hold much of interest. But Greenberg's elementary errors in interpreting criminal statistics—confusing simple "offenses against public order," for example, with evidence of seditious activity, even rebelliousness—seriously limits his credibility as interpreter. So does his insistence upon forcing his provocative materials into the routine channels dictated by conventional views about provincial history.

Michael Hindus, in contrast, has handled his colonial materials in intelligent fashion. In writing about Massachusetts and South Carolina, 1767 to 1878 (1975), he is able to make a complex series of comparisons about two different—or indeed three different—societies over time. South Carolina's patterns of black/white, male/female, interpersonal/property offenses, while revealing, did not much change. But Massachusetts in the late eighteenth and in the mid-nineteenth centuries was in effect two quite different places. William E. Nelson (1967) had earlier found a shift in the operations in the justice system, as following the American Revolution the commonwealth grew less concerned with offenses against morals and more with offenses against property. Hindus, in refining and expanding this argument, finds the shift related in part to changing attitudes among the authorities who "labeled" offenses, as Massachusetts moved from Puritan province to leading industrial state. But, more important, it indicates real changes in popular behavior inspired by the same economic transformation. As a result of finding more jail committals of all sorts in Boston than elsewhere, and no clear drop in the statewide indices of "real" criminality until well after the Civil War, Hindus tends to doubt at least the timing of the change I had described in my first article (1968). But perhaps as a result of his legal training he is also more careful than most to remind readers of the many variables, some the result of small procedural differences, which affect his numbers—and, by extension, all of those available to any of us.

What is a caveat for Hindus, doing a modest comparative study, is a major complaint for Eric Monkkonen, attempting an ambitious one (forthcoming). Monkkonen has surveyed the work of 11 scholars, covering 14 jurisdictions in 13 quantitative studies, ancient and modern. All are plagued by certain unavoidable problems. It is of course impossible, using the nineteenth-century records, to get as close to the actual commission of an offense as it is today. There is no full record of "crimes known to the police." Arrests date only from the establishment of professional departments, which in some smaller jurisdictions never occurred. Scholars as a result have used indictments, committals, and imprisonments, as available, in state and local jurisdictions with widely differing policies. Less excusable, Monkkonen finds, virtually none have tried to frame their research in such a way as to enable comparison or testing. For example, each defines "crime" in his or her own fashion, dividing the aggregate figures along equally idiosyncratic lines.

A vigorous debate, moreover, ranges over the very fundamental issue—and, given the circumstances, the range of possibilities is even greater than among students of contemporary deviance— about whether or how far official statistics may be used as measures of "real" behavior. J. J. Tobias, the pioneering Briton (1967), insists that, quite apart from theoretical considerations, the records were so badly kept—even invented by harried clerical cogs in the justice system—as to be worthless. He relies instead largely on the descriptive accounts of contemporary experts, cops and reformers, in estimating the level and direction of criminal activity. David Philips (1977), in reply, points out that the experts themselves relied upon statistics rather than personal experience alone, however, so that Tobias is merely retailing the official figures at one remove. John Beattie (1974), a pioneer in studying pre-nineteenth-century figures in England, believes that the "dark figure," or proportion of unreported offenses, may be regarded as a constant whatever its magnitude, so that relative changes in the magnitude of offenses may be measured with some accuracy.[7] Eric Monkkonen (forthcoming) argues that at least for heuristic purposes we must assume that "bad behavior"— "crime" is only that which is so labeled officially—is a constant. And those four represent only a sampling of the opinions that have been advanced.

Virtually all of us, too, in the modern era have assumed that class considerations have in some way influenced the definition of crime, and that public policy has shaped the attempt to control it. But Philips, again (1977), in studying the mid-Victorian "Black Country," surely one of the most tightly class-bound of subsocieties, points out that although those in charge of the justice system clearly violated popular tradition in prosecuting industrial "pilferage," for example, most common-law offenses were prosecuted by private persons, usually of the same working

---

[7] There is considerable difficulty in dealing with figures for a period before the nineteenth century. Beattie (1974) has done a careful job, but a study such as that of the Middle Ages by James B. Given (1977) reveals the dangers of generalizing from the very uncertain data of an earlier era. This is a problem which may be dealt with either by displaying great sensitivity, as done by Barbara A. Hanawalt (1979), or by largely relying upon illustration and anecdote, and being very careful to qualify any quantitative generalizations, as done by John G. Bellamy (1973).

class as the offenders, and there seems no clear class difference in attitudes toward ordinary assault or theft. It remains true, however, that an official increase in recorded offenses, especially minor ones, may indicate that fewer rather than more such offenses are being committed (Lane 1968). While no truly hardcore labeling theorist has attempted a serious historical study, and most historians would probably take a commonsensical approach which suggests that some reported offenses are more reflective of "real" behavior than others—homicide and robbery versus gambling and drunkenness—important differences remain. Even in relatively homogeneous England there is an argument as to whether a survey of national figures, such as that done by Gatrell and Hadden for 1805–92 (1972), is relatively reflective of "real" levels of crime because local variations cancel out, or whether, as Philips insists, local studies are essential because local changes may be accounted for.

Parallel to this debate, which has its counterparts in this country as well, is one over the relative accuracy of long- and short-term studies. Thus Gatrell and Hadden suggest that with procedural change discounted, long-term fluctuations may be less trustworthy than short, since official labeling practices may change imperceptibly over the decades. Most of those dealing with single jurisdictions, however, and trying to account for such official changes in interaction with the statistical record, would probably agree with Michael Hindus (1975) that short-term fluctuations may reflect unnoted procedural changes, such as the term of an aggressive prosecutor, and that long-term trends are thus more reliable.

No one has as yet even attempted to solve some of the most fundamental problems involved in the continued effort to distinguish between "real" and merely "labeled" offenses, moreover. Both Eric Monkkonen and I, for example, draw rather different lines between these, and I have even drawn different lines in different pieces. For both the principle is the same: we try to distinguish between acts which genuinely harmed individuals and those which were without victims. While robbery, say, poses few problems, what of assault, or disorderly behavior? What proportion of assault arrests were made by policemen on their own initiative, what proportion as the result of complaints by aggrieved losers? How many "order" arrests, even, represent felt needs, responses to community demands, and how many represent attempts to impose alien values, to suppress a neighborhood's enjoyment of its regular Saturday night fights? The statistics in themselves offer few clues.

One possible way out of this dilemma is to try to bypass criminal statistics in favor of other measures of behavior. Thus in a recent book on *Violent Death in the City: Suicide, Accident, and Murder in Nineteenth Century Philadelphia* (1979), I have outlined the patterns and incidence of violently reckless behavior in its noncriminal as well as criminal forms. The two noncriminal indices, suicide and accident, are linked with that for homicide, generally considered the "hardest" of criminal offenses, the one least susceptible to changing practices and definitions. Modern studies have shown that young people prone to accident are psychologically and emotionally very similar to those inclined to commit violent offenses including manslaughter (Waller 1969). Further, as indicated by psychologist Martin Gold (1958), inventor of the so-called "Suicide-Murder Ratio," the inclination to homicide or to suicide, among both individuals and groups, is linked in an opposite way. Both are means of expressing aggressive impulses, the one internally and the other externally, and are heavily influenced by the way in which a group or society trains its members to deal with these impulses. The finding is that, with technological accident discounted, there was little clear movement in the rates of any of these forms of violent death until after the Civil War, when homicide and especially accidents went down sharply and the suicide rate nearly doubled. All three indices seem closely linked, as suggested in my early work, to the growth of compulsory schooling and of supervised factory and bureaucratic employment, a hypothesis tested by comparing the changing occupations and ethnicity of victims.

As a solution to the problem of reliance upon criminal statistics, however, this effort is only partially successful. Only the accident index is truly value-free. Although I believe I have found ways of discounting the problems, suicide is of course a social index notoriously open to changing labels. Even homicide turns out on close examination to be much more susceptible to such changes than previously believed. A changing threshold of tolerance resulted in labeling many late-nineteenth-century killings "homicide" which would earlier have been ignored or labeled "accident," while it seems that massive numbers were ignored or semi-intentionally mislabeled by the coroner simply because the machinery of detection and prosecution was unable to handle them successfully. However critics react to the study as a whole, one sure result will be to underline the degree to which the official indices are uncertain reflectors of actual behavior.

Despite the manifold difficulties, however, it is possible to find a rough pattern among most of the extant studies, at least with respect to the single issue of trend over time. Of the studies which Monkkonen has surveyed, Augustus Kuhlman (1929) found all felonies rising in the state of Missouri between 1850 and 1920, and Hindus (1977) finds all felonies rising in Massachusetts between 1836 and 1873. Every other study tends to show that, when measured over any considerable period of the nineteenth century, serious crime, however defined, was either declining or, at worst, stable. In England the situation is clearer—all the recent surveys show falling crime rates, in whatever jurisdiction, lending statistical confirmation to the earlier accounts.

Two recent studies, finally, the most ambitious yet attempted, seem to confirm the downward pattern for the previous century —while simultaneously raising another set of questions about our own.

Monkkonen's forthcoming study comprises a number of elaborate statistical analyses of the published records of the twenty-three largest American cities for the period 1860–1920. It also surveys most of the relevant earlier hypotheses in the course of offering its own richly complex and provocative explanations for, among other things, the several statistically significant "crime waves" he discovers, and their relation both to "real" conditions and to such bureaucratic variables as police strength. In contrast to my own earlier findings about the commonwealth of Massachusetts (including a large number of places just beginning to employ their own cops), he finds that "order arrests" in big cities tended to decline. And his best estimate—based on the number of crimes with victims, and especially homicides—is that "real" criminal activity followed a pattern easily described as a U-curve. There was a fall, that is, through the late nineteenth century, and a rise beginning late in the nineteenth or early in the twentieth.

The evidence for the U-curve is even more impressive in *The Politics of Crime and Conflict* by Ted Gurr and others (1977), which traces the history of the justice systems of four major cities from the late eighteenth century to the present. Calcutta is sui generis, for a number of reasons, but the rates of interpersonal violence and theft in London, Stockholm, and Sydney seem to have fallen through most of the nineteenth century and, indeed, much of the twentieth, only to turn up about the time of World War II. Despite some tendency, here and elsewhere (Gurr 1979), to rely rather uncritically on official sources, Gurr's evidence is too massive to deny. The impressively cross-national pattern he has revealed accords also with my own findings for homicide in Philadelphia and, by extension, for the United States as a whole (1979). It may be that Monkkonen's discovery of an earlier upturn is premature, the result of a number of relatively short-term factors or of others, such as better reportage or police procedures, which would affect reported rates but not "real" ones. If so, his study may fit with the others to suggest the exciting possibility that there is a single comprehensive explanation for long-term trends in criminal behavior in the Western world as a whole over the past two centuries.

Such an explanation, if it does prove possible to demonstrate and elaborate, will necessarily be complex. The possible existence of an overarching U-curve does not deny that war, for example, and a number of other influences affect the shape of the crime rates over shorter time spans (Gurr 1979). Criminal behavior has clearly differed over time in a number of respects, quite apart from its overall incidence. But the differences may themselves be patterned. The Gurr studies suggest that during the twentieth century upswing on the U-curve, for example, the incidence of crimes against property has often tended to rise during periods of prosperity, exactly reversing the correlations usually found for the previous century, on the downswing. Both Gurr and Monk-konen find important differences, during the downswing and up-swing phases, in the degree to which serious crime rates appear to have responded to police activity. Evidence of this sort helps at the least to validate the importance of historical perspective, illustrating the basic fact that patterns change, that purely contemporary studies are necessarily limited in application. At the same time, the upswing-downswing differences may in themselves be evidence for an explanation which indicates that some combination of conditions in a developing(?) modernizing(?) industrializing(?) society tends to drive down the level of criminal activity, while a different set in a postindustrial(?) mature(?) aging(?) society tends to drive it up.

It must be stressed, however, that although such an explanation now seems conceivable—indeed to me it is the best available hypothesis—there is, quite apart from its accuracy, no reason to suppose that it will be accepted or even explored in depth. Some of the difficulties may be illustrated through a brief examination of a subsidiary issue—the degree to which police activity may be held responsible for "controlling" crime.

There is, as noted, little disagreement that the early police enjoyed at least some success in curbing riot and the excesses of street gangs. There is considerable agreement, too, about the role of big city police in "controlling"—that is regulating—professional crime and especially vice. But with respect to ordinary crime, there is none—no more than there is agreement about matters of definition or measurement.

In England, a long tradition credits the bobbies with at least some responsibility for the decline in ordinary criminality which marked the nineteenth century. Gurr, in a chapter of Gurr, Grabosky, and Hula (1977), is the most recent exponent of this tradition, and has attempted to demonstrate it statistically, not only for London but for Stockholm and Sydney, by correlating increases in police strength with decreases in serious crime. (The proposition does not hold for the upswing, post-1940 period.) There remains considerable variation, however, as to what share of the credit should go to the police as distinct from such factors as moral campaigns, fuller employment, schooling, and factory discipline. In the larger view, the word "credit" is itself problematic; while some scholars have celebrated the pacification of the British population, others have denounced the often brutal repression of working-class habits and customs which it entailed.

Among Americans there is less agreement yet. It is possible, as we have seen, to write extensively about cops without much mention of crime and, equally significant, to write about crime with virtually no mention of cops. It may be inferred, for example, that Michael Hindus (1975), believes police impact on non-"order" offenses was minimal. Samuel Walker (1977) and Robert M. Fogelson (1977) are almost contemptuous about the efficacy of patrol, Walker pointing out that the thin blue line was too thin to make much difference, Fogelson insisting that the duty was more often shirked than shouldered. Eric Monkkonen (forthcoming), whose method is a more sophisticated version of Gurr's, finds as Gurr does that police strength has some apparent impact on "real" crimes on the downslope of the U-curve but none on the upslope. David Johnson (1979) vaguely implies, as did Richardson and I in our early cop books, that patrol was at least partially effective in maintaining public "order," but without advancing much hard evidence. My own more fully matured position would be that the cops "worked" only as part of the demand —created fundamentally by a changing economic order—for a more disciplined society and workforce. Acting alone, or out of phase, with this deeper economic need, as in an age of labor surplus, their impact was (and still is) minimal.

Failure of consensus on this one representative point is partly the result of trying to prove a negative—we cannot measure, historically, the deterrent effect of uniformed patrol. It is partly, too, the result of gaps in the records. And it is partly of our own making, the result of the careless or ad hoc research designs, the noncomparable results and incompatible definitions for which Monkkonen rightly scolds us. But at bottom many of the problems in the field seem currently insoluble for the most fundamental of reasons: all questions escalate. The definition of "crime" leads to the issue of who or what governs the justice system, then the society, ultimately the course of history. And for each of us at some point a level of emotional or ideological conviction is attained which is beyond the reach of empirical evidence, beyond the reach of social science.

The problems, then, will remain. There is no question but that a progressive awareness of the work of other social scientists has enriched the work of historians and will continue to do so. Each of us has more tools in the kit, more perspectives to consider. We will find or disallow more and more testable middle-level generalizations in ways that most of us can agree on. American (and perhaps, even more, British) scholars can profit from paying more attention to the clues offered by societies other than their own. I hope in particular that the implications of the U-curve hypothesis will be tested fully and comparatively. But at present we seem little closer to a comprehensive synthesis than we were before, and whatever the rate and direction of the traffic across that bridge to the social sciences, there seems no immediate prospect that it will take us to such a goal.

REFERENCES

Banton, Michael. 1964. *The Policeman in the Community*. New York: Basic Books.
Beattie, John M. 1974. "The Pattern of Crime in England 1660–1800," *Past and Present* 62:47–95.
Bell, Daniel. 1960. "Crime as an American Way of Life." In *The End of Ideology: On the Exhaustion of Political Ideas in the 'Fifties*, ed. Daniel Bell. Glencoe, Ill.: The Free Press.
Bellamy, John G. 1973. *Crime and Public Order in England in the Later Middle Ages*. London: Routledge & Kegan Paul.
Benson, Lee. 1961. *The Concept of Jacksonian Democracy*. Princeton: Princeton University Press.
Bogue, Allan G., Jerome M. Clubb, and William H. Flanigan. 1977.

"The New Political History," *American Behavioral Scientist* 21: 201–20.

Bordua, David, ed. 1967. *The Police: Six Sociological Essays*. New York: John Wiley.

Chesney, Kellow. 1970. *The Victorian Underworld*. London: Maurice Temple Smith.

Cook, Adrian. 1974. *The Armies of the Streets: The New York City Draft Riots of 1863*. Lexington: University of Kentucky Press.

Feldberg, Michael. 1975. *The Philadelphia Riots of 1844: A Study of Ethnic Conflict*. Westport, Conn.: Greenwood Press.

Ferdinand, Theodore N. 1967. "The Criminal Patterns of Boston Since 1849," *American Journal of Sociology* 73:84–99.

Fogelson, Robert M. 1977. *Big-City Police*. Cambridge, Mass.: Harvard University Press.

Gatrell, V. A. C., and T. B. Hadden. 1972. "Criminal Statistics and Their Interpretation." In *Nineteenth-Century Society: Essays in the Use of Quantitative Methods for the Study of Social Data*, ed. E. A. Wrigley. Cambridge, England: Cambridge University Press.

Given, James B. 1977. *Society and Homicide in Thirteenth-Century England*. Stanford: Stanford University Press.

Gold, Martin. 1958. "Suicide, Homicide, and the Socialization of Aggression," *American Journal of Sociology*, 63:651–61.

Graff, Harvey J. 1977. "Pauperism, Misery, and Vice: Illiteracy and Criminality in the Nineteenth Century," *Journal of Social History* 11:245–68.

Greenberg, Douglas. 1976. *Crime and Law Enforcement in the Colony of New York, 1691–1775*. Ithaca: Cornell University Press.

Gurr, Ted Robert. 1979. "On the History of Violent Crime in Europe and America." *Violence in America: Historical and Comparative Perspectives*, rev. ed., ed. Ted Robert Gurr and Hugh Graham. Beverly Hills: Sage Publications.

Gurr, Ted Robert, Peter N. Grabosky, and Richard C. Hula. 1977. *The Politics of Crime and Conflict: A Comparative History of Four Cities*. Beverly Hills: Sage Publications.

Haller, Mark. 1971a. "Organized Crime in Urban Society: Chicago in the Twentieth Century," *Journal of Social History* 5:210–34.

———. 1971b. "Civic Reformers and Police Leadership: Chicago, 1905–1935." In *Police in Urban Society*, ed. Harlan Hahn. Beverly Hills: Sage Publications.

Haller, Mark, and John V. Alviti. 1977. "Loansharking in American Cities: Historical Analysis of a Marginal Enterprise," *American Journal of Legal History* 21:125–56.

Hanawalt, Barbara A. 1979. *Crime and Conflict in English Communities, 1300–1348.* Cambridge, Mass.: Harvard University Press.

Handlin, Oscar. 1951. *The Uprooted.* Boston: Little, Brown.

Harring, Sidney L. 1979. "Class Conflict and the Suppression of Tramps in Buffalo, 1892–1894." In *Criminology Review Yearbook I,* ed. Sheldon L. Messinger and Egon Bittner. Beverly Hills: Sage Publications.

Harring, Sidney L., and Lorraine M. McMullin. 1975. "The Buffalo Police 1872–1900: Labor Unrest, Political Power and the Creation of the Police Institution," *Crime and Social Justice* 1975:5–14.

Hindus, Michael. 1975. "Crime, Justice, and Authority in Massachusetts and South Carolina, 1767–1878." Ph.D. dissertation, University of California, Berkeley.

———. 1977. "The Contours of Crime and Justice in Massachusetts and South Carolina, 1767–1878," *American Journal of Legal History* 21:212–37.

———. 1979. "The History of Crime: Not Robbed of Its Potential, But Still on Probation." In *Criminology Review Yearbook I,* ed. Sheldon L. Messinger and Egon Bittner. Beverly Hills: Sage Publications.

Inciardi, James A., Alan A. Block, and Lyle A. Hallowell. 1977. *Historical Approaches to Crime.* Beverly Hills: Sage Publications.

Johnson, Bruce. 1976. "Taking Care of Labor: The Police in American Politics," *Theory and Society* 3:89–117.

Johnson, David R. 1979. *Policing the Urban Underworld: The Impact of Crime on the Development of the American Police, 1800–1887.* Philadelphia: Temple University Press.

Kennett, Lee, and James LaVerne Anderson. 1975. *The Gun in America: The Origins of a National Dilemma.* Westport, Conn., and London: Greenwood Press.

Kuhlman, Augustus. 1929. "Crime and Punishment in Missouri: A Study of the Social Forces in the Trial and Error Process of Penal Reform." Ph.D. dissertation, University of Chicago.

Lane, Roger. 1967. *Policing The City: Boston, 1822–1885.* Cambridge, Mass.: Harvard University Press.

———. 1968. "Crime and Criminal Statistics in Nineteenth Century Massachusetts," *Journal of Social History* 2:156–63.

———. 1974. "Crime and the Industrial Revolution: British and American Views," *Journal of Social History* 7:287–303.

———. 1979. *Violent Death in the City: Suicide, Accident, and Murder in Nineteenth Century Philadelphia.* Cambridge, Mass.: Harvard University Press.

Laurie, Bruce. 1973. "Fire Companies and Gangs in Southwark:

The 1840's." In *The Peoples of Philadelphia: A History of Ethnic Groups and Lower Class Life, 1790–1840*, ed. Allen F. Davis and Mark Haller. Philadelphia: Temple University Press.

Levett, Allan E. 1975. "Centralization of City Police in the Nineteenth Century United States." Ph.D. dissertation, University of Michigan.

Levine, Jerald E. 1971. "Police, Parties, and Polity: The Bureaucratization, Unionization, and Professionalization of the New York City Police, 1870–1917." Ph.D. dissertation, University of Wisconsin.

Liebman, Robert, and Michael Polen. 1978. "Perspectives on Policing in Nineteenth Century America," *Social Science History* 12:346–60.

Maier, Pauline. 1970. "Popular Uprisings and Civil Authority in Eighteenth-Century America," *William and Mary Quarterly* 27: 3–35.

Maniha, John F. 1973. "Structural Supports for the Development of Professionalism among Police Administrators," *Pacific Sociological Review* 16:315–43.

Miller, Wilbur R. 1977. *Cops and Bobbies: Police Authority in New York and London, 1830–1870*. Chicago: University of Chicago Press.

Monkkonen, Eric. 1975. *The Dangerous Class: Crime and Poverty in Columbus, Ohio, 1860–1885*. Cambridge, Mass.: Harvard University Press.

———. 1977. "Toward a Dynamic Theory of Crime and the Police: A Criminal Justice System Perspective," *Historical Methods Newsletter* 10:157–65.

———. 1979a. "Systematic Criminal Justice History: Some Suggestions," *Journal of Interdisciplinary History* 9:451–64.

———. 1979b. "Recent Historical Studies of Crime and Crime Control in the United States," *Quantum Information*, forthcoming.

———. Forthcoming. *Hands Up: American Policing, 1860–1920*.

Morn, Frank. 1975. "Discipline and Disciplinarians: The Problem of Police Control in the Formative Years." Paper read at winter 1975 meeting of the American Historical Association.

Muraskin, William A. 1976. "The Social Control Theory in American History: A Critique," *Journal of Social History* 11:559–68.

Nelli, Humbert. 1976. *The Business of Crime: Italians and Syndicate Crime in the United States*. New York: Oxford University Press.

Nelson, William E. 1967. "Emerging Notions of Modern Criminal Law in the Revolutionary Era: An Historical Perspective," *New York University Law Review* 42:450–82.

Pepinsky, Harold E. 1978. "Social Historians: Write Your Crimi-
nologists." Paper read at fall 1978 meeting of the Social Science
Historical Association.
Philips, David. 1977. *Crime and Authority in Victorian England:
The Black Country, 1835–1860*. Totowa, N.J.: Rowman and Lit-
tlefield.
Powell, Elwin H. 1966. "Crime as a Function of Anomie," *Journal
of Criminal Law, Criminology, and Police Science* 57:161–71.
Radzinowicz, Leon. 1948–68. *A History of English Criminal Law
and Its Administration from 1750*. 4 vols. London: Stevens.
Reichard, Maximillan. 1975. "The Origins of Urban Police: Free-
dom and Order in Antebellum St. Louis." Ph.D. dissertation,
Washington University.
Richardson, James F. 1970. *The New York Police: Colonial Times
to 1901*. New York: Oxford University Press.
———. 1974. *Urban Police in the United States*. Port Washington,
N.Y.: Kennikat Press.
Rudé, George. 1964. *The Crowd in History: A Study of Popular
Disturbances in France and England, 1730–1848*. New York: John
Wiley.
Schneider, John. 1978. "Public Order and the Geography of the
City: Crime, Violence, and the Police in Detroit, 1845–1875,"
Journal of Urban History 4:183–208.
Silberman, Charles E. 1978. *Criminal Violence, Criminal Justice*.
New York: Random House.
Skolnick, Jerome. 1966. *Justice Without Trial*. New York: John
Wiley.
Sutherland, Edwin. 1937. *The Professional Thief*. Chicago: Univer-
sity of Chicago Press.
Tobias, J. J. 1967. *Crime and Industrial Society in the Nineteenth
Century*. New York: Schocken Books.
Walker, Samuel. 1977. *A Critical History of Police Reform: The
Emergence of Professionalism*. Lexington, Mass.: Lexington Books.
Waller, Julian A. 1969. "Accidents and Violent Behavior: Are They
Related?" In *Crimes of Violence: A Staff Report Submitted to
the National Commission on the Causes and Prevention of Vio-
lence*, vol. 12. Washington: U.S. Government Printing Office.
Westley, William A. 1970. *Violence and the Police: A Sociological
Study of Law, Custom, and Morality*. Cambridge, Mass.: M.I.T.
Press.
Wilson, James Q. 1968. *Varieties of Police Behavior: The Manage-
ment of Law and Order in Eight Communities*. Cambridge, Mass.:
Harvard University Press.

Douglas Hay

Crime and Justice in Eighteenth- and Nineteenth-Century England

ABSTRACT

Recent historical studies concerned with the period of the English industrial revolution illuminate many relationships between crime and the criminal law, and social and economic change. The creation and abolition of the capital code and the invention of the penitentiary and the police suggest the importance of threats to political authority in deciding policy. Other studies emphasize the place of crime in popular culture, while quantitative work shows the importance of economic fluctuations, moral panics, war and the new police in explaining the level of prosecutions. Most suggestive for further work is the upper class assault on popular mores, poor men's property, and old economic orthodoxies. New legislation and new levels of enforcement, as well as less premeditated changes in English capitalism, created crimes where none had existed, and probably caused a crisis of legitimacy for the English criminal law. What emerged may have been not only a modern system of criminal law and enforcement, but a modern criminal.

Recent histories of crime and criminal law make little use of criminology, partly because it is notably indifferent to what interests historians most: cultural, political, and economic change. More important, much criminology seems still to be infected with the belief that the civilized legal order must represent the healthy, or the collective conscience, or some more recent formulation of the norm.[1] From the assumption that criminal law broadly expresses the social norm, it is easy to conclude that

Douglas Hay is Associate Professor, Memorial University of Newfoundland, and currently Visiting Professor, Yale Law School.

[1] See Diamond (1974) for a critique by an anthropologist.

crime of all kinds is deviance. And deviance too easily comes to seem a homogeneous quality of those so labeled.[2]

Historians are perhaps more inclined to see norms as partial, transient, ambiguous, and contested. They do not expect to find social consensus in the societies they study. They are acutely aware that mores as well as governments and economies undergo remarkable changes. And they spend a great deal of time reading the correspondence of elites who were attempting to impose their will on the social order. From this perspective, the criminal law looks less like a common social property with a self-evident purpose.

In eighteenth-century England, government was in the hands of a small group of men with enormous economic and political power. Less than 3 percent of the adult male population were rich enough to be legally entitled to act as justices of the peace, or even to hunt game, another prerogative of gentlemen. An even smaller proportion of the most wealthy, the two hundred families of the peerage, dominated both houses of Parliament. Only the House of Commons was fitfully responsible to an electorate, an electorate that was small, manipulated, and unrepresentative. These groups together comprised "the public," the political nation. They enacted a very extensive capital code in the eighteenth century, and replaced it by the penitentiary in the nineteenth. The rest of the population, the majority, were known simply as "the labouring poor" when they were quiet, and as "the mob" when they were not. Without political rights, they were also the object of the abundant criminal legislation of the period.

It is easy, if unwise, to assume consensus about the criminal law in a modern society, but Englishmen clearly did not share such a consensus in the two centuries after 1700. The upper class hold on power remained strong throughout the period, in spite of a vastly widened franchise and a growing trade union movement in the nineteenth century. And in their attitudes to property and popular custom, and hence to crime, the aristocracy,

[2] As it seems to do in the large literature on labeling theory, much of which virtually ignored crimes against property.

gentry, and prosperous middle class were exceptional minorities in England. They were bent on a remaking of the English economy and of English society. In the process they enclosed ancient common lands by parliamentary act, destroying a whole corpus of local customary law. They sharpened prosecutions for poaching, although taking game was popularly believed to be a right. They redefined certain customary parts of the wage as theft, suppressed popular amusements as threats to order and productivity, outlawed trade unions for much of the period, dismantled protective apprenticeship laws and resisted factory legislation, repealed laws against speculators in food, labored to make charity punitive, and impressed thousands into the army and navy to fight great commercial wars. In these and in many other ways incident to the growth of capital and industry they violated old and widely held community values. In the eyes of many Englishmen it was their rulers—landowners, entrepreneurs, magistrates, and judges—who were deviant. And it was inevitable, therefore, that legal definitions of crime did not correspond closely to the norms of a large part, perhaps the majority, of the population.

Questions like these have not much concerned legal historians, working to understand the institutional and doctrinal growth of the law. But in recent years a rapidly growing literature has tried to situate historical crime in an intelligible context of class relations, collective mentalities, and economic structure. All of these were transformed over the modern period, and with them the behavior stigmatized by the law changed too. At the same time a related but partly autonomous evolution of law constructed and reconstructed both the definition and incidence of crime. The scope of this work is international, but England in this period perhaps commands attention as a special case and as a standard of comparison. It was the seat of the Common Law and of a criminal procedure widely admired in Europe. It was the first nation to industrialize, and spawned what was then the largest city in the world. And the rapid and pervasive transformation of England's economy and society was reflected in the criminal law, in criminal behavior, and in the complex relationship between the two.

What follows is a review of recent writing on this period, especially where it illuminates these themes.[3] A section on the criminal law and its administration deals with the creation and then abolition of a capital code, the emergence of recognizably modern trial procedure, and the invention of the penitentiary and the police. A second section discusses some of the writing on crime as part of popular culture. Here riot is important, not only because of its great significance in this period, but because it suggests approaches to other offenses. I also consider some of the findings and problems of quantitative studies of historical crime. Finally, a third section sketches some of the emerging explanations of the relations between crime, the criminal law, and long-run structural change in this period. At issue was the legitimacy of the law itself.

I. The Criminal Law and Its Administration

Between 1700 and 1900 a system familiar to our eyes emerged as a result of important changes in substantive law, procedure, punishment, and prosecution. At the beginning of the eighteenth century the only police were parish householders who took turns as constables. They did little more than assist the private citizen who was the victim of a theft or other crime and who himself paid for the prosecution and largely organized it. If he was undaunted by the cost and trouble, he got the thief before a jury, for a full criminal trial was necessary in most cases of even simple theft. There the defendant was denied legal counsel, but the jurors were more than likely to acquit or greatly reduce the charge because of their scruples about the severity of the law. For if they convicted outright, the prisoner was fairly likely to be sentenced to death. Most serious felonies and many lesser offenses were capital in 1700, and many more became so in the course of the eighteenth century. Even if sentenced to death, however, the convict still had about an even chance of a royal

[3] Recent work on earlier centuries is found in Hanawalt (1979) for the medieval period, and in Wrightson and Levine (1979) and contributors to Cockburn (1977) on the Tudor and Stuart period. For other studies see the references in Knafla (1977) (to 1800), Cornish (1978) (nineteenth century), and Bailey (1980).

pardon, conditional on his transportation to the American colonies. If he had any initiative, he was fairly likely to be back in England long before his sentence was up: he might even return to take revenge on his prosecutor. On the other hand, returning from transportation was a capital offense too. If caught again he was likely to be hanged. He then became one of the one or two hundred Englishmen publicly executed every year as "terrible examples" to those contemplating crime. Eighteenth-century penal practice was based largely on the supposed efficacy of such infrequent, but theatrical, examples: a few hundred were hanged each year, and perhaps a few score pilloried, a few thousand publicly flogged. But most known offenders were never prosecuted, and most of those convicted of serious crime were simply shipped overseas.

Two hundred years later, public executions had long been abolished, and the few men and women still hanged were almost all convicted murderers. They died behind the massive walls of penitentiaries, labyrinths which traced in brick and stone a penal theory remarkably different from that of eighteenth-century England. For almost all Englishmen convicted in the courts now served terms of imprisonment, under an austere discipline. Imprisonment, hardly used in 1700, had displaced all the eighteenth-century punishments: public whipping, the pillory, transportation, hanging. There had been equally striking changes in trials. Lawyers now spoke for the accused whenever he could afford it, but juries were considerably more likely to convict nonetheless. Far fewer prisoners went before juries in any case, since summary proceedings before magistrates now accounted for far more cases. Partly as a result, a greater proportion of known crime was probably prosecuted. But equally important was the most remarkable change of all. Private prosecution had been almost entirely displaced by police prosecution. A professional police, tightly organized and under close supervision, now epitomized for many Englishmen the virtues of Victorian society. It was incredible to them that less than a hundred years before it had been the opinion of almost everyone that police forces were the invention of European tyrants, and that England must never accept one.

The chronology of these changes, and some of their interconnections, are well known. But many of the older accounts were based largely on literary memoirs, newspapers, statutes and reported cases. The results were often anecdotal, sometimes shocking, and oddly incurious. The filiations of ideas from one writer to another somehow produced "reform," and an irrational and bloody criminal law yielded to "progress." Teleology informs even more recent writing on the history of the criminal law. Thus Radzinowicz asserts in the preface to his indispensable work that the history of the criminal law forms part of "the history of progress" and that "the criminal law of England has always been sensitive to the needs and aspirations of the English people" (1948–68, 1: 9). But when we examine the place of the criminal law in English society as a whole, and move deeper into the archival sources, both those claims seem less self-evident.

A. The Capital Code

The number of capital statutes greatly increased from the late seventeenth until the early nineteenth century, and the growth of the capital code has been charted in detail (Radzinowicz 1948–68, vol. 1). But far less has been written to explain the motives behind Parliament's bloody enthusiasm. The several hundred new capital offenses (no exact count is possible) were responsible for less than a third of the executions in the eighteenth century (unpublished findings of J. M. Beattie and D. Hay). The new statutes did make it possible to stage exemplary hangings when it was thought necessary to deal harshly with particular offenses: not all horse thieves were hanged, but more were when horse theft became too common. Some new statutes simply restored the death penalty where it had been eroded by benefit of clergy;[4] others created new offenses to deal with new kinds of appropriation, such as the forging of banknotes. But the marked acceleration of capital legislation after the beginning of the eighteenth century is so pronounced, the number of new statutes so

[4] Benefit of clergy—the right to plead exemption from execution for a first conviction of lesser felonies—was extended to the literate layman in medieval times and then to all accused in 1706. See Baker (1977), p. 41.

many, that it seems likely that deeper changes in property relations and in attitudes were affecting Parliament.

Our only close study of a capital statute, the most sanguinary
of the lot, suggests explanations which may be relevant to other
acts as well (Thompson 1975b). The Waltham Black Act (9
George I c.22, 1723) punished with death scores of offenses
against rural property, from poaching hares to arson, if the criminal was armed or disguised. It also significantly eroded safe-
guards to the accused: among other provisions, it allowed capital
sentences to be passed and carried out without a trial if the accused had failed to surrender when ordered to do so. The Black
Act was passed very quickly by Parliament at a particular con-
juncture of economic and political change. As Walpole consolidated his position as the first and most powerful of British prime
ministers, shortly after the accession of the Whigs, he and his
supporters were anxious to curtail customary rights over lands
in the royal forests and particularly in the royal forest of Wind-
sor. The inhabitants, who were increasingly prosecuted for taking turf or wood while they suffered the destruction caused by
the royal deer, retaliated with more poaching and the use of
force, much of it against the property of the local representatives
of the Whig oligarchy. The resulting "emergency" was politically useful to Walpole, and the act passed to deal with it was
agreeable to his intimates and doubtless to the king himself. The
arson, poaching, and murder against which the act was directed
was not the work of an existing "criminal subculture," but a
protest by foresters, using desperate means, against a concerted
attack on their economy and what they knew to be their rights.
But Parliament made the laws. Not only was the Black Act
passed almost overnight as a temporary measure; it was reen-
acted and broadened by judicial interpretation until it became
"a versatile armoury of death apt to the repression of many forms
of social disturbance" (Thompson 1975b, p. 192).

In this it may have been a model for later statutes. Government in the eighteenth century was unprotected by a regular
police, and hence the discretionary use of the death penalty, and
its aggravated forms, was an essential instrument in maintaining

order. A quick hanging, perhaps followed by hanging the body to rot from a gibbet, or dissecting it at a public lecture, could arrest further trouble. When the temper of the crowd was more dangerous, it was important to discriminate the moment when terror should be succeeded by mercy, and a royal pardon granted. The prerogative of mercy was as important as the shock of terror in creating submission, and the more crimes that were punishable by death, the more readily was the theater of a hanging, or a reprieve and pardon, staged (Radzinowicz 1948–68, vol. 1, chaps. 4, 5; Hay 1975a; Linebaugh 1975). But beyond this general explanation we need more detailed studies of individual statutes, and not only of those imposing death. Case law too has hardly been examined for its ties with shifts in the forms of property and the class relations surrounding it.[5]

B. Prosecution and Conviction

The daily operation of the unreformed criminal law is becoming clearer. Radzinowicz emphasized the host of expedients used to move the ordinary citizen to prosecute, or the criminal to impeach his colleagues: rewards, promises of pardon, exemption from onerous public offices such as that of constable (Radzinowicz 1948–68, vol. 2). All were designed to avoid both the expense and the dangers of a police and public prosecution. The distinctive fact that England had no public prosecutors meant that the law was used more readily for private as well as public ends, and was in sharp contrast to continental practice. This is a theme that has not been much explored.[6] On the other hand, much more is emerging about other aspects of courts and trials. Older work on justices of the peace (Webb and Webb 1963) is being enriched by local studies but there is also a fairly recent synthesis (Zangerl 1971; Philips 1976; Moir 1969). The justice of the peace, the unpaid lay magistrate on whom most of the administration of the law fell, emerges often as a paternalist, but

[5] One study of redefinitions of larceny in case law (Hall 1952), while sketchy in its account of the wider economic context, is useful and almost unique.

[6] On continental practice see Langbein (1977) and the works cited there. On vexatious use of the law in an earlier period see Ingram (1977, pp. 118 ff.). On nineteenth-century English practice the best introduction is still Maitland (1885).

also as a man who colluded or cooperated with fellow landowners or manufacturers to effect convictions (Philips 1976, pp. 175ff.; Hay 1975b, pp. 240–44).[7] The higher courts were much less arbitrary, and by the eighteenth century had generated an immense body of case law respecting procedure, forms of indictment, and evidence.[8] But until recently we knew little about what actually happened in court, at least before the nineteenth century, when extensive press reports begin to appear.

We know now that the older accounts, based largely on the few "state trials", for sedition and similar offenses, are quite unrepresentative (Howell 1816–31; Pike 1968; Stephen 1977). Ordinary people in the eighteenth century were tried for the most serious crimes with amazing speed: a score in a day, before experienced jurors who heard several cases before considering verdicts, and who showed much deference to very directive judges. In most cases conviction or acquittal turned on quick assessments of the plausibility of the charge. The basis for decision therefore tended to be a rapid assessment of the character of the accused,[9] rather than a sifting of the evidence before the court. Two things followed. The trial resembled to a surprising extent the inquisitorial procedure of the continent, where character and social standing were explicitly germane to the methods of establishing guilt and fixing punishments.[10] Secondly, there was a lack of evi-

[7] Assessments of the justice of the peace are scattered throughout the literature on the gentry: see the relevant sections of Chaloner and Richardson (1976).

[8] There is an older account of quarter sessions, the lowest court with jury trials, for the period 1688–1834 (Webb and Webb 1963). An excellent recent treatment of assizes from 1558 to 1714 (Cockburn 1972) describes the personnel, proceedings, and political significance of the circuit court, which tried most serious offenses. The highest criminal court, King's Bench, is neglected, but see Blatcher (1978) for an earlier period, and Innes (1980) on its prison. Church courts trying morals and defamation cases are not studied for this period, but see Marchant (1969) for their earlier history. On criminal procedure see the succinct and learned summary in Baker (1977); on trials and the nature of verdicts see the important account in Beattie (1977).

[9] On the special case of insanity see Walker (1968).

[10] With the important differences that English trials were public, openly confronted the accused with his accuser in all cases, and did not countenance distinctions such as the French rule that allowed torture to be used against vagabonds where it could not be used against others, or the principle that the social status of both parties must be considered in determining punishment (Langbein 1977, pp. 13, 150).

dentiary rulings such as may now dominate a criminal trial
(Cockburn 1972, chap. 6; Beattie 1977, pp. 164–74). A study of
the Old Bailey sessions papers suggests that the growth of the
law of evidence was in large part the result of increasingly common representation of defendants by counsel. Once allowed into
the courtroom (in law, not completely until 1836 but in practice
long before) the lawyers shaped trial procedure increasingly into
an adversarial mold as they took part in more trials (Langbein
1978; Philips 1977, pp. 104–5). The question has more than a
purely legal significance. The public trial was the principal source
of popular knowledge about the workings of the law. The increasing formality, more scrupulous attention to evidence, and
greater impartiality of judges must therefore have served to
heighten the popular legitimacy of the courts as arbiters of men's
affairs (Hay 1975a).

C. The Invention of the Penitentiary

The end of the eighteenth century saw the beginning of the
great changes in legislation, enforcement, and punishment which
made the nineteenth-century criminal law not much different
from our own. In punishment the change was virtually complete
by the 1860s. But most capital statutes were not touched until
the 1830s and 1840s, after at least a century of complaint that
prosecutors were deterred by the severity of the punishment. The
delay in dismantling the capital code was partly due to the unsatisfactory results of transportation and whipping, which were
uncertain in their effects but the only real alternative to hanging.
Probably more important, however, was the belief of government
that some discretionary hangings might always be necessary, as
a deterrent or to restore order. Certainly the ideological functions
of pardons and death sentences continued to be exploited long
after the capital code proved ineffective in preventing crime
(Hay 1975a).[11] But from 1783, when processions to the gallows

[11] For the ideological significance of the criminal law in justifying the social
order in this period see also Thompson (1975b, pp. 258–69), with a somewhat
different emphasis. For the difficulties of realizing the ideological functions of
Anglo-American criminal law in another society, see Genovese (1974, pp. 25–
49).

in London were ended because of frequent riots, until 1868, when the hangman was finally hidden in the prison, public execution fulfilled less and less its purpose as a dignified and terrible example (Linebaugh 1975; Cooper 1974). By the later date its two functions of deterrence and punishment had been wholly assumed by the police and the penitentiary.

The penitentiary epitomized order. It was also expected to be more certain in its effects than transportation: more punitive, and more reformative.[12] Some such solution became increasingly necessary due to the interruptions to transportation that resulted from the American revolution, the French wars at the end of the eighteenth century, and the final refusal of the Australian colonies to accept more convicts by the mid-nineteenth century. The expedient used to supplement transportation from 1774 to the early 1850s, old warships moored as floating prisons, was repeatedly attacked as ineffective and inhumane (Johnson 1970). The prison evolved as an answer to all these difficulties.

But the form taken by the penitentiary was not obvious. Transportation and the hulks had been cheap, but the new prison architecture of separate wards and single cells was not. Nor was there precedent in England for such massive jails. Before the nineteenth century, prisons and houses of correction held only those awaiting trial, debtors, and a few vagrants, petty thieves, and unwed mothers locked up for short terms. Guards were few and corrupt, and the prisoners made many of the rules (Sheehan 1977; Ignatieff 1978; Innes 1980). Explanations for the calculated discipline of Pentonville and the other new prisons thus must be sought in larger changes in English society.

The evolution of the prison (and other European punish-

[12] Studies of transportation tend to emphasize special cases such as political protestors (Rudé 1978) or the voyage and colonial experience (Smith 1947; Bateson 1969; Barry 1958; Robson 1965; Shaw 1966, 1972; Martin 1976). We know less about how it was regarded by the ordinary Englishman, or even by those administering the criminal law (Radzinowicz 1948–68, vol. 1). But it was crucially important as the expedient which allowed England to delay longer than Europe or America in building penitentiaries (Langbein 1977, chap. 2; Rothman 1971). The most common punishment for serious offenses, transportation was neither public and exemplary like so many punishments of the eighteenth century, nor expressly designed to remold character by the new scientific-religious methods invented in the nineteenth.

ments) has been explained as a partial expression of problems of capitalist labor supply (Rusche and Kirchheimer 1968). It is a suggestive analysis, which needs much closer testing in the light of more exact knowledge of English economic history. Another account (Foucault 1977) sees the transition from capital punishment to imprisonment throughout Europe as one expression of a profound change in modes of power. The ancien régime staged executions and spectacular torture to celebrate the irresistible will of the sovereign. By the nineteenth century, however, the new "science" of criminology, using exact techniques in the laboratory of the "carceral system," was expected instead to reshape criminal character. Even when it failed to do so, the prison could be justified as an attempt to segregate the most dangerous criminals from the rest of the working class, and served to create the idea of "the delinquent" as a man or woman radically different from others. The argument is rich in insights, but it scorns chronology and tends to reduce modes of power to a self-explanatory (and unexplained) principle of social organization.

Closer studies have established much more about the origins of English penitentiaries in particular, and the theories and motives of their creators. At once punitive and humane, psychically destructive and hygienically sound, a secular invention marked deeply by religious purposes, the penitentiary fused some of the main strands of European and English cultural development. It expressed the renewed belief that criminality was a product of criminal character, not of circumstance. And to remake character it created an unremitting discipline, based on the religious experience of conversion, a psychology of perceptions, and the practical experience of factory masters instilling discipline in another institutional setting. Elimination of squalid living conditions seemed compatible with a merciless attack on personality, both in the name of humane reform. But as the architecture became more elaborate and the isolation of the prisoner more complete, more prisoners went insane and the evidence of character reformation became unconvincing (Henriques 1972; Tomlinson 1978; Ignatieff 1978).

The subsequent evolution of prison policy, after mid-century,

is less clear. Increasing punitiveness in both the legislation determining sentences and in the administration of prisons was apparently closely tied to the level of crime and the ebb and flow
of middle-class confidence that the threat from the dangerous
class could be contained. In the 1850s and 1860s the end of transportation alarmed the middle class: all criminals would eventually
be released in England. And a press campaign not only attacked
the idea of rehabilitation but probably created waves of arrests
and convictions by generating public alarm and increased police
activity. Such reinforcing fears also helped bring about the en-
actment of rigorous legislation such as the Penal Servitude Act
and the Habitual Criminals Act (Davis 1980). In the prison system a hard régime prevailed to the end of the nineteenth century,
and what moderation there was in the harshness of the law came
about largely as a result of a decline in the length of sentences
from the 1860s, and some attempts to correct the very wide disparities in sentences passed by different judges (Radzinowicz and
Hood 1979, p. 1323, n. 131, and *passim;* Gatrell 1980, appendix
B).

But all conclusions about the evolution of punishments over
the whole period of the eighteenth and nineteenth centuries must
be tentative until we know exactly how convicts were dealt with.
Even the statistics on capital punishment are incomplete, and we
have very little information, especially for the eighteenth century, on the incidence and timing of whipping, transportation,
and shorter or longer terms of imprisonment.[13]

D. The New Police

The progressive reduction of capital punishment, changes in
procedure that gave greater protection to defendants, and the
invention of the penitentiary were projects usually supported by
the same men. But "reformers" (an unsatisfactory characteriza-

[13] Philips (1977) gives six-year averages for larceny sentences in the Black
Country, 1835–60, but aggregates the figures for the whole period when discussing particular offenses. Gatrell (1980, appendix B) provides quinquennial distributions of sentences for felonious and malicious wounding, and property
offenses with and without violence, for England, 1834–1914. A firm basis for
eighteenth-century comparisons will be found in J. M. Beattie's forthcoming
work on sentences in three counties between 1660 and 1800.

tion that still peppers the literature) were much less agreed about police. The deep Whig prejudices against executive coercion by a political police continued well into the nineteenth century, while a precarious order was maintained by parish constables, troops, private watchmen, and the yeomanry. The property of the rich was guarded by their servants. And a radical working class movement, harassed by government spies and informers in the first three decades of the century, denounced all proposals for a new police as an extension of those methods. Only increasing urban and rural disorder, and the threat of it, rising rates of prosecutions, and astute parliamentary tactics allowed Peel to create the metropolitan London police force in 1829. Continued parsimony and suspicion delayed the creation of provincial forces for another ten years, and sometimes much longer (Miller 1977a; Stevenson 1977; Silver 1967; Hart 1955, 1956; Radzinowicz 1948–68, vols. 1 and 4; Mather 1959; Darvall 1969).

Middle-class fears of police tyranny evaporated, but working-class hostility was largely reinforced. For the new police were frequently the agents of a middle-class assault on popular mores, not just crime or riot, and they introduced constant surveillance into working-class communities which had long since escaped the knowledge of squire and parson. Their establishment in new areas was thus a sensitive issue in class politics, and a frequent cause of riots (Foster 1974; Donajgrodzki 1977; Storch 1975). Their deployment became a carefully calculated policy, and the consent of the community was courted through rigid discipline and a policy of restraint.

The police became central to all subsequent discussion of the criminal law, and they incidentally transformed the nature of the historical evidence, notably the criminal statistics (see below, pp. 62–68). Both the metropolitan and provincial forces evolved from undisciplined groups with a high turnover to effective bureaucracies under close discipline and, in London, central control (Radzinowicz 1948–68, vol. 4; Philips 1977; Miller 1977). They assumed quickly the main responsibility for prosecutions, and enabled the government to dispense with troops when faced with disorder. Their usefulness in dealing with riot helps explain the relative lack of disorder in the later Victorian years, compared to the massive confrontations of the early decades, and the endemic riot of the eighteenth century. But riot was endemic in the eighteenth century not just because government was weak. Many riots enjoyed a great degree of legitimacy, or expressed popular convictions so deep that no police, had one existed, could have suppressed them. The social history of riot is a sharp reminder that crime, though defined by laws, is also a result of traditions and practices with their own cultural histories. The law creates crime, but often does not understand what it has created.

II. Riots and Crime

The crime of riot began to undergo substantial reinterpretation twenty years ago, and the results now inspire work on other offenses. The reasons have to do with both historiography and the nature of English society. For a long time, riot was just another crime to historians, a crime committed by an anonymous "mob" that was hardly differentiated from an equally anonymous "criminal element" (Rudé 1964, p. 8). As more work was done to identify rioters, they emerged as more respectable than expected, and the riot often turned out to be an organized instance of political pressure or economic negotiation, or even an assertion of constitutional rights. The crowd was usually disciplined and informed about its aims, and discriminating in the property destruction it sometimes organized. The very idea of a "crowd" was severely qualified by the demonstration that there were many different kinds of participants in riot, with very specific motives. And a taxonomy of food riots, church and king riots, Jacobite and Jacobin riots quickly developed. In each case, deeper understanding of motive and cultural context proved to be crucial to historical explanation (Rudé 1964, 1973; Rose 1960, 1961; Hobsbawm 1959).

The food riot is a good example, and an important one, as the most common kind of disturbance until the early nineteenth cen-

tury and one for which the incidence and geographical distribution is quite well known.[14] It can no longer be characterized as
a "simple" riot "without ideas" (Hobsbawm 1959, pp. 110–11).
It was almost always a well-organized demand for government
regulation of food prices and sales, regulation which was provided for in Tudor and Stuart statutes, but increasingly unen-
forced in the face of the developing integration of national and
international markets. When prices rose or wholesalers threatened to buy up short supplies, the crowd increasingly had to act
itself, threatening buyers, seizing and selling grain at a fixed price,
halting wagons and barges en route to the ports or to London.
And much of this direct action was considered legitimate by both
the crowd and the local magistrates. Both knew that the law provided a remedy but that it was not enforced. Their agreement
about the old "moral economy" of paternalist protection for the
consumer, and often their common suspicion of dissenting millers
and wholesalers, allowed for negotiation. A few mills were destroyed or granaries pillaged, and then the gentry met the mob.
Charity was promised, some tenets of political economy explained, prosecutions of speculators announced. Except in the
worst years the crisis passed quickly. Few gentlemen feared revolution except in years of very widespread riot, such as 1766.
Only in the context of the French revolutionary threat, and the
massive distress of 1795 and 1800–1801, did it seem to government that the food riot threatened the constitution itself (Thompson 1971).

The riot emerges in this account as an act with a cultural and
political and economic history, as it does also in accounts of
political protests in the early eighteenth century (Holmes 1976;
Rogers 1978), the massive agricultural disturbances of 1830
(Hobsbawm and Rudé 1969), distinctive Welsh disorders (Williams 1955; Jones 1973) and attacks on the Salvation Army in
late Victorian England (Bailey 1977). These diverse episodes,
each with distinctive purposes and methods, are only a small part
of the popular activity now being studied. (For an overview of

[14] Establishing the chronology showed that official sources were very incomplete; cf. Gurr, Grabosky, and Hula (1977, pp. 16, 29).

the period 1700–1870, see Stevenson 1979.) And the whole corpus of work on riot has important implications for the study of historical crime in general.

It has revealed that the official record of "disorder" is very incomplete, and that its dimensions can only be approximated by using a very wide range of sources. It is clear too that riot was very often recorded as theft or other offenses for which charges could be laid. For both these reasons, correlations of "disorder" with "crime" are unlikely to explain much about either (see, e.g., Gurr, Grabosky, and Hula 1977, pp. 666ff.; Rudé 1973, pp. 10ff.). The historiography of riot suggests that it may be wrong to distinguish "public order" offenses from "ordinary crime" as sharply as is sometimes done. The motivations of many rioters are now much clearer to us, but that many other crimes are less understood should not lead us to assume that criminals were a different species from rioters. Both were criminals in the eyes of the law; more important, recent work increasingly suggests that a wide range of other crime enjoyed broad community sanction. Thus poachers, smugglers, pillagers of wrecked ships, and makers of counterfeit coin all worked collectively within communal definitions that legitimized their crimes (Munsche 1977; Hay 1975b; Winslow 1975; Rule 1975; Styles 1980). All these groups too, at times, used riot, destruction of property, or violence against others while defending their distinctive economies.

As with riot, the reconstruction of the systems of beliefs that surround particular crimes illuminates economies, group interests, and local practices, rather than "crime" or "deviance." Other offenses that have been made comprehensible in human terms include witchcraft, arson, and infanticide (Thomas 1971; Macfarlane 1970; Hobsbawm and Rudé 1969; Jones 1968; Malcolmson 1977). Sexual offenses, female crime, and the organizations of London master thieves and receivers have also been the subject of recent studies (Gilbert 1976; Harvey 1978; Storch 1977a; Beattie 1975; Howson 1970). As the literature grows we reawaken to the diversity of what the criminal law proscribes, and as our understanding of different crimes matures we become more and more aware of the importance of specific historical context to explanations. None of the areas described has approached the maturity of the work on riot, with the possible exception of that on witchcraft.[15] But as more is understood of popular mentalities and class relations, we begin, as with riot, to transcend the myopia of the criminal law, which sees only—crime.[16] Simple larceny too becomes less simple and less individualistic an act when its context is more fully understood (see below, pp. 72–73).

A. Rates of Prosecution

The work on the popular culture of crime has been paralleled by a somewhat separate growth of quantitative studies, which have begun to establish the main trends in levels of prosecutions, and some of their connections with long-term structural change and short-run fluctuations in economic conditions. Quantitative studies seem inevitable for crime, and not only because of the long positivist tradition which colors contemporary criminology as well as history. The English sources demand sophisticated quantitative treatment, for the oral procedure of English courts generated remarkably few detailed accounts. What remains are arid and stylized indictments and recognizances, which yield up useful conclusions only through careful statistical analysis. Scrupulous preliminary examination of these and other documents has exposed their formal nature (Cockburn 1975, 1978; Baker 1980; Beattie 1972). Close attention has also been given to biases introduced by changes in the law, by incentives for prosecution, and by the creation of the police (Beattie 1974, 1980; Philips 1977; Gatrell and Hadden 1972). But there are serious gaps in most of the quantitative studies that have appeared so far. Few

[15] See also Boyer and Nissenbaum (1974) for a full exploitation of local sources for the Salem trials in Massachusetts, which provide some interesting contrasts with the English experience.

[16] Some recent quantitative studies take too pessimistic a view of the sources. Thus Gurr, Grabosky, and Hula 1977: "Historical studies of crime and public order are limited to what can be observed mainly in records of public (especially official) policies and actions and to aggregate measures of demographic and economic conditions. Information on the beliefs, social wants, and opportunities of less advantaged historical groups is scanty" (p. 749).

discuss the ratio of prosecuted to unprosecuted behavior, the discretion of the police with respect to different crimes, or how different kinds of criminals run different risks. Categorization of crimes is idiosyncratic; rates and ratios are usually not comparable from one study to another. Most serious is the failure to employ much statistical sophistication in what are statistical arguments. Correlations of rates of crime with other social facts have been based mostly on visual comparisons, and the logic or construction of other time-series (such as economic indicators) is rarely explained.

Nonetheless some patterns emerge. Over the longer period rates in the early eighteenth century were much lower than they had been a hundred years earlier. Probably this was partly a consequence of the considerable growth of summary jurisdiction, and other changes related to the marked decentralization and informality of local government after the restoration of the Stuart kings. But the direction of secular change was upward during the eighteenth century, at least for serious offenses. (A very large and unknown number of summary convictions were never recorded.) In the nineteenth century, high levels after the Napoleonic wars persisted through the 1840s, followed by a long decline for almost a century, only reversed in the late 1930s. Not much discussion of these very long-term trends has yet developed, but there is disagreement as to what degree they represent changes in court structure, attitudes of prosecutors and police, or behavior of those groups among whom the accused were found (Cockburn 1977; Beattie 1974; Philips 1977; Gatrell and Hadden 1972; Gurr, Grabosky, and Hula 1977; Gatrell 1980).

It seems likely that these problems will remain particularly acute in studies of long-term trends, which may be thought of as the product of successive systems of criminal law and successive social structures, complicated by evanescent economic and political events. In short, the number of variables is very large, and we do not yet know much about many of them for very many points in these two hundred years. On the other hand, more seems certain about the effects on crime of short-term economic change, for periods when the administration of the criminal law, social structure, and mentalities can be assumed to have been static.[17]

The importance of the police to this argument must be emphasized. Short-term variations may be more reliable than long-term ones only in societies without such highly organized enforcement bureaucracies. Thus in eighteenth-century England, recorded crime is the sum of many, largely independent, decisions to prosecute taken by private individuals for the most part. Once organized police were established, in the jurisdiction of any given force and sometimes in several, decisions taken at the center affected both enforcement and recording procedures for all offenses. Changes in police practice cause remarkable changes in crime rates, as do similar changes in the judicial bureaucracy or in public opinion. And after about 1850 this was increasingly the situation in England (Davis 1980).

But while the police and the Home Office and the press may have introduced distortions into short-term variations in crime rates, it has been convincingly argued that the long-term trend of Victorian crime is more trustworthy. Again the police are a large part of the explanation. From the evidence that there was greater popular acceptance of a more efficient police and judicial system as the decades passed, it follows that there was a deeper penetration of the criminal law into the recesses of Victorian society, and that the gap between criminal acts and recorded crime must therefore have narrowed. And since the trend in the statistics is steadily downward, they must reflect a real decline in most kinds of crime (Gatrell 1980).

Short-run changes can be shown to correlate very well with other events. In the eighteenth century and until the end of Napoleonic wars, rates of indictable offenses leaped upward at the end of every war. Demobilization of the armed forces was feared by the propertied for precisely this reason, and the pattern is clear wherever it has been investigated (Cockburn 1977; Beat-

[17] Compare Gatrell and Hadden (1972, pp. 360–61) (but see also Gatrell 1980). The opposite view is taken in Hindus (1977, p. 213) and Gurr, Grabosky, and Hula (1977, p. 21, but see also p. 52).

tie 1974; Gatrell and Hadden 1972). But we do not yet know the relative importance of labor surplus, brutalization in the forces, demobilization of criminals who had been conscripted, or increased prosecution through fear.

A second relationship that obtains until the early nineteenth century is the fluctuation of indictments for property crime with changes in food prices caused by harvests and markets. The harvest cycle is then superseded by the violent trade and invest-ment cycles of industrial capitalism (a transition well known to economic historians), and property crime shifts accordingly. At the same time, in the nineteenth century, assault and drunkenness exhibit an inverse correlation with economic hardship (Beattie 1974; Gatrell and Hadden 1972; Philips 1977). Earlier sugges-tions that economic changes were irrelevant to crime rates (Tobi-as 1967) are quite wrong, for variations in police or judicial practice cannot possibly explain the strong correlations ob-served.[18] The pattern disappears sometime between 1850 and 1880, depending on the sources used. So far, published accounts disagree about whether this is an artifact of change in the ad-ministration of the law (Philips 1977, p. 146) or a real effect of the improvement in living standards after mid-century (Gatrell and Hadden 1972, pp. 368–69). New evidence suggests the lat-ter, because rates of offenses show remarkable responsiveness to new economic conditions later in the century. In the 1880s there is a negative correlation between theft and hardship, but in the harsher economic conditions of the decade before the First World War, and again between the wars, the positive correlation reap-pears. Equally striking, positive correlations between theft and hardship occur in periods when the general trend of thefts is up-ward (before 1850) or steady (after 1900). But during the pe-riod when the general trend is steadily downward (1850–1900) there is no relationship, or an inverse one, between theft and economic conditions. The plausible explanation is that in the periods of strong correlation there was a coincidence of employ-

[18] In the Midland county of Stafford in the later eighteenth century, fully 80 percent of the variance in simple larceny can be explained by fluctuations in local grain prices, controlling for effects of demobilization after wars (my unpublished findings).

ment and subsistence crises, and perhaps the creation of a more permanent criminal class through increased policing (Gatrell 1980).

B. Counting Crimes

The quantitative work mentioned here is clearly only first soundings, though the initial findings are sufficiently suggestive to show the value of critical and careful statistical studies.[19] But in some recent writing an argument is developing that we should eschew all attempts to distinguish the quantitative dimensions of "real crime" from the effects of judicial systems. The argument is strongly influenced by labeling theory: the undoubted fact that lawmakers and police create "official crime," and alter behavior itself, by identifying actions and actors as criminal. In this view criminal statistics are always "indices of organization processes rather than of the incidence of certain forms of behavior" (Monkkonen 1979, p. 456, quoting Cicourel and Kitsuse 1963; also cited in Philips 1977, p. 45). The problem of unrecorded crime is largely dismissed, either because it is not crime (behavior so recorded), or at least not socially significant crime (because policy-making elites react to recorded behavior). Instead of serial study of crime rates in one society, we are urged to make cross-sectional comparisons of different societies, lifting the discussion "from a groundless argument about the value of the indicators to a systematic and substantive discussion of differing criminal justice systems, or of differences between geopolitical areas and social structures" (Monkkonen 1979, p. 459, citing Gurr, Grabosky, and Hula 1977 and the work of Michael Hindus as examples.)

There are two problems with this program. It may not in fact reveal much about social structure; and, if followed literally, it rules out research into the most interesting questions about the place of crime in popular culture. Certainly there is ample evidence that the bureaucracies of the law, particularly the police,

[19] Tobias's wholesale dismissal of the nineteenth-century statistical returns (1967, appendix) was effectively demolished by Gatrell and Hadden (1972), at least for national aggregates. The problems with more local studies are discussed below.

do label, do create offenders, do markedly affect the criminal statistics. But there is a simultaneous (and real) evolution of the kinds of behavior which are susceptible to prosecution. And unless the histories of both are investigated, the meaning of their net result, "official crime," remains obscure. An implicit recognition of this fact causes some advocates of an interactionist perspective to return in practice to discussions of "real crime" (Philips 1977). On the other hand, comparisons of different legal systems (or, presumably, particular ones at different times) may not tell us much about social structures or popular attitudes precisely because police and courts are so important in shaping the record of crime. For two legal bureaucracies are often more similar in organization, and the elites controlling them more like in their attitudes, than the societies that they respectively police. Two such bureaucracies may therefore process and record rather similar samples of cases, even when those samples are unrepresentative (in different ways) of the different crime in each jurisdiction. In short, criminal statistics may suggest a spurious identity of crime and punishment in very different societies.[20]

This argument too is unproven, but it does not seem self-evident that cross-cultural comparisons, or those between different jurisdictions, are any less dangerous than assessments of the relation between official and real crime. But there is a more important reason why we cannot abandon the attempt to isolate the latter. Understanding "real" crime is shorthand for understanding a large part of the culture of the poor, of the working class, of the dangerous class—all those most visited by the police and most knowledgeable about the social significance of the criminal law. And the disjunction between their experience and the interpretations of the judiciary and police is the root of the legitimacy that the law has, or does not have, in different societies

[20] One thinks of the rapid diffusion in Europe and America of "delinquency" as an explanatory category in the nineteenth century. Similar levels of state formation may also have created spurious similarities in the judicial records in earlier periods, A small example: it appears that sixteenth-century France, and eighteenth-century England, New France, and post-conquest Quebec, with very different legal systems, social structures, and constitutions, all imposed the death penalty at the rate of 1 execution per 100,000 population per year (Hay 1980).

or at different times. In short, criminal-legal history will only reach its full development as part of a total social history.

But how can we penetrate behind the flawed statistics? The short (but not simple) answer has three parts. The effects of judicial and police procedures must be closely studied. Sophisticated quantification must seek to understand connections with other social facts such as economic conditions, or police strength. But most important may be the reconstruction, from a wide range of other sources, of the social histories of the communities in which the crime and prosecution took place. Recent work on living standards and poverty cycles has been fruitful because it has been based on close local work, where such sources as the manuscript census returns allow reconstitution of neighborhoods or parishes (e.g., Foster 1974). There are greater difficulties in using the criminal statistics for such small areas than with the national aggregates, which smooth out anomalies (Gatrell and Hadden 1972). But aggregates, while suggestive of important trends, are averages and cannot be linked into clear causal chains with much other social change. For the historical experience of English industrialization is staggeringly diverse: local mores, highly distinctive congregations of workers in particular trades, local economies only gradually immeshed with national market structures, popular beliefs and trade practices peculiar to a town or parish. All these are likely to be important in explaining patterns of local crime, both "real" and "official." This texture is almost wholly lost in series compiled on a national or even regional level. And until we recover it, full explanations of national trends will be difficult to make.

III. Emerging Explanations: Capitalism and Crime

From close local work, more subtle quantitative analysis, and comparative work on specific offenses, we may expect answers to begin emerging about the effects of long-run structural change on crime. English historians have not been particularly interested in paradigms used elsewhere. There has been little comment on the preoccupation of French historians, the apparent secular decline in crimes of violence and increase in crimes of guile (LeRoy

Ladurie 1973). Nor has the American obsession with urbanization as an explanatory category aroused much interest, either because sociology has had so little impact on English academic
work, or because the concept itself seemed hardly applicable to
the complex local history of London.[21] But more important is the
fact that, for England, the process of capitalist industrialization
so clearly set the bounds of social development that its primary
significance for crime has been assumed. Recent work suggests
that the assumption was correct, and that the meaning of the
criminal law was equally affected.

Nevertheless, there has not been much work yet that explicitly
relates stages of economic growth to the development of crime
between the Restoration and the twentieth century. One typology of full-time thieves constructs four ideal types of criminal
organization (picaresque, craft, project, and business) which are
associated with a very general framework of economic growth
(McIntosh 1971, 1975). Its specific relevance to the eighteenth
and nineteenth centuries has not been much tested.[22] More work
has been done on the Victorian preoccupation with the growth
of a "dangerous class," its influence on the infant science of
criminology, and the problem of casual labor, which made it
seem a persuasive explanation (Tobias 1967; Foucault 1977;
Stedman Jones 1971; Bailey 1975). Some preliminary evidence
suggests that the nineteenth century did see a growing distinction between an increasingly "respectable" working class, and
a separate culture of the criminal and "rough."[23] There are a
range of possible explanations: the effect of imprisonment in
creating an identified "delinquent" group; working-class political
and trade union organization; rising real wages after mid-century

[21] See Lane (1974) for the relative preoccupation of American historians
with urbanization, an emphasis which has since undergone much questioning.

[22] Gatrell (1980) discusses it in relation to serious crimes against property
in the late 19th century.

[23] Gatrell and Hadden (1972, pp. 381–83) observe a higher proportion of
former convicts in the prison population later in the century, suggesting development of a criminal class. But this may have been an effect of a more efficient police. And mitigation of sentences from 1860 to 1900 released first offenders more rapidly, or resulted in sentences other than imprisonment (Gatrell
1980).

for some workers; greater dangers to less professional thieves from the new police. All these require more examination (Davis 1980; Gatrell 1980). But over a much longer period there were also changes in definitions of property and the wage, aspects of the growth of industrial capitalism, which created sharper demarcations of crime. In this process the law may have succeeded in creating both the concept of delinquency and the life histories that exemplified the concept.

The most persuasive evidence begins with an examination of the convicted, particularly in London. Certainly there were full-time thieves in London for centuries before this, and groups of them, organized by skilled tacticians of crime, distinguished by cant or working methods, and probably related through long chains of kinship.[24] But important recent work on the collective biography of those hanged in London finds little difference in origins or experience from the great mass of the laboring poor.[25] Men and women ended up at Tyburn when they lost their precarious security through trade depressions, technological or commercial displacement, or sharp rises in the costs of necessities. Whole trades could be so affected; thus changes in the meat trade could cause butchers to be disproportionately represented on the gallows. And this common occurrence undoubtedly legitimized some crimes (such as highway robbery) among a whole class of men not formerly involved, and caused many hangings to become occasions of class and trade or (for the Irish) national solidarity (Linebaugh 1975).

Moreover, other groups of workers entered the criminal court records through activities which suddenly became illegal. There is much evidence that masters and landlords, dismayed by the relative shortage of labor early in the eighteenth century, were convinced of the need for tighter labor discipline and a reduction of wages. One form this took was a prolonged campaign, per-

[24] A recent critique of cant, however, argues that thieves' languages are largely a fiction of genre literature (Curtis and Mannsaker 1980).

[25] This and the next paragraph are a bald outline of two themes developed with a wealth of detail in Peter Linebaugh's unpublished study of *Crime and the Wage in the 18th Century*. On the identity of the laboring poor and criminal poor, see also Philips (1977).

haps sharper in this period but seen in a variety of trades at different times over the next century and a half, to rationalize wage payment. The motive was to eliminate traditional perquisites, that part of the raw materials or finished product claimed by the worker as part of the wage. Perquisites, although sanctioned by long custom, were therefore increasingly redefined, in many trades, as theft. Parliament enacted a large number of embezzlement statutes in the course of the century, to allow easier prosecution of workers taking materials, and justices and juries enforced them.[26]

A similar case was the enclosure of open-field parishes, particularly where there were large numbers of poor commoners with extensive customary rights to firewood, furze, nuts and berries, turf or other goods (depending on local custom). Enclosure of open fields and wastes by act of parliament extinguished those rights, commuting them into small parcels of land where commoners could prove a full case, or removing them without compensation where custom had not been clearly enough established in the courts in earlier centuries. As a consequence, commoners often rioted, tearing down and burning new fences, sometimes destroying the books of the surveyors. But enclosure also increased local "crime" when commoners tried to continue taking wood or turf. Immemorial custom had become trespass and theft, and new prosecuting associations of the larger landowners were not slow to press charges (Thompson 1975b; Reaney 1970; Neeson 1977).

The struggle against customary rights on land and in wage payment was also partly an expression of a wider concern to create a disciplined industrial proletariat, the first in the world. Common rights or perquisites both conferred independence from the wage, and independence (to work or not, to change employers, to leave work uncompleted) was anathema to the early factory masters (Pollard 1965). They worked in close cooperation with magistrates to close pubs, eliminate popular amusements, and increasingly regulate a level of "disorder" which

---

[26] Unpublished work by Raphael Samuel describes the continuing struggle over perks in the 19th century; there is a brief discussion in Philips (1977).

formerly had been tolerated or even considered part of national tradition. Religious motives also fueled the attack on "low amusements," but there was often a satisfactory convergence of economic and moral principle for a dissenting factory master (Malcolmson 1973; Storch 1977b, 1976; Reid 1976). By the later nineteenth century a disciplined and usually tractable labor force existed which responded to wage incentives, had few options to do otherwise, and pursued class aims in trade unions (now legalized) and in politics.[27] But until that shift into the relative acquiescence of the heavily policed and more prosperous society of the later nineteenth century, a vigorous plebeian culture posed a politically disturbing and economically frustrating challenge to those with power.

IV. Legitimacy and Justice

A central issue raised by this evolution of criminal laws is the legitimacy of particular crimes, and the legitimacy of the criminal law as a whole, in the minds of ordinary Englishmen. Workers resisting the criminalization of perks, or commoners trespassing on what had been their communal property, did not believe they were defying justice: their employers and landlords were. In a similar way, other crimes were regarded as perfectly legitimate activities by almost the entire population (poaching, smuggling) or by particular communities (wrecking, coining) (see references at p. 61 above). A distinction is sometimes made between such "social crime" (enjoying community sanction or carried out collectively) and "ordinary crime" (such as thefts committed by individuals, from which men of all classes suffered). The dichotomy takes several forms, from that of the honest versus the dishonest poor (distinguished by squires excusing smugglers), or social protesters versus real criminals (suggested by some historians), or proletariat versus lumpenproletariat (in some Marxist writing) (Society for the Study of Labour History 1972; Hirst 1972; Rudé 1973). But such distinctions are much less clear in the evidence from local studies. We now

---

[27] Nonmonetary income could still be surprisingly important, however, in particular communities even in the late nineteenth century (Samuel 1975).

understand why many riots were considered legitimate and why some other offenses were thought so by certain groups, and it seems likely that the same kinds of distinctions obtained in many communities about the most ordinary kinds of theft or assault. Whether sheepstealing was legitimate or not depended on whose sheep were stolen, by whom, and what the relation of the two was known to be. It depended as well on whether many in the community felt themselves exposed to that particular form of theft, which in turn could be a reflection of the distribution of wealth or the structure of common rights. In short, agreed distinctions about the legitimacy of certain offenses, or offenses in certain circumstances, obtained in particular villages, trades, and streets of cities. And "ordinary" crime (illegal individual behavior) thus could be collective in the sense that a large part of the community might engage in it sometimes, or at least would not think of denouncing such acts by others. Because we do not understand the circumstances of much theft, we should not therefore assume that most of it was the work of isolated individuals, or that it enjoyed no communal sanction.

The legitimacy of the criminal law as a whole must be closely related to these questions, but the connections are still unclear. Much class conflict found its locus in the courts, perhaps particularly so in the eighteenth century (which in the historiography of popular movements was something of a hiatus before the riot came under scrutiny). But whether the criminal law as a whole was perceived by the poor as the creation of a class enemy is far less certain. Recently it has been argued that the poor concurred in the justice of the criminal law, at least in the Black Country in Victorian times, because some 20 percent of the prosecutors were unskilled working men (Philips 1977, pp. 127–28). But there are two difficulties with this argument. One is the specific and partial nature of legitimacy already mentioned. The other is the probability that crimes enjoying communal sanction were difficult to prosecute and hence underrepresented in the court records. It follows that prosecutions by the poor against offenses not popularly tolerated or endorsed may be overrepresented, all else being equal. Moreover, without knowing the circumstances of each case brought by a poor prosecutor, it is difficult to know whether they represent personal disputes, malice, or have other meanings beyond the prosecution of "crime."

We are reminded again that crimes represent the judicial response to an enormously wide range of human behavior, behavior which may have nothing in common beyond the fact that it can be prosecuted. That is, of course, an important common characteristic, as any six men hanged at Tyburn for different offenses would have testified at the gallows. Moreover, the common punishment meted out to different offenses, and the fact that the criminal law was through most of this period the creation of the propertied and the powerful, did create solidarities where none had existed before. It is likely, for example, that the illegality of trade unionism caused many workers in early nineteenth-century England to be better acquainted with revolutionary doctrine than otherwise would have been the case (Thompson 1968, pp. 546ff.). And criminal definitions constructed by elites do create crimes of specific kinds. Much of the history of crime can be thought of as a succession of different kinds of labeling, stigmatizing in turn heretics, vagabonds, witches, masterless men, the mob, the dangerous class, and delinquents.

But the crucial point remains: these are elite definitions. Popular attitudes are likely to be quite different, and the superficial identities of crimes in the official record are largely a product of the fact that "legal institutions are . . . responsible for bringing a logical order to deviancy which lacks this order in its pristine form" (Rock 1973, p. 57). Popular culture had its own definitions, practiced its own labeling. Much more is now understood about the rituals of popular justice, in England and Europe (Thompson 1972). Wife-beating, breaking trade union solidarity, unseemly marriages, and a wide range of other behavior were the object of ritualistic public humiliation. Less openly (because it was illegal), a community could ostracize, threaten, or actively persecute members who transgressed its moral codes concerning property. The more public and violent forms of "rough music" were part of the popular culture increasingly repressed as the state sought to impose its version of "order" throughout the nineteenth century. But the tradition, even when it went underground or assumed other forms, endured. Recovering it is part of the historical task of reconstructing popular legitimacies.

The poor imposed their norms not only on one another but, to an extent, on the powerful as well. The Gordon rioters of 1780 virtually controlled London for five days. They freed the prisoners in Newgate jail, burned the house of the Lord Chief Justice, destroyed Catholic chapels and residences of the rich, and threatened Parliament itself. The starving rural laborers of the 1830s and 1840s destroyed machinery and barns by riot and arson, terrified hundreds of farmers, clerics, and magistrates, and in anonymous letters (Hobsbawm and Rudé 1969, p. 210) rebuked them for their greed and egoism:

> Sir, Your name is down amongst the Black hearts in the
> Black Book and this is to advise you and the like of you,
> who are Parson Justasses, to make your Wills
>   Ye have been the Blackguard Enemies of the People
> on all occasions, Ye have not done as ye ought.
>   Swing

On these and countless less dramatic occasions the powerful were forced to respond, sometimes with hangings or mantraps, but also by making charity less mean or the poor laws less brutal. Riot and arson and the secret and anonymous destruction of property were popular attempts to impose definitions of right and wrong on the rulers of England. There was not a consensus about authority, property, and crime. Two different conceptions of justice were embodied in the corpse of an executed rioter, rotting in chains, and in the burning barns and slaughtered horses of a hated magistrate.

REFERENCES

Bailey, Victor. 1975. "The Dangerous Classes in Late Victorian England." Ph.D. dissertation, Warwick University.
———. 1977. "Salvation Army Riots, the 'Skeleton Army' and Legal

Authority in the Provincial Town." In *Social Control in 19th-Century Britain*, ed. A. P. Donajgrodzki. London: Croom Helm.

——. 1980. "Crime, Criminal Justice and Authority in England: a Bibliographical Essay," *Bulletin of the Society for the Study of Labour History* (Spring 1980).

Baker, J. H. 1977. "Criminal Courts and Procedure at Common Law 1550–1800." In *Crime in England 1550–1800* (see Cockburn 1977).

——. 1978. *Legal Records and the Historian*. London: Royal Historical Society.

——. 1980. "The Refinement of English Criminal Jurisprudence, 1500–1848." In *Crime and Justice in Europe and Canada*, ed. Louis A. Knafla. Montreal: Wilfred Laurier Press.

Barry, John Vincent. 1958. *Alexander Maconochie of Norfolk Island: a Study of a Pioneer in Penal Reform*. Melbourne: Oxford University Press.

Bateson, Charles. 1969. *The Convict Ships, 1787–1868*. 2d ed. Glasgow: Brown, Son & Ferguson.

Beattie, J. M. 1972. "Towards a Study of Crime in 18th Century England: A Note on Indictments." In *The Triumph of Culture*, ed. Paul Fritz and David Williams. Toronto: A. M. Hakkert, Ltd.

——. 1974. "The Pattern of Crime in England, 1660–1800," *Past & Present* 62: 47–95.

——. 1975. "The Criminality of Women in Eighteenth-Century England," *Journal of Social History* 8:80–116.

——. 1977. "Crime and the Courts in Surrey 1736–1753." In *Crime in England 1550–1800* (see Cockburn 1977).

——. 1980. "Judicial Records and the Measurement of Crime in Eighteenth Century England." In *Crime and Justice in Europe and Canada* (see Baker 1980).

Blatcher, Marjorie. 1978. *The Court of King's Bench, 1450–1550: A Study in Self-help*. London: Athlone Press.

Boyer, Paul, and Stephen Nissenbaum. 1974. *Salem Possessed: the Social Origins of Witchcraft*. Cambridge, Mass.: Harvard University Press.

Chaloner, W. H., and R. C. Richardson. 1976. *British Economic and Social History: a Bibliographical Guide*. Totawa, N.J.: Rowman and Littlefield.

Cicourel, Aaron V., and John I. Kitsuse. 1963. "A Note on the Uses of Official Statistics," *Social Problems* 11:131–39.

Cockburn, J. S. 1972. *A History of English Assizes, 1558–1714*. Cambridge: Cambridge University Press.

——. 1975. "Early-modern Assize Records as Historical Evidence," *Journal of the Society of Archivists* 5:215–31.

——. 1977. "The Nature and Incidence of Crime in England 1559–

1625." In *Crime in England 1550–1800*, ed. J. S. Cockburn. London: Methuen; Princeton, N.J.: Princeton University Press.

——. 1978. "Trial by the Book? Fact and Theory in the Criminal Process 1558–1625." In *Legal Records and the Historian*, ed. J. H. Baker. London: Royal Historical Society.

Collins, Philip. 1965. *Dickens and Crime*. 2d ed. London: Macmillan.

Cooper, David D. 1974. *The Lesson of the Scaffold: The Public Execution Controversy in Victorian England*. London: Allen Lane.

Cornish, W. R., Jenifer Hart, A. H. Manchester, and J. Stevenson. 1978. *Crime and Law in Nineteenth Century Britain*. A volume in the series "Government and Society in Nineteenth Century Britain: Commentaries on British Parliamentary Papers." Dublin: Irish University Press.

Curtis, Tim, and Frances Mannsaker. 1980. "Anti-social Stereotyping in Early Modern England." In *Crime and Justice in Europe and Canada* (See Baker 1980).

Darvall, Frank O. 1969. *Popular Disturbances and Public Order in Regency England*. New York: A. M. Kelley.

Davis, Jennifer. 1980. "The London Garotting Panic of 1862: A Moral Panic and the Creation of a Criminal Class in Mid-Victorian England." In *Crime and the Law in Western Societies: Historical Essays*, ed. V. A. C. Gatrell, B. Lenman, and G. Parker. London: Europa.

Diamond, Stanley. 1974. "The Rule of Law versus the Order of Custom." In *In Search of the Primitive: a Critique of Civilization*, ed. Stanley Diamond. New Brunswick, N.J.: Transaction Books.

Donajgrodzki, A. P. 1977. " 'Social Police' and the Bureaucratic Elite: a Vision of Order in the Age of Reform." In *Social Control in Nineteenth Century Britain*, ed. A. P. Donajgrodzki. London: Croom Helm.

Dunbabin, J. P. D. 1974. *Rural Discontent in Nineteenth Century Britain*. New York: Holmes & Meier.

Foster, John. 1974. *Class Struggle and the Industrial Revolution: Early Industrial Capitalism in Three English Towns*. London: Weidenfeld & Nicolson.

Foucault, Michel. 1977. *Discipline and Punish: the Birth of the Prison*. New York: Pantheon.

Gatrell, V. A. C. 1980. "The Decline of Theft and Violence in Victorian and Edwardian England." In *Crime and the Law in Western Societies: Historical Essays*, ed. V. A. C. Gatrell, B. Lenman, and G. Parker. London: Europa.

Gatrell, V. A. C., and T. B. Hadden. 1972. "Criminal Statistics and their Interpretation." In *Nineteenth Century Society: Essays in the Use of Quantitative Methods for the Study of Social Data*, ed. E. A. Wrigley. Cambridge: Cambridge University Press.

Genovese, Eugene D. 1974. *Roll, Jordan, Roll: The World the Slaves Made*. New York: Pantheon.

Gilbert, Arthur N. 1976. "Buggery and the British Navy, 1700–1861," *Social History* 10:72.

Gillis, John R. 1975. "The Evolution of Juvenile Delinquency in England, 1890–1914," *Past & Present* 67: 96–126.

Gurr, Ted Robert, Peter N. Grabosky, and Richard C. Hula. 1977. *The Politics of Crime and Conflict: A Comparative History of Four Cities*. Beverly Hills and London: Sage.

Hall, Jerome. 1952. *Theft, Law, and Society*. 2d ed. Indianapolis: Bobbs-Merrill.

Hanawalt, Barbara. 1979. *Crime and Conflict in English Communities, 1300–1348*. Cambridge, Mass.: Harvard University Press.

Hart, Jenifer. 1955. "Reform of the Borough Police, 1835–1856," *English Historical Review* 70:411–27.

———. 1956. "The County and Borough Police Act, 1856," *Public Administration* 34:405–17.

Harvey, A. D. 1978. "Prosecutions for Sodomy in England at the Beginning of the Nineteenth Century," *Historical Journal* 21: 939–48.

Hay, Douglas. 1975a. "Property, Authority and the Criminal Law." In *Albion's Fatal Tree: Crime and Society in Eighteenth-Century England*, ed. Douglas Hay, Peter Linebaugh, and E. P. Thompson. New York: Pantheon.

———. 1975b. "Poaching and the Game Laws on Cannock Chase." In *Albion's Fatal Tree* (see Hay 1975a).

———. 1980. "The Meanings of the Criminal Law in Quebec, 1764–1774." In *Crime and Justice in Europe and Canada* (see Baker 1980).

Henriques, U. R. Q. 1972. "The Rise and Decline of the Separate System of Prison Discipline," *Past & Present* 54:61–93.

Hindus, Michael. 1977. "The Contours of Crime and Justice in Massachusetts and South Carolina, 1767–1878," *American Journal of Legal History* 21:212–37.

Hirst, Paul Q. 1972. "Marx and Engels on Law, Crime, and Morality," *Economy and Society* 1:28–56.

Hobsbawm, E. J. 1959. *Primitive Rebels*. New York: Norton.

Hobsbawm, E. J., and George Rudé. 1969. *Captain Swing*. London: Lawrence & Wishart.

Holmes, Geoffrey. 1976. "The Sacheverell Riots: the Crowd and the

Church in Early Eighteenth Century London," *Past & Present* 72: 55–85.

Howell, T. B., ed. 1816–31. *A Complete Collection of State Trials.* London: Hansard.

Howson, Gerald. 1970. *Thief-Taker General: the Rise and Fall of Jonathon Wild.* London: Hutchinson.

Ignatieff, Michael. 1978. *A Just Measure of Pain: the Penitentiary in the Industrial Revolution, 1750–1850.* London: Macmillan.

Ingram, Michael. 1977. "Communities and Courts: Law and Disorder in Early Seventeenth-Century Wiltshire." In *Crime in England 1550–1800* (see Cockburn 1977).

Innes, Joanna. 1980. "The King's Bench Prison in the Later Eighteenth Century: Law, Authority and Order in a London Debtor's Prison." In *An Ungovernable People: The English and Their Law in the 17th and 18th Centuries*, ed. John Brewer and John Styles. New Brunswick, N.J.: Rutgers University Press.

Johnson, W. Branch. 1970. *The English Prison Hulks.* 2d ed. London and Chichester: Phillimore.

Jones, David J. V. 1968. "Thomas Campbell Foster and the Rural Labourer: Incendiarism in East Anglia in the 1840s," *Social History* 1:1–43.

——. 1973. *Before Rebecca: Popular Protests in Wales, 1793–1835.* London: Allen Lane.

——. 1979 "The Poacher: A Study in Victorian Crime and Protest," *Historical Journal* 22:825–60.

Knafla, L. A. 1977. "Crime and Criminal Justice: A Critical Bibliography." In *Crime in England, 1550–1800* (see Cockburn 1977).

Lane, Roger. 1974. "Crime and the Industrial Revolution: British and American Views," *Journal of Social History* 7:287–303.

Langbein, John H. 1977. *Torture and the Law of Proof: Europe and England in the Ancien Régime.* Chicago: University of Chicago Press.

——. 1978. "The Criminal Trial Before the Lawyers," *University of Chicago Law Review* 45: 263–316.

LeRoy Ladurie, E. 1973. "La décroissance du crime au xviiie siècle: bilan d'historiens," *Contrepoint* 9:227–33.

Linebaugh, Peter. 1975. "The Tyburn Riot against the Surgeons." In *Albion's Fatal Tree* (see Hay 1975a).

——. 1977. "The Ordinary of Newgate and His *Account*." In *Crime in England 1550–1800* (see Cockburn 1977).

——. Unpublished. *Crime and the Wage in the Eighteenth Century.*

Macfarlane, Alan. 1970. *Witchcraft in Tudor and Stuart England.* New York: Harper & Row.

McIntosh, Mary. 1971. "Changes in the Organization of Thieving." In *Images of Deviance,* ed. Stanley Cohen. Harmondsworth, England: Penguin.

———. 1975. *The Organisation of Crime.* London: Macmillan.

Maitland, F. W. 1885; new ed. 1974. *Justice and Police.* New York: AMS Press. (Originally published 1885. London: Macmillan).

Malcolmson, Robert W. 1973. *Popular Recreations in English Society 1700–1850.* Cambridge: Cambridge University Press.

———. 1977. "Infanticide in the Eighteenth Century." In *Crime in England 1550–1800* (see Cockburn 1977).

Marchant, Ronald Albert. 1969. *The Church under the Law: Justice, Administration and Discipline in the Diocese of York 1560–1640.* Cambridge: Cambridge University Press.

Martin, Ged. 1976. "Economic Motives Behind the Founding of Botany Bay," *Australian Economic History Review,* 16:128–43.

Mather, Frederick Clare. 1959. *Public Order in the Age of the Chartists.* Manchester: Manchester University Press.

May, Margaret. 1973. "Innocence and Experience: the Evolution of the Concept of Juvenile Delinquency in the mid-19th Century," *Victorian Studies* 17(3):7–29.

Miller, Wilbur R. 1977a. *Cops and Bobbies: Police Authority in New York and London, 1830–1870.* Chicago: University of Chicago Press.

———. 1977b. "Never on Sunday: Moralistic Reformers and the Police in London and New York City, 1830–70." In *Police and Society,* ed. David H. Bayley. Beverly Hills: Sage Publications.

Moir, Esther. 1969. *The Justice of the Peace.* Harmondsworth, England: Penguin.

Monkkonen, Eric. 1977. "Toward a Dynamic Theory of Crime and the Police: a Criminal Justice Systems Perspective," *Historical Methods Newsletter* 10:157–65.

———. 1979. "Systematic Criminal Justice History: Some Suggestions," *Journal of Interdisciplinary History* 9:451–64.

Munsche, P. B. 1977. "The Game Laws in Wiltshire 1750–1800." In *Crime in England, 1550–1800* (see Cockburn 1977).

Neeson, Jeanette. 1977. "Common Right and Enclosure in Eighteenth Century Northamptonshire." Ph.D. dissertation, Warwick University.

Peacock, A. J. 1965. *Bread or Blood: The Agrarian Riots in East Anglia 1816.* London: Gollancz.

Philips, David. 1977. *Crime and Authority in Victorian England: The Black Country, 1835–1860*. London: Croom Helm.

——. 1976. "The Black Country Magistracy, 1835–60: a Changing Elite and the Exercise of its Power," *Midland History* 3:161–90.

Pike, Luke Owen. 1968. *A History of Crime in England, Illustrating the Changes of the Laws in the Progress of Civilisation*, 2 vols. Montclair, N.J.: Patterson Smith. (Originally published 1873–76, London.)

Pollard, Sidney. 1965. *The Genesis of Modern Management*. Cambridge, Mass.: Harvard University Press.

Radzinowicz, Leon. 1948–68. *A History of English Criminal Law and its Administration from 1750*. 4 vols. London: Stevens.

Radzinowicz, Leon, and Roger Hood. 1979. "Judicial Discretion and Sentencing Standards: Victorian Attempts to Solve a Perennial Problem," *University of Pennsylvania Law Review* 127:1288–1349.

Reaney, Bernard. 1970. *The Class Struggle in 19th Century Oxfordshire: The Social and Communal Background to the Otmoor Disturbances of 1830 to 1835*. Oxford: History Workshop.

Reid, Douglas A. 1976. "The Decline of Saint Monday 1766–1876," *Past & Present* 71:76–101.

Robson, L. L. 1965. *The Convict Settlers of Australia: An Enquiry into the Origin and Character of the Convicts Transported to New South Wales and Van Diemen's Land, 1787–1852*. Melbourne: Melbourne University Press.

Rock, Paul. 1973. *Deviant Behaviour*. London: Hutchinson.

Rogers, Nicholas. 1978. "Popular Protest in Early Hanoverian London," *Past & Present* 79:70–100.

Rose, R. B. 1960. "The Priestley Riots of 1791," *Past & Present* 18:68–88.

——. 1961. "Eighteenth Century Price Riots and Public Policy in England," *International Review of Social History* 6:277–92.

Rothman, David. 1971. *The Discovery of the Asylum: Social Order and Disorder in the New Republic*. Boston: Little, Brown.

Rudé, George. 1964. *The Crowd in History: A Study of Popular Disturbances in France and England 1730–1848*. New York: Wiley.

——. 1970. *Paris and London in the Eighteenth Century: Studies in Popular Protest*. London: Collins. (also published 1973, New York: Viking Press).

——. 1973. "Protest and Punishment in Nineteenth Century Britain," *Albion* 5:1–23.

——. 1978. *Protest and Punishment: The Story of the Social and Political Protesters Transported to Australia, 1788–1868.* Oxford: Clarendon Press.

Rule, John G. 1975. "Wrecking and Coastal Plunder." In *Albion's Fatal Tree* (see Hay 1975a).

Rumbelow, D. 1971. *I Spy Blue: The Police and Crime in the City of London from Elizabeth I to Victoria.* London: Macmillan.

Rusche, Georg, and Otto Kirchheimer. 1968. *Punishment and Social Structure.* New York: Russell & Russell. (Originally published 1939. New York: Columbia University Press.)

Samuel, Raphael. 1975. " 'Quarry Roughs': Life and Labour in Headington Quarry, 1860–1920. An Essay in Oral History." In *Village Life and Labour,* ed. Raphael Samuel. Boston: Routledge & Kegan Paul.

Shaw, A. G. L. 1966. *Convicts and the Colonies: A Study of Penal Transportation from Great Britain and Ireland to Australia and Other Parts of the British Empire.* London: Faber & Faber.

——. 1972. "Reformatory Aspects of the Transportation of Criminals to Australia." In *Law and Crime: Essays in Honour of Sir John Barry,* ed. Norval Morris and Mark Perlman. New York: Gordon & Breach.

Sheehan, W. J. 1977. "Finding Solace in Eighteenth-Century Newgate." In *Crime in England, 1550–1800* (see Cockburn 1977).

Silver, Allan. 1967. "The Demand for Order in Civil Society: A Review of Some Themes in the History of Urban Crime, Police, and Riot." In *The Police: Six Sociological Essays,* ed. David. J. Bordua. New York: Wiley.

Smith, A. E. 1947. *Colonists in Bondage: White Servitude and Convict Labor in America, 1607–1776.* Chapel Hill, N.C.: University of North Carolina Press.

Society for the Study of Labour History. 1972. "Conference Report," *Bulletin* 25:5–17.

Stedman Jones, Gareth. 1971. *Outcast London: a Study in the Relationship between Classes in Victorian Society.* Oxford: Oxford University Press.

Stephen, James F. 1977. *A History of the Criminal Law of England.* 3 vols. New York: B. Franklin. (Originally published 1883.)

Stevenson, John. 1977. "Social Control and the Prevention of Riots in England, 1789–1829." In *Social Control in 19th-Century Britain* (see Donaigrodski 1977).

——. 1979. *Popular Disturbances in England, 1700–1870.* New York: Longman.

Stevenson, John, and R. Quinault, eds. 1974. *Popular Protest and Public Order*. London: Allen & Unwin.

Storch, Robert D. 1975. "The Plague of the Blue Locusts: Police Reform and Popular Resistance in Northern England, 1840–57," *International Review of Social History* 20:61–90.

———. 1976. "The Policeman as Domestic Missionary: Urban Discipline and Popular Culture in Northern England, 1850–1880," *Journal of Social History* 9:481–509.

———. 1977a. "Police Control of Street Prostitution in Victorian London: A Study in the Contexts of Police Action." In *Police and Society*, ed. David H. Bayley. Beverly Hills: Sage Publications.

———. 1977b. "The Problem of Working-class Leisure. Some Roots of Middle-class Moral Reform in the Industrial North, 1825–50." In *Social Control in 19th-century Britain* (see Donajgrodzki 1977).

Styles, John. 1980. "Our Traiterous Moneymakers." In *An Ungovernable People: The English and Their Law in the 17th and 18th Centuries*, ed. John Brewer and John Styles. London: Hutchinson.

Thomas, Keith. 1971. *Religion and the Decline of Magic: Studies in Popular Beliefs in Sixteenth and Seventeenth Century England*. London: Weidenfeld & Nicolson.

Thompson, E. P. 1968. *The Making of the English Working Class*. rev. ed. Harmondsworth, England: Penguin.

———. 1971. "The Moral Economy of the English Crowd in the Eighteenth Century," *Past & Present* 50: 76–136.

———. 1972. " 'Rough Music': Le Charivari anglais," *Annales: Economies, Sociétés, Civilisations*, 27th year, pp. 285–312.

———. 1975a. "The Crime of Anonymity." In *Albion's Fatal Tree* (see Hay 1975a).

———. 1975b. *Whigs and Hunters: The Origins of the Black Act*. New York: Pantheon.

Tobias, John J. 1967. *Crime and Industrial Society in the 19th Century*. New York: Schocken Books.

Tomlinson, Heather. 1978. "Prison Palaces: A Re-appraisal of Early Victorian Prisons, 1835–77," *Bulletin of the Institute of Historical Research* 51:60–70.

Walker, Nigel. 1968. *Crime and Insanity in England*. Vol. 1: *The Historical Perspective*. Edinburgh: Edinburgh University Press.

Webb, Sidney, and Beatrice Webb. 1922. *English Prisons under Local Government*. London and New York: Longman's, Green.

———. 1963. *English Local Government from the Revolution to the*

Municipal Corporations Act. Vol. 1: *The Parish and the County.*
London: Cass. (Originally published 1906.)

Williams, David. 1955. *The Rebecca Riots: A Study in Agrarian
Discontent.* Cardiff: University of Wales Press.

Winslow, Cal. 1975. "Sussex Smugglers." In *Albion's Fatal Tree*
(see Hay 1975a).

Wrightson, Keith, and David Levine. 1979. *Poverty and Piety in an
English Village: Terling, 1525–1700.* New York: Academic Press.

Zangerl, Carl H. E. 1971. "The Social Composition of the County
Magistracy in England and Wales, 1831–1887," *Journal of British
Studies* 11:113–25.

Sarnoff A. Mednick and Jan Volavka

Biology and Crime

*. . . Man with all his noble qualities, with sympathy which
feels for the most debased, with benevolence which extends
not only to other men but to the humblest living creature,
with his godlike intellect which has penetrated into the
movements and constitution of the solar system—with all
these exalted powers—man still bears in his bodily frame
the indelible stamp of his lowly origin.*
—Charles Darwin
The Descent of Man

ABSTRACT

Research into biological factors in the etiology of crime has long
been out of favor in the United States. Yet all human behavior
is partly the result of physiological causes, and it is a reasonable
hypothesis that both nature and nurture influence antisocial
behavior. Recent research has tested that hypothesis and results
seem to confirm it. A growing body of research has consistently
found that identical twins are likelier both to have criminal
records than are fraternal twins. Adoption studies have found
that, controlling for the criminality of the adoptive parents,
adopted children whose biological parents had criminal records
are likelier themselves to have criminal records than are adopted
children of noncriminal biological parents. Psychophysiological
studies of the autonomic nervous system, primarily using skin

Sarnoff A. Mednick is Professor of Psychology, University of Southern California and Director of the Psykologisk Institut in Copenhagen. Jan Volavka is
Professor of Psychiatry, New York University School of Medicine.

The preparation of this paper was in part supported by NIMH grant number 31433 from the Center for Research on Crime and Delinquency and LEAA
Contract Number 78-NI-AX-0088. The comments of Malcolm Klein, Irving
Gottesman, Dan Glaser and Saleem Shah to a first draft of this essay were extremely valuable. The work of Ms. Vicki Pollock in preparation of the neurophysiology and biochemistry portions of the paper was of great help. The
assistance of Ms. Temi Moffit and Bill Gabrielli with the editing of the manuscript is acknowledged.

conductance measures, suggest that repetitively antisocial people tend to have low arousal levels and slow skin conductance recovery. These factors may play a role in learning to avoid antisocial behavior. The consensus of neurophysiological research findings is that criminals' electroencephalograms (EEG) are more often abnormal than are those of noncriminals and that there is some slowing of EEG frequency in habitual offenders. Research into the relations among epilepsy, EEG, and aggression has produced no clear consensus. There are similarities in the skin conductance and EEG research: both slow alpha frequencies and diminished skin conductance responsiveness are associated with low arousal states. There is no question that biochemical and pharmacological factors contribute to antisocial behavior, but the extent of their contribution, relative to social and other environmental factors, is unclear. Drugs and other endogenous materials are not intrinsically criminogenic but elicit antisocial behavior under particular cultural, social, and personal circumstances. Taken together, research into the relation between biology and crime leaves no doubt that social and biological variables, and their interactions, are important to our understanding of the origins of antisocial behavior.

This essay reviews selected studies on biological factors relevant to criminological concerns. At a time when there is a drift toward vigorously punitive attitudes in relation to crime—a political posture often unnecessarily and wrongly linked to an increasing belief in the significance of biological factors to crime (Holden 1978)—it is essential that criminologists be better informed on this body of literature.

Likewise, criminal law doctrine and practice may be influenced by the emerging understanding of biological factors in crime. The criminal law, deeply rooted in an eighteenth-century belief in the autonomy of free will, suffers tension as insights emerge of the influence of biology on behavior. Few now see free will as an unfettered determinant of behavior, but the criminal law clings to its classical hypothesis.

The XYY flare-up focused attention on this issue (*Georgetown Law Journal* 1969). If an individual's violent conduct cannot be ascribed solely to his conscious intent but is to a degree influenced by his genetic structure, then his responsibility in law seems at least to be reduced. If genetic or acquired biological factors have a partial role in the etiology of crime, what variations must be made to doctrines of intent, of *mens rea?*

And there are very practical concerns of crime prevention which, ineluctably, have directed the attention of criminologists to biological issues. One suggested approach to the primary prevention of serious crime is the early identification and treatment of individuals at high risk for future criminal behavior. This approach, replete with social, legal, and political pitfalls, has never been carefully tested. Social, behavioral, and familial factors predict adult crime with reasonable validity, explaining perhaps 30 per cent of the variance (Ratcliff and Robins 1979); but, for a variety of reasons, intervention based on such predictions demands high predictive validity, higher than has been achieved, and even then raises a host of problems. But certainly, if predictive validity can be increased by combining biological measures with social, behavioral, and familial factors, that process must be studied.

The fundamental point is that biological factors are relevant to criminality, and their exclusion from policy consideration is a function of fear and of prejudice which perhaps should be resisted. As an example: Carlsson (1977) has argued that if social factors were solely responsible for crime, we might expect the frequency of criminal behaviors to be more or less evenly distributed in the population (at least among men). This does not seem to be the case in Stockholm (Carlsson 1977), Philadelphia (Wolfgang, Figlio, and Sellin 1972), Copenhagen (from our unpublished population studies) and London (Farrington 1979). Over 50 percent of crimes seem to concentrate in a small subgroup of men. Carlsson suggests that this small active group of men may be driven by individual (biological) factors not shared by most other men. Responsible, data-based arguments like this merit more consideration than they have received. It is the purpose of this essay to facilitate such a consideration.

Before we present and discuss research findings, some caveats are in order concerning definitions, our criteria for inclusion of studies for review, and the range of materials covered.

Criminal behavior. Much of the biological crime research has treated "crime" generically or ambiguously. Both the shoplifting of a can of tuna and the rape-murder of a three-year-old girl are crimes. This should not, however, be construed as suggesting that we are incapable or unwilling sharply to distinguish these acts. On the contrary, we believe that progress in understanding the causes of crime will require that specific antecedents be linked to specific criminal outcomes. Numerous differentiations of criminal behavior have proved useful in biological research: violent and nonviolent; violence against strangers and violence against relatives or friends; recidivist and single offender; forger and other; and theft and other. In most of the research to be cited, the types of crime were unfortunately not fully delineated by the authors. We hope that such specification will accompany the maturation of this field.

Mental illness. We exclude discussions of mental illness except for psychopathy. The diagnosis of psychopathy is given to men who are among the most recidivist and conscienceless of the criminal population (Hare 1978a). It is therefore appropriate to include studies of psychopaths in this review. Problems with this diagnostic category include the variety of definitions used in the literature and the frequent lack of attention to establishing the reliability of the diagnosis; Hare's work (1970) is an outstanding exception.

Definition of subject population and controls. We expect authors to describe their methods of sampling of subjects and the characteristics of the resultant subject groups; only those studies which include some form of control group have been considered.

Definition of biological factors. By the term "biological factors" we will refer to nonsocial, nonbehavioral aspects of man's constitution and functioning. In this essay we discuss genetic, autonomic nervous system, central nervous system, and biochemical factors as correlates or influences of criminal behavior. We exclude behaviorally defined characteristics (such as intelligence) which may have a partial biological origin.

If genetic factors play any role in the etiology of antisocial behavior, then this relationship *must* be mediated by biological factors. For this reason we begin with a review of the literature linking heredity and crime which demonstrates that genetic factors do play an etiological role in antisocial behavior. We then summarize the criminological research literature in selected areas of biological investigation. Here is the outline of the entire essay:

I. Genetic studies
   A. Sex chromosomal abnormalities
   B. Family and twin studies
   C. Adoption studies
   D. Gene-environment influences in adoption
   E. Conclusions from genetic studies

II. Autonomic nervous system studies (skin conductance)
   A. Emotionality and emotional responsiveness
      1. Basal level emotionality
      2. Spontaneous responses
      3. Skin conductance responses to stimulation
   B. Anticipation of negative experiences
   C. Failure to learn from punishment; a biosocial theory of antisocial behavior
   D. Skin conductance recovery
   E. Conditioning studies using punishment

III. Neurophysiological studies
   A. Clinical EEG abnormality
   B. Slowing of the EEG frequency
      1. Slowing of alpha activity
      2. EEG activity below 8 Hz
   C. Epilepsy, EEG, and aggression
   D. Activation techniques and event-related potentials

IV. Biochemical and psychopharmacological factors
   A. Testosterone
   B. Hypoglycemia
   C. Alcohol
   D. Amphetamines
   E. Marijuana

F. Opiates and endorphins
G. Other substances
V. Summary and conclusions

Some research topics not considered. Some areas of research were arbitrarily excluded from this review because of the authors' limited expertise, because of space constraints, or for other reasons. The section on biochemical and psychopharmacological factors is brief and selective. We omit discussion of immunology, pituitary-adrenal hormones, and many neural transmitters. The reader may find these topics discussed in detail in Moyer (1976). Another major new area of research concerns the neuropsychological functioning of criminals. Yeudall et al. (1979) have provided a summary of this work.

I. Genetic Studies

The mass media in highly developed societies are a potent force in producing common conceptions and conformity of thought; 37,000,000 Americans simultaneously think almost identical thoughts as they watch prime time television. Two forces resist these pressures for homogeneity: unique life experiences and genetics. In this section we consider one of these forces, genetics, and its relation to criminal behavior.

The mechanisms governing the human gene pool maximize uniqueness. There is one chance in 73,000,000,000 that a human couple will produce two children with identical genotypes other than identical twins. The genes selected from this vast pool help to determine the individual's biological construction. The *possibilities* for the color of the eyes, the length of the fingers, the diameter of the brain arteries, the structure of the nerve cells, and the biochemical substances in the brain are all stated in a double helix blueprint. This helix of potential interacts with the specific food, air, water, love, and rejection which each life provides to mold a unique person. The interplay between experience and the blueprint produces variation in specific characteristics; when we measure these characteristics in a representative population, their distribution is almost invariably bell-shaped. There are tails to these distributions so that a few people are tall, a few are short; but most are in a middle range. Some persons have a very reactive nervous system while others have a phlegmatic one.

Almost all human behavioral characteristics result from an interaction of life experiences and a conglomerate of genetic factors. There are extremely rare, dominant-gene-determined states, such as Huntington's Disease, in which genes directly determine whether the disease will appear. But even in these cases the environment helps shape the course of the illness. On the other hand, the environment may incline a person toward alcoholism, but if he has a genetically fragile liver, he may not go very far! In the case of behavior disorders, recent studies have emphasized the interactive role of environment and genes in the development of alcoholism (Goodwin et al. 1974; Goodwin et al. 1977) and schizophrenia (Kety et al. 1968).

It would seem to be a reasonable, testable hypothesis that interactions between nature and nurture might influence deviance expressed as a consistent pattern of antisocial behavior. In 1855, Auguste Comte accepted this general proposition as a given. "The whole social evolution of the race must proceed in entire accordance with biological laws. . . . No sociological view can therefore be admitted . . . that is contrary to the known laws of human nature" (p. 487). But since 1855, Western philosophy and science have been exposed to a superficial Social Darwinism and to poorly founded social adaptations of the doctrine of "survival of the fittest." In 1878, Herbert Spencer enraged social reformers by his prostitution of evolution for the preservation of privilege. Spencer applauded the "shouldering aside of the weak by the strong" as just another step in the glorious improvement of the race. These simplistic perceptions rationalized and justified privilege, encouraged racism, and inhibited scientific understanding of the gene-environment relations in human behavior.

In the United States early in this century, such expedient ethics —as expressed, for example, in early interpretations of intelligence test results—helped write the immigration laws of the 1920s. The Nazis of the 1930s drove an almost final nail in the coffin of biological and social interactionism; among social scientists, biological factors became expressly excluded from consideration in the same context as social variation. Haller (1968) suggests that part of the reason for this is that many of those who had been pointed to as inferior (the new immigrants to the United States and their offspring) had belied the dire predictions of their antagonists and had struggled to the top of the heap, including the academic heap. Politically and emotionally, they turned away from biology. Haller suggests that besides these personal, affective reasons for neglecting biological explanations of human behavior there was little credible empirical evidence on hereditary variables that could help us understand social man. The student in social sciences or psychology in the 40s and 50s learned that genes played a role in determining whether one would become a turtle or a human, but once a human, genetic factors could safely be ignored.

The evidence on genetic influences on social functioning consisted mainly of some inadequate and ignored twin studies (some tainted by their origins in Nazi Germany or pre–World War II Japan) and some entertaining, well-written, and inventive analogies to observations of animal behavior. Haller's point is well taken; genetic factors tainted by political considerations were not only affectively repulsive but, coincidentally, also not intellectually compelling. Recently, however, there have been developments in behavior genetics which are worthy of the attention of the social scientist and criminologist. In this section we present recent findings which bear on the intellectual attractiveness of the notion of genetic influences in antisocial behavior.

A. Chromosomal Abnormalities

The XYY chromosome affair may have been one of the most publicized criminological events of this century. Men usually have 46 chromosomes. Two of these are the sex chromosomes, one X and one Y. The usual notation for this chromosomal configuration is XY. That there are XYY men who have two Y chromosomes was first announced by Sandberg et al. (1961). This historic XYY man was *not* a criminal. Surveys began to suggest, however, that XYY men are disproportionately represented in maximum security hospitals. The descriptions presented of the crimes perpetrated by some of these XYY men would supply material for a series of horror films. An image quickly developed of a huge, dangerous hulk of a "supermale" with super aggressiveness spurred on by his extra male chromosome. Other hospital studies contradicted these findings. The true facts would have some critical consequences aside from their scientific interest. If the XYY-aggression relation were reliably established, the legal implications would be of some importance (see *Georgetown Law Journal* 1969).

Sophisticated observers soon realized that the inconsistent findings resulted from the arbitrary, small samples being investigated (Kessler and Moos 1970). Other observers were politically opposed to the possibility of any "internal causality" in "the causes of crime," referring to the XYY research as "Demonism revisited" (e.g., Sarbin and Miller 1970). Sarbin and Miller called for a study which would "eliminate the sampling bias by obtaining XYY subjects from the general non-institutionalized population. . . . This in itself would be an overwhelming project, requiring the chromosomal typing of possibly thousands of potential subjects."

Precisely such a study was undertaken by Witkin et al. (1977) at the Psykologisk Institut, Kommunehospitalet, Copenhagen, Denmark. A cohort was identified consisting of all the 31,436 men born in the municipality of Copenhagen in 1944, 1945, 1946, and 1947. All those men who were 184 cm or above in height (N = 4,139) were visited in their homes. Blood samples were taken and karyotypes (systematically arranged photographs of their chromosomes) prepared. This process yielded 12 XYY men. The XYYs and their controls were checked in the official Danish criminality records. There was little or no recorded evidence of violent behavior by XYY men. They did, however, evidence significantly more criminal behavior than did the XY men of their age, height, intelligence, and social class. Their low intelligence did not fully explain this excess criminality. An ongoing extensive examination of their electrical brain activity indicates that, in comparison to a control group, the XYY subjects evidence remarkably slow alpha and excessive theta activity (Volavka et al. 1977c). Their EEG driving response to visual stimulation is inadequate (Volavka et al. 1979). They also show very low skin conductance responsiveness and a slow rate of recovery. (EEG and skin conductance research are discussed in sections II and III below.)

Note that this study selected all of the XYYs from a total birth cohort of Danish tall men. The results are reliable (despite the small yield of XYYs) and generalizable to the population represented by the cohort. Careful genetic investigation (also from other laboratories) helped explode a disagreeable myth and tended to relieve a class of men (albeit a small group) of a nasty label and perhaps of other unpleasant consequences.

But the XYY man is an exceedingly infrequent fellow. The critical question is whether more commonly observed criminality and psychopathy are influenced by genetic factors.

B. Family and Twin Studies

It has long been observed that antisocial parents raise an excessive number of children who also become antisocial. In the classic study by Robins (1966), the father's criminal behavior was one of the best predictors of antisocial behavior in a child. In terms of genetics very little can be concluded from such family data as it is difficult to disentangle hereditary and environmental influences. The criminogenic effects of social and economic adversity mask the possible influence of genetic factors.

Twin studies comparing identical, monozygotic (MZ) twins with fraternal, same-sex, dizygotic (DZ) twins offer a somewhat better separation of genetic and environmental effects. MZ twins are genetically identical; DZ twins have 50 percent of their genes in common (the same as siblings). In almost all studies the twins are reared together. The research design assumes that the effect of hereditary factors is demonstrated if MZ twins have greater concordance for criminality than do DZ twins, that is, if MZ twins are likelier both to have criminal records than are DZ twins. Problems of this method will be discussed below.

In the first twin-criminality study, the German psychiatrist

Lange (1929) found 77 percent concordance for criminality for his MZ twins and 12 percent concordance for his DZ twins. Lange concluded that "heredity plays a quite preponderant part among the causes of crime." Subsequent studies of twins (until 1961 there were eight in all) have tended to confirm Lange's results. About 60 percent concordance has been reported for MZ and about 30 percent concordance for DZ twins (see table 1). For a detailed discussion of these twin studies the reader may turn to Christiansen (1977a).

These eight twin studies suffer from their haphazard sampling methods. Several were carried out in Germany during a politically unfortunate period. They report too high a proportion of MZ twins. Concordant MZ pairs are more likely to be brought to the attention of the investigator. Twinship is usually easier to · detect in identical twins, especially if they end up in the same prison. All of these factors tend to inflate MZ concordance rates in nonsystematic studies. The recent and continuing study initiated by the late Christiansen, and being continued by Mednick,

TABLE 1

Twin Studies of Psychopathy and Criminality
(MZ and same-sexed DZ twins only)

	Monozygotic			Dizygotic		
Study and Location	Total Pairs	Pairs Concor- dant	% Concor- dant	Total Pairs	Pairs Concor- dant	% Concor- dant
Lange 1929 (Bavaria)	13	10	77	17	2	12
Legras 1932 (Holland)	4	4	100	5	1	20
Rosanoff 1934 (U.S.A.)	37	25	68	28	5	18
Stumpfl 1936 (Germany)	18	11	61	19	7	37
Kranz 1936 (Prussia)	32	21	66	43	23	54
Borgstrom 1939 (Finland)	4	3	75	5	2	40
Slater 1953 (Psychopathy) (England)	2	1	50	10	3	30
Yoshimasu 1961 (Japan)	28	17	61	18	2	11
Total	138	92	67.2	145	45	31.0

Gottesman, and Hutchings in Copenhagen, minimizes these sampling problems. Christiansen (1977b) studied 3,586 twin pairs (the study has since been updated to include 5,111 twin pairs) born in a well-defined area of Denmark between 1881 and 1910. He used a complete national criminality register. Christiansen notes that "there are several important characteristics of the Danish law enforcement process that relate to its statutory uniformity regarding treatment of the offender and sentencing by the court. Police officers are legally *required* to report cases if they have a suspect. They are not permitted to make judgments in such matters. An elaborate court appeals system is aimed at achieving national uniformity of sentencing. The social status of a Danish police officer is comparatively high; they are regarded as being incorruptible" (p. 93).

Christiansen (1977b) reports 52 percent concordance for MZ (male-male) pairs and 22 percent concordance for the DZ (male-male) pairs. These rates are probandwise which can be directly compared with the population base rate for non-twins. (Pairwise rates were 35 percent and 12 percent.) The MZ probandwise concordance rate is lower than in previous studies; almost as many cases are discordant as concordant. Nevertheless, the MZ concordance rate is 2.4 times the DZ rate and 5 times the population rate. This result suggests that MZ twins show some genetically controlled biological characteristic (or characteristics) which increases their common risk of being registered for criminal behavior.

This is not some mysterious force as is implied by the title of the first twin study, "Crime as destiny" (Lange 1929). For example, height is partly genetically determined. If tall men were more likely to commit crimes, be apprehended, or both, we would expect MZ concordance for criminality to be higher than DZ concordance because DZ twins are less likely to be of the same height. Similarly, if alcohol addiction increased the probability of antisocial behavior and alcohol addiction had some partial genetically based predisposition, then twin research might yield positive genetic findings. Or positive genetic findings may be observed if the child's learning of law abidance is facilitated by some neurophysiological characteristic, the functioning of which is influenced by genetic factors.

A recent study of 85 pairs of Norwegian male-male twins reports 41 percent MZ and 26 percent DZ probandwise concordance; pairwise rates were 26 and 15 percent (Dalgaard and Kringlen 1976). Though the MZ-DZ differences are smaller than in previously reported studies, they are in the same direction. Dalgaard and Kringlen explain the difference exists because "MZ pairs usually are brought up more similarly than DZ." (Christiansen [1977a] also discusses this problem.) This group of Norwegian twins seems to have been drawn disproportionately from the lower classes; they have a "less-than-normal degree of education, they are to a lesser degree married; and frequency of alcoholism seems higher in this group than in the general population" (p. 221). In Christiansen's larger Danish twin investigation, MZ-DZ concordance differences were considerably lowered in subgroups characterized by these sorts of variables. It would seem prudent for Dalgaard and Kringlen to sample additional segments of the Norwegian twin register (which contains 33,000 twin pairs) in order to attempt to overcome this social and deviance skew.

Sarnoff Mednick, Irving Gottesman, and Barry Hutchings are attempting to expand Christiansen's study to include approximately 13,000 twin pairs alive at age 15. This number should be sufficient for a more detailed analysis (e.g., by type of crime) than has been possible before. Despite the limitations of the twin method, the results of these studies are compatible with the hypothesis that genetic factors account for some of the variance associated with antisocial behavior.

C. Adoption Studies

A great weakness of the twin studies is that genetic and environmental factors are not well separated in the overwhelming number of cases. A design which does a better job in this regard studies individuals adopted at birth. A register of all nonfamilial adoptions in Denmark in the years 1924–47 has been established in Copenhagen at the Psykologisk Institut by a group of American and Danish investigators (See Kety et al. 1974). The register records 14,427 adoptions and includes information on the adoptee and his biological and adoptive parents. Thus, the register contains information on approximately 72,000 persons. (Only about 80 percent of the biological fathers are definitely identified.)

This adoption register may help us determine whether genetic factors influence human characteristics. For example, if male criminal adoptees have disproportionately high numbers of criminal biological fathers (given appropriate controls), this would suggest a genetic factor in criminality. This is especially true since in almost all instances the adoptee has never seen the biological father and does not know who he is; the adoptee may not even realize he has been adopted. Another research possibility is to study adoptees whose biological parents are criminal and who were placed with noncriminal adoptive parents. Or we can take adoptees whose biological parents are not criminal and who were placed with criminal adoptive parents. This design is called the "cross-fostering" model and is useful for comparison of the effectiveness of genetic and certain environmental criminogenic forces. The adoptive method permits reasonable separation of environmental and hereditary influences. The method has some problems which will be discussed below.

Two completed investigations studied the subpopulation of adoptees born in Copenhagen. From 5, 483 Copenhagen adoptees, Schulsinger (1977) identified 57 psychopaths from psychiatric registers and police files. He also selected 57 nonpsychopath control adoptees matched for sex, age, social class, neighborhood of rearing, and age of transfer to the adoptive family. The numbers are small, but among the relatives the biological relatives of the psychopathic adoptees manifest the most psychopathy. Since the postnatal contact between the adoptee and the relative (especially male relative) was in most cases nonexistent, environmental factors probably did not play a very important role in this relationship. The existence of some heritable factor seems the most reasonable interpretation.

Using the same adoptee register, Hutchings and Mednick (1977) studied the registered criminality of a pilot sample of the 1,145 male adoptees born in Copenhagen between 1927 and 1941.

Of these 1,145 male adoptees, 185 had been convicted of a violation of the Danish penal code. Of these 185 criminal-adoptees we were able to identify 143, for each of whom we were certain of the biological father's identity (including date and place of birth) and that he had been born after 1890 (there are better police records after 1890). To each of these 143 criminal adoptees we matched a noncriminal adoptive son for age of child and social class of adoptive father. For the criminal and noncriminal groups, the age of parents and the age of child at adoption proved to be about the same. There was, in most cases, no contact between the adoptee and the biological father. Table 2, part A, indicates that the heaviest weight of the registered criminality in the fathers is in the cell of the biological fathers of the criminal adoptees. Again we have evidence that genetic factors play some role in the etiology of registered criminality.

Table 2, part B, presents this information in a different form, analogous to the cross-fostering paradigm. In this table minor

TABLE 2

Criminality in Male Adoptees and Their
Biological and Adoptive Fathers

A.
Registered criminality in biological and adoptive fathers
of criminal adoptees.

	Biological Father	Adoptive Father
Criminal adoptive sons (N=143)	70	33
Control adoptive sons (N=143)	40	14

B.
"Cross fostering" analysis: Tabled values are percentage
of adoptive sons who are registered criminals.

		Is Biological Father Criminal?	
		Yes	No
Is adoptive father criminal?	Yes	$\frac{21}{58}=36.2\%$	$\frac{6}{52}=11.5\%$
	No	$\frac{46}{214}=21.5\%$	$\frac{35}{333}=10.5\%$

---

offenses are omitted. As can be seen in the lower righthand cell, if neither the biological nor the adoptive father is criminal, 10.5 percent of their sons are criminal. If the biological father is not criminal but the adoptive father is, this figure rises to only 11.5 percent. In the lower left hand corner of table 2, part B, note that 21.5 percent of the sons are criminal if the adoptive father is not criminal and the biological father is criminal. The 21.5 percent and 11.5 percent figures are not quite significantly different (.05 level). Note that in this table the influence of the adoptive father's criminality is statistically significant only in those sons whose biological fathers were also criminal (36.2 percent versus 21.5 percent). These cross-fostering comparisons are replicated and are statistically significantly different in preliminary analyses involving the total population of 14,427 adoptions recorded in the Copenhagen adoption register (Mednick and Hutchings 1977).

Thus the comparison analogous to a cross-fostering experiment seems to support a partial genetic-etiology hypothesis. We must caution, however, that simply knowing that the adoptive father has been a criminal does not tell us how criminogenic the adoptee's environment has been. On the other hand, at conception, the potential genetic influence of the father is already complete. Thus as we have arranged the cross-fostering table it is not a fair comparison between environmental and genetic influences. But the genetic effect does seem to exist.

A third adoptee project has been completed by Crowe (1975) in Iowa. This investigation finds evidence of a relation between criminality in an adopted child and his or her biological mother. Crowe further notes an apparent similarity in the types of crimes of the biological mother and the index cases. This suggests some form of specificity of genetic effect. Study of the 14,427 Copenhagen adoptees and their 58,000 (approximately) adoptive and biological parents and of Christiansen's 14,000 twin pairs should permit more precise answers to the question of genetic specificity of type of crime.

Cadoret (1978) has reported on 246 Iowans adopted at birth. He indicates that antisocial behavior in the adoptees is significantly related to antisocial behavior in the biological parents. His data were gathered by telephone interviews with the adoptive parents and adoptee. It is difficult to judge how this method influenced the reported results. Bohman (1978), in a study of Swedish adoptees, originally found no significant relation between criminality in the biological parents and the adoptees; further analysis, distinguishing between biological parents' levels of severity of criminality, has identified subgroups of adoptees whose criminal behavior is partly explained by their biological parents' criminality (Bohman, personal communication, 1980).

Taken as a whole, the family, twin, and adoptee investigations do not allow one to discard the hypothesis that a genetic factor is involved in the predisposition to antisocial behavior. The family and twin studies are often criticized because the criminal probands and relatives almost always share both genes and environment. This criticism is less justified in the case of the adoption studies, which therefore seem to have a greater face validity.

D. Gene-Environment Independence in Adoptions

If anything were to be found which lessened the independence of genetic and environmental influences in the adoption studies, this would serve to temper the impact of the findings just described. The major adoptive agency in Denmark had a policy of attempting to match the biological and adoptive families for vaguely defined social characteristics (Hutchings 1972). That they partially succeeded is evidenced by the significant correlation of the social class of biological and adoptive fathers ($r[880] = .22, p < .001$). To what extent does this correlation between the social classes of the biological fathers and the sons' adoptive families explain the "genetic" findings? By determining the chronological order of entry of the adoptive and biological fathers' criminality and social class into a multiple regression analysis, all three of these variables were shown to have significant and independent effects on the criminality of the adopted sons (Hutchings and Mednick 1977, p. 139). The social class linkage apparently does not explain away the "genetic" effect.

Another factor to be considered in interpreting the strength of the genetic influence is that much of the research took place in relatively homogeneous Denmark. The laboratory experimenter in behavior genetics reduces the variance ascribable to environmental influences when he wishes to explore the effects of strain differences. As environmental variance increases, the genetic effects become more and more masked. We would suggest that the amount of variability in Denmark for most crime-related environmental dimensions is less than that of many other countries. It follows, then, that extrapolation of our Danish findings to other national situations must be conducted with caution. We must exercise extreme restraint in extrapolation to a nation like the United States with relatively large variations in social circumstances.

We must also recall that the adoptive process involves screening of the biological and adoptive parents and the adoptee by the adoptive agencies. Such screening can produce skewed populations; this possibility must be checked and taken into account in application of findings to nonadopted populations. The 1946–47 annual report of the largest Danish state adoption organization notes:

> Before a child is cleared for adoption, it is investigated with respect to health, and an attempt is made to obtain detailed information on the child's family background and to form an impression of its developmental potential. Not only for the adoptive parents, but also for the child itself, these investigations are of great importance for its correct placement. Information is obtained on the child's mother and father; on whether or not there is serious physical or mental illness in the family background; criminal records are obtained for the biological parents; and in many cases school reports are obtained. By means of personal interview with the mother an impression of her is formed. Where information is uncovered on convicted criminality or on mental retardation, mental illness, etc., in the family background, the case is referred to the Institute of Human Genetics of Copenhagen University, with whom there exists a valuable cooperation for advice on the advisability of adoption.
> (Mothers Aid Organization for Copenhagen 1946, p. 13)

One important problem suggested by this statement is that the adoptive family may have been told that the biological family was deviant. It is clear from some of the old adoption files that serious deviance in the biological parents was more or less routinely reported to the prospective adoptive parents unless they refused the information. This could result in interpretation of the adoptee's behavior in accordance with this information and in consequent labeling of the adoptee, which might affect the probability that the adoptee will be deviant. This form of correlation between the biological and adoptive parents is not wanted in this research design. What effect might result from such information?

If the biological father's criminal career *began the year after* the birth of the child, this criminality information could not have been transmitted to the adoptive parents. If the biological father's criminality started *before* the birth of the adoptee, the information probably was communicated and could have affected the probability of criminality in the adoptee. Of the 347 criminal biological fathers in the adoptee pilot study, 67 percent had their first registration for criminality before the birth of the child and 33 percent began their criminal career after the birth of the adoptee. For all of the 347 criminal biological fathers the probability of their biological son becoming a criminal is 23 percent. Where the biological father committed his first offense *before* the birth of the adoptee, 23 percent of the adoptees became criminal. Where the biological father committed his first offense *after* the birth of the adoptee, 23 percent of the adoptees did become criminal (Mednick and Hutchings 1977). We can tentatively conclude from this simple analysis of Danish adoption studies that the *possibility* that the adoptive family was informed of the biological father's criminality does not alter the likelihood that the adoptive son will become a criminal.

E. Conclusions from Genetic Studies

The cumulative evidence of the family, twin, and adoption studies does not allow rejection of the hypothesis that some genetically transmitted factor increases the likelihood that an individual will behave in an officially noticed, antisocial manner. Rather, this hypothesis received support from such studies. How might such a genetic factor operate? Perhaps the genetic factor affects a biological system involved in the early learning of law-abiding behavior. In this manner it may impair the learning of inhibition of antisocial acts. We would expect that the effect of this genetic factor would vary. Those not affected or minimally affected might be expected to respond normally to social training forces (society, peers, family). Those somewhat more affected may need more training time, more stringent training, or more dramatic training conditions (perhaps one or two disagreeable contacts with the juvenile or criminal justice system) before they become reliably law-abiding. Those who are more heavily affected by the "factor" may have great difficulty in learning to avoid or to control antisocial behavior and may eventually find themselves considered chronic offenders.

Thus, from the proposition that the "factor" influences the child's general learning of law abidance we would expect to observe the genetic influence across many types of crime. We would also expect to observe the critical biological effects of this "factor" to be most manifest in repetitive psychopathic criminals.

There are other possibilities. Perhaps the "factor" affects some special biological system (or systems) which, in turn, is related to a specific type (or types) of crime (such as violent or sexual crimes). In this case we would expect to observe genetic transmission only for certain types of crimes and would expect to find similarity in the crimes of biological parents and offspring. The relation with recidivism would also be expected in this case but only within specific types of crimes.

Recidivistic criminals tend to exhibit a variety of criminal modes. Taken with the empirical results showing stronger genetic effects for recidivists without regard to type of crime (Christiansen 1977b; Hutchings and Mednick 1977), this suggests that the first speculation—a general disability in morality learning aptitude—may warrant further consideration. Autonomic nervous system insufficiency is one form such a learning disability could take. Autonomic system recovery (explained below) is genetically influenced (Bell et al. 1977). Children with criminal fathers tend to evidence slow autonomic nervous system recovery (Mednick 1977).

II. Autonomic Nervous System Studies (Skin Conductance)

The psychopath is described by Hare (1978a) as being among the most aggressive, dangerous, and recidivist clients of a prison. While there is low agreement about the diagnosis, most clinicians describe the psychopath as unsocialized and callous; he feels no guilt, remorse, or shame; lacks emotion; and is incapable of love. He does not alter his behavior as a result of punishment and fails to learn from punishing experiences. He is unable to control impulses and cannot anticipate consequences (American Psychiatric Association 1968; Craft 1965; Cleckley 1976; Buss 1966). Many of these symptoms describe a lack of emotional expression (no guilt, no emotionality, inability to love, callousness). Other symptoms relate to emotion-mediated learning (failure to learn from punishment, inability to anticipate negative consequences, lack of socialization).

Psychophysiologists have techniques appropriate to systematic study of emotions and emotional learning.[1] Inevitably, some psychophysiologists became curious to determine whether this clinically described psychopathic lack of emotion was expressed in lower levels of objectively measured physiological indices of emotional expression such as heart rate, blood pressure, respiration, and skin conductance. This section reviews physiological research with antisocial individuals relating to three of these clinical characteristics: lack of emotionality or emotional responsiveness, callousness; inability to anticipate negative consequences; and failure to learn from punishment, lack of socialization.

Psychophysiology is most concerned with studying peripheral signs of activity of the autonomic nervous system (ANS). The ANS mediates physiological activity associated with emotions;

[1] We do not pretend to cover every relevant article. We have tried to write nontechnically for a lay audience. There have been four recent reviews of research on the psychophysiology of antisocial individuals to which we can direct the interested reader (Shah and Roth 1974; Siddle 1977; Hare 1970, 1978b).

hence its importance to the study of psychopathy. Examples of peripheral manifestations of ANS activity include changes in heart rate, blood pressure, respiration, muscle tension, pupillary size, and electrical activity of the skin.

The measurement of exodermal electrical properties (called GSR—galvanic skin resistance—or skin conductance) is the most commonly used peripheral indicant of ANS activity in psychophysiology generally and in criminology. There are several reasons for this. Technically, it is relatively simple to obtain reliable skin conductance recordings. There is a sizable methodological literature for procedural guidance. The responses are typically recorded as waves that have a relatively slow rate of change and are consequently readily amenable to hand scoring. If we administer a stimulus, we typically observe a discrete response which can be readily and immediately identified. (Heart rate responses, by contrast, consist of *changes in rate*, which, in the raw record, are very difficult to see.)

The skin conductance response as it is usually measured is most heavily dependent on the activities of the sweat glands of the palms. Individuals who are often emotionally aroused, anxious, and fearful tend to have clammy, wet, handshakes because their emotional responsiveness is reflected in overactivity of the sweat glands of their palms. Such emotional individuals usually exhibit high skin conductance even when they are not stimulated. Very calm, unemotional people typically have very low skin conductance. (This "emotional" perspiration is also abundant in the soles of the feet but is typically less evident because most people wear shoes most of the time. The soles and palms are called the volar areas.)

When frightened or otherwise emotionally aroused, normally calm individuals will evidence episodes of volar sweating. This sweating moistens the skin with a salt solution that increases its electrical conductivity. (More detailed information can be found in Venables and Christie 1975.) If a weak current (generated by a battery) is leaked through the fingers, we can monitor the electrical resistance (or its inverse, conductance) of the skin to the passage of this current. If we stimulate the individual to become emotionally aroused, as by shooting off a gun behind his back, his ANS will activate his volar sweat glands. The skin will be profused with perspiration, which will increase its conductance; if we are monitoring this conductance on a polygraph, we will see an excursion of the pen which will be proportionate to some degree to the ANS arousal experienced. Subjects who are relatively unaroused by the gunshot will evidence little or no pen excursion. Individuals who are highly aroused will evidence a substantial pen excursion. The extent of pen excursion can be calibrated so that it can be expressed in electrical units of conductance. This process yields an objective score which reflects, at least to some substantial extent, the subject's degree of emotional arousal and ANS activation. A considerable body of methodological literature describes application of this technique; there is good standardization of technique which makes it possible, with due caution, to compare results from different laboratories.

All of these considerations have made skin conductance the most frequently measured psychophysiological characteristic of antisocial individuals. The patterns of results reported regarding certain characteristics of the skin conductance of antisocial persons has been relatively consistent across many laboratories, nations, experimental procedures, and definitions of antisocial behavior. For these reasons this review is restricted, in the main, to a discussion of skin conductance.

Much of the reported work involved prisoners as subjects. The prisoners are typically divided and compared on the basis of level of assessed psychopathy, seriousness of criminality, recidivism, type of crime, or some combination. Nonprisoner controls are rarely assessed.

Some studies have compared the skin conductance of college students who have scored high or low on a socialization scale or a personality inventory. We restrict ourselves here to research which is more manifestly relevant—research with criminals—and refer to other types of research only where it is conceptually or methodologically useful.

Studies on the skin conductance of prisoners or nonincarcerated criminals must be interpreted with considerable caution. The criminal life and the prison experience very likely affect a person's emotional response patterns (D'Atri 1978). Thus, skin conductance deviance in antisocial individuals may result from their criminal careers or incarceration. Etiological interpretations of such data must be very cautiously proffered. However, some tiny beginnings of prospective research have been undertaken in which young people are assessed and the results related to their delinquency years later. Assessments of prisoners have also been related to their subsequent recidivism. These few studies are emphasized in this review.

A. Emotionality and Emotional Responsiveness

The descriptions of the callous, remorseless, unfeeling psychopath present a challenge to the psychophysiologist to produce an objective measure which might make it possible to subject this clinical description to analytic study. The psychophysiologist has responded by investigating the psychopath's customary (relatively unprovoked) or *basal level* of emotionality, and his emotional *responsiveness* when provoked by a variety of challenging stimuli.

Basal level emotionality. To measure basal level emotionality, the subject is brought into the laboratory and appropriate electrodes are applied; his skin conductance level is then continuously recorded under conditions of no special stimulation. The psychopathic prisoner tends to evidence a slightly lower level of skin conductance than the nonpsychopathic prisoner. For some studies this difference is statistically significant (Blankenstein 1969; Dengerink and Bertilson 1975; Hare 1965; Mathis 1970; Schalling et al. 1973). In other studies the difference, while not statistically significant (perhaps in part because of the low reliability of the psychopathy diagnosis), is usually in the direction of a lower skin conductance for the psychopath (Hare 1972, 1975; Hare and Craigen 1974; Fox and Lippert 1963; Hare and Quinn 1971; Hare, Frazelle, and Cox 1978; Hare, Cox, and Frazelle, in press; Borkovec 1970; Schalling et al. 1968; Schmauk 1970; Parker et al. 1975; Lippert and Senter 1966; Sutker 1970). Hare, noting this consistent but weak tendency, combined the results from eight independent studies in his laboratory. In most of these studies statistically significant basal level skin conductance was *not* observed, though all the investigators found that the psychopath had lower skin conductance. The combined results are statistically significant (Hare 1978b).

Loeb and Mednick (1977) report on a ten-year follow-up and delinquency ascertainment of a group of 104 normal Danish adolescents. In 1962, these adolescents had been subjected to a skin conductance examination; in 1972, their officially recorded delinquency was ascertained from the Danish National Police Register—which has been described by Wolfgang as "probably the most thorough, comprehensive and accurate in the Western world . . . the reliability and validity of the Danish record-keeping system are almost beyond criticism" (Wolfgang 1977). At ten-year follow-up, seven boys of the 104 adolescents had been registered for mildly delinquent acts. Seven of the other boys were matched to these mild delinquents for social factors and age. The predelinquency basal skin conductance level of six of the seven delinquents was below that of all the controls. (A t-test between the delinquents and nondelinquents was not significant.) Note that, in this study, mild registered delinquency, not psychopathy, defined the groups.

Spontaneous skin conductance responses. After a subject is attached to the skin conductance recording device, he is usually permitted a five- to ten-minute rest. During this time, continuous recording of his skin conductance takes place. Although no stimulation is being systematically provided, the subject will almost always exhibit episodic increases in skin conductance. These are called spontaneous responses. They may be instigated by thoughts, images, sounds outside of the laboratory, or unknown physiological factors. Subjects who are more aroused and anxious tend to exhibit more spontaneous responses (Szpiler and Epstein 1976).

As in the case of basal level, the results of several experiments lean slightly toward the conclusion that psychopaths have fewer spontaneous responses during a pre- or postexperimental rest period. (Hare 1968; Hare and Quinn 1971; Schalling et al. 1968, 1973). Fox and Lippert (1963) observed that antisocial psychopaths exhibit less spontaneous activity than do inadequate psychopaths. Lippert and Senter (1966) did not find significant differences between psychopaths and controls. Hemming (1977) found no differences between prisoners and students. Siddle et al. (1973) report no spontaneous response differences between groups varying in degree of delinquency. Hare (1978b) combined the results of several of studies from his laboratory in which the psychopath tended to evidence fewer spontaneous responses but still did not obtain statistically significant differences.

If the studies just reviewed had found consistent evidence of lower skin conductance basal level and fewer spontaneous responses for the psychopath, this would have suggested that he continuously experiences an underaroused, unemotional state of being. The picture, unfortunately, is inconsistent. Cumulatively, the studies suggest that if indeed the basal skin conductance of the psychopathic prisoner *is* relatively low, the differences from the nonpsychopathic prisoner are not very great or consistent. Inspection of the reported variances in some studies suggests that the psychopathic group may have a greater range of basal levels and number of spontaneous responses. This may reflect the possibility that a subgroup of the psychopaths consistently lowers the group means. The Fox and Lippert (1963) study suggests that the subgroup may consist of the aggressive, antisocial psychopaths.

It is a pity that most of these studies do not include nonprisoner comparison groups. This would give us a frame of reference for evaluation of the results. The differences within prisoner populations may be totally dwarfed by the differences between prisoners and noncriminal populations. Evidence for such a difference has been mentioned by Hare (1978b).

The assumption underlying both the basal level and spontaneous response studies is that the observed skin conductance behavior is unstimulated. Actually, as experimenters fully realize, subjects are heavily stimulated by being introduced and attached to the apparatus. These basal measures may be heavily influenced by responsiveness characteristics.

Skin conductance responses to stimulation. Cleckley (1976) has described the psychopath as characterized by general poverty of emotional reactiveness. Psychophysiologists have attempted to confirm this description by use of physiological recordings of psychopaths' skin conductance responses to stimuli, such as simple tones, loud noises, electric shock, insertion of a hypodermic needle, and slides of horrible facial injuries. The results of most of these studies are consonant: antisocial individuals identified in a variety of ways (the psychopath, the prisoner, the criminal, and the delinquent) are decidedly emotionally hyporeactive to stimulation (Blankenstein 1969; Hare 1972; Mathis 1970; Sutker 1970; Aniskiewicz 1973; Hare and Craigen 1974; Schalling 1975; Borkovec 1970; Siddle, Nicol, and Foggitt 1973; Hinton and O'Neill 1978; Hare 1975; Hare and Quinn 1971; Hodgins-Milner 1976; Hemming 1977).

Hare, Cox, and Frazelle (in press) report that in their studies psychopaths only exhibit diminished responsiveness to exceptionally loud noise (120db). Their research is carried out in a prison. Subjects were selected by inviting 250 prisoners to participate in the research. Of these, 87 volunteered and 64 were finally tested. The investigators recognize the difficulty of generalizing from such a selected population. Moreover, all of these subjects, both psychopaths and controls, were serious law violators. Perhaps this is why differences between psychopaths and nonpsychopaths were apparent only under extreme stimulus conditions. In another study using similar subject selection methods, Hare (1975) reports no differences between psychopaths and nonpsychopaths. Lippert and Senter (1966) also report no differentiation of psychopaths by skin conductance amplitude.

In the one published *prospective* study (Loeb and Mednick 1977), skin conductance amplitude was measured on a group of 104 Danish adolescents some ten years before delinquency was ascertained. Predelinquent skin conductance amplitude of the seven delinquents was markedly (and statistically significantly) lower than that of controls. In 1962, the mean amplitude of response of the nondelinquent controls was five to ten times as great as that of the boys who eventually evidenced delinquency; the transgressions involved were mild.

Cleckley's clinical description is consistent with the physiologically assessed emotional responsiveness of not only the psychopath but also the criminal and the delinquent. The finding is substantially consistent across a considerable variety of national settings, laboratory procedures, levels, and definitions of antisocial behavior. The single prospective study has a pitifully small group (seven) of mild delinquents, but the results do not contradict the hypotheses and are bolstered considerably by the other cited literature.

The robustness of the cross-sectional findings encourages the inclusion of skin conductance responsiveness among the reliable characteristics of individuals who are officially noted as having transgressed. The single prospective finding suggests that ANS responsiveness should not be excluded from the group of variables of potential etiological significance in the *development* of antisocial behavior.

B. Anticipation of Negative Experiences

The psychopath is marked by his inability to foresee the negative consequences of his acts for himself and for his victims. Psychophysiologists have attempted to create laboratory situations in which foreseeable negative consequences (e.g., electric shock, very loud noises) could be anticipated. Skin conductance responses are then monitored to test whether antisocial individuals evidence normal emotional apprehension in anticipation of the shock or noise.

In 1957, Lykken reported that psychopaths evidence relatively small skin conductance responses in anticipation of electric shock. Hare (1965) presented prisoners with numbers (1–12) in serial order and warned them that they would experience an electric shock at the number 8. The nonpsychopathic prisoners evidenced strong electrodermal responses early in the number sequence preceding 8. The psychopaths evidenced little or no anticipation until just before 8. The nonpsychopaths also demonstrated greater responsiveness immediately before the electric shock. In a more recent study (Hare, Frazelle, and Cox 1978) prisoners were warned that they would experience a very loud (120db) aversive "blast" of noise after a twelve-second countdown. The psychopathic prisoners did not begin to show anticipatory skin conductance responding until just before the blast, and even then their responses were rather weak. The nonpsychopathic prisoners exhibited substantial skin conductance anticipation after three seconds. The highest mean level of skin conductance anticipation reached by the psychopathic subgroup just before the "blast," twelve seconds, was at the mean level reached by the nonpsychopaths after just over six seconds.

This lack of emotional anticipation by psychopaths of (to-be-experienced) pain or aversive stimulation is well documented (Hare and Craigen 1974; Lippert and Senter 1966; Schalling and Levander 1967; Hodgins-Milner 1976; Schalling, Levander, and Dahlin-Lidberg 1975). Tharp et al. (1978) repeatedly presented trials consisting of a countdown followed by a very loud noise (95db). After a few countdown-noise trials, the psychopaths showed no skin conductance response in anticipation of the aversive loud noise. The controls (nonprisoners in this study) continued to evidence skin conductance anticipation of the impending noise.

There are other ways to measure ANS functioning in anticipation of stress which do not deal with skin conductance. Lidberg et al. (in press) observed catecholamine levels in the blood of Swedish men just before they were to appear in criminal court to be tried. Catecholamine levels in normals are highly elevated during ANS excitation such as states of anxiety or fear; it would be expected that men just before such a court trial would have elevated levels. The pretrial men were divided into groups high and low in psychopathy. The more psychopathic men evidenced no heightening of their catecholamine levels just prior to the trial. The less psychopathic men had strongly elevated levels. The anticipation of the court trial evoked in the psychopaths no physiological inkling of anxiety or fear.

A second non–skin conductance study concerned the delinquents in a "sample of 5362 single-born, legitimate, live births drawn from all 13,687 births occurring between March 3 and 9 in England, Wales and Scotland" in 1946 (Wadsworth 1976).

This classic longitudinal birth cohort study was begun by Douglas (Douglas and Blomfield 1958). Wadsworth (1975) described the cumulative, officially recorded delinquency in this birth cohort at twenty-one years of age and then examined the relationship of this delinquency to a predelinquency measure of ANS response to anticipation of stress. The survey members were subjected to a school medical examination at age eleven. The period during which they waited for this examination was designed to be somewhat stressful. Their pulse rates were measured to assess the effects of this anticipation. Delinquents were defined as those who "either made a court appearance or were formally cautioned by the police between the ages of 8 and 21 years" (Wadsworth 1976, p. 249). Those who were *later* registered as delinquents had a lower anticipatory pulse rate. The delinquent–not delinquent differences were significant for those committing indictable offenses and sexual and violent offenses. Wadsworth reported an interesting biosocial interaction in these data. He assessed whether the children had experienced broken homes. Within the group of boys who had experienced broken homes early in life, anticipatory pulse rate did not distinguish the delinquents. Anticipatory pulse rate was highly significantly lower for the delinquents among the boys who did not experience broken homes. This type of interaction of biological (pulse rate) and social (family disruption) data was predicted by Sellin (1938) and has been observed repeatedly in our research in Copenhagen. The biological factors predict best in those areas and situations, or among those groups, in which social factors (e.g., stable home, middle-class status) do not "explain" antisocial behavior. In those situations, areas, or groups in which the social variables (broken home, or lower-class status) do predict antisocial behavior, the biological variables are less predictive.

The Wadsworth study is important because it is based on a large, national birth cohort and the results must be seen as representative. The data on pulse rate were gathered by hundreds of different physicians in different schools using primitive methods. Not all of these measurements were equally accurately taken. About ten years intervened between the recording of the pulse rate and the ascertainment of delinquency. The hypothe-sized results emerged despite these conditions—which in most re-search do not tend to inflate positive findings. The antisocial in-dividuals evidenced a low level of emotional, ANS, physiolog-ically measured, anticipation of an aversive experience. Those who did not suffer anticipatory "fear" before the examination were those boys who later were more likely to become delin-quent. Perhaps this anticipatory fear was also lacking before they committed the act or acts which placed them in the delinquent group.

One other feature of the Wadsworth study warrants emphasis. Because of the ten-year period between pulse rate reading and ascertainment of delinquency, the delinquency experience is un-likely to have produced the low pulse rates. The prospective nature of the study establishes low pulse rate in anticipation of stress as a variable worthy of consideration as a potential etio-logical factor in delinquency.

How salient a predictive factor is pulse rate? Not very. In the Wadsworth study it predicts delinquency about as well as does the variable "broken home." It is naive to expect that any variable alone, whether biological or social, will explain large amounts of delinquency variance. Delinquency is likely to be as complex in its causation as it is in its manifestation. When, however, the biological interactive effect of pulse and family is assessed, pre-diction improves remarkably.

In some studies the subjects have the opportunity to anticipate that others are about to be shocked or blasted with noise. Sutker (1970) studied noninstitutionalized psychopaths and controls while they observed an individual experiencing an electric shock when a countdown from number 1 reached 4. The psychopaths displayed no or minimal skin conductance response in anticipa-tion of the other's pain. Nonpsychopaths showed strong anticipa-tion. This result has been replicated by House and Milligan (1976) in a study on prisoners. Similar results have been ob-tained by Aniskiewicz (1973) and Hare and Craigen (1974).

Psychopaths, prisoners, and delinquents evidence reduced physiological signs that they are apprehensive about a forthcoming painful or aversive stimulus to themselves or to others. Non-psychopathic (or less psychopathic) prisoners and individuals not officially registered as delinquent evidence more physiological anticipation of such events. The intended analogy of these laboratory confrontations to the development of "real life" acts of lawlessness is clear. Of course, most elements of criminal acts in the "field" are only remotely modeled by this laboratory paradigm. Yet the relatively consistent results of these studies cannot be ignored. They give no reason to reject the hypothesis that lack, or diminution, of a "normal" ANS-fear reaction anticipating negative or painful consequences may be partly responsible for the relative ease with which certain individuals commit deviant acts.

As pointed out above, the evidence in support of this hypothesis is all correlative. A more rigorous examination of the role of this variable in the etiology of antisocial behavior can only be carried out in the context of a prospective, *experimental-manipulative* project (primary or secondary prevention). Training techniques could be tested which improve a young person's ability to foresee emotionally the aversive consequences of his acts. The more effective the training techniques (taking into consideration social factors and initial level of emotional anticipation), the greater should be the reduction of delinquency. Given use of an adequate control group in such a study, this experimental-manipulative approach (as opposed to the traditional weak correlative approach) would improve our capacity to test this hypothesis.

C. Failure to Learn from Punishment: A Biosocial Theory of Antisocial Behavior

The clinical characteristic of the psychopath that is perhaps most critical to understanding the origins of his condition is his reputed inability to learn from punishment. This failing certainly relates to his hectic recidivism; but, even more important, it suggests a mechanism which would make the young psychopath-to-be relatively unresponsive to one of society's important moral training forces, namely, family and peer punishment for transgressive acts. The argument would also apply to other types of antisocial individuals.

This section presents a mini-theory[2] of the bases and consequences of some individuals' inability to learn from punishment. Viewed inversely, the theory is an attempt to explain the development and learning of law abidance. The theory postulates the interaction of specific social factors and specific ANS aptitudes. After presenting the theory, we present skin conductance evidence relating to the theory and to the examination in laboratory situations of the ability of the antisocial individual to learn from punishment.

Perhaps it would do no great harm to begin with a discussion of how we define morality and law abidance. An early publication on this topic was chipped in stone and brought down from Mount Sinai. The major thrust of that message was negative, "Thou shalt *not*. . . ." While subsequent moral authorities have added *some* positive acts as prescriptions of moral behavior (e.g., "Love thy neighbor"), they have retained the original, basic, inhibitory definitions of law abiding acts.

People must have evidenced, and still do, tendencies toward aggression, adultery, and avarice. In self-defense, society has set up moral, social, legal, and religious codes and has struggled to teach its children to *inhibit* impulses leading to transgression of those codes.

Following the excellent exposition of Gordon Trasler (1972), we would suggest that the avoidance of transgression (that is, the practice of law-abiding behavior) demanded by the moral commandments is probably mainly learned from punishments administered by society, family, and peers. The critical inhibitory training forces in childhood likely are (1) the punishment of antisocial responses by family, society, and friends, and (2) the child's individual capacity to *learn* to *inhibit* antisocial responses.

Using the example of aggressive impulses, the minitheory attempts to explain how children learn to inhibit antisocial impulses. Frequently, when child A is aggressive to child B, child

[2] An earlier statement of this mini-theory appears in Mednick (1977).

A is punished by a peer or a parent. Eventually, after enough punishment, just the thought of aggression should produce a little anticipatory fear in child A. If the fear response is large enough, the raised arm will drop and the aggressive response will be successfully inhibited.

Our theory suggests that what happens in this child after he has successfully inhibited such an antisocial response is critical for his learning of civilized behavior. Let us consider the situation again in more detail.

1. Child A contemplates aggressive action.
2. Because of previous punishment or the threat of punishment he suffers fear.
3. Because of fear he inhibits the aggressive response.
4. *Since he no longer entertains the aggressive impulse, the fear will begin to dissipate, to be reduced.*

Fear reduction is the most powerful, naturally occurring reinforcement that psychologists have discovered. The reduction of fear (which immediately follows the inhibition of the aggression) can act as a reinforcement for this *inhibition* and will result in the learning of the inhibition of aggression. The powerful reinforcement associated with fear reduction increases the probability that the inhibition of the aggression will occur in the future. After many such experiences, the normal child will learn to inhibit aggressive impulses. Each time such an impulse arises and is inhibited, the inhibition will be strengthened by reinforcement, since the fear elicited by the impulse will be reduced following successful inhibition.

What does a child need in order to learn social norms effectively?

1. A censuring agent (typically family or peers), and
2. An adequate fear response, and
3. The ability to learn the fear response in anticipation of an anti-social act, and
4. Fast dissipation of fear to provide a natural reinforcement for the inhibitory response.

We have earlier summarized evidence that suggests that the antisocial individual exhibits an abnormally diminished ANS response to frightening (or neutral) stimuli (point 2 above) and is relatively unable emotionally (ANS) to anticipate negative events (point 3). Below we discuss point 4, the antisocial individual's ability to experience a normally fast dissipation of an (ANS) fear response and be reinforced for inhibiting the antisocial response.

The speed and size of a reinforcement determines its effectiveness (Mednick 1964). An effective reinforcement is one which is delivered immediately after the relevant response. The faster the reduction of fear, the faster the delivery of the reinforcement. The fear response is, to a large extent, controlled by the ANS. ANS activity can be estimated by use of peripheral indicants such as skin conductance.

A child who has an ANS that characteristically recovers very quickly from fear will receive a quick and large reinforcement for inhibiting the aggression response and will learn inhibition quickly. If he has an ANS that recovers very slowly, he will receive a delayed, small reinforcement and will learn to inhibit aggression slowly, if at all. This perspective would predict that (holding constant training, social status, criminal associations, poverty level, and similar factors), those who commit antisocial acts should tend to be characterized by slow autonomic recovery. The slower the recovery, the less the learned inhibition and the more serious and repetitive the antisocial behavior predicted.

D. Skin Conductance Recovery

There was little precedent for measuring skin conductance recovery when in 1962 we (Mednick and Schulsinger 1964) began examining its functioning characteristics. It was a critical element in a theory of inhibition learning in schizophrenia (Mednick 1962, 1974). We examined 104 normal adolescents (controls for children at high risk for schizophrenia) with a variety of assessment devices including skin conductance. The seven adolescents (of the 104) who some years later were registered for mild delinquent acts had a distinctly and significantly slower rate of skin conductance recovery than their controls (Loeb and Mednick 1977).

Siddle, Nicol, and Foggitt (1973) examined skin conductance responsiveness of 67 English Borstal inmates, divided into high, medium, and low antisocial groups. When Siddle learned of our recovery hypothesis, he rescored his data for skin conductance recovery; speed and rate of recovery varied inversely as a function of the degree of antisocial behavior. Recovery measured on a single trial was surprisingly effective in differentiating the three groups (Siddle, Mednick, Nicol, and Foggitt 1977). Bader-Bartfai and Schalling (1974) also reanalysed skin conductance data from a previous investigation of criminals, finding that criminals who tended to be more "delinquent" on a personality measure tended to have a slower recovery. Hare (1975) reports slow recovery (for a novel tone) for psychopaths among prison inmates. There have been other supportive findings reported (Hemming 1977; Hinton, O'Neill, and Webster 1977; Eisenberg 1976; Plovnick 1976; Waid 1976). Hare, Cox, and Frazell (in press) and Hare, Frazelle, and Cox (1978) found that prison psychopaths evidence slow recovery both in anticipation of a loud noise (120db) and to the noise itself. Levander et al. (1977), Lidberg et al. (1977), and Levander et al. (1980) report slow skin conductance recovery in psychopaths among criminals and delinquents.

Hare's studies find that the psychopaths from prison populations evidence slow ANS recovery under extreme stimulus conditions. In one study he compared prisoners with college students. There are serious difficulties of interpretation in such comparisons, but it is nevertheless interesting that the students' average recovery speed was more than twice that of the prisoners. "Thus, while it may be possible to differentiate between psychopathic and non-psychopathic inmates in terms of electrodermal recovery to intense stimuli, it may be easier to differentiate between criminals and non-criminals or between groups who show marked differences in asocial behavior" (Hare 1978a, p. 128).

One more prospective study can be cited. In 1964, Hare examined skin conductance in prisoners (all in a maximum security prison). Ten years later he checked to see how recidivist the prisoners subsequently became. Skin conductance recovery in 1964 was used to predict degree of recidivism. As might be expected, the relation between skin conductance and recidivism within this group composed exclusively of serious offenders is not great ($r = .24$, $p < .05$, one-tail test). Interestingly enough a small group of the slowest recoverers was almost entirely composed of individuals repeatedly convicted of fraud (Hare 1978a). This attempt to link specific antecedents with specific types of offender characteristics is a research mode worth emulating.

The relation between slow recovery and antisocial behavior seems robust across national boundaries, experimental procedures, and definitions of "antisocial." Prospective studies (supported by the cross-sectional findings) do not contradict the hypothesis. Siddle (1977) notes: "The results concerning skin conductance recovery and anti-social behavior appear to be quite consistent. Subjects who display anti-social behavior (psychopaths, adult criminals, and adolescent delinquents) also display significantly slower SCR recovery than do matched controls" (pp. 206–7).

Hare, reporting some semicontradictory evidence, finds reliable differences between psychopathic and nonpsychopathic serious criminals only under specific, usually extreme, stimulus conditions. The mini-theory described above, however, relates only to moral training and subsequent law abidance and is not confounded by the discovery that it is difficult to observe recovery differences between two groups which have both exhibited behavior reflecting somewhat negatively on the adequacy of their moral training. The theory assumes that skin conductance recovery reflects central ANS processes. Bundy (1977) has argued that recovery is related mainly to peripheral sweat gland activity and does not reflect central processes. Levander et al. (1980) later tested this criticism and concluded that skin conductance recovery *is* in large part controlled by central factors.

Several studies have tested the hypothesis that antisocial behavior is associated with slow ANS recovery, and none unequivocally refutes it. Two *prospective* studies suggest that slow ANS recovery precedes the onset of recorded delinquency and predicts recidivism. Consequently, slow ANS recovery must be included among the factors that may be etiologically related to antisocial behavior.

E. Conditioning Studies Using Punishment

The classic research in the field of ANS factors in antisocial behavior is the 1957 study by Lykken. Lykken demonstrated that antisocial individuals could learn to negotiate a "push button" maze as well as controls do. In the Lykken task, one type of maze error caused a red light to flash, thus indicating to the subject that he had made a mistake; another type of maze error subjected the subject to an unpleasant electric shock. The controls quickly learned to avoid the buttons which resulted in shock. The antisocial individuals showed little evidence of learning to avoid the shock button.

Schachter and Latane (1964) and Schmauk (1970) replicated the Lykken findings. Schmauk's study demonstrated again that the psychopath has normal ability to learn skin conductance conditioning with positive reinforcement (rewards). When shock or social censure (i.e., punishment) was involved, the psychopath evidenced poor skin conductance conditioning. In other words the psychopath's deficiency is most apparent where an ANS response is needed to mediate learning. This result has been observed by several other investigators (Hare 1970; Hare and Quinn 1971; Rosen and Schalling 1971; Schoenherr 1964). The Loeb and Mednick (1977) *prospective* study also found that those boys who later became delinquent evidenced poor skin conductance conditioning in adolescence.

Several explanations for the psychopath's deficit in ANS-mediated learning have been mentioned in the literature. It is known, for example, that conditioning of skin conductance response is facilitated if the subject is consciously aware that the conditioned stimulus tone will be followed by an electric shock (Dawson 1973; Dawson and Faredy 1976). It has been argued that the psychopath is simply not able to verbalize this contingency. Studies by Syndulko et al. (1975) and Ziskind, Syndulko, and Maltzman (1978), however, indicate that even when the psychopaths were clearly aware of the contingencies and could verbalize them, they still evidenced a deficit in skin conductance conditioning.

It has also been suggested that the psychopaths are at such a low level of arousal that they are unable to condition. It is not clear why this low arousal level does not affect learning involving positive reinforcement. In support of this interpretation, Schachter (1971) has demonstrated that imprisoned psychopaths who evidence poor skin conductance conditioning will show normal conditioning under the influence of an injection of adrenaline. The adrenaline will of course increase the subject's state of ANS arousal. (Hare [1973] has offered some cogent criticisms of the bases of this study.) Chesno and Kilman (1975) noted that psychopaths who evidence poor ANS conditioning under low background noise will learn normally under high background noise stimulation. Background noise increases level of ANS arousal. Allen et al. (1976) reasoned that if the delinquent's problem is low ANS arousal, perhaps recidivism would be decreased by administration of a drug which would increase arousal. They report that a small pilot trial with delinquents seemed exceptionally promising.

The antisocial individual evidences relatively poor skin conductance conditioning. This finding is reliable and not contradicted. In discussions of this literature there has been a tendency to imply that the psychopath simply cannot learn an ANS conditioned response. Perhaps it would be more accurate to say that at equivalent levels of aversive stimulation (noise or electric shock), the antisocial individual evidences a deficit in ANS conditioning. This deficit has generated hypotheses regarding the etiology of the failure of moral learning. It also suggests that if rehabilitation or prevention programs are contemplated, consideration should be given to arousal manipulation to improve emotional learning.

III. Neurophysiological Studies

The most frequently used measures of neurophysiological functioning in research with antisocial individuals have concerned

various aspects of electrical brain activity. The electroencephalogram (EEG), recorded under resting conditions from the scalp,
has been used to investigate criminal populations since the early
forties. Later on, various chemical substances (e.g., alpha chloralose) were introduced to activate the EEG; this method has
been particularly fruitful in the study of episodic behavioral disorders (Monroe 1970). The more recently developed methods
of scalp recording under various conditions of sensory stimulation (e.g., evoked potentials) have been used very rarely with
criminals. Intracerebral recordings have not been used to explore
criminal populations. However, selected patients whose brain
disease was accompanied by aggressive behavior were examined
with electrodes inserted in various parts of the brain; these studies are mentioned because of their potential implications for antisocial behavior.

A. Clinical EEG Abnormality

Before we discuss EEG abnormalities, a brief review of spontaneous electrical activity of the normal brain may be in order.
Most of the surface EEG reflects the activity of neuronal groups
which are located in the cerebral cortex. The rhythmic nature
of that activity is determined by pacemaker mechanisms which
involve subcortical structures, primarily the thalamus. The EEG
represents a complex signal composed of a number of rhythms
and transient discharges. The EEG and its components may be
described in terms of location of electrodes on the scalp (or on
the cortical surface) from where it is recorded, and the amplitude, and frequency of the brain waves. The frequency is given
in cycles per second. This unit of frequency is sometimes called
the Hertz (Hz). Most of the EEG activity occurs at frequencies
between 0.5 and 30 Hz. This frequency range is subdivided by
electroencephalographers into several bands, designated by Greek
letters. These conventional bands are as follows: delta (0.5–3
Hz); theta (4–8 Hz); alpha (8–13 Hz); and beta (14 Hz and
above).[3]

[3] These bandwidths are taken from a recent standard EEG text (Kooi,
Tucker, and Marshall 1978), which also provides additional information on
normal and abnormal EEG. Other authors may use slightly different bandwidths.

One of the earliest reports to indicate a relation between abnormal brain function and criminal behavior was a dramatic case history of a man who murdered his mother (Hill and Sargant 1943). The man was not suffering from any manifest illness, and there was no apparent motive for the murder. However, the EEG revealed that under conditions of low blood sugar content, this man's brain produced abnormal electrical discharges which were associated with clouding of consciousness. These discharges could be elicited whenever the blood sugar content dropped below a certain level (which happened when he was temporarily deprived of food). Since the crime was committed when the accused had not eaten for some time, the jury returned the verdict of "guilty but insane," essentially on the basis of the EEG and biochemical (blood sugar) evidence.

This and similar cases have inspired a series of EEG studies, many of which share certain similarities. The subjects had committed an antisocial (usually violent) act. They were then sent to a penal institution, at which they received a neuropsychiatric examination, including an EEG. The EEG was evaluated by *visual inspection* by a physician, who classified it as "normal" or "abnormal." A qualitative description of the abnormalities was sometimes included.

All of the studies mentioned above used visual assessment of the EEG. Unfortunately, the reliability of visual assessments of EEG abnormality is not very high (Volavka et al. 1973), and this problem may have been partly responsible for the wide range of estimates of prevalence of EEG abnormality in criminal populations. Another reason for these differences is the sampling bias inherent in the various methods used within institutions to select criminal subjects for the EEG test (e.g., consecutive admissions, self-selection, or selection by medical or other officers) as well as unknown differences between various institutions in the characteristics of subjects. Most of these studies agree that the EEG in criminals is likely to be abnormal (e.g., Silverman 1944; Hill and Pond 1952; DeBaudouin 1961; Small 1966; Sayed, Lewis, and Brittain 1969; Williams 1969; Okasha, Sadek, and Moneim 1975). In probably the best study of this type, Williams (1969) evaluated

333 delinquents referred by prison authorities because they used violence in their crimes. He divided this sample into those who were habitually aggressive and those who had committed a single violent act. Sixty-four percent of the first group showed EEG abnormalities and only 24 percent of the second group. When those who were mentally retarded, who had epilepsy, or who had a major head injury were removed, the EEG was abnormal in 57 percent of the habitual aggressors, but in only 12 percent of the persons who had committed a single violent crime. Williams states that 12 per cent is the proportion of abnormalities to be expected in the population at large.

Several studies, however, reported no EEG differences between criminal and noncriminal populations (Jenkins and Pacella 1943; Gibbs, Bagchi, and Bloomberg 1945; Driver, West, and Faulk 1974). To some extent, these negative findings resulted from misinterpretation of data.

The Gibbs, Bagchi, and Bloomberg study, in particular, was taken by many authors (Forssman and Frey 1953; De Baudouin 1961; Hill 1963; Knott 1965) as an example of a disagreement in the literature regarding the abnormality of EEG in criminals. This widely cited study compared the EEGs of 452 prisoners with those of 1,432 nonprisoner controls. The subjects were divided into three age groups. Comparisons did not yield significant differences between prisoners and controls. The rationale for the age grouping was that "in both prisoners and controls, normal EEGs were commoner in the young than in the older groups" (Gibbs, Bagchi, and Bloomberg 1945, p. 296). This rationale does not receive much support from their table III: the percentage of normal EEGs in young, middle-aged, and older control subject groups is 82 percent, 81 percent, and 82 percent respectively. Furthermore, the differences between the criminals and the controls show the same tendency in all three age groups. We therefore collapsed the three age groups into one, and found a significant difference between prisoners and controls ($\chi^2(3) = 10.5$, $p < .02$). Most of the difference was due to the greater proportion of abnormally fast EEGs among the prisoners. Moreover, the percentages of normal recordings in the control groups used for this study were quite low. Using the same method of

EEG evaluation, Gibbs and Gibbs (1950) found 84.2 percent normal EEGs in 1,000 controls. Even that percentage is low compared with other estimates (Cobb 1963; Williams 1969). Thus a spuriously high percentage of EEG abnormalities in the control groups might have reduced the contrast with the criminals. We conclude that Gibbs, Bagchi, and Bloomberg have collected a large amount of interesting material, which was misinterpreted.

The weight of research findings strongly supports a conclusion that criminals' EEGs are more frequently classified as abnormal than those of noncriminal control subjects. In order to explore the implications of this finding, we have to review the type of EEG abnormalities reported to occur in criminal populations, and try to trace the relation of these electrical abnormalities to specific types of antisocial behavior.

B. Slowing of the EEG Frequency

Almost all studies of the resting EEG in criminals report some slowing of the EEG frequency. This slowing may involve a relatively small frequency decrease within the alpha frequency range (8–13 Hz), it may mean an increased occurrence of theta waves (4–8 Hz), or even slower delta waves (0.5–3 Hz). The slow activity may occur diffusely (i.e., over large scalp areas without constant location), or in a focus (a limited region). The slow activity may be more or less continuous throughout the EEG record (i.e., background slowing), or it may occur in bursts. These properties impart various types of functional significance to the slow rhythms.

Slowing of alpha activity. Statistically significant background slowing of alpha activity was reported to occur in juvenile delinquents (Forssman and Frey 1953; Verdeaux 1970) and also in a series of ninety-seven adult murderers (De Baudouin 1961). Another group which measured the alpha frequency (Gibbs, Bagchi, and Bloomberg 1945) demonstrated no statistically significant difference between prisoners and controls, but their data indicate a tendency for prisoners to have a slightly slower alpha activity. Many other authors have reported diffuse EEG slowing in criminals without any attempt at quantitative measurement;

it seems fair to assume that the slowing of alpha activity is probably a fairly frequent finding in persons who exhibit antisocial behavior.

Alpha slowing is not specifically related to antisocial behavior; it may occur in a wide variety of psychiatric and neurological diseases as well as in symptom-free XYY men (Volavka et al. 1977a; Volavka et al. 1977b). Average frequency of alpha activity increases as a function of age between five and twenty years; thus it may be considered an indicator of brain maturation. Normative data on this development of alpha activity in normal children and adolescents are available (Lindsley 1939; Matousek and Petersen 1973).

The most obvious hypothesis to explain alpha slowing in criminals involves a developmental lag. It is possible that brain maturation proceeds at a slower rate in these individuals than in noncriminals, or that maturational processes stop earlier. The idea that physiological brain immaturity may be related to certain forms of antisocial behavior is not new. Hill and Watterson (1942) reported a number of EEG abnormalities in aggressive and other psychopaths. They suggested that both behavioral and EEG abnormalities may be explained on the basis of a "cortical immaturity" (p. 64). Hill's work is discussed below in more detail.

An alternative hypothesis to account for alpha slowing would be that alpha frequency was normal until several weeks or months prior to the onset of antisocial behavior. At that time, a brain disorder developed (e.g., a tumor, epilepsy, or an injury) which caused the alpha frequency to slow and the antisocial behavior to occur. Since the alpha slowing in criminals is generally not associated with any coarse brain disorder, this hypothesis is not tenable.

The hypothesis based on developmental lag may be correct but does not explain much in itself. The causes of the developmental lag may be genetic, they may involve pre- or perinatal events, postnatal diseases, or injuries. We do not know whether the slowing of alpha activity precedes the development of antisocial behavior or occurs later. This is a pivotal question: if the alpha slowing is an antecedent of antisocial behavior, one might hypothesize that it is a predisposing factor for the development of such behavior. Lower frequency of alpha activity is generally associated with lower levels of arousal—which earlier in this essay was hypothesized to be related to the development of antisocial behavior.

The only way to establish whether the alpha slowing precedes the development of antisocial behavior is to examine and follow a number of persons, some of whom will become criminals. In other words, a longitudinal prospective study is needed to answer this question. No such study has been published. Our preliminary data indicate that such an approach may be fruitful (Mednick et al. 1980). In 1971–73 we recorded EEGs in 129 boys in Copenhagen, aged eleven to thirteen, as a part of a prospective study of factors predisposing to delinquency. The EEGs were subjected to computerized period analyses; partial results were published (Itil et al. 1974), and the data were filed. We were able to obtain information from police records about the delinquent behavior of these 129 boys through 1978. Preliminary results indicate that a significant portion of the variance of convictions for theft and for traffic violations can be predicted by the relative amount of EEG activity between 8 and 10 Hz (i.e., slow alpha). We are preparing a study to replicate these results in a larger sample.

It should be noted that the slowing of alpha activity is associated with a variety of antisocial behavior ranging from theft to murder. It is possible that the alpha slowing is associated with a generalized predisposition to poorly controlled behavior, including antisocial behavior. The development of specific types of such behavior may be determined by other factors (social, cultural, various biological factors).

EEG activity below 8 Hz. An excessive amount of theta activity (4–8 Hz) is a classical finding reported in persons who exhibit antisocial behavior. Hill (1952) reviewed EEGs of psychiatric patients with varied types of abnormal behavior and concluded that a "large percentage have shown aggressive, dangerous, antisocial conduct . . . fugue states . . . or withdrawal, stupor, and mutism" (p. 419). In that paper, which discusses sets of patients he reported on previously (Hill and Pond 1952), Hill describes four types of EEG abnormality which, in his opinion, suggest maturational defect. All four involve an excess of slow activity: (1) excessive central temporal theta activity; (2) alpha variants (i.e., waves at subharmonic frequencies of alpha rhythm) occurring predominantly over occipital areas; (3) posterior temporal slow wave focus; (4) theta-dominant record (i.e., diffuse theta activity with little or no alpha activity present).

The possible significance of maturational defects was discussed earlier in this section. There is good evidence that the amount of diffuse theta activity decreases with age in normal subjects (Matousek and Petersen 1973, Matousek et al. 1967). Retardation of that decremental process may be viewed as a developmental lag. Subjects in Hill's sample were not selected for criminality, and definitions of behavioral abnormalities were imprecise. However, most of his findings have been replicated in criminal populations. Fenton et al. (1974) have found temporal slow activity in EEGs of residents of a penal-mental institution. Many studies supporting Hill's findings have been reviewed elsewhere (Monroe 1970).

C. Epilepsy, EEG, and Aggression

Epilepsy is frequently associated with paroxysmal changes in the EEG as well as with abnormal behavior. The relation between epilepsy, EEG, and antisocial (particularly aggressive) behavior has now been debated for more than thirty-five years; no clear consensus has been reached. Temporal lobe epilepsy has been particularly interesting for criminologists, since abnormalities of temporal lobe function may be associated with complex seizures (sometimes called "psychomotor" seizures); during such seizures as well as between them, patients may exhibit aggressive behavior. Mark and Ervin (1970) have reported that patients suffering from temporal lobe epilepsy are prone to perform aggressive acts, either as a part of their seizure or in the immediate postseizure state. However, Rodin (1973) photographed epileptic seizures in 150 patients, 42 of whom had ictal, psychomotor automatism during a seizure and 15 of whom had psychomotor automatism immediately following the seizure. There was no instance of aggressive behavior in that study.

Although neither of these reports is explicit about patient selection, it was well known that Mark and Ervin were primarily interested in violence; it is reasonable to assume that violent behavior was an important reason why patients were referred to them. Rodin, on the other hand, is a leading expert in epilepsy, and patients were probably referred to him primarily because of seizures.

Methodological problems involved in subject sampling and in definitions of aggressive behavior and of temporal lobe epilepsy have been reviewed by Klingman and Goldberg (1975). These problems are so overwhelming that their literature review does not provide any conclusion as to whether temporal lobe epilepsy is associated with aggressive behavior either during seizures or between them. Temporal lobe epilepsy appears to be a heterogenous group of disorders; aggressive behavior may of course be determined by a very large number of factors.

If temporal lobe epilepsy is related to aggression, an interaction between social and biological factors can be expected. Low socioeconomic status of parents may expose children to inferior medical care. This may increase the risk for pre- and perinatal injuries, which in turn may increase the risk for temporal lobe epilepsy.

The syndrome of "episodic dyscontrol" is used to describe certain types of antisocial, particularly violent, behavior (Monroe 1970, p. 29). There is a partial overlap between the syndrome of episodic dyscontrol and temporal lobe epilepsy; a large proportion of persons with episodic dyscontrol have focal EEG abnormalities over temporal lobes. Some of these EEG features are known as "positive spikes" or "14- and 6-per-second positive spikes." They appear in bursts over posterior temporal areas, mostly in drowsiness or light sleep. EEG features in the episodic dyscontrol syndrome were reported by Monroe (1970), and Bach-y-Rita et al. (1971).

It is clear that a large proportion of persons who show clinical signs of temporal lobe epilepsy or of episodic dyscontrol will not have paroxysmal features in their routine clinical EEG. If these "false negative" cases are investigated with more elaborate techniques, abnormalities of electrical brain function may emerge. Such techniques include either the use of intracerebral electrodes, or various methods of EEG activation.

The scalp electrodes used in the routine clinical EEG are relatively distant from the sources of neuronal discharges which give rise to the clinical signs of temporal lobe epilepsy or episodic dyscontrol. Therefore they give only an approximate and incomplete picture of the electrical events which are the bases of such behavioral phenomena. Techniques are available for the insertion of electrodes into the brain during surgical procedures. Such electrodes can be used to record simultaneously with the routine scalp electrodes in the same person. Comparison of such records makes it clear that many subcortical discharges are not adequately reflected in the scalp electrodes.

Recordings from certain subcortical structures, such as the amygdala and the septal region, have demonstrated paroxysmal activity in cases of episodic rage (e.g., Heath and Mickle 1960; Mark and Ervin 1970). Subcortical electrodes may also be used for electrical stimulation of selected structures such as the amygdala, and such stimulation may elicit or interrupt aggressive behavior (Mark and Ervin 1970). The use of intracerebral electrodes is too complicated to become widespread. Ethical concerns have been raised about the potential use of these techniques in criminal populations.

D. Activation Techniques and Event-Related Potentials

The sensitivity of EEG readings can be increased by use of various activation techniques, pharmacological or other manipulations which elicit latent EEG abnormalities. Monroe has pioneered the use of alpha chloralose as an activation agent which brings out paroxysmal EEG features in persons who exhibit episodic violent behavior (Monroe 1970; Monroe 1974). Bilateral paroxysmal slow activity with a frontal predominance was a frequent EEG finding in his "dyscontrol" patients. Another substance used for EEG activation is pentamethylenetetrazol. Kido (1973) found that relatively small doses of this drug elicited paroxysmal EEG features in juvenile multiple offenders and in juvenile murderers. These and other drugs used for EEG activation decrease the seizure threshold. It should be noted that similar effects may be achieved by the ingestion of alcohol, by lowering the blood level of glucose, and by other manipulations. This is discussed in the section on biochemistry.

If a stimulus is repeatedly administered to a subject and the brain response is monitored, the average of blocks of these trials assumes a recognizable and replicable wave form. Since the brain response is instigated by a stimulus, the response is called evoked potential (EP). Very little is known about EP in persons who exhibit antisocial behavior. Dobbs and Speck (1968) reported an increase of amplitude of a component of visual EP in a small group of nonpsychotic male prisoners. Filimonova (1978) saw an increase of a late positive EP component in "psychopaths" (in comparison with controls). This was dependent on the informational content of the stimulus. Similar results are referred to by Ivanitskii (1976), who, however, presents no data to support his claims. Syndulko et al. (1975) reported essentially negative EP observations. In the same paper, these authors also present negative data on Contingent Negative Variation (CNV)—an event-related potential specific to anticipation of a stimulus, thus not confirming a previous report by McCallum (1973).

These methods have an advantage over the resting EEG in that they explore brain activity under various sensory and cognitive loads. Further research will show whether they are useful in the study of antisocial behavior.

Research on neurophysiological bases of criminal behavior is fraught with major methodological problems. The main difficulties are that criminal behavior is extremely varied and that the neurophysiological measures are not well defined. The available evidence indicates that episodic violent behavior may be associated with abnormal electrical discharges in certain parts of the brain, particularly in the temporal lobe. This relatively specific relationship has been widely recognized. A small, relatively permanent decrease of the average frequency of the EEG alpha activity may reflect a general propensity for a wider variety of antisocial behavior. Whether such antisocial behavior is of a violent or nonviolent nature may depend on additional social and biological factors. The paroxysmal features and alpha slowing may coexist, or they may occur independently of each other. The hypothesis related to alpha slowing is testable, and we are pursuing it.

IV. Biochemical and Pharmacological Factors

In this section we review some endogenous and exogenous substances which may be important for antisocial behavior. The endogenous substances include testosterone and glucose. Among the exogenous substances, we discuss alcohol, amphetamines, marijuana, and opiates. We intend to give the reader merely a brief overview of this burgeoning topic and provide basic references. Space does not permit in-depth treatment of biochemical and pharmacological topics.

A. Testosterone

Testosterone is the principal androgenic steroid hormone. Preliminary evidence suggests that its plasma levels and production rate may be related to criminal aggressive behavior in human males. Kreuz and Rose (1972) studied a sample of prisoners and reported that the plasma testosterone levels were higher in those men who had committed violent offenses than in the other men. Similar results were obtained by Rada, Laws, and Kellner (1976) who classified rapists and child molesters according to the degree of violence manifested while committing their offenses. The more violent rapists had higher testosterone plasma levels than the less violent ones or than the child molesters.

Various psychological tests purporting to measure aggression or hostility were administered to prisoners and nonprisoner control subjects, and the results of such tests were compared with the plasma testosterone levels. Some of these experiments suggested a positive relation between aggressivity/hostility and testosterone (Persky, Smith, and Basu 1971; Ehrenkranz, Bliss, and Sheard 1974). However, other studies did not confirm the existence of such a relation (Kreuz and Rose 1972; Meyer-Bahlburg et al. 1974; Doering et al. 1975; Rada, Laws and Kellner 1976; Monti, Brown, and Corriveau 1977).

Several substances exhibiting antiandrogenic activity have been used to control sex-related aggression in men. Cyproterone acetate and Medroxyprogesterone (marketed as Provera) decrease plasma testosterone levels by mechanisms which are not completely understood. Each of these substances decreases sexual interest and sexual activity in men. Laschet (1973) reported therapeutic success using cyproterone acetate in males convicted of sexual assault. Medroxyprogesterone was used by Money (1970) and by Blumer and Migeon (1973) to reduce illicit sexual behavior in male offenders.

The long-term side effects and risks of these treatments are not known. It seems that the antiandrogenic effect is reversible on discontinuation of the treatment. More information about the safety and efficacy of these treatments is needed.

B. Hypoglycemia

Under normal conditions the plasma levels of glucose are maintained within a certain range (70–115 mg%, depending on the assay method). The brain is dependent on blood glucose for its energy supply. If the glucose in the blood decreases to an abnormally low level (that state is called hypoglycemia), brain function will be altered. Hypoglycemia may be induced by an injection of insulin, it develops during starvation, it may be a symptom of various (mostly endocrinological) diseases, and sometimes it occurs without any apparent cause. The initial effects of hypoglycemia include fatique, irritability, aggressivity, and sometimes rage. Various types of criminal behavior may occur under the influence of hypoglycemia; this relationship was reviewed by Wilder (1947). We earlier mentioned the Hill and Sargant (1943) study of a murderer whose EEG showed paroxysmal features only when he became hypoglycemic. It is well known that hypoglycemia may elicit a variety of other EEG abnormalities (Dawson and Greville 1963). It is possible that hypoglycemia exerts some of its behavioral effects by means of the epilepsy-like mechanisms discussed in the preceding section on neurophysiology.

It is difficult to estimate the relative importance of hypoglycemia as a causative or contributory factor in the development of criminal behavior. There is no doubt that certain crimes occur under the partial influence of hypoglycemia, but there is little evidence that this biochemical abnormality represents a major threat to law and order.

C. Alcohol

Two main types of offenses are committed under the influence of alcohol: assaults and traffic offenses. There is an overlap between these two. The role of alcohol in violent crime has been studied by a large number of researchers; this work has been reviewed by Tinklenberg (1973) and Moyer (1976). One of the best known and largest studies is that of Wolfgang (1958), who analyzed 588 homicides and reported that the offender had been drinking just prior to the crime in 55 percent of the cases. Tinklenberg et al. (1974) studied the drug involvement in criminal assaults by adolescents. In twenty-three of fifty-six assaults studied, the assailant was reported to be under the influence of alcohol (alone or in combination with other drugs). These very thorough studies also exemplify a principal problem of this type of research: they rely only on reports of alcohol use rather than on measurements of alcohol blood levels. More direct evidence linking alcohol ingestion with crime was provided by Shupe (1954), who studied urine or blood samples obtained from suspects immediately after their arrests. Alcohol was detected in 144 of 163 suspects charged with violent crimes. This study also shows that the likelihood of arrest for violent crime under the influence of alcohol is an inverted U-shape function of the blood alcohol concentration (BAC). The likelihood increases from zero BAC up to 0.20–0.29 percent, and then decreases with increasing BAC. This goes along with clinical observations of severe impairment of motor coordination at higher BAC; such impairment reduces the subject's capability to cause bodily harm to others.

The usual dose-response relations do not apply in cases of "pathological intoxication," which is characterized by an acute disruption of behavior elicited by a small quantity of alcohol. The suddenness of the onset, disorientation, impairment of consciousness, and subsequent loss of memory of the attack make this phenomenon clinically similar to psychomotor epilepsy. Whether paroxysmal EEG discharges can be triggered in these cases by drinking alcohol is a controversial issue. It seems that persons prone to temporal lobe dysfunction may be at high risk for EEG and clinical manifestations of epileptiform pathological intoxication. The proneness to such dysfunction may be due, for example, to a head injury. A large collection of clinical cases supports this notion (Marinacci and Von Hagen 1972).

Bach-y-Rita, Lion, and Ervin (1970) studied ten men who received the diagnosis of pathological intoxication. None of these ten patients had a history of epilepsy. The experimenters administered alcohol intravenously while routine scalp EEG was being recorded, and no paroxysmal features were detected in any of the ten subjects. Two additional subjects were studied; both of them were known to have temporal lobe epilepsy. EEGs in these two patients were recorded simultaneously from depth (amygdala), nasopharyngeal, and surface electrodes. Alcohol infusion increased the preexisting EEG abnormalities; this effect was most expressed in (but not limited to) the depth electrodes. In this experiment the syndrome of pathological intoxication was not elicited in any of these twelve subjects. This study therefore cannot provide any answer to the question of possible epileptiform mechanisms of pathological intoxication. The most interesting implication of these observations is that internal and external cues (perhaps alcohol taste and a social setting) are apparently needed to trigger the syndrome of pathological intoxication.

No available study provides a proof that alcohol ingestion alone elicits criminal behavior. In Shupe's study (1954), 88 percent of the suspects (144 of 163) used alcohol prior to the offense. However, how many law-abiding citizens of the same socioeconomic class, race, age, and sex also used alcohol at the same time of day? Alcohol use or abuse may be an effect of the same social or other environmental factors which cause the individual to engage in criminal activity. The question unanswered by the existing literature is whether alcohol ingestion accounts for a portion of variance of criminal behavior independently of environmental factors. This comment applies to many other attempts to link biological factors to crime and to explain crime exclusively by reference to environmental factors.

D. Amphetamines

Chronic abusers of amphetamines frequently become irritable and suspicious. These features may range from mild uneasiness to a paranoid psychosis accompanied by outbursts of rage and counterattacks against imagined enemies. Violent behavior of amphetamine abusers was reported by Connell (1958), Angrist and Gershon (1969), and many others, as reviewed by Moyer (1976). Ellinwood (1971) reported histories of thirteen amphetamine abusers who committed homicide. In eight of these cases, the murderers acted under the influence of paranoid delusions. These subjects took unusually high doses of amphetamine prior to the killing, but it is difficult to be sure about the time elapsed between the last dose of amphetamine and the murder. These murders may have taken place during an actual intoxication, or in a period of drug withdrawal. Ellinwood concluded that amphetamine abusers move through several phases leading to a violent act. Chronic amphetamine abuse causes gradual personality change with paranoid thinking and fears. During this period the abuser frequently obtains a weapon. The next phase involves a sudden increase of amphetamine dosage, use of other drugs, and loss of sleep. Paranoid tendencies become suddenly much more expressed, and this results in increased anxiety. Under these conditions, a minor incident can trigger violence.

At the present time, we have no basis for an estimate of the relative importance of amphetamine abuse in criminal behavior. Ellinwood's suggestion that every person arrested for a violent crime should have a urine test for drugs of abuse is certainly worthwhile.

E. Marijuana

There is a long history of allegations connecting marijuana and other cannabis preparations (e.g., hashish) with violent crime (Kaplan 1970). Such allegations were used to support the prohibition of marijuana. "How many murders, suicides, robberies, criminal assaults, holdups, burglaries, and deeds of maniacal insanity it causes . . . can only be conjectured," asserted Harry J. Anslinger, Commissioner of Narcotics, in 1937 (Kaplan 1970, p. 89). We are still waiting to see the deeds of maniacal insanity caused by marijuana. The acute effect of marijuana on mood can be described as a "high" or as pleasant euphoria. Marijuana smoking may elicit anxiety, particularly at higher doses (Volavka et al. 1973). However, feelings of hostility or overt aggression are not caused by marijuana under either experimental or "real life" conditions. Except for violation of laws regulating use of cannabis, criminal behavior is not increased in chronic hashish users (Boulougoris et al. 1977).

Many opiate addicts report that they had used marijuana prior to their first experience with heroin. Such statements gave rise to the so called "stepping stone" theory (Kaplan 1970, p. 233) which states—with various degrees of explicitness—that marijuana use somehow causes the development of heroin addiction. This is a controversial issue. Marijuana smoking in the U.S.A. is widespread, and obviously only a small fraction of marijuana users progress to opiates. Longitudinal prospective studies of drug users may be helpful in testing the "stepping stone" theory.

F. Opiates and Endorphins

The notion that opiate (e.g., heroin) addiction is a major cause of violent crime is very popular. Opiates and similar substances are seen as intrinsically criminogenic. We believe that the latter notion is untrue and the former questionable.

Addicts, of course, break the law by possessing and sometimes selling opiates. Money needed for the purchase of drugs is no doubt often acquired by dealing, and sometimes by stealing. However, we do not know whether addicts engage in violent crime more frequently than nonaddicts of the same age, sex, race, and socioeconomic status. Addicts who are able to obtain drugs through legitimate channels and who have adequate funds may function reasonably well in social and occupational situations. Cutting (1942) described a physician who was functioning well both physically and mentally after sixty-two years of addiction. That narcotic analgesics are not intrinsically criminogenic can be demonstrated by the example of methadone. Gearing and Schweitzer (1974) studied 17,500 patients who were maintained on methadone. The maintenance treatment was associated with a decrease in antisocial behavior and increased social productivity. It should be noted that heroin and methadone have very similar pharmacological effects. Both substances produce physical dependence, and a very unpleasant withdrawal syndrome develops when they are suddenly discontinued. Methadone has a longer duration of action than heroin and produces less of a "high"; this difference is mainly because it is given by mouth whereas heroin is self-administered intravenously. However, the main difference is in the attitude of our society. Heroin is a "drug." Methadone is "medication." Heroin use is a disease. Methadone use is a treatment. A heroin habit may cost more than $100 a day. Methadone is free.

In contradistinction to alcohol, the acute administration of opiates does not increase aggressivity. Injection of heroin intravenously to an addict usually elicits mental clouding, euphoria, sedation, relaxation, talkativeness, and reduction of respiratory rate. We have administered heroin to ex-addicts on hundreds of occasions in our laboratory (Volavka et al. 1974; Volavka et al. 1976; Volavka et al. 1978) and have never observed increased hostility or aggression. If there was any effect in this respect, heroin made these persons more friendly.

The addicts' lives revolve around the drug in a cyclic fashion. The cycle of addiction starts when tolerance (and drug dosage) is increasing. This is followed by a plateau phase and then dose reduction with an attendant withdrawal syndrome. The dose is then increased again (or the drug is restarted), and the cycle goes on.

The withdrawal syndrome from opiates is unpleasant. The symptoms include loss of appetite, insomnia, fatigue, and irritability (Jaffe 1975). The irritability in the withdrawal stage is frequently too pronounced to be explained as an epiphenomenon of physical discomfort. Workers in drug abuse treatment programs are familiar with irritable, hostile, and sometimes aggressive clients in withdrawal. Occasionally a psychotic episode accompanied by rage may develop. These manifestations disappear when opiates are administered.

An ex-addict schizophrenic patient who showed attacks of rage failed to respond to routine antipsychotic treatment; she improved dramatically on methadone (Berken, Stone, and Stone 1978). The potential role of opiates in the treatment of various mental disorders is discussed elsewhere (Verebey, Volavka, and Clouet 1978).

Since the discovery of endogenous opiate-like substances (endorphins) (Wahlstrom 1974; Hughes, Smith, and Kosterlitz 1975), various roles in the pathogenesis of opiate addiction have been hypothesized for them. Is there a segment of the population who have an endorphin deficiency, and may this deficiency constitute a predisposing factor for addiction? Do addicts simply attempt to replace a substance which they are missing (Goldstein 1976)? Adequate function of the endorphin system may be necessary for psychological homeostasis; if that function is impaired, abnormal behavior is likely to occur (Verebey, Volavka, and Clouet 1978). Can this speculation be expanded to include certain forms of antisocial behavior, such as violent crime? Sensitive and reliable assays for plasma levels of endorphins are not yet generally available, but we expect them to arrive within several years. The speculations outlined above will then become amenable to verification.

G. Other Substances

Barbiturates may elicit irritability, hostility, and overt aggression. Tinklenberg et al. (1974) reported on drug involvement in criminal assaults by adolescents. In all ethnic groups, alcohol and secobarbital, used alone or in combination with other drugs, were most often implicated in assaults. These adolescents over-whelmingly selected secobarbital as the drug most likely to en-hance assaultive tendencies.

Benzodiazepines (marketed, e.g., as Librium) usually reduce anxiety and hostility, but in some individuals they paradoxically increase hostility. The reaction is sometimes quite pronounced, and the term "paradoxical rage" has been used for it. This was reviewed by Moyer (1976, pp. 87–88).

Phencyclidine (PCP, Angel Dust) intoxication may present as a schizophreniform psychosis, and preliminary evidence indicates that more or less bizarre acts of violence may be committed un-der its influence. It is too early to estimate the relative impor-tance of this substance for criminal behavior.

Biochemical and pharmacological factors play a role in some anti-social behavior by several mechanisms. These involve the effects on drives, weakening of impulse control, generation of hostility and aggression, psychotic reactions, or drug craving. There is no question that these factors do contribute to antisocial behavior, but their importance (relative to social and other environmental factors) has yet to be established. No drugs or endogenous sub-stances are intrinsically criminogenic; they elicit antisocial be-havior in a set of cultural, social, and personal circumstances. In-teractions between biochemical (or pharmacological) and socio-economic factors are incompletely understood and require fur-ther research.

V. Summary and Conclusions

The preceding discussion may be summarized as follows:

1. The cumulative evidence of the family, twin, and adoption studies suggests that some biological factor (or factors) is genet-ically transmitted which increases the likelihood that an individ-ual will behave in an antisocial manner.

2. Antisocial individuals, identified in a variety of ways, evi-dence few or no physiological signs that they are apprehensive about a forthcoming aversive stimulus. They also respond auto-

matically at a reduced level to the presentation of a neutral or aversive stimulus.

3. The recovery from an ANS response is abnormally slow in antisocial individuals.

4. The preceding two statements support a biosocial learning theory of the development of delinquent behavior.

5. Criminals' electroencephalograms are more frequently classified as clinically abnormal than are those of noncriminal controls. Much of the abnormality is accounted for by slowing of the EEG frequency in criminals. This slowing is reliably observed within the alpha (8–13 Hz) frequency band.

6. Findings of skin conductance and EEG research with antisocial individuals are similar. Both slow alpha frequencies and diminished skin conductance responsiveness may be viewed as characteristics associated with low arousal states. This similarity of conclusion from two independent fields of investigation is supported by four prospective studies (Hare 1978a; Loeb and Mednick 1977; Mednick et al. 1980; Wadsworth 1976) which found that low arousal antedates antisocial and recidivistic behavior by some years. Low arousal and associated characteristics should be included among variables of potential etiological significance to delinquent and criminal behavior.

7. The relationship between epilepsy and crime is unresolved. There is a subgroup of epileptics who repeatedly display aggressive behavior in conjunction with abnormal electrical brain discharges. While study of affected individuals may yield hypotheses and possibilities for treatment and prevention, the size of the subgroup is probably too small to make a major impact on crime statistics.

8. Biochemical and pharmacological factors play a role in the development or expression of antisocial behavior, but no drugs or substances are intrinsically criminogenic.

A half century of research and common sense leaves no doubt that social and cultural factors play a considerable role in the etiology of crime. The biological factors reviewed in this essay must be seen as another set of variables involved in the etiology of crime. Both social and biological variables *and their interactions* are important for our complete understanding of the origins of antisocial behavior. Specific examples of such interactions are provided in the body of the essay. Study of biological factors in their social context may yield information needed for the design of useful treatment and prevention strategies. The early detection of persons at high risk for repetitive criminal behavior may be an important feature of such strategies.

The development of early detection techniques from existent research data assumes that the critical factors differentiating the criminal were characteristic of him in his precriminal state. Unfortunately almost all the studies reviewed examined criminals in prisons. Such studies are obviously incapable of distinguishing between antecedents and consequences of criminal behavior. For example, very distinctive ANS changes are observed as a function of prison conditions (D'Atri 1978). Variables which are consequences, rather than causes, of criminal behavior will be less useful in the understanding, treatment, and prevention of antisocial acts than will be factors which antedate the inception of criminal behavior. Distinguishing characteristics of persons who will later be engaged in criminal activity can be developed *only* in prospective, longitudinal investigations. Studies reported in this review suggest that such predictive characteristics may well exist.

The study of biological factors in relation to antisocial behavior has been relatively unpopular among criminologists. Perhaps the most important reason for this bias has been the fear that in the wrong hands positive biological findings could be misused politically as a pretext for not ameliorating the racial, social, and cultural disadvantages associated with high crime rates. Individuals who wish to misuse information for this purpose, however, will be successful in finding a pretext, whether it be the product of social, psychological, or biological research. Fear of facts has never helped advance the cause of social justice; it merely retards the development of understanding.

REFERENCES

Allen, Harry, S. Dinitz, T. W. Foster, H. Goldman, and L. A. Lindner. 1976. "Sociopathy: an Experiment in Internal Environmental Control," *American Behavioral Scientist* 20:215–26.

American Psychiatric Association. 1968. "Diagnostic and Statistical Manuals for Mental Disorders." Washington, D.C.: American Psychiatric Association.

Angrist, B. M., and S. Gershon. 1969. "Amphetamine Abuse in New York City—1966 to 1968," *Seminars in Psychiatry* 1(2):195–207.

Aniskiewicz, A. 1973. "Autonomic Components of Vicarious Conditioning and Psychopathy." Ph.D. dissertation, Purdue University.

Bach-Y-Rita, George, J. R. Lion, C. E. Climent, and F. Ervin. 1971. "Episodic Dyscontrol: A Study of 130 Violent Patients," *American Journal of Psychiatry* 127(11):1473–78.

Bach-Y-Rita, George, J. R. Lion, and F. R. Ervin. 1970. "Pathological Intoxication: Clinical and Electroencephalographic Studies," *American Journal of Psychiatry* 127(5):698–703.

Bader-Bartfai, A., and D. Schalling. 1974. *Recovery Times of Skin Conductance Response as Related to Some Personality and Physiological Variables.* Stockholm: Psychological Institute, University of Stockholm.

Bell, B., S. A. Mednick, I. I. Gottesman, and J. Sergeant. 1977. "Electrodermal Parameters in Young, Normal Male Twins." In *Biosocial Bases of Criminal Behavior*, ed. S. A. Mednick and K. O. Christiansen. New York: Gardner Press.

Berken, Gilbert H., M. M. Stone, and S. Stone. 1978. "Methadone in Schizophrenic Rage: A Case Study," *American Journal of Psychiatry* 135(2):248–49.

Blankenstein, K. R. 1969. "Patterns of Autonomic Functioning in Primary and Secondary Psychopaths." M.A. Thesis, University of Waterloo.

Blumer, D., and C. Migeon. 1973. "Treatment of Impulsive Behavior Disorders in Males with Medroxy-Progesterone Acetate." Paper presented at the annual meeting of the American Psychiatric Association.

Bohman, Michael. 1978. "Some Genetic Aspects of Alcoholism and Criminality," *Archives of General Psychiatry* 35: 269–76.

Borgström, C. A. 1939. "Eine Serie von kriminellen Zwillingen," *Archiv für Rassenbiologie.*

Borkovec, T. 1970. "Autonomic Reactivity to Sensory Stimulation in Psychopathic, Neurotic, and Normal Juvenile Delinquents," *Journal of Consulting and Clinical Psychology* 35:217–22.

Boulougoris, J., A. Liakos, D. Madianou, and C. Stefanis. 1977. "Characteristics of Hashish Users and Controls: Social, Family, and Personal." In *Hashish—Studies of Long-Term Use*, ed. C. Stefanis, R. Dornbush, and M. Fink. New York: Raven Press.

Bundy, R. S. 1977. "Electrodermal Activity as a Unitary Phenomenon." A paper presented at the 1977 meetings of the Society for Psychophysiological Research, Philadelphia.

Buss, A. 1966. *Psychopathology*. New York: Wiley.

Cadoret, Remi J. 1978. "Psychopathology in Adopted-Away Offspring of Biologic Parents with Antisocial Behavior," *Archives of General Psychiatry* 35:176–84.

Carlsson, G. 1977. "Crime and Behavioral Epidemiology. Concepts and Applications to Swedish Data." In *Biosocial Bases of Criminal Behavior*, ed. S. A. Mednick and K. O. Christiansen. New York: Gardner Press.

Chesno, F., and P. Kilman. 1975. "Effects of Stimulation Intensity on Sociopathic Avoidance Learning," *Journal of Abnormal Psychology* 84:144–50.

Christiansen, K. O. 1977a. "A Review of Studies of Criminality among Twins." In *Biosocial Bases of Criminal Behavior*, ed. S. A. Mednick and K. O. Christiansen. New York: Gardner Press.

———. 1977b. "A Preliminary Study of Criminality among Twins." In *Biosocial Bases of Criminal Behavior*, ed. S. A. Mednick and K. O. Christiansen. New York: Gardner Press.

Cleckley, Hervey. 1976. *The Mask of Sanity*. 5th ed. St. Louis: Mosby.

Cobb, W. A. 1963. "The Normal Adult EEG." In *Electroencephalography*. 2d ed., ed. J. D. N. Hill and G. Parr. London: Macdonald.

Comte, A. 1855. *The Positive Philosophy of Auguste Comte*, translated by Harriet Martineau. New York: Blanchord.

Connel, P. H. 1958. *Amphetamine Psychosis*. London: Chapman & Hall.

Craft, Michael J. 1965. *Ten Studies into Psychopathic Personality*. Bristol: John Wright.

Crowe, R. 1975. "An Adoptive Study of Psychopathy: Preliminary Results from Arrest Records and Psychiatric Hospital Records." In *Genetic Research in Psychiatry*, ed. R. Fieve, D. Rosenthal, and H. Brill. Baltimore: Johns Hopkins University Press.

Cutting, W. C. 1942. "Morphine Addiction for 62 Years," *Stanford Medical Bulletin* 1:39–41.

Dalgaard, Odd S., and E. A. Kringlen. 1976. "A Norwegian Twin Study of Criminality," *British Journal of Criminology* 16:213–32.

D'Atri, D. A. 1978. "Psychophysiological Responses to Crowding in Prisons." In *Colloquium on the Correlates of Crime and the Determinants of Criminal Behavior*, ed. Laura Otten. Rosslyn, Va.: Mitre Corporation.

Dawson, M. 1973. "Can Classical Conditioning Occur without Contingency Learning? A Review and Evaluation of the Evidence," *Psychophysiology* 10:82–86.

Dawson, M., and J. Faredy. 1976. "The Role of Awareness in Human Differential Autonomic Classical Conditioning: The Necessary Gate Hypothesis," *Psychophysiology* 13:50–53.

Dawson, M. E., and G. D. Greville. 1963. "Biochemistry." In *Electroencephalography.* 2d ed., ed. J. D. N. Hill and G. Parr. London: Macdonald.

DeBaudouin, Haumonte, Bessing, and P. Geissman. 1961. "Study of a population of 97 confined murderers . . . ," (in French), *Annales Medico-Psychologiques* 119(1):625–86.

Dengerink, H. A., and H. S. Bertilson. 1975. "Psychopathy and Physiological Arousal in an Aggressive Task," *Psychophysiology* 12:682–84.

Dobbs, Dorothy S., and L. B. Speck. 1968. "Visual Evoked Response and Frequency Density Spectra of Prisoner-Patients," *Comprehensive Psychiatry* 9(1):62–70.

Doering, C. H., H. K. H. Brodie, H. C. Kraemer, R. H. Moos, H. B. Becker, and D. A. Hamburg. 1975. "Negative Affect and Plasma Testosterone: A Longitudinal Human Study," *Psychosomatic Medicine* 37(6):484–91.

Douglas, J. W. B., and J. M. Blomfield. 1958. *Children under Five.* London: Allen & Unwin.

Driver, M. V., L. R. West, and M. Faulk. 1974. "Clinical and EEG Studies of Prisoners Charged with Murder," *British Journal of Psychiatry* 125:583–87.

Ehrenkranz, J., E. Bliss, and M. H. Sheard. 1974. "Plasma Testosterone: Correlation with Aggressive Behavior and Social Dominance in Man," *Psychosomatic Medicine* 36(6):469–75.

Eisenberg, J. 1976. "Criminality and Heart Rate: A Prospective Study." Ph.D. dissertation, New School for Social Research, New York.

Ellinwood, Everett H., Jr. 1971. "Assault and Homicide Associated with Amphetamine Abuse," *American Journal of Psychiatry* 127 (9):1170–75.

Farrington, David P. 1979. "Longitudinal Research on Crime and

Delinquency." In *Crime and Justice: An Annual Review of Research*, ed. Norval Morris and Michael Tonry, 1:289–348.

Fenton, G. W., T. G. Tennent, P. B. C. Fenwick, and N. Rattray. 1974. "The EEG in Antisocial Behavior: A Study of Posterior Temporal Slow Activity in Special Hospital Patients," *Psychological Medicine* 4:181–86.

Filimonova, T. D. 1978. "Features of the Dynamics of Evoked Cerebral Electrical Activity in Psychopathic Personalities . . . ," *Zhurnal Nevropatologii i Psikhiatrii Imeni S. S. Korsakova* 78(2): 222–27.

Forssman, Hans, and T. S. Frey. 1953. "Electroencephalograms of Boys with Behavior Disorders," *Acta Psychologica et Neurologica Scandinavica* 28:61–73.

Fox, R., and W. Lippert. 1963. "Spontaneous GSR and Anxiety Level in Sociopathic Delinquents," *Journal of Consulting Psychology* 27:368.

Gearing, F. R., and M. D. Schweitzer. 1974. "An Epidemiologic Evaluation of Long-Term Methadone Maintenance Treatment for Heroin Addiction," *American Journal of Epidemiology* 100:101–12.

Georgetown Law Journal, Note. 1969. "The XYY Chromosome Defense," *Georgetown Law Journal* 57:892–922.

Gibbs, Frederic A., B. K. Bagchi, and W. Bloomberg. 1945. "Electroencephalographic Study of Criminals," *American Journal of Psychiatry* 102:294–98.

Gibbs, Frederic A., and E. L. Gibbs. 1950. *Atlas of Electroencephalography*, vol. 1: *Methodology and Controls*. 2d ed. Cambridge, Mass.: Addison-Wesley.

Goldstein, A. 1976. "Opioid Peptides (Endorphins) in Pituitary and Brain," *Science* 193:1081–86.

Goodwin, Donald W., F. Schulsinger, N. Moller, L. Hermansen, G. Winokur, and S. B. Guze. 1974. "Drinking Problems in Adopted and Nonadopted Sons of Alcoholics," *Archives of General Psychiatry* 31:164–69.

Goodwin, Donald W., F. Schulsinger, J. Knop, S. A. Mednick, and S. B. Guze. 1977. "Alcoholism and Depression in Adopted-Out Daughters of Alcoholics," *Archives of General Psychiatry* 34: 751–55.

Haller, Mark H. 1968. "Social Science and Genetics: A Historical Perspective." In *Genetics*, ed. D. Glass. New York: Rockefeller University Press.

Hare, Robert D. 1965. "Temporal Gradient of Fear Arousal in Psychopaths," *Journal of Abnormal Psychology* 70:442–45.

——. 1968. "Psychopathy, Autonomic Functioning and the Orienting Response," *Journal of Abnormal Psychology, Monograph Supplement* 73:1–24.

——. 1970. *Psychopathy: Theory and Research.* New York: Wiley.

——. 1972. "Psychopathy and Physiological Responses to Adrenalin," *Journal of Abnormal Psychology* 79:138–47.

——. 1973. "The Origins of Confusion," *Journal of Abnormal Psychology* 82:535–36.

——. 1975. "Psychophysiological Studies of Psychopathy." In *Clinical Applications of Psychophysiology,* ed. D. C. Fowles. New York: Columbia University Press.

——. 1978a. "Psychopathy and Crime." In *Colloquium on the Correlates of Crime and the Determinants of Criminal Behavior,* ed. Laura Otten. Rosslyn, Va.: Mitre Corporation.

——. 1978b. "Electrodermal and Cardiovascular Correlates of Psychopathy." In *Psychopathic Behavior: Approaches to Research,* ed. R. D. Hare and D. Schalling. London: Wiley.

——. In press. "Psychopathy and Violence." In *Violence and the Violent Individual,* ed. J. R. Hays, K. Roberts, and K. Soloway. New York: Spectrum.

Hare, R. D., D. N. Cox, and J. Frazelle. In press. "Psychopathy and Electrodermal Responses to Nonsignal Stimulation," *Biological Psychology.*

Hare, R. D., and D. Craigen. 1974. "Psychopathy and Physiological Activity in a Mixed-Motive Game Situation," *Psychophysiology* 11:197–206.

Hare, R. D., J. Frazelle, and D. N. Cox. 1978. "Psychopathy and Physiological Responses to Threat of an Aversive Stimulus," *Psychophysiology* 15:165–72.

Hare, R. D., and M. J. Quinn. 1971. "Psychopathy and Autonomic Conditioning," *Journal of Abnormal Psychology* 77:223–35.

Heath, R. B., and W. A. Mickle. 1960. "Evaluation of Seven Years' Experience with Depth Electrode Studies in Human Patients." In *Electrical Studies on the Unanesthesized Brain,* ed. E. R. Ramey and D. S. O'Doherty. New York: P. B. Hoeber.

Hemming, H. 1977. "Comparison of Electrodermal Indices Theoretically Relevant to Anti-Social Behavior in a Selected Prison Sample and Students." Paper presented to the British Psychophysiological Association, Exeter.

Hill, D. 1952. "EEG in Episodic Psychotic and Psychopathic Behavior," *Electroencephalography and Clinical Neurophysiology* 4(4):419–42.

——. 1963. "The EEG in Psychiatry." In *Electroencephalogra-*

phy. 2d ed., ed. J. D. N. Hill and G. Parr. London: Macdonald.

Hill, D. and D. A. Pond. 1952. "Reflexions on 100 Capital Cases Submitted to Electroencephalography," *Journal of Mental Science* 98(410):23–43.

Hill, D., and W. Sargant. 1943. "A Case of Matricide," *Lancet* 244 (1):526–27.

Hill, D., and D. Watterson. 1942. "Electro-encephalographic Studies of Psychopathic Personalities," *Journal of Neurology and Psychiatry* 5(1–2):47–65.

Hinton, J., and M. O'Neill. 1978. "Pilot Research on Psychophysiological Response Profiles of Maximum Security Hospital Patients," *British Journal of Social and Clinical Psychology* 17:103.

Hinton, J., M. O'Neill, and S. Webster. 1977. "Electrodermal Indices of Psychopathic Recidivism and Schizophrenia in Maximum Security Patients." Paper presented to the British Psychological Society, Exeter.

Hodgins-Milner, S. 1976. "Psychopathy: A Critical Examination." Ph.D. dissertation, McGill University.

Holden, C. 1978. "The Criminal Mind: A New Look at an Ancient Puzzle," *Science* 199:511–14.

House, T. H., and W. L. Milligan. 1976. "Autonomic Responses to Modeled Distress in Prison Psychopaths," *Journal of Personality and Social Psychology* 34:556–60.

Hughes, J., T. W. Smith, and H. W. Kosterlitz. 1975. "Identification of Two Related Pentapeptides from the Brain with Potent Opiate Agonist Activity," *Nature* 258(18):577–79.

Hutchings, B. 1972. "Genetic and Environmental Factors in Psychopathology and Criminality." M.Phil. thesis, University of London.

Hutchings, B. and S. A. Mednick. 1977. "Criminality in Adoptees and Their Adoptive and Biological Parents: A Pilot Study." In *Biosocial Bases in Criminal Behavior*, ed. S. A. Mednick and K. O. Christiansen. New York: Gardner Press.

Itil, T. M., W. Hsu, B. Saletu, and S. Mednick. 1974. "Computer EEG and Auditory Evoked Potential Investigations in Children at High Risk for Schizophrenia," *American Journal of Psychiatry* 131(8):892–900.

Ivanitskii, A. M. 1976. "Nekotorye Mekhanizmy Narusheniia Otsenki Vneshnikh Signalov Pri Psikhopatiiakh," *Zhurnal Nevropatologii i Psikhiatrii Imeni S.S. Korsakova (Moskva)* 76(11): 1669–73.

Jaffe, J. H. 1975. "Drug Addiction and Drug Abuse." In *The Pharmacological Basis of Therapeutics*, ed. L. Goodman and A. Gilman. New York: MacMillan.

Jenkins, R. L. and B. L. Pacella. 1943. "Electroencephalographic Studies of Delinquent Boys," *American Journal of Orthopsychiatry* 13:107–20.

Kaplan, John. 1970. "Marijuana and Aggression." In *Marijuana: The New Prohibition*, ed. J. Kaplan. New York: World Publishing Company.

Kessler. S., and R. H. Moos. 1970. "The XYY Karotype and Criminality: A Review," *Journal of Psychiatric Research* 7:153–70.

Kety, S. S., D. Rosenthal, P. H. Wender and F. Schulsinger. 1968. "The Types and Prevalence of Mental Illness in the Biological and Adoptive Families of Adopted Schizophrenics." In *The Transmission of Schizophrenia*, ed. D. Rosenthal and S. S. Kety. Oxford: Pergamon.

———. 1974. "The Types and Prevalence of Mental Illness in the Biological and Adoptive Families of Adopted Schizophrenics." In *Genetics, Environment and Psychopathology*, ed. S. A. Mednick, F. Schulsinger, J. Higgins, and B. Bell. Amsterdam: North Holland/Elsevier.

Kido, M. 1973. "An EEG Study of Delinquent Adolescents with Reference to Recidivism and Murder," *Folia Psychiatrica et Neurologia Japanica* 27(2):77–84.

Klingman, D., and D. A. Goldberg. 1975. "Temporal Lobe Epilepsy and Aggression," *Journal of Nervous and Mental Disease* 160(5): 324–41.

Knott, J. R. 1965. "Electroencephalograms in Psychopathic Personality and in Murderers." In *Applications of Electroencephalography in Psychiatry*, ed. W. P. Wilson. Durham, N.C.: Duke University Press.

Kooi, Kenneth A., R. R. Tucker, and R. E. Marshall. 1978. *Fundamentals of Electroencephalography*. 2d ed. Hagerstown, Md.: Harper & Row.

Kranz, H. 1936. *Lebensschicksale krimineller Zwillinge*. Berlin: Springer.

Kreuz, L. E., and R. M. Rose. 1972. "Assessment of Agressive Behavior and Plasma Testosterone in a Young Criminal Population," *Psychosomatic Medicine* 34(4):321–32.

Lange, J. 1929. *Verbrechen als Schicksal*. Leipzig: Georg Thieme. English edition. London: Unwin, 1931.

Laschet, U. 1973. "Antiandrogen in the Treatment of Sex Offenders: Mode of Action and Therapeutic Outcome." In *Contemporary Sexual Behavior: Critical Issues in the 1970's*, ed. J. Zubin and J. Money. Baltimore: John Hopkins University Press.

Legras, A. M. 1932. *Psychese en Criminalitet bij Twellingen*. Utrecht: Kemink en Zonn. N.B. A summary in German can be found in "Psychosen und Kriminalität bei Zwillingen," *Zeitschrift für die gesamte Neurologie und Psychiatrie*, 1933, 198–228.

Levander, S. E., L. Lidberg, D. Schalling, and Y. Lidberg. 1977. "Electrodermal Recovery Time, Stress and Psychopathy." Manuscript.

Levander, S. E., D. Schalling, L. Lidberg, A. Bader-Bartfai, and Y. Lidberg. 1980. "Skin Conductance and Personality in a Group of Criminals," *Psychophysiology* 17:105–11.

Lidberg, L., S. Levander, D. Schalling, and Y. Lidberg. 1977. "Necker Cube Reversals, Arousal, and Psychopathy," *British Journal of Social and Clinical Psychology*.

———. Forthcoming. "Urinary Catecholamines, Stress, and Psychopathy—A Study of Arrested Men Awaiting Trial," *Psychosomatic Medicine*.

Lindsley, D. G. 1939. "A Longitudinal Study of the Occipital Alpha Frequency in Normal Children: Frequency and Amplitude Standards," *Journal of Genetic Psychology* 55:197–213.

Lippert, W. W., and R. J. Senter. 1966. "Electrodermal Responses in the Sociopath," *Psychonomic Science* 4:25–26.

Loeb, J., and S. A. Mednick. 1977. "A Prospective Study of Predictors of Criminality: 3. Electrodermal Response Patterns." In *Biosocial Bases of Criminal Behavior*, ed. S. A. Mednick and K. O. Christiansen. New York: Gardner Press.

Lykken, D. T. 1957. "A Study of Anxiety in the Sociopathic Personality," *Journal of Abnormal and Social Psychology* 55:6–10.

Marinacci, A. A., and K. O. Von Hagen. 1972. "Alcohol and Temporal Lobe Dysfunction," *Behavioral Neuropsychiatry* 3(11–12): 2–11.

Mark, V. H., and F. R. Ervin. 1970. *Violence and the Brain*. New York: Harper & Row.

Mathis, H. 1970. "Emotional Responsivity in the Antisocial Personality." Ph.D. dissertation, George Washington University.

Matousek, M., and I. Petersen. 1973. "Frequency Analysis of the EEG in Normal Children and Adolescents." In *Automation of Clinical Electroencephalography*, ed. P. Kellaway and I. Petersen. New York: Raven Press.

Matousek, M., J. Volavka, J. Roubicek, and Z. Roth. 1967. "EEG Frequency Analysis Related to Age in Normal Adults," *Electroencephalography and Clinical Neurophysiology* 23:162–67.

McCallum, C. 1973. "The CNV and Conditionability in Psychopaths," *Electroencephalography and Clinical Neurophysiology* 33:337–43.

Mednick, S. A. 1962. "Schizophrenia: A Learned Thought Disorder." In *Clinical Psychology*, ed. G. Nielsen. Proceedings of XIV International Congress of Applied Psychology. Copenhagen: Munksgaard.

——. 1964. *Learning*. Englewood Cliffs: Prentice-Hall. 2d ed. 1973.

——. 1974. "Electrodermal Recovery and Psychopathology." In *Genetics, Environment and Psychopathology*, ed. S. A. Mednick, F. Schulsinger, J. Higgins, and B. Bell. Amsterdam: North-Holland, Elsevier.

——. 1977. "A Bio-Social Theory of the Learning of Law-Abiding Behavior." In *Biosocial Bases of Criminal Behavior*, ed. S. A. Mednick and K. O. Christiansen. New York: Gardner Press.

Mednick, S. A., J. Higgins, and J. Kirschenbaum. 1974. *An Exploration of Behavior and Experience*. New York: Wiley.

Mednick, S. A., and B. Hutchings. 1977. "Some Considerations in the Interpretation of the Danish Adoption Studies." In *Biosocial Bases of Criminal Behavior*, ed. S. A. Mednick and K. O. Christiansen. New York: Gardner Press.

Mednick, S. A., and F. Schulsinger. 1964. "A Preschizophrenic Sample," *Acta Psychiatrica Scandinavica* 40: 135–39.

Mednick, S. A., J. Volavka, W. F. Gabrielli, and T. Itil. 1980. "EEG as a Predictor of Antisocial Behavior." In Press. *Criminology*.

Meyer-Bahlburg, H. F. L., D. R. Nat, D. A. Boon, M. Sharma, and J. A. Edwards. 1974. "Aggressiveness and Testosterone Measures in Man," *Psychosomatic Medicine* 36(3):269–74.

Money, J. 1970. "Use of an Androgen-Depleting Hormone in the Treatment of Male Sex Offenders," *The Journal of Sex Research* 6:165–72.

Monroe, Russell R. 1970. *Episodic Behavioral Disorders: A Psychodynamic and Neurophysiologic Analysis*. Cambridge: Harvard University Press.

——. 1974. "Maturational Lag in Central Nervous System Development as a Partial Explanation of Episodic Violent Behavior," *Psychopharmacology Bulletin* 10(4):63–64.

Monti, Peter M., W. A. Brown, and D. P. Corriveau. 1977. "Testosterone and Components of Aggressive and Sexual Behavior in Men." *American Journal of Psychiatry* 134(6):692–94.

Mothers Aid Organization for Copenhagen. Copenhagen County and Frederiksberg County. Annual Report for 1946–47.

Moyer, K. E. 1976. *The Psychobiology of Aggression*. New York: Harper & Row.

Okasha, A., A. Sadek, and S. A. Moneim. 1975. "Psychosocial and

Electroencephalographic Studies of Egyptian Murderers," *British Journal of Psychiatry* 126:34–40.

Parker, D. S., R. Syndulko, I. Maltzman, R. Jens, and E. Ziskind. 1975. "Psychophysiology of Sociopathy: Electrocortical Measures," *Biological Psychology* 3:185–200.

Persky, H., K. D. Smith, and G. K. Basu. 1971. "Relation of Psychologic Measures of Aggression and Hostility to Testosterone Production in Man," *Psychosomatic Medicine* 33(3):265–77.

Plovnick, N. 1976. "Autonomic Nervous System Functioning as a Predisposing Influence on Personality, Psychopathy and Schizophrenia." Ph.D. dissertation, New School for Social Research, New York.

Rada, R. T., D. R. Laws, and R. Kellner. 1976. "Plasma Testosterone Levels in the Rapist," *Psychosomatic Medicine* 38(4):257–68.

Ratcliff, K. S., and Lee N. Robins. 1979. "Risk Factors in the Continuation of Childhood Antisocial Behavior into Adulthood," *International Journal of Mental Health* 7:96–116.

Robins, Lee N. 1966. *Deviant Children Grown Up*. Baltimore: William and Wilkins.

Rodin, E. A. 1973. "Psychomotor Epilepsy and Aggressive Behavior," *Archives of General Psychiatry* 28:210–13.

Rosanoff, A. J., L. M. Handy, and F. A. Rosanoff. 1934. "Criminality and Delinquency in Twins," *Journal of Criminal Law and Criminology* 24:923–34.

Rosen, A., and D. Schalling. 1971. "Probability Learning in Psychopathic and Non-Psychopathic Criminals," *Journal of Experimental Research in Personality* 5:191–98.

Sandberg, A. A., G. F. Koepf, T. Ishihara, and T. S. Hauschka. 1961. "An XYY Human Male," *The Lancet*, Aug. 26, 1961, 488–89.

Sarbin, T. R., and J. E. Miller. 1970. "Demonism Revisited: The XYY Chromosomal Anomaly," *Issues in Criminology* 5:195–207.

Sayed, Z. A., S. A. Lewis, and R. P. Brittain. 1969. "An Electroencephalographic and Psychiatric Study of Thirty-two Insane Murderers," *British Journal of Psychiatry* 115:1115–24.

Schachter, Stanley. 1971. *Emotion, Obesity and Crime*. New York: Academic Press.

Schachter, S., and B. Latane. 1964. "Crime, Cognition and the Autonomic Nervous System." In *Nebraska Symposium on Motivation*, ed. M. R. Jones. Lincoln: University of Nebraska Press.

Schalling, D. 1975. "The Role of Heart Rate Increase for Coping with Pain as Related to Impulsivity." Unpublished manuscript, University of Stockholm.

Schalling, D., and S. Levander. 1967. "Spontaneous Fluctuations in EDR during Anticipation of Pain in Two Delinquent Groups Differing in Anxiety Proneness." Report no. 238 from the Psychological Laboratory, University of Stockholm.

Schalling, D., L. Lidberg, S. E. Levander, and Y. Dahlin. 1968. "Relations between Fluctuations in Skin Resistance and Digital Pulse Volume and Scores on the Gough Delinquency Scale." Unpublished manuscript, University of Stockholm.

———. 1973. "Spontaneous Autonomic Activity as Related to Psychopathy," *Biological Psychology* 1:83–97.

Schalling, D., S. Levander, and Dahlin-Lidberg. 1975. "A Note on the Relation between Spontaneous Fluctuations in Skin Conductance and Heart Rate, and Scores on the Gough Delinquency Scale." Unpublished manuscript, University of Stockholm.

Schmauk, F. J. 1970. "Punishment, Arousal and Avoidance Learning in Sociopaths," *Journal of Abnormal Psychology* 76:325–35.

Schoenherr, J. C. 1964. "Avoidance of Noxious Stimulation in Psychopathic Personality." Ph.D. dissertation, University of California, Los Angeles.

Schulsinger, F. 1977. "Psychopathy: Heredity and Environment." In *Biosocial Bases of Criminal Behavior*, ed. S. A. Mednick and K. O. Christiansen. New York: Gardner Press.

Sellin, T. 1938. *Culture, Conflict and Crime*. New York: Social Science Research Council.

Shah, S. A., and L. H. Roth. 1974. "Biological and Psychophysiological Factors in Criminality." In *Handbook of Criminology*, ed. D. Glaser. Chicago: Rand McNally.

Shupe, L. M. 1954. "Alcohol and Crime," *Journal of Criminal Law, Criminology, and Police Science* 44:661–64.

Siddle, D. A. T. 1977. "Electrodermal Activity and Psychopathy." In *Biosocial Bases of Criminal Behavior*, ed. S. A. Mednick and K. O. Christiansen. New York: Gardner Press.

Siddle, D. A. T., S. A. Mednick, A. R. Nicol, and R. H. Foggitt. 1977. "Skin Conductance Recovery in Antisocial Adolescents." In *Biosocial Bases of Criminal Behavior*, ed. S. A. Mednick and K. O. Christiansen. New York: Gardner Press.

Siddle, D. A. T., A. R. Nicol, and R. H. Foggitt. 1973. "Habituation and Over-Extinction of the GSR Component of the Orienting Response in Antisocial Adolescents," *British Journal of Social and Clinical Psychology* 12:303–8.

Silver, Larry B., C. C. Dublin, and R. S. Lourie. 1969. "Does Violence Breed Violence? Contributions from a Study of the Child Abuse Syndrome," *American Journal of Psychiatry* 126:404–7.

Silverman, D. 1944. "The Electroencephalogram of Criminals," *Archives of Neurology and Psychiatry* 52(1):38–42.

Slater, E. 1934–35. "The Incidence of Mental Disorder," *Annals of Eugenics* 6:172–86.

Small, Joyce G. 1966. "The Organic Dimension of Crime," *Archives of General Psychiatry* 15:82–89.

Smith, S. M., L. Honigsberger, and C. A. Smith. 1973. "EEG and Personality Factors in Baby Batterers," *British Medical Journal* 7:20–22.

Spencer, H. 1878. *Social Statistics*. New York: Appleton-Century-Crofts.

Stumpfl, F. 1936. *Die Ursprünge des Verbrechens. Dargestellt am Lebenslauf von Zwillingen.* Leipzig: Goerg Thieme.

Sutker, F. 1970. "Vicarious Conditioning and Sociopathy," *Journal of Abnormal Psychology* 76:380–86.

Syndulko, K., D. A. Parker, R. Jens, I. Maltzman, and E. Ziskind. 1975. "Psychophysiology of Sociopathy: Electrocortical Measures," *Biological Psychology* 3:185–200.

Syndulko, K., D. Parker, I. Maltzman, and E. Ziskind. 1975. "Central and Autonomic Nervous System Measures of Conditioning in Sociopaths and Normals." Paper presented at the Science Fair of the Society for Psychophysiological Research, Toronto, Canada.

Szpiler, J. A., and S. Epstein. 1976. "Availability of an Avoidance Response as Related to Autonomic Arousal," *Journal of Abnormal Psychology* 85:73–82.

Tharp, V., K. Syndulko, I. Maltzman, and E. Ziskind. 1978. "Skin Conductance and Heart Rate Measures of the Gradient of Fear in Non-Institutionalized Compulsive Gamblers, Socio-Paths."

Tinklenberg, J. R. 1973. "Alcohol and Violence." In *Alcoholism: Progress in Research and Treatment,* ed. P. G. Bourne and R. Fox. New York: Academic Press.

Tinklenberg, Jared R., P. L. Murphy, P. Murphy, C. F. Darley, W. T. Roth, and B. S. Kopell. 1974. "Drug Involvement in Criminal Assaults by Adolescents," *Archives of General Psychiatry* 30(5):685–89.

Trasler, G. 1972. "Criminal Behavior." In *Handbook of Abnormal Psychology,* ed. H. J. Eysenck. 2d ed. London: Putnam.

Venables, P. H., and M. J. Christie. 1973. "Mechanism, Instrumentation, Recording Techniques and Quantification of Responses." In *Electrodermal Activity in Psychological Research,* ed. W. F. Prokasky and D. C. Raskin. New York: Academic Press.

———, eds. 1975. *Research in Psychophysiology.* New York: Wiley.

Verdeaux, G. 1970. "Electroencephalography in Criminology," *Médecine Legale et Dommage Corporel* (Paris) 3(1):39–46.

Verebey, Karl, J. Volavka, and D. Clouet. 1978. "Endorphins in Psychiatry: An Overview and a Hypothesis," *Archives of General Psychiatry* 35:877–88.

Volavka, Jan, P. Crown, R. Dornbush, S. Feldstein, and M. Fink. 1973. "EEG, Heart Rate and Mood Change ("High") after Cannabis," *Psychopharmacologia* (Berl) 32:11–25.

Volavka, J., R. Levine, S. Feldstein, and M. Fink. 1974. "Short-Term Effects of Heroin in Man," *Archives of General Psychiatry* 30:677–81.

Volavka, J., M. Matousek, S. Feldstein, J. Roubicek, P. Prior, D. F. Scott, V. Brezinova, and V. Synek. 1973. "The Reliability of EEG Assessment," *Z EEG-EMG* 4(3):123–30.

Volavka, J., S. A. Mednick, J. Sergeant, and L. Rasmussen. 1977a. "Electroencephalograms of XYY and XXY Men," *British Journal of Psychiatry* 130:43–47.

——. 1977b. "EEG Spectra in XYY and XXY Men," *EEG and Clinical Neurophysiology* 43:798–801.

——. 1977c. "EEGs of XYY and XXY Men Found in a Large Birth Cohort." In *Biosocial Bases of Criminal Behavior*, ed. S. A. Mednick and K. O. Christiansen. New York: Gardner Press.

Volavka, J., S. A. Mednick, L. Rasmussen, and T. Teasdale. 1979. "EEG Response to Sine Wave Modulated Light in XYY, XXY, and XY Men," *Acta. Psychiatrica Scandinavica* 59:509–16.

Volavka, J., S. A. Mednick, L. Rasmussen, T. Teasdale, and D. Owen. In Preparation. "Evoked Potentials in XXY and XYY Men."

Volavka, J., R. Resnick, R. Kestenbaum, and A. Freedman. 1976. "Short-Term Effects of Naltrexone in 155 Heroin Ex-Addicts," *Biological Psychiatry* 11:679–85.

Volavka, J., K. Verebey, R. Resnick, and S. Mule. 1978. "Methadone dose, Plasma Level and Cross-Tolerance to Heroin in Man," *Journal of Nervous and Mental Diseases* 166(2):104–9.

Wadsworth, Michael. 1975. "Delinquency in a National Sample of Children," *British Journal of Criminology* 15:167–74.

——. 1976. "Delinquency, Pulse Rates and Early Emotional Deprivation," *British Journal of Criminology* 16:245–56.

Wahlstrom, G. 1974. "Inhibitor(s) of Narcotic Receptor Binding in Brain Extracts and Cerebral Spinal Fluid," *Acta Pharmacologia et Toxicologica* 35(suppl. 1):55.

Waid, W. M. 1976. "Skin Conductance to Both Signalized and Unsignalized Noxious Stimulation Predicts Level of Socialization," *Journal of Personality and Social Psychology* 34:923–29.

Wilder, J. 1947. "Sugar Metabolism in its Relation to Criminology." In *Handbook of Correctional Psychology*, ed. S. Linduer and B. J. Selinger. New York: Philosophical Library.

Williams, D. 1969. "Neural Factors Related to Habitual Aggression —Consideration of Differences between those Habitual Aggressives and Others Who Have Committed Crimes of Violence," *Brain* 92:503–20.

Witkin, H. A., S. A. Mednick, F. Schulsinger, E. Bakkestrom, K. O. Christiansen, D. R. Goodenough, K. Hirschhorn, C. Lundsteen, D. R. Owen, J. Philip, D. B. Rubin, and M. Stocking. 1977. "Criminality, Aggression and Intelligence among XYY and XXY Men." In *Biosocial Bases of Criminal Behavior*, ed. S. A. Mednick and K. O. Christiansen. New York: Gardner Press.

Wolfgang, Marvin E. 1958. *Patterns in Criminal Homicide.* Philadelphia: University of Pennsylvania Press.

———. 1977. "Foreword." In *Biosocial Bases of Criminal Behavior*, ed. S. A. Mednick and K. O. Christiansen. New York: Gardner Press.

Wolfgang, M. E., R. M. Figlio, and T. Sellin. 1972. *Delinquency in a Birth Cohort.* Chicago: University of Chicago Press.

Yeudall, L. F., O. Fedora, S. Fedora, and D. Wardell. 1979. "A Neurosocial Perspective on the Assessment and Etiology of Persistent Criminality." In *Perspectives in Prison Psychiatry*, ed. C. Roy. London: Oxford University Press.

Yoshimasu, S. 1961. "The Criminological Significance of the Family in the Light of the Studies of Criminal Twins," *Acta Criminologiae et Medicinae Legalis Japanica* 27.

Ziskind, E., K. Syndulko, and I. Maltzman. 1978. "Aversive Conditioning in the Sociopath," *Pavlovian Journal* 13:199–205.

Richard F. Sparks

A Critique of Marxist Criminology

ABSTRACT

Within the past few years, a marxist school of criminology has
developed in England and the United States. In both countries, this
school arose in part because of a dissatisfaction with "mainstream"
criminology; especially in the United States, political radicalism
provoked by the turmoil of the sixties also played a part. The
theoretical antecedents of marxist criminology include "labeling"
and "conflict" theories of crime and the origins of the criminal
law. Though its writings to date have too often been marred by
vacuous rhetoric and polemic, the marxist school has usefully
called attention to a number of important questions, in particular
questions concerning the relations between social structures and
economic systems and the criminalization of certain forms of
behavior. To date, relatively little empirical research has been done
by marxist criminologists; much of the important scholarly
writing on crime from a marxist perspective has in fact been done
by social historians. Marxist criminologists tend to be committed
to *praxis*, and a desire for radical social reform; but this
commitment is not entailed by the scientific claims which marxists
make, and it has sometimes led to those claims being improperly
suspect. Marxists claim both that the criminal law is affected by
the social relations of production in capitalist societies, and that
the criminal law is an instrument by which capitalist social order
is maintained. There is some truth in each of these propositions,
but each needs to be qualified in important respects. There are
signs that marxist criminology may be moving toward something
nearer to what Marx himself wrote; but it remains to be seen what
effect this will have on marxist theories of crime and crime control.

Richard F. Sparks is Professor, School of Criminal Justice, Rutgers University.
Among colleagues and students who read and commented on an earlier draft
of this paper and helped to improve it, James Garofalo, David Greenberg, Alex
Greer, Sheldon Messinger, Albert Reiss, Fred Roth, Michael Tonry, and Andrew von Hirsch are gratefully acknowledged.

Within the past decade, a new school of criminology has come into being. I use the term "school" here in its somewhat figurative sense, to refer to a group of people held together by certain shared beliefs, teachings, and opinions; that is, I use it in the same sense as it was used of the Italian "positivist" school of criminology of a century ago. Within its brief life, this new school has been referred to in a variety of ways. It has been said to propound a "new" criminology; a "radical" criminology; and a "critical" criminology. For a variety of reasons, however, none of these terms seems to me to be particularly satisfactory. For one thing, there is nothing very new about the ideas which this school espouses; nor do they have a monopoly on radical or critical views—always assuming, of course, that the terms "radical" and "critical" have any meaning left at all, in political and social discourse. For another thing, claims to novelty, in criminology as elsewhere, are bound by nature to be pretty transient things: somebody, someday, is going to come along with a newer criminology, a still newer criminology, a newest criminology, and so on.[1] But the basic objection to all three terms is that they do little to clarify the character of the criminological views of the school in question: for the most part, the members of that school are (or at least claim to be) marxists.

The term "marxist" is itself not free from ambiguity, of course. Among those who are called (or call themselves) by that name, there are many theoretical and doctrinal differences: there are also crypto-marxists, neo-marxists, and (for all I know) quasi-marxists, as well as Maoists, Leninists, Trotskyites, Stalinists and so on. All too often, there is only the most tenuous relation between the views of these groups and the political and social theories of Marx himself; and as is well known those theories them-

---

[1] This has already happened. Professor James Q. Wilson, in his introduction to Thomas Reppetto's (1974) book *Residential Crime* writes that "there is slowly arising a 'new criminology' to supplant traditional criminology." Wilson tells us that this new criminology "considers crime from the point of view of the victim, treats particular kinds of offenses (e.g. residential burglaries, stranger-to-stranger assaults), and considers explicitly the effectiveness of alternative preventive strategies." He adds that Reppetto's book "is a good example of the new criminology." In fact, about all that Reppetto's book shares with Taylor, Walton, and Young's book *The New Criminology* is that both books are printed on paper.

selves underwent several changes during and after Marx's life. Nonetheless, it seems appropriate to refer to the school of criminology discussed in this paper as marxist—or as *marxisant*, to use Douglas Hay's felicitous term (Hay 1975a, p. 61). Several of the leading members of this school now call themselves marxists, though they did not all do so originally; and many of the main theories and concepts which they employ in their attempts to explain crime and societal reaction to crime are undoubtedly ones which are commonly imputed to Marx. (In particular, they place great emphasis on the social relations of production, and employ a concept of "class" based on those relations.) But given the considerable doubt which still surrounds at least some of the writings of Marx and Engels (see, e.g., Hirst 1975; Singer 1979), and some reservations (to be discussed further below) about the relations between those writings and the criminological writings with which I shall be concerned, it seems best not to assume a priori that those relations are necessarily very close; hence I shall write the word "marxist" with a small *m* throughout, except where reference is to Marx himself.

It is also important to note that I am not here concerned to question the cogency, coherence, or correctness of marxist social theories in general.[2] Though undoubtedly important, such a task is far beyond the scope of this paper. My concern is rather with the application of those theories to criminological problems, including problems about the origins, nature, and enforcement of the criminal law. The school of criminology whose works I shall review may be marxist; but it is also a school of *criminology*, though not all of those whom I shall discuss describe themselves professionally as criminologists. Why are certain acts defined as criminal? Why nonetheless do certain people commit those acts? What is done to those people, and why? It is with questions of that kind that we (and the marxist school of criminology) are concerned.

[2] Or in particular, e.g., the "theory of surplus value," according to which capitalists exploit labor by extracting surplus value from their work in the form of profits—a theory first expounded by Marx in 1865 (Marx and Engels 1968). I cannot see any conditions under which this "theory" might turn out to be false; in any case, it appears to entail little by way of predictions about crime.

The purpose of this essay, then, is to analyze the criminological theories and claims of a group of writers, most of whom are marxists or approach the study of crime from a marxist perspective. I begin by describing the intellectual origins of the new marxist school. I describe the central tenets which most members of this group appear to hold. I then describe some empirical work done by these criminologists, and related work done by historians, sociologists and other scholars, which has many affinities with marxist criminology. I offer a brief critique of some of the views of this school, and conclude with a provisional assessment of the impact which marxist criminology has had to date.

A caveat is in order at the outset. I think it is illuminating to compare the contemporary marxist school of criminology with the *Scuola Positiva* which revolutionized criminology a century ago. But the analogy may be unfair and misleading if it is pressed too far. Contemporary marxist criminologists do not refer to themselves as a "school," so far as I know; and they are by no means as self-consciously united in opinion as were Lombroso, Ferri, and Garofalo.[3] On the contrary, they differ among themselves on a number of points, and they may well regard some of those differences as important. I shall try to document some of this diversity of opinion, even though it is mainly with areas of agreement that I shall be concerned; and wherever possible I shall cite chapter and verse from specific writers for specific views. Those views should not necessarily be imputed to anyone else.

I. Origins of the Marxist School of Criminology
In order fully to appreciate a body of social or philosophical theory, it is often helpful to begin by considering its intellectual history and the circumstances in which it arose. This is clearly so in the case of recent marxist criminology. Thus, if one were to choose a single book by which to date the birth of the contemporary marxist school, that book would undoubtedly be *The New Criminology*, by Ian Taylor, Paul Walton, and Jock Young,

---

[3] There were, of course, important differences of opinion between Lombroso, Ferri, and Garofalo. For a discussion see Mannheim (1960), especially pp. 23–29.

which was first published in England in 1973. But in order to appreciate *that* book, and its impact on contemporary criminology (at least in English-speaking countries), it is necessary to go back to about 1968—a vintage year for dissent of whatever variety—and to consider Britain and the United States separately.

It was in 1968 that a group of younger British sociologists formed the National Deviancy Conference (NDC), a group—consisting, at its largest, of about three hundred members—which sponsored a number of symposia on crime and deviance over the next few years. Membership in the NDC was by no means confined to academics. In addition, the group included a motley of social workers, journalists, self-confessed deviants, and political activists of various kinds; indeed, at some meetings the academic element was rather hard to find, amidst the clamoring for the reform or destruction of "the system" from radical hangers-on. Yet there was an academic group within the NDC, and one with a serious purpose. What motivated, and to some extent united, this group was a profound dissatisfaction with British criminology of the time—as represented chiefly by the Home Office Research Unit and the Cambridge University Institute of Criminology. That criminology was distrusted by the NDC sociologists because of its "applied" and system-serving character, and because of what they saw as its atheoretical[4] approach to the study of crime; no doubt much of it also struck them as dead boring, or at least I hope it did. Many NDC sociologists also hoped to rescue the study of crime from what they saw as its pariah status within British sociology; at this they had some measure of success, when the 1971 annual meeting of the British Sociological Association was largely given over to discussion of crime, deviance and social control. (See Rock and McIntosh 1974, for a selection of papers from this meeting; other evidence on the early history of the NDC is contained in Cohen 1971, Taylor and Taylor 1973, and Downes and Rock 1979.)

[4] As exemplified by, e.g., Radzinowicz (1966). In part, however, they were concerned by what they saw as the conservative implications of "Establishment" criminology, which they saw as a consequence of too-cozy relations with the Home Office (then, as now, the principal source of funding for criminological research in Britain).

The NDC did not originally have a marxist orientation. Its members were much influenced by interactionist theory and labeling theory, by the work of Howard Becker[5] and David Matza (whose reputation then was for some reason much higher in Britain than in the United States). They maintained what Stanley Cohen, in his introduction to *Images of Deviance* (1971), the first published volume of NDC conference papers, called a "skeptical" approach to the study of deviant behavior. This involved several things. To begin with, it involved a rejection of the idea that deviance was a manifestation of individual pathology. On the contrary: in Becker's words, "deviance is *not* a quality of the act the person commits, but rather a consequence of the application by others of rules and sanctions to an 'offender.' The deviant is one to whom that label has successfully been applied; deviant behavior is behavior that people so label" (Becker 1973, p. 9). This approach also called attention to ways in which social control might actually give rise to deviant behavior rather than being a response to it. It also involved a rejection of what Matza (1969) had called "correctionalism"; instead of being studied in order that they should be "reformed," deviants were to be "appreciated" for their contribution to human diversity, which would be studied chiefly through ethnography and participant observation. A second volume of NDC conference papers, *Politics and Deviance* (Taylor and Taylor 1973), was much more explicitly concerned with the political nature of social control. This volume contained papers on subjects ranging from social control in Cuba to university psychiatric services, the Weathermen, hippies, and American corporate crime. Like *Images of Deviance*, it was a far cry from the studies of XYY chromosomes, psychopathy, and the "effectiveness" of penal measures which still preoccupied so many "mainstream" criminologists in Great Britain.

Gradually, however, something of a schism began to develop

[5] Who gave one of the keynote speeches at the 1971 B.S.A. meetings. Ironically, this paper—which is reprinted in the 1973 edition of *Outsiders*—is the one in which Becker conceded that his original definition of deviance was mistaken, and that labeling theory was not a theory but a perspective. See Becker 1973, pp. 181, 186–87.

within the NDC. As Plummer (1979, p. 85) has noted, inter-actionist and labeling theories "moved from being the radical critic of established orthodoxies to being the harbinger of new orthodoxies to be criticized"—in particular, to be criticized from a marxist perspective. Some of those associated with the founding of the NDC—the writers represented in Downes and Rock (1979) are a fair sample—continued to approach the explanation of crime and deviance from a broadly interactionist perspective. Others—the best-known of them being Taylor, Walton, and Young—rejected this approach (and pretty well all others), in favor of what eventually developed into a self-proclaimed marxist criminology.

Meanwhile, in the United States, a self-proclaimed "new," "radical," "critical" criminology had begun to emerge, among a group of scholars some (though not all) of whom were located at the School of Criminology at the University of California at Berkeley. Prominent among this group were Anthony Platt, Richard Quinney, Herman and Julia Schwendinger, Paul Takagi, and William J. Chambliss. The animus of this group was very different from that of the NDC and English marxist criminolo-gists. As Krisberg (1975, p. 167) has written,

> As social scientists committed to the application of new knowledge to social relations, we were confronted with the nightmares of political murders, race riots, increasing political repression, and the moral dilemmas of a tragic war in Southeast Asia. In this period most of the powerful and most of the officials of the criminal justice system became symbols of the reactionary mode that appeared to settle upon the nation. In this period the liberation struggles of oppressed peoples, particularly people of color, created the greatest tension in our consciences. Committed as we were to civil rights, racial equality, and social justice, how could we interpret the role of the criminal justice system in suppressing dissent, enforcing human misery, and preventing social change? The theories we had learned did not seem to apply; the history we had taken for granted was disputed and

shown to be full of lies. Many of our scientific heroes of
the past, upon rereading, turned out to be racists or,
more generally, apologists for social injustice. In response
to the widespread protests on campuses and throughout
society, many of the contemporary giants of social science
emerged as defenders of the status quo and vocally dismissed
the claims of the oppressed for social justice. The crisis of
disbelief widened and deepened as some of us felt compelled
to understand "what was going on within ourselves and
within our society." [See also Platt 1974a, p. 2.]

The theoretical antecedents of this group were similar to those
of their British counterparts. In addition to Becker and other
labeling theorists, they had no doubt been influenced by the
"conflict" perspective embodied in the writings of Coser (1956)
and Dahrendorf (1959), and in the criminological theories of
Turk (1969) and Quinney (1970). They had no great corpus
of marxist scholarship on which to draw, not least because it was
not then (and is not now) prudent to proclaim oneself a marxist
in most American universities. (Indeed, even the "radicalism"
avowed by some of this group could be dangerous to one's ten-
ure; there is reason to believe that this played some part in the
closing of the School of Criminology at Berkeley in 1976. For
one version of this story see Schauffler 1974a, 1974b.) There
were some sociological thinkers of an older generation (left-
wing "radical" thinkers in an era when that word still had meaning) with whom American "new" criminologists could feel an
affinity of purpose and perspective: C. Wright Mills, Irving Louis
Horowitz, and Alvin Gouldner are examples.[6] But what most
united the group, it seems, was an extreme disenchantment—for
reasons which Krisberg's statement makes clear—with official
"liberal" criminology in the United States, as represented by the
1967 President's Commission on Law Enforcement and Administration of Justice and the later governmental commissions on

---

[6] In particular, Mills's work on power elites (Mills 1959), Horowitz's writings
on deviance and political marginality (Horowitz and Liebowitz 1968) and
Gouldner's attacks on "value-free" sociology (Gouldner 1962, 1968). See, for
example, Krisberg 1975, pp. 3–6.

violence, civil disorder, and pornography. There is, I think, another important attribute of the American "new" criminologists (and one which they shared with the British sociologists of the NDC): to wit, they occupied a very marginal position within their profession. Crime and deviance were certainly very much more respectable objects of sociological study in the United States in the 1960s than they were in Britain; but they were not in the same league as, say, stratification.[7]

The purpose of this brief discussion has been to sketch the context in which contemporary marxist criminology first developed, in Britain and the United States. I believe that that historical context helps to explain the popularity of certain aspects of marxist thought among the writers I have mentioned—in particular, the generally oppositional tone of some of their writings, and a concomitant commitment to *praxis*.[8] But—as we shall see—marxist criminology has by no means been static; it continues to develop, and at a theoretical level may be moving toward a much more subtle and complete appreciation of what Marx himself actually wrote. In any case, a description of the context and origins of theories is not an argument—even an ad hominem argument—for or against the theories themselves; those need to be examined on their own merits, preferably in the light of empirical evidence. To this task I now turn.

II. From New Criminology via Criticism to Marx

Taylor, Walton, and Young's book *The New Criminology* was not an avowedly marxist work. In retrospect, having read the later writings of its authors, it is easy to see where their sympathies lay in 1973; but the book itself does not go far toward propounding an explicitly marxist view. (Indeed, there are almost as many references to Marx in Alvin Gouldner's fourteen-page introduction to the book, as in its three hundred pages of

[7] There are, I think, two marginalities involved here. First, it was not easy to make a career in "mainstream" sociology as a specialist in crime or deviance; second, most American "new" criminologists (like the NDC sociologists) were on the margin of the subfield of criminology. The latter may arguably have resulted from the positions they took, rather than being a cause of them.

[8] *Praxis*, n. Marxist jargon for practicing what you preach. See below, "The Commitment to Praxis."

text and notes.) *The New Criminology* propounded *no* criminological theory of its own. Described by its authors as an "immanent critique" of existing theories of crime, deviance, and social control,[9] the book is mainly taken up with exposition and criticism of other "schools" of criminology, from Beccaria to such recent "conflict" theorists as Chambliss and Turk. The concluding chapter then attempts to spell out what its authors describe as "certain *formal* and *substantive* requirements of a fully social theory of deviance, a theory that can explain the forms assumed by social control and deviant action in 'developed' societies (characterized—we have argued—by the domination of a capitalist mode of production, by a division of labour involving the growth of armies of 'experts,' social workers, psychiatrists and others who have been assigned a crucial role in the tasks of social definition and social control, and, currently, by the necessity to segregate out—in mental hospitals, prisons and in juvenile institutions—an increasing variety of its members as being in need of control)" (Taylor, Walton, and Young 1973, p. 269). Earlier chapters of the book deal successively with classicism and positivism, Durkheim and Merton, the Chicago and ecological schools, differential association, symbolic interactionist and labeling theory, "American naturalism" (i.e. Matza 1969), and phenomenology. There is a chapter on Marx, Engels, and Bonger; but in this the authors were forced to admit (p. 217) that "Marx's authentic position on crime is never really fully spelt out."[10]

The chief opponent or stalking-horse of *The New Criminology* was "positivism"—characterized, in this case, by an emphasis on the quantification of behavior, the "objectivity" of the (social) scientist, and a species of "determinism" which applied to both the social and physical worlds. To these attributes were added a belief in a social or political consensus, or both, of values

[9] It is not clear what this meant; perhaps the word "immanent" was used in its secondary, and now rare, sense of "an act which is performed entirely in the mind of the subject, and produces no external effect" (*OED*, s.v.).

[10] Bonger fared even worse, being described as "avowedly a Marxist but in reality . . . a positivist." The main ground for this curious conclusion appears to be that Bonger treated "egoism" or "criminal thoughts" as an intervening variable, mediating between the socioeconomic system and crime. He is also accused of "correctionalism" (see Taylor, Walton, and Young 1973, pp. 222–36).

and interests, or at least an absence of conflict about those things. (Cf. Taylor, Walton, and Young 1973, pp. 11, 31–40.) In particular, the book argued against biological "positivism" as represented by (inter alia) Lombroso, Hans Eysenck, and Gordon Trasler, who are the demons of the early chapters in which the scene is set for almost all of the later theoretical critiques in the book.

It may be questioned how far the kind of "positivism" attacked in *The New Criminology* was of any real importance, for criminologists in either Britain or the United States, when that book appeared. Twenty years earlier, when the predominant influences on British (but *not* American) criminology had come from the work of psychiatrists and clinical psychologists,[11] attacks on biological "positivism" might have had some force; by 1973, however, they seemed like the flogging of a very dead horse.[12] Moreover, some of the theories discussed in *The New Criminology* were caricatured in order to be rhetorically demolished. Ironically—in view of a valid criticism which the authors of *The New Criminology* made about the insularity of much criminological theory—this element of caricature came about in part because Taylor, Walton, and Young sometimes aimed exclusively at the *criminological* versions of the theories in question. Thus, as Rock (1979, p. 79) has noted,

> *The New Criminology* can discuss symbolic interactionism without invoking the neo-Kantianism of Simmel . . . and without citing Dewey, Blumer, Hughes and Strauss. It can exclude even the relatively minor strains of interactionist sociology. The self is not lodged in its dialectical background. Phenomenalism is ignored. . . . An interactionism without those authors and themes is a sociological corpse which

[11] In addition to Eysenck and Trasler, psychiatrists such as E. I. Glover, Peter Scott, John Bowlby, and T. C. N. Gibbens were influential, not only through their writings but in the British Society of Criminology: the work of D. K. Henderson on psychopathic personality, and of Burt, were also influential, especially on criminal justice practitioners.

[12] Though, paradoxically, genetic theories have more recently made something of a comeback—not to mention the growing influence of sociobiology (e.g., Wilson 1978).

lacks any robustness or life. It can be dismissed with ease. Phenomenology, too, has been examined as if Husserl, Renouvier, Bergson, Kant, Heidegger, Jaspers and Merleau-Ponty had never written.

Nonetheless, whatever the force of these and other criticisms (see, e.g., Currie 1974), *The New Criminology* was an impressive and influential work. It attempted a critical survey of criminological theories, on a scale far exceeding that of any textbook of criminology published during the preceding half-century (with the possible exception of Vold 1958); and it drew—indeed, dragged—the attention of many students of criminology to theories and perspectives which they probably would not otherwise have noticed.

Running through the book, moreover, were a number of themes which reappeared in the later writings of Taylor, Walton, and Young and of other marxist criminologists. In particular, there was an emphasis on *rule making* (and, to a lesser extent, *rule enforcing*), rather than *rule breaking*, as the most important subject with which the study of crime and deviance should be concerned. Concomitantly, there was an emphasis on the social structure, in the sense of "structures of power, domination and authority . . . and the initiative of the state, and its entrepreneurial representatives, in defining and sanctioning certain forms of behavior at certain points in time" (p. 268). And finally there was a view of the criminal or deviant as heroically *challenging* these structures of authority and power, and in so doing asserting "the facts of human diversity." In the final paragraph of the book, the authors state that

> For us, as for Marx and for other new criminologists, *deviance* is normal—in the sense that men are now consciously involved . . . in asserting their human diversity. The task is not merely to "penetrate" these problems, not merely to question the stereotypes, or to act as carriers of "alternative phenomenological realities." The task is to create a society in which the facts of human diversity, whether personal,

organic or social, are not subject to the power to criminalize (Taylor, Walton, and Young 1973, p. 282).

The first two of the themes just noted reappear in a somewhat modified form in *Critical Criminology*, a collection of essays edited by Taylor, Walton, and Young which appeared in 1975. In the first chapter in this volume, those authors reject both orthodox (or "conservative") criminology, and what they stigmatize as "Fabian criminology,"[13] on the grounds of their inherent "correctionalism." They also reject, however, the "Romantic" notion that deviants are attempting, through their deviance, to assert some form of control over the "normalized repression" inherent in their worlds. The "appreciation" of deviance is dismissed as a form of "moral voyeurism" (cf. Taylor, Walton, and Young 1973, p. 18). In its place, the authors argue for a criminology committed to the analysis and abolition of a social system in which "radical diversity" can be defined as deviant. They then come out of the critical closet, so to speak, with a more or less explicit statement of a marxist perspective:

It is now our position not only that these processes [involved in rule creation and rule breaking] are *fully social* in nature, but also that they are paramountly conditioned by the facts of *material reality*. Breaking with individual (that is, genetic, psychological and similar) explanations into social explanations has thrust upon us the political economy as the primary determinant of the social framework. We shall argue later that the processes involved in crime-creation are bound up in the final analysis with the *material* basis of contemporary capitalism and its structures of law. . . . Albeit by implication [!], the insistence in *The New Criminology* was that, insofar as the crime-producing features of contemporary capitalism are bound up with the inequities and divisions in material production and ownership, then it

[13] By this the authors mean criminology associated with the Fabian Society, i.e., with (I think) the right-center of the British Labour Party, or maybe it is just the center of it. Anyway, the body of thought in question is described as "essentially *liberal*" in its ideology, "meritocratic" and "social-work oriented." Taylor, Walton, and Young 1975, pp. 11–14.

must be possible via social transformations to create social
and productive arrangements that would abolish crime.
[Taylor, Walton, and Young 1975, p. 20; emphasis in original.]

They go on to assert (p. 44) that

we have argued for a criminology which is normatively
committed to the abolition of inequalities in wealth and
power. And we have strongly argued also that any theoretical
position which is not minimally committed to such a view
will fall into correctionalism (i.e. individual rehabilitation
or tangential social reform). . . . The task we have set
ourselves, and other criminologists, is the attempt to create
the kind of society in which the facts of human diversity
are not subject to the power to criminalize.

They further assert (pp. 44–45) that

If criminology is to advance as a science, it must be free to
examine not only the causes of crime, but also of the norms
which, in a primary sense, create crime—that is, legal norms.
The unquestioning acceptance of a given legal system and
given legal norms has been the general tendency in
positivist criminology, and the result has been disastrous
for criminology's claim to scientificity. . . . Ignoring or
displacing the propertied nature of crime, criminologists
unwilling or unable to confront the facts of inequality in
ownership of property have been driven back to individualistic
explanations of the differences between criminals and
conformists—a task which has proven (not surprisingly) to
be unilluminating and inconclusive. . . . The analysis of
particular forms of crime, or particular types of criminal,
outside of their context in history and society has been
shown, in our view, to be a meaningless activity; and the
analysis of propertied crime without reference to the demands
placed by a propertied society on its members especially
diversionary. We have ourselves been forced, logically, to
turn for such an analysis (and such a criminology) to Marx.

Substantially similar themes are further developed by Young in an essay on "working-class criminology," and in papers by other contributors—in particular, Anthony Platt and Richard Quinney —in the same volume.

Undoubtedly the most extreme statements of the position of contemporary marxist criminologists are to be found in the writings of Richard Quinney (1970, 1975a, 1975b, 1977, 1978). Much of Quinney's book *Class, State and Crime* (1977) is taken up with documenting (somewhat erratically)[14] the increase in federal spending on criminal justice in the United States in recent years, and with drawing appropriately radical conclusions from this. Thus, in the opening chapter of the book Quinney warns that "The criminal justice movement is . . . a state-initiated and state-supported effort to rationalize mechanisms of social control. The larger purpose is to secure a capitalist order that is in grave crisis, likely in its final stage of development" (p. 10). The final chapter is more optimistic: "As criminal justice falters with the development of capitalism, new socialist forms of justice emerge. Rather than a justice based on the needs of the capitalist class, to the oppression of everyone else, a justice develops under socialism that satisfies the needs of the entire working class" (pp. 145–46). The criminologist's job is to provide the theory and practice that will bring about this change: "In understanding criminal justice—its theory and practice under capitalism—we provide a theory and a practice that have as their objective changing the world. The importance of criminal justice is that it moves us dialectically to reject the capitalist order and to struggle for a new society. We are engaged in socialist revolution" (p. 165).

Sandwiched between those apocalyptic pronouncements is a set of assertions which, taken together, provide something which might, with a minimum of charity, be called a contemporary marxist theory of crime. Paraphrased—to save the reader's patience and mine—this theory goes approximately as follows. In capitalist societies, the state arose, and exists, in order to protect

---

14 As Steinert (1978) has pointed out, several of Quinney's figures do not add up; they are moreover uncorrected for inflation.

and promote the interests of the dominant class, namely the class that owns and controls the means of production. The state thus is a device for controlling the exploited class, namely the working class which labors for the benefit of the ruling class; the exploitation, of course, consists in the appropriation by capitalists of the surplus value created by the workers' labor. The criminal law (and "legal repression") are the means by which the dominant capitalist class enforces and protects its interests; crime control in capitalist society is accomplished by a governmental elite, representing ruling-class interests, for the purpose of establishing domestic order and allowing capitalists to go on accumulating capital at the expense of those who work. This domestic order is not imposed by brute force alone, but by the imposition of an ideology on the working class, such that the capitalist world is accepted as legitimate. In the course of exercising its domination of the working class, the ruling capitalist class itself commits crimes. These include crimes of *control*, e.g., those committed by the police and others in the name of the law; crimes of *government*, e.g., Watergate; crimes of *economic domination*, e.g., price fixing and environmental pollution; and, in addition, many social injuries—involving racism, sexism, and economic exploitation—which the capitalist ruling class has managed to assure are not legally defined as crimes at all. On the part of the working class—or, more correctly, the lumpenproletariat[15]—there are crimes which occur within the context of capitalist oppression: these include *predatory* crimes, such as burglary, robbery, and drug dealing, which are pursued out of a need to survive; *personal* crimes, such as murder and rape, which are committed by those brutalized by the conditions of capitalism; and a few rather heroic "defensive actions" committed by alienated workers, e.g., industrial sabotage. In the conditions of "advanced" capitalism, there is a surplus population of unemployed and underemployed;

[15] Quinney actually does admit that in addition to "lumpen crimes" there are crimes committed by the working class: these however constitute "a struggle, however conscious or unconscious, against the exploitation of the life and activity of the worker"; they are "crimes of resistance" (1977, pp. 54–55). Otherwise, however, he appears to follow Marx in holding that lower-class criminals are to be found exclusively in the lumpenproletariat.

it is this segment of the working class that most readily turns to crime in the struggle for survival, despite ruling-class efforts to control it through the criminal justice system or the social welfare system or both (Quinney 1977, chaps. 2, 3).

This summary is by no means intended as a parody. I am not suggesting that Quinney's work is representative of contemporary marxist criminology; on the contrary, I have quoted his views in part because they are extreme. Less extreme (and less polemical) treatments of theoretical issues are now emerging; some of these will be discussed below. Quinney's work has been severely criticized, even by some marxist criminologists (see, e.g., Mankoff 1978; Steinert 1978); on nonmarxists he tends to have rather the same effect as a red rag on a bull (see, e.g., Klockars 1979). But Quinney's work is widely read; and it is not exactly unrepresentative of marxist criminology, at least as it was in the late middle 1970s. Many of his theoretical claims—and much of his revolutionary rhetoric—can be found in a more diffuse form, in the writings of others of the marxist school (see, e.g., Werkentin, Hofferbert, and Bauermann 1974; Platt 1974; Chambliss 1976; Hepburn 1977). In any case, despite all of the claptrap and cant which he uses to express his views, Quinney—like the other writers to whom I have so far referred—calls attention to a number of serious and important questions which until recently had been largely neglected by criminologists; and he, and they, make a number of claims to which attention must be paid.

The questions by and large concern the *origins* of criminal laws and the relations between social structures and economic systems and the criminalization of certain forms of behavior. Instead of asking why individuals or groups obstinately behave in ways that break rules of the criminal law, the writers we have been considering tend to ask: *why were those forms of behavior ever made criminal in the first place?* A separate but parallel question is: why are certain activities, demonstrably harmful, *not* criminalized? If one believes, with some sociologists, that the answer to these questions is that the criminal law merely reflects some preexisting moral consensus, then one will naturally be led to look for an explanation of rule breaking in some kind of "pathology," whether individual or social. If, however, one begins by taking as problematic the process by which certain forms of behavior are declared to be "criminal," with all that that normally entails by way of social action nominally on behalf of the state, then it becomes natural to ask: what interests wanted such-and-such a law; why did they want it; and *how did they manage to get their way?* These questions had been raised by Becker (1973) and other labeling theorists; but they have been much more clearly and emphatically considered by marxist criminologists.

The answers given by marxist criminologists to the questions just mentioned are also important, though they are not uncontentious. Most marxists would assert, more or less emphatically, that the criminal law tends to reflect the interests of the powerful and privileged; specifically, that it reflects (and reinforces) the interests of the propertied ruling class—those who own or control the means of production, or both—vis-à-vis the rest of society. At a minimum, they would assert that there is a connection between class conflict, as defined by the social relations of production which obtain in a given society, and the form of the criminal law in that society. It is by no means obvious that these claims are true, in any nontrivial sense. Nonetheless, given the historical context in which the above questions have been asked, and given the societies about which they have been asked, it is of obvious importance to inquire how far a particular form of political economy—roughly speaking, Western industrial capitalism, as it has developed over the past three hundred years or so—has influenced the form of the criminal law as we know it, and (more generally) to ask what are the relations between capitalism and the paraphernalia of "criminal justice." In asking this question, marxist criminologists take up where labeling theorists (and conflict theorists) left off.[16]

---

[16] For a somewhat different view of the theoretical antecedents of marxist criminology, see Meier 1977.

III. Empirical Work of the Contemporary Marxist School

In *Critical Criminology*, Taylor, Walton, and Young wrote that "in the immediate future, empirical radical research is likely to be minimal," adding for good measure that "radical criminology must move beyond the *mere* collection of empirical data" (1975, pp. 28, 43; my emphasis). The first of these statements has so far turned out to be broadly correct: relatively little empirical work has yet been done by marxist criminologists in the admittedly brief time since the statements just quoted were made. A depressingly high proportion of the writing of members of the marxist school has been polemical or programmatic (or both) in character; and much time has been taken up with "replies to critics," i.e., with arguments (often intemperate on both sides) about the validity or value of the marxist perspective.[17] There have also been some important and interesting attempts to formulate more cautious and detailed marxist theories on deviance, social control, or both (see, e.g., Greenberg 1980; Spitzer 1975; Bierne 1979; Humphries and Greenberg 1979).

It would not be correct to say, however, that there has been no empirical work done by marxist criminologists in which marxist concepts and methods have been brought to bear on the analysis or explanation of specific criminal justice phenomena. On the contrary, there is a small but growing corpus of empirical work done within this perspective, much of which has appeared in dissertations, journal articles, and conference papers within the last two or three years. (A recent useful collection is Greenberg 1980; see also Inciardi 1979.)

Much of this work has been historical in character, and has—consistent with a marxist perspective—focused on the development of criminal laws or criminal justice institutions, and their relations to the economic systems (and associated power structures) in which they took their particular forms. Thus, for example, Harring has studied the development of municipal police

---

[17] See, in particular, Klockars 1979, and the fifteen papers critical of "radical" criminology cited there, adding Wheeler (1976).

forces in Buffalo and other American cities during the latter half of the nineteenth century, and has documented the relations between the mayors and police commissioners of those cities and their business communities. He has argued that the forms of police organization, patrolling practices, etc., were to some extent influenced by a desire to control "the labor problems" of those cities in a time of industrial development, rather than to deal with an actual or perceived increase in the rate of serious crime (Harring and McMullin 1975; Harring 1976, 1977, 1980). A similar study of the more recent history and organization of policing— including the part played in the funding and coordination of police in the United States by the Law Enforcement Assistance Administration—has been carried out by a group at the Center for Research on Criminal Justice at Berkeley (1977).[18] A similarly skeptical analysis has been carried out by Barak (1974, 1975) of the origins and development of the public defender system in the United States; by Currie (1975) of the reformatory movement during the period 1865–1920; and by Takagi (1975) of the development of state prison systems in relation to the political economy. Much the same perspective is taken by Platt, in his studies of the "child saving" movement and the origins of the juvenile court (Platt 1974; cf. Platt 1977; see also Jankovic 1977, an attempt to test Rusche and Kirchheimer's theories about unemployment and imprisonment; Chambliss 1974, 1975).

While most of the work done so far by marxist criminologists has focused on social control and on criminal justice institutions rather than on criminal, delinquent, or deviant behavior there are exceptions: one is David Greenberg's study of the age distribution of delinquency (1977b). Beginning with evidence of the considerable variation in age-specific participation rates in crime and delinquency (as measured by arrest rates in the United States), Greenberg notes that contemporary sociological theories of delinquency shed little light on the reasons for this variation,

[18] See also Speiglman's (1977) study of psychiatry at the California Medical Facility at Vacaville; and the study by Jacobs and Britt (1979) of inequality and police-caused homicides.

and in particular on the decline in criminal behavior in late adolescence or early adulthood. He suggests that adolescent theft
occurs in part because of a disjunction between the desire to
participate in social activities with peers, and the absence of legitimate sources of funds to finance that participation, as well as
by a need to gain self-esteem in contexts such as the school. He
then notes the important structural role played by the exclusion
of juveniles from the world of adult work, which simultaneously
exaggerates their dependence on peers' approval and deprives
them of funds to support leisure-time activities. This exclusion—
a consequence of child-labor laws, compulsory education, mini-
mum-wage laws, changing patterns of industrial work, and so
on—is much greater today than it was in the last century; and
Greenberg suggests that this may be part of the reason for the
greater participation of juveniles in crime at present, as compared
with earlier years. He goes on to argue that the prolongation
of education has, in turn, been historically associated with the
contraction of the labor market; and suggests that "the high and
increasing level of juvenile crime we are seeing in the present-day
United States and other Western countries originates in the
structural position of juveniles in an advanced capitalist economy" (Greenberg 1977b, p. 220; see also Schwendinger and
Schwendinger 1976; Chambliss 1978).

Greenberg's paper is of special interest since, as he points out,
it illustrates the general compatibility of marxist and nonmarxist
approaches to problems of crime causation. Indeed, it shows the
extent to which the two bodies of theory tend to offer answers
to different questions; there is no necessary incompatibility between causal roles given to such things as peer groups, the school
or the family, and the influence of relations to the means of
production.

This list of empirical works by marxist criminologists is by
no means intended to be exhaustive.[19] There is, for example, an

---

[19] I have excluded work by authors identified in one way or another with
the marxist perspective (e.g., by publishing in *Crime and Social Justice*) which
make no use of marxist theories or concepts: an example is Weis (1976).

extensive series of papers by researchers—some (but not all) of whom would probably regard themselves as marxists in the sense used in this paper—on sentencing, which have purported to test "marxist class conflict" theories of disparity in sentencing (see, e.g., Hagan and Leon 1977; Greenberg 1977a; Lizotte 1978; Carter and Clelland 1979; Hagan and Bernstein 1979). But as Bierne (1979) has pointed out, it is not clear that all of these researchers are applying (or testing) a marxist theory; some, at least, appear to be dealing instead with "conflict" theories (of the kind propounded by, e.g., Turk 1966, 1969; Chambliss and Seidman 1971; Chambliss 1974) which are based on rather different notions of class and class conflict (see also Balbus 1973). These papers illustrate, however, that the scope of empirical application and testing of marxist criminological theories is, even now, wider than the limited work of the marxist school itself would suggest.

IV. The Ancestors and Siblings of Contemporary Marxist Criminology

The issues we have been considering have fortunately been considered by others besides the contemporary marxist criminologists so far discussed. Indeed, to appreciate fully the work of that school, it is necessary to see it in relation to a wider body of scholarship, much of it by persons who would probably not be correctly described as marxists, and who would certainly not be described—or describe themselves—as criminologists. This wider corpus includes such earlier studies as Rusche and Kirchheimer's *Punishment and Social Structure* (1939) and more recent works such as those of Eric Hobsbawm (1959) and George Rudé (1964), all of which have influenced the contemporary marxist school (see, e.g., Platt 1975; Krisberg 1975). Still more recently, it includes the work of E. P. Thompson and his colleagues, many of whom were earlier connected with the Centre for the Study of Social History at the University of Warwick (England). In particular, Thompson's book *Whigs and Hunters* (1975), a study of the origins of the Waltham Black Act, and the collection of essays titled *Albion's Fatal Tree* (Hay et al. 1975) are essential reading for anyone concerned with the theoretical issues raised by marxist criminologists (see also Linebaugh 1976; Pearson 1978).

Running through these works are several interconnected themes. To begin with, the authors argue (convincingly, to at least one nonhistorian) that in eighteenth-century England the criminal law was very often not a mere codification of a peaceful consensus, but was instead the outcome of conflict, often brutal, between different factions of that supposedly harmonious society. There were many instances in which the state—acting on behalf of the propertied classes who controlled its machinery—imposed laws on a populace which resented those laws and, so far as it could in the circumstances, resisted them with often remarkable ferocity. Thus, for example, the Sussex smugglers discussed by Winslow (in Hay et al. 1975) not only regarded it as "no crime" to import wine or tea without paying customs duties; they also regarded attacks on Customs Houses as "gallant expeditions" on which they embarked to the applause of their neighbors. It was of course true that smuggling was profitable—especially in comparison with the legitimate incomes then open to the rural poor. But it was also regarded by many as a *right*, in accordance with custom and tradition; their pursuit of that "right," and the Duke of Richmond's efforts to deny it to them, much more closely resembled guerrilla warfare than it did the suppression of "common crime." Similarly, the Cornish miners and others who engaged in the plunder of wrecked vessels—and who were not above creating shipwrecks when Nature would not oblige—showed "how strong was the local strength of tradition, if such a form of criminal action could be persistently employed by whole communities, when its only legitimacy lay in the realm of custom" (Rule, in Hay et al. 1975, p. 186). As Hay (1975a, pp. 207–8) has pointed out, much the same thing was true of poaching, which was by no means confined to the impoverished: this was widely regarded as a right, while at the same time there were strong communal sanctions against casual theft.

A related theme is the extent to which the criminal law was

employed by the propertied classes as a weapon with which to protect their lands and themselves: the game laws, and in particular the infamous Black Act, are the clearest examples of this. As Thompson (1975, p. 196) has remarked, the Black Act was "an astonishing example of legislative overkill": it created at least fifty separate capital offenses, and furnished a model for the vast expansion of capital statutes passed by Parliament during the rest of the eighteenth century. Yet the available evidence—inevitably not as full as it might ideally be—by no means suggests an emergency of that magnitude: instead it suggests "the repeated public humiliation of the authorities; the simultaneous attacks upon royal and private property; the sense of a confederated movement which was enlarging its social demands . . . [and] the symptoms of something close to class warfare, with the loyalist gentry in the disturbed areas objects of attack and pitifully isolated in their attempts to enforce order. . . . It was this displacement of authority, and not the ancient offence of deer-stealing, which constituted, in the eyes of Government, an emergency" (pp. 190–91).

Further, the law "existed in its own right, as ideology; as an ideology which not only served, in most respects, but which also legitimized class power. The hegemony of the eighteenth-century gentry and aristocracy was expressed, above all, not in military force, not in the mystifications of a priesthood or the press, not even in economic coercion, but in the rituals of the study of the Justices of the Peace, in the quarter-sessions, in the pomp of Assizes and in the theatre of Tyburn" (Thompson 1975, p. 262). As Hay has put it, "the criminal law, more than any other social institution, made it possible to govern eighteenth-century England without a police force and without a large army. The ideology of the law was crucial in sustaining the hegemony of the English ruling class" (1975a, p. 56).

Other recent and relevant works by social historians working within a more or less explicitly marxist perspective, on the development of the criminal law and criminal justice systems, include Ignatieff's (1978) study of the development of the English prison system during the years 1750–1850, and Foucault's (1975) somewhat parallel study of the origins of the penitentiary system in France during approximately the same period; and Tigar and Levy's (1977) ambitious study of the development, from medieval times onward, of the "bourgeois law" which eventually supplanted feudalism in Western Europe. These works, like those of Thompson and his colleagues, are essentially concerned with social *change*—with the replacement of one social order by another, over more or less extended periods of time. But there are other historical analyses of a more static or structural kind, which have fruitfully analyzed particular social institutions from a marxist point of view, and which contain many insights into the working of the criminal law and other mechanisms of social control: the writings of Eugene Genovese (1965, 1971, 1973, 1974) on the political economy of slavery are examples.[20]

This too-brief synopsis of noncriminologists' studies of crime and the criminal justice system does not pretend to do justice to the subtlety, range, or variety of those authors' work; nor does it purport to be exhaustive of the research and scholarship which touch on criminological questions from a broadly marxist perspective. Instead, it is intended merely to emphasize two closely related points which should be borne in mind when assessing contemporary marxist criminologists. The first is that the study of crime and societal reaction to crime is by no means the monopoly of persons who describe themselves professionally as "criminologists"; indeed, anyone wanting wisdom (as distinct from mere truth) on those subjects might do well to put criminologists—whether marxist or nonmarxist—near the bottom of the list of people whom he would seek to consult. The second, and intrinsically related, point is that crime and the criminal law cannot be yanked from their social and economic contexts and studied in isolation—as one might study, for example, a diseased liver or a particularly exotic tumor after their extraction from

---

[20] See also Sellin 1976. Relevant research on media interpretations of deviant and criminal behavior is also being carried out at the Center for Contemporary Cultural Studies at the University of Birmingham, England: see, e.g., Clarke et al. 1978, and the series of Occasional Papers obtainable from the Centre, P.O. Box 363, Birmingham B15 2TT England. I am indebted to Mr. Ian Taylor for this reference.

the body in which they were nurtured. One of the great merits of the modern marxist criminologists is that they have refocused interest on important questions which traditional criminologists have too long neglected. Another is that they have shown that the answers to many of those questions require an understanding of much broader social, economic, and political issues than have heretofore been considered by the majority of those who have studied crime—either to correct it or to appreciate it.

V. The Commitment to Praxis

At this point, before examining further the central theoretical and empirical claims of contemporary marxist criminologists, it is important to dispose of one theme which recurs, in various forms, throughout their writings, but which is nonetheless irrelevant to the rest of their work. This is their announced commitment to *praxis*—to the bringing about, through social action, of "socialist revolution" or some other such visionary transformation of society's current arrangements, at least where crime and the criminal justice system are concerned. As Taylor, Walton, and Young (1975, p. 24) have put it, "most importantly, radical social science must neither simply describe nor prescribe (in the passive, liberal sense); it must engage in theory and research as *praxis*." Similarly, according to Platt (1975, p. 105), "A radical commitment to practice consists of 'practical critical activity' and participation in ongoing political struggles." And for Quinney (1975b, p. 200), "To think critically and radically today is to be revolutionary. To do otherwise is to side with repression. Our understanding of the legal order and our actions in relation to it must be to remove that oppression, to be a force in liberation."

I have no wish to disparage, let alone discourage, these ambitions. But it should be clear that they do not entail, nor are they entailed by, the *scientific* views of contemporary marxist criminologists. Political activism of a "radical" kind is compatible with a wide range of beliefs about how the social world works; per contra, a marxist view of the way that society works is compatible with a great many political platforms.

In *The New Criminology* Taylor, Walton, and Young spent a great deal of time excoriating "positivism," partly on the ground that it was an inherently conservative doctrine which—tacitly or explicitly—led to an unquestioning acceptance of the legal status quo, in which the capitalist ruling class exercised its power to criminalize the "facts of human diversity" and "corrected" those who continued to deviate. This suggests that "positivist" explanations of crime and deviance have an intrinsic connection with conservative, consensualist programs of social defense; or, at a minimum, that these explanations lend themselves exclusively to a conservative ideology. To see that this is not so, we need only consider the original criminological "positivists" of a century ago, and their sociological contemporaries. At the first international congress of sociology in 1894, for example, Enrico Ferri argued passionately for a marxist position, and subsequently published his views in a monograph called *Socialism and Positive Science*. There may have been some criminologists of that day who were more thoroughly committed to *praxis* than the Italian criminologists who called themselves "positivists," but, if so, history has failed to record just who they were.[21]

This is not to say, of course, that there is no connection between social-scientific theory and evidence and political views about the criminal justice system. It is to say that the connections which may exist are many and various, and that neither one can be very accurately predicted from the other.

I make this point in part, I suppose, out of liberal pique at the arrogant assumption that it is only marxists who will ever get to heaven. But it is also true that radical criminologists' commitment to *praxis* has been a focus of much criticism (see, in particular, Turk 1979; Akers 1979), and at least some of the critics seem to have assumed that marxists' theoretical or empirical claims were somehow suspect, purely because of marxists' political or value preferences. This is surely a mistake—though it is

[21] However, the relations between marxist social thought, and "positivism" in the Comtean sense of that term, are complex: see the discussion in Bottomore 1975, pp. 9–19. Ferri and his contemporaries were in fact unacquainted with much of the writing of Marx, which had then not been translated: cf. Greenberg 1980.

one which may have been encouraged by statements like those quoted above. Marxist writers certainly make no secret of their political views, and often argue forcefully for reforms; but they are at least candid about this, and state their premises clearly. Policy recommendations—equally based on value preferences— are also made by nonmarxist criminologists; sometimes the values in question are explicit (e.g., Van den Haag 1975); sometimes they are not.[22] For either group, there is a necessary distinction between fact and value. Thus, the current shift from "treatment" to "justice" in sentencing in the United States has received criti- cal attention from marxists (Clarke 1978; Greenberg and Hum- phries 1980) as well as from liberals (e.g., Morris 1974; Von Hirsch 1976) and conservatives (Wilson 1975; Van den Haag 1975). The prescriptions of these three groups tend to differ: but all of those prescriptions are logically distinct from empirical questions such as those concerning the effects of determinate sentencing.

VI. Capitalism and the Criminal Law

One claim made by some marxist criminologists is that *criminal behavior* is a consequence of the repression, brutalization, etc., of capitalism; the optimistic concomitant of this claim is a prediction that crime committing will cease (or at least sharply diminish) once a "genuine" socialist revolution takes place. (See, e.g., Quin- ney 1975a, pp. 50–59; to much the same effect, Werkentin et al. 1974.) More cautious marxist theorists would assert that there is at least a connection between the *patterns* of criminal behavior displayed by certain groups, and those groups' relations to the means of production (Greenberg 1977b; Spitzer 1975); they

---

[22] Consider, for example, the following: "With respect to the charge of de- fending 'middle-class values,' let me stress that the analysis of 'neighborhood' offered here makes no assumptions about the substantive values enforced by the communal process. On the contrary, the emphasis is on the process itself; in principle, it could be used to enforce any set of values. . . . Lower-class persons (by definition, I would argue) attach little importance to the opinions of others; they are preoccupied with the daily struggle for survival and the immediate gratifications that may be attendant on survival and are inclined to uninhibited, expressive conduct. A lower-*income* person, of course, is not neces- sarily lower-*class*. . . ." (Wilson 1975, pp. 29, 37; emphasis in original).

would concede that there are certainly crime and criminal justice agencies in many countries that call themselves socialist, though they might give various accounts of the reasons for this (Greenberg 1980).

Of equal theoretical interest—and more fully articulated—is the concern of the writers discussed here with relations between capitalism and *the criminal law*. This concern takes a variety of forms; and in evaluating the views of marxist criminology it is necessary to distinguish between two different claims which can be made about the criminal law in capitalist societies. (1) It can be argued that the criminal law is influenced by capitalism: that is, that the content of the law reflects the interests of those who own the means of production, or control them, or both. (2) It is also sometimes argued that the criminal law helps to perpetuate capitalism—or that the criminal justice system is an important means by which the propertied and privileged maintain their dominant position over the working class. It would caricature these two propositions to put them in causal-modeling terms; but were they put in those terms, the arrows indicating causation would run in opposite directions: in proposition (1) from capitalism to criminal law, in proposition (2) from criminal law to capitalism.

Examples of proposition (1) are numerous in the writings so far discussed. Young (1975, p. 87) for example, writes that "the criminal statistics represent the end-result of the deployment of social-control agencies by the powerful"; in the same volume Chambliss (1975, p. 168) "suggests" that "acts are criminal because it is in the interests of the ruling class so to define them." Quinney puts it this way: "That the legal system does not serve society as a whole, but serves the interests of the ruling class, is the beginning of a critical understanding of criminal law in capitalist society" (1975b, p. 195). At an empirical level, the work of Thompson and his colleagues, and of the other social historians discussed earlier, has been directed to showing how, in certain times and places, the criminal law and related institutions—the juvenile justice system, the public defender system, the courts—have been shaped in ways that reflect the interests of property owners, corporations, or whatever.

Examples of proposition (2) also abound. Thus Quinney (1975a, p. 45) writes that "the coercive force of the state, embodied in law and legal repression, is the traditional means of maintaining the social and economic order"; elsewhere he has written (Quinney 1975b, p. 199) that "criminal law in the USA can be critically understood in terms of the preservation of the existing social and economic order." To like effect is Hay's hypothesis that "the criminal law, more than any other social institution, made it possible to govern eighteenth-century England without a police force and without a large army" (Hay 1975a, p. 56).

Evidently propositions (1) and (2) are compatible, so that a writer (like Quinney) who asserts both is not contradicting himself. But the two propositions are independent; neither entails the other. They say quite different kinds of things about the relations between capitalism and the criminal law or criminal justice system. The important question is whether—or, rather, under what conditions—either proposition is true.

Consider first proposition (1), that in capitalist societies the criminal law reflects the interests of the dominant capitalist class. I do not think that it can be doubted that there are *some* conditions under which this proposition is true; and—as I have already suggested—that truth was too long ignored by traditional criminologists, with the exception of Sutherland (1940, 1941, 1949). Studies such as Thompson's analysis of the Black Act (1975), or Hay's analysis of the laws on poaching on Cannock Chase (1975b) leave no room for doubt that in eighteenth-century England the criminal law developed in just the way that marxists assert: it criminalized behavior of the lower orders which threatened the interests of the ruling class. It would seem, however, that proposition (1) needs to be spelt out in some detail by marxist criminologists, so that the specific influence of *capitalism* is made clear. Otherwise, it becomes no more than an instance of a more general proposition that the rules tend to be made by the powerful (cf. Quinney 1970); on which the only possible comment is, What else is new? What might one predict, for example, from that more general proposition, for a socialist society? Presumably not a failure to criminalize such "facts of human diversity" as rape. But one might predict a different *definition* of rape from that found in (some) capitalist societies, varying perhaps as a consequence of the different social and economic position of women. Reflection on such matters from a marxist point of view might help to clarify the distinction between prohibitions aimed at protecting the essential conditions of organized existence, without which group life would be impossible, and prohibitions necessary for particular *forms* of social existence, e.g., those dependent on a particular economic system.[23]

Marxist criminologists hypothesize that the power relations in question are a consequence of the social relations of production; it is precisely here that they make an important advance over the "conflict" theories which preceded them. But even in capitalist societies the matter is by no means as simple as some marxist criminologists have made it seem. As Greenberg (1976, p. 614) has asked, "is it *always* true that the State's reaction is *necessary* to the maintenance of production and reproduction? Might the State or those on behalf of whom it acts not sometimes be mistaken, thinking a reaction necessary when it isn't? Or, on the other hand, might it not fail to recognize the necessity of some measure and so fail to react? Where steps are taken, what determines whether legislation is civil or criminal, and the level of penalties? Are these always determined by 'necessity'? How would that be demonstrated?" As Greenberg points out, crude marxist accounts (such as those of Werkentin, Hofferbert, and Bauermann [1974], whom he is considering) "assume a level of governmental omniscience that even Marxist social scientists equipped with the tools of 'scientific socialism' have yet to attain." As Greenberg also points out, there are many forms of

---

[23] E.g., state capitalism, in which we would expect to find that theft of public property was sanctioned more severely than theft of private property; this is said to be the case in Poland and other Eastern European countries, at least so far as penalties provided by law are concerned.

deviance that do not threaten upper-class interests; the interests threatened may be those of other groups, in which case the ruling class may not care much one way or another about the outcome. He gives an example of this: a couple of years ago there was a campaign in New York City to pass a civil rights bill for homosexuals. This was defeated by an alliance of the Catholic Church, the Orthodox Jewish rabbinate, and the city's firemen's union, none of whom could be said to represent the ruling class. It is also true that there are many kinds of crime and deviance that affect units (e.g., the family) that are found in all classes. It does not seem sensible to attempt to explain prohibitions on, say, incest by reference to ruling-class interests—though there are no doubt some marxists who would try.[24]

Moreover, some care is needed with the concept of "the ruling class"; control of the state by those who own or control the means of production is problematic, and not automatic as some marxists have made it seem. For one thing, some degree of separation of ownership from control of the means of production is now conceded, even by marxists, to exist in most capitalist societies. It is not enough to show—as Miliband (1969), for example, has done—that the functionaries of the state have the same social origins as those who own or control property and the means of production. Undoubtedly that is generally true. But it must surely be shown that those who run the state act *on behalf of* the capitalist class; and that is not shown merely by demonstrating that the two groups went to the same schools and belong to the same clubs. Finally, some account must be taken of the fact that capitalists sometimes lose in the legislative arena: trustbusters, consumerists, environmentalists, and others do occasion-

[24] Marxist analyses of laws relating to such things as abortion and homosexuality usually assert that these practices threaten the continued existence of the nuclear family and thus the labor supply needed by capitalism; perhaps a similar argument could be made for the prohibition of incest. On the other hand, sociobiologists such as Wilson (1978, p. 36) argue that incest taboos originate in a sexual aversion between persons who grew up together before the age of six—as if the taboo would be necessary if such an aversion did in fact generally exist. Forced to choose between these two explanations, I do not know what I would do.

ally succeed in getting laws passed which are plainly not in the interest of capital.[25]

In any event, as Thompson has pointed out, in real life even the use of law by the ruling class is a complex matter:

> To be sure, I have tried to show, in the evolution of the
> Black Act, an expression of the ascendancy of a Whig
> oligarchy, which created new laws and bent old legal forms
> to legitimize its own property and status; this oligarchy
> employed the law, both instrumentally and ideologically,
> very much as a modern structural Marxist should expect it
> to do. But this is not the same thing as to say that the
> rulers had need of law, in order to oppress the ruled,
> while those who were ruled had need of none. What was
> often at issue was not property, supported by law, against
> no-property; it was alternative definitions of property rights:
> for the landowner, enclosure—for the cottager, common
> rights; for the forest officialdom, "preserved grounds" for the
> deer; for the foresters, the right to take turfs. (Thompson
> 1975, pp. 260–61; the whole concluding section of this book,
> pp. 258–69, should be read daily at breakfast by those
> who think it enough to assert that "the ruling class
> makes the law" and leave it at that.)

[25] The problem here involves much more than giving ad hoc explanations of laws like the Sherman and Clayton Acts, or the Environmental Protection Act. The point is that it is only in a capitalist society that *capitalists' crimes* (like those created by the statutes just mentioned) can take place. But it is well known that at least some such crimes have analogues in socialist societies, such as those of present-day Eastern Europe and China, in which the state has not (yet) "withered away." It would seem that marxist criminologists need to show that there would not also be analogous crimes in a "pure" socialist society—and why this would be the case, if it were so. Would a genuine socialist revolution necessarily involve new forms of industrial organization, for example, so that there would no longer be factories which polluted the atmosphere while making cars that exploded when hit from behind? Or would the concept of property somehow be made to disappear completely, so that there *could* be no theft because there were not even short-term use rights in artifacts or other commodities in one's physical possession? Or that there *would* be no theft, because there would be a superabundance of property of every kind? *Some* account of what would happen if there were no capitalism is necessary, if the proposition that "capitalism causes crime" is to be at all plausible; and no marxist criminologist, so far as I am aware, has yet even attempted to provide such an account.

With these reservations, we may perhaps accept proposition (1) as containing some truth—albeit of a complex kind. What about proposition (2), which says (roughly) that the criminal law is an important instrument for preserving the capitalist social and economic order? The logician Frank Ramsey once said of a certain philosophical theory that it had "only to be questioned to be doubted";[26] and I think that this is certainly the case where proposition (2) is concerned. It all depends upon the strength or generality with which the proposition is asserted.

There may well be *some* limited range of cases in which the proposition is true in a fairly strong form. For example: Hay's and Thompson's arguments as to the ideological importance of the criminal law in England in the early eighteenth century— the appeals to "Justice" and the legitimation of inequality, played out in the theaters of Assizes and Quarter Sessions—are certainly convincing to me. Again, we know from rare but (for that very reason) compelling cases that when the criminal law—or, more strictly, its enforcement machinery, a.k.a. the legitimate use of naked force—is absent, then chaos threatens: let anyone witness a *real* riot, and assert with a straight face that the criminal law and its associated paraphernalia are not "useful," to capitalists and proletarians alike. Further, there are altogether too many incidents, even within recent memory, in which the machinery of criminal justice has been used on behalf of the state or the capitalist class, without even a redeeming trace of cynicism: the history of American labor relations in the twentieth century yields too many examples. Indeed, perhaps these examples furnish a clue as to the importance of the criminal justice system for the preservation of capitalists' social order: it is *organized* threats to that order that are most likely to be met with force. Individual deviance seldom poses a problem, unless of course it is perceived to be endemic—as it arguably was among the "dangerous classes" in the last century (cf. Ignatieff 1978, pp. 179–87). Finally, there is an ideological borderline at which the criminal law may be

26 He was talking about Johnson's and Russell's theories on the subject-predicate distinction. See Ramsey 1931, p. 116.

all too useful to a dominant class or group: what are, by their intentions, *political* challenges to the legitimacy of a ruling order may with a bit of luck be neutralized if they can be defined as "merely" criminal. (In contemporary socialist societies, read: merely psychotic.)

When all of that is said and done, however, it seems clear that the criminal law assumes such importance only at the *margins* of social life;[27] and that in day-to-day affairs it is not all that important to the maintenance of late industrial capitalism's social order. Even in eighteenth-century England, I think, it can be argued that the laws most important to the propertied classes were those laws—created some centuries earlier—which permitted the transfer of land and the income it generated from one generation to the next. It is perhaps plausible to assume that kings and nobles could seize land and hold it by force of arms, for a while; but the creation of great estates in feudal times, and after, was not possible without the laws which made *estates* possible, and those laws were not criminal laws. In more modern times, give me the law of contracts (including contracts of employment), and you can have all of the rest of the statute book. No doubt the criminal law, and in particular the law of larceny, is often a convenient thing for the propertied classes to have at their disposal. But it is scarcely possible to conceive of a law of larceny which is not primarily based on an asportation, i.e., the physical taking up and carrying away of an object; and you cannot steal very much if you literally have to carry it away with you. Thus an industrialist might find it handy to be able to prosecute for theft or embezzlement those workmen who rip

[27] It is of course arguable that that these margins are in a strong sense fundamental: that is, that unless some minimum element of order were coercively maintained, the primarily contractual relations which characterize all societies except the most primitive could never have developed in the first place. That does not, I think, falsify the general point being made in the text, which is that in the course of day-to-day affairs in reasonably stable societies (including those of Western industrial capitalism) the norms of the criminal law, and the machinery used to enforce them, are by no means the most important techniques of social control. Industrialists do not often have to shoot strikers; nor does the Roman Catholic Church often find itself compelled to excommunicate heretics.

off tools (or finished products) from his factory;[28] he will, I suggest, find it infinitely more useful to be able to define the terms on which those workmen work there at all. The importance of the law of contract can be seen in many other examples. Thus, it is generally agreed that the common law of contract (like most of the Roman law of contract) rests on the fiction that the two contracting parties are of approximately equal strength, dealing under no compulsion, and at arm's length. But what about the standard form contract—exemplified in the airline ticket, for instance? What if one of the two contracting parties is the airline that printed the ticket, and the other is some poor wretch who merely wants to get from Newark to San Francisco? The passenger cannot negotiate the terms on which he will accept the company's offer to transport him; it is literally an offer he cannot refuse, unless of course he refuses to travel at all.

In summary, it seems to me that proposition (2) is in need of considerable qualification, and that in protecting the interests of those who own or control the means of production, or both, the most generally useful laws are likely to be the ones that define that ownership and control, and not some ancillary laws that promise to thump individuals for rather trivial kinds of tampering with those means. (Attention was recently called to a variety of "improper" payments made by multinational companies to agents of foreign governments; some of these payments were bribes intended to influence legislators to pass laws favorable to the companies concerned. But it is highly unlikely that a bribe was ever paid to insure the passage of a *criminal* statute; what multinationals tend to want is laws that permit transfer payments, restrict or permit imports, give tax breaks, and the like.) Even in the case of poaching, as Hay's (1975b) essay makes clear, what was at stake was not merely the use of the criminal law, but the property qualifications which underlay the game laws in general.

---

[28] For a discussion of the development of statutes prohibiting embezzlement, in relation to the "outworking" system in eighteenth-century England, see Ignatieff 1978, esp. pp. 26–27.

I do not doubt the *ideological* importance of a very strong form of proposition (2); it makes a handy stick to beat the Establishment with, especially for those old enough to remember the 1960s. Scientifically, however, it seems clearly to need to be qualified: state sanctions for misbehavior are merely the hand-maiden of economic dominance.

VII. Methodological Considerations: History and Criminology

In his essay on "Prospects for a Radical Criminology in the United States," Anthony Platt (1975, p. 104) noted that

> the field of criminology is long overdue for serious historical scholarship. The history of the police is unwritten, with the exception of "house" histories and a few microscopic case studies; the history of the criminal courts has been systematically neglected; we know very little about the modern prison system, its variations over time, its relationship to other institutions, or its impact on the lives of prisoners; finally, we know even less about the nature and impact of "criminal" behavior in the USA before the twentieth century, even though European scholars have demonstrated the importance of such studies. Radical criminologists recognize this deficiency and we are beginning to develop a historical analysis in our writings and courses.

There was certainly truth in Platt's charge of neglect; and the attention to history since paid by marxist criminologists is an extremely valuable contribution. There is an important respect in which it is true that "the nature and content of crime and law *cannot* be grasped without a thorough analysis of its evolution historically" (Taylor, Walton, and Young 1975, p. 47; emphasis in original). As we have seen, some of the most important work in this field has been carried out by professional social historians.

Historical research is as characteristic of the contemporary marxist school as ethnography and participant observation were, or are, of labeling and interactionist theorists.

The question is whether that is the *only* methodology appropriate to the marxist school's theories. It may be that they emphasize historical studies out of deference to Marx's own view on historical materialism; or it may be that they are motivated by an ideological interest in showing how the criminal justice systems of late capitalist societies got in the shape they are in; or that the kinds of changes in crime and social control predicted by their theories are of a kind which take place over a fairly long period of time, and can thus only be seen in historical perspective.[29] However that may be, it is striking that so little research of other kinds has yet been done by members of the contemporary marxist school. There has been very little use of ethnographic research, for instance; nor is much use made of survey methods (perhaps because they are too tainted by "positivism").[30] Yet to the extent that marxist theories of crime or law are true, they should surely generate predictions about the here and now, of a kind that are testable by participant observation, by experiment, or through cross-sectional surveys.

That this is so can be seen—if it is not obvious—by considering

[29] For an interesting methodological discussion of research of this kind, see Humphries and Greenberg 1979, pp. 61–63, where it is suggested that one might assess the importance of historical factors by performing the *Gedankenexperiment* of asking what *might* later have occurred if something had *not* occurred earlier (e.g., if Sir Robert Peel had died before becoming prime minister, would the British police have developed as they did?). An obvious problem of this approach is that there is no such thing as a *complete* account of "what happened" in history; one tends to "see" only what one is looking for. But it is precisely here, I think, that marxist historians perform their greatest service in the present state of social science: they see what others have chosen not to. As Humphries and Greenberg (1979, pp. 61–62) write, "Someone who assumes *a priori* that subordinate classes can never have an impact on social control will never look for their influence, and consequently will never discover it. If ideology is believed to be nothing more than a mask for class interests and carries no weight of its own, then it too can be neglected. As long as the state is thought to be controlled by a single class whose will it carries out, then there is no need to examine the constraints of social control imposed by the form of the state, or to take account of its partial autonomy."

[30] There are admittedly difficulties involved in using most traditional social science data-collection methods to test marxist theories. It is difficult to use orthodox field methods to study the intentions of the powerful, because the powerful tend to be very good liars; large-scale "attitude" surveys, which might be useful in providing data on interclass normative consensus, have well-known validity problems of their own. Yet surely it is better to have imperfect data, than no data at all?

a recent paper by Mann (1970), on the problem of social co-hesion in liberal democracies. Mann notes that even "conflict" theorists agree that some minimal degree of value consensus exists in liberal democratic societies, permitting them to handle con-flicts and remain stable. Marxists attribute this consensus to "false consciousness," asserting that acceptance of ruling-class norms is "false" in the sense that it leads workers to ignore their true in-terests. As Mann points out (p. 425), "the concept of false con-sciousness is tenable if we can demonstrate two of three things: that an indoctrination process has occurred, palpably changing working-class values, or that the indoctrination process is incom-plete, leaving indoctrinated values in conflict with 'deviant' ones in the mind of the worker; and thirdly, in *both* cases we still have to be able to rank the rival sets of values in order of their 'authenticity' to the worker if we are to decide which is more 'true.'"

Mann then proceeds to test the "false consciousness" hypothe-sis empirically, by means of a reanalysis of findings from a variety of surveys carried out in Britain and the United States, on value commitment. While the findings of those surveys lead Mann to reject more extreme marxist theories, he concludes that they nonetheless give some support to those theories: "a significant measure of consensus and normative harmony may be necessary among ruling groups, but it is the absence of consensus along lower classes which keeps them compliant" (p. 437). Discussing the role of the educational system in Britain and the United States, he notes that "the most common form of manipulative socialization by the liberal democratic state does not seek to change values, but rather to perpetuate values that do not aid the working class to interpret the reality it actually experiences. These values merely deny the existence of group and class con-flict within the nation-state society and, therefore, are demon-strably false" (p. 437).

I have cited Mann's paper primarily as a methodological ex-ample; but its subject is surely one that is highly relevant to marxist criminology. The question of consensus or dissensus on crime, and the related problem of "false consciousness," are crucial to marxist criminology.[31] Taylor, Walton, and Young (1975, pp. 42–43) cite one British study (Moorhouse and Chamberlain 1974) which claimed to find that "the lower class in Britain have attitudes to property ownership which are opposed, and in some ways constructively opposed, to those which are dominant in society." Yet in a survey which my colleagues and I carried out at about the same time in London, we found that lower-class respondents gave scores (on a 1–11 scale) indicating that they thought property crimes were *more* serious than middle-class respondents did (Sparks, Genn, and Dodd 1977, pp. 187–89). Some notion of "false consciousness" may well explain that finding (assuming it to be valid)—even though it is pretty plainly true that the lower classes do have a genuine interest in hanging on to their property, as well as an interest in not being raped, robbed, or murdered. (See also Young 1975.) My point is that the origin of value consensus or dissensus is an empirical question—and one that can be studied by conventional social survey methods, as Mann's paper shows.

I am not suggesting, of course, that marxist criminologists' historical work is not "empirical" (though it is certainly true that their work *looks* very different from the empirical work of nonmarxist criminologists, e.g., in the virtual absence of quantitative data or methods).[32] It may be that, as Platt (1975, pp. 106–7) and others have suggested, academic repression and limited access to federal or other research grant support are in part responsible for marxists' relatively infrequent use of other (and

[31] It is thus astonishing that Humphries and Greenberg (1979, p. 9) should state that marxism cannot be refuted by empirical evidence that there is agreement among classes about the wrongfulness of certain criminal offenses. Would they not, one wonders, have claimed that marxist theories were *supported* if the empirical evidence had shown substantial *dissensus?*

[32] For an exception, see Jankovic (1977, 1978); in general, however, marxist criminologists make only minimal use of quantitative methods. This is surprising, since at least some of them are highly skilled at such methods (see, e.g., Greenberg 1979); and since recent work by historical demographers has shown that historical analyses and multivariate analysis are not in the least antithetical (see, e.g., Tilly 1978).

more expensive) research methods.[33] Whatever the explanation, it is to be hoped that the imbalance will not persist; to the extent that it does, there is a danger that marxist *criminology* will self-destruct, or become no more than a specialized area of social historiography.

VIII. Assessing the Impact of Marxist Criminology

It is still too early to attempt any but the most provisional assessment of the impact of the contemporary marxist school of criminology. Books like *The New Criminology* have certainly had an impact on the teaching of criminology in English and American universities—enough to justify Stanley Cohen's (1979, p. 23) complaint about the "vacuous rhetoric with which, as forty earnest students tell me each year, 'Matza's view of man' (or something like that) is 'inadequate' and has to be replaced by a 'fully social' picture." (My own experience of teaching criminology over the past fifteen years fully confirms Cohen's view: Taylor, Walton, and Young have now supplanted Merton, Cohen, and Cloward-and-Ohlin as the Unholy Trinity of second-rate students' exams.)

Their impact on the rest of criminology and sociology is less clear. In part this may be because relatively little of their work has yet appeared in the "mainstream" journals devoted to those subjects—compare, for example, the large number of articles on some aspect of "labeling theory" which appeared in those journals in the 1960s. This may be, as Platt (1975) and Krisberg

---

[33] Greenberg (1980) has suggested that funding for criminological research has been "geared primarily to work that poses no intellectual threat to the government or the capitalist economy." This may perhaps be true of most research funded by the Law Enforcement Assistance Administration, which usually puts out Requests for Proposals for research it wants done. Some years' experience in reviewing proposals for the Crime and Delinquency Center of the National Institute of Mental Health, however, leads me to doubt that Greenberg's view is true for that agency. I do not recall ever having seen a grant proposal submitted to NIMH by a marxist criminologist; colleagues involved in reviewing unsolicited proposals for the National Institute of Justice report the same thing. Much the same thing was true of the NDC sociologists discussed in an earlier section of this paper, in the late 1960s: they complained vociferously about the failure of the British Home Office to support their research, yet they seldom applied for Home Office grant support.

(1975) have charged, because of a conspiracy on the part of "mainstream" sociologists, journal editors, university administrators, and the like; or it may not. Either way, the fact remains that much of the work of the marxist school of criminology is difficult for many students and teachers to find; it tends to appear in journals with titles like *The Insurgent Sociologist* which are not (to put it mildly) widely available. Two journals—*Crime and Social Justice*, and *Contemporary Crises*—are largely devoted to marxist criminology; these too are not available in many university and college libraries.[34] There have been sessions devoted to "radical" criminology at recent meetings of the American Society of Criminology and other professional associations (see, for example, the February 1979 issue of the journal *Criminology*). In Britain, at least one volume of essays critical of "radical" criminology has recently appeared (Downes and Rock 1979); and numerous papers critical of the marxist school's work have been published in the United States (see above, n. 17). Overall, however, the impact of the marxist school on criminology in Britain and the United States has not been very great.

This is not to say that it has been nonexistent. A sharp difference between the marxist school and the sociology of deviance of the 1960s and early 1970s is the emphasis which the marxists have placed on *crime* as their object of study. *The New Criminology* was subtitled "For a Social Theory of Deviance"; but the book's focus was on acts which had been prohibited by the criminal law, and not on violations of other social norms, expectations, or various forms of (merely) deviant behavior. This emphasis is obviously a consequence of the marxists' interest in the role of the criminal law and the criminal justice system, and their theoretical views on the importance of "criminalization" as an aspect of class conflict. (Of course it is not merely prohibition, arrest, incarceration and so on which are important here: the operation of the law as ideology, to which Hay, Thompson, and

---

[34] *Contemporary Crises* is published by Elsevier Scientific Publishing Co., in Amsterdam; *Crime and Social Justice* (which absorbed the periodical *Issues in Criminology* when the School of Criminology at the University of California at Berkeley ceased to exist in 1976) can be obtained by writing to P.O. Box 4373, Berkeley, California 94704.

their colleagues have drawn attention, is of enormous importance. See also Jock Young's discussion of "the soft machine" in his essay on "Working-Class Criminology" [1975, pp. 82–85].)

Whatever its causes, this shift in focus of attention has, I believe, been both important and salutary. Reading back over the literature of the sociology of deviance throughout the preceding decade—in particular, in the journal *Social Problems*—one cannot help but be struck by the *triviality* of much that was studied and written about then. It is not merely the vast number of papers on marijuana use, homosexuality, and other "victimless" crimes that strikes one; it is also papers on the management of respectability in nudist camps (Weinberg 1966, 1970) and on breakfast with topless barmaids (Ames, Brown, and Weinberg 1970) that give substance to Young's charge of "voyeurism." As he remarks, "Utilitarian crime is of little interest to the new deviancy theory. Indeed, it is engaged in an astonishing accomplishment—the development of a criminology that does not deal with property crime, and a criminology whose subjects live not in a world of work but in a world of leisure" (Young 1975, pp. 68–69; see also Liazos 1972).

This does not mean that marxist criminologists focus entirely on acts that have already been declared officially to be crimes, of course. On the contrary, many of them have called attention to "the crimes of the powerful" (e.g., Quinney 1975b; Pearce 1976; Platt 1975; Schwendinger and Schwendinger 1970), i.e. those acts of corporations, government officials, professionals and other powerful and prestigious persons which are—because of their power—not criminal at all. In the post-Watergate era it should scarcely be necessary to draw anyone's attention to the misbehavior of the powerful; but criminologists arguably are professionally socialized into a habit of ignoring what is obvious to everyone else, so the reemphasis on "white-collar crime" is probably beneficial. But marxist criminologists have not yet done any work on contemporary corruption of the caliber of Thompson's (1975) study of Walpole and the Hanoverian Whigs. It is not clear, moreover, that the conceptual structure used by some marxist criminologists is especially helpful to them in this task. In a well-known essay, Herman and Julia Schwendinger (1970) suggested that legal definitions of crime should be rejected in favor of definitions based on "human rights," which would include "imperialistic war, racism, sexism and poverty" as crimes.[35] It is difficult indeed to see how such a definition facilitates the practical task of criminalizing the kinds of behavior in question, still less the analytical task of explaining why those kinds of behavior are not now crimes in everybody else's sense of that term.

The ultimate question to be asked is whether future empirical research by marxist criminologists will be found to support the claims of their theories; but the answer to this question will depend in large measure on what those theories turn out to be. It may be, as Greenberg (1980) has recently suggested, that marxist criminological theory is moving away from the cruder "instrumental" position summarized earlier, toward something nearer to what Marx himself actually wrote; but it remains to be seen how far this will help in the effort to formulate theories of crime and crime control. The qualifications made by "structural" marxists to the proposition that the capitalist class makes the law are plainly necessary; the problem is that they may lead to the proposition being qualified out of existence, and so to throwing out the baby with the bathwater.[36] In particular, the central propositions of marxist theory concerning the relations between the means of production and the rest of social life seem in need of clarification. It may be, as Greenberg (1980) and others have argued, that Marx himself did *not* assert that the legal and political superstructure of society is determined by its economic

[35] The Schwendingers have since adopted a "proletarian" definition of crime: see Schwendinger and Schwendinger 1977.

[36] Thus Bierne (1979), after having refuted "instrumental" marxists by citing "structuralist" marxist theorists, goes on to cite marxist jurists such as Pashukanis to the effect that dominant modes of production determine only the *form* of law, not its *content*, which may vary within "determinate limits." As an example, Bierne says that under the capitalist mode of production there could be no law which abolished rent, interest, or profit, since such laws would abolish capital itself; but he concedes that the *level* of interest, etc., may vary for a variety of reasons. Yet surely a law prohibiting interest or rent would have the same *form* as a law prohibiting rape or murder.

base.[37] However that may be, *some* clear statement of those relations would seem necessary; and it is not clear what such a statement will turn out to entail about crime and the criminal law. Marxists' embedding of crime in its economic and social context is important; but it must surely do more by way of explanation than to point out that certain kinds of economic or social institutions are necessary to provide the opportunities for certain kinds of crimes. It is not very illuminating, for example, to be told that there would not be laws against forgery if there were not first documents which could be forged (cf. Ignatieff 1978, p. 17).

Is it likely that the contemporary marxist school of criminology will *ever* have as much impact or influence as the Italian positivist school did in its day and subsequently? We shall have to wait and see; but my guess is that it will not. It is true that "success" for some marxist criminologists would involve basic structural changes in society, and that this is a much more ambitious target than the reforms of the criminal justice system which the positivists set out to bring about. It is also true that much (though not all) of the influence of Lombroso, Ferri, and Garofalo came about through their being proved *wrong* about such things as atavism; marxists would presumably prefer not to achieve immortality in quite the same way. But at least the Italian positivists had a theory, which *could* be proved wrong; nobody ever accused them of having a mere "perspective."

[37] Yet in support of this contention Greenberg quotes from a well-known passage from Marx's *Contribution to the Critique of Political Economy* which states, in part, that "the mode of production in material life determines the general character of the social, political and spiritual processes of life." "Determines" and "general character" are obviously the difficult concepts here. Most marxists who discuss these words of Marx refer somewhat nervously to the metaphor of (economic) "base" and (social) "superstructure" which he used; they do little to clarify it, however.

204   Richard F. Sparks

REFERENCES

Akers, Ronald L. 1979. "Theory and Ideology in Marxist Criminology," *Criminology* 16:527–44.
Ames, Richard G., Stephen W. Brown, and Norman L. Weinberg. 1970. "Breakfast with Topless Barmaids." In *Observations of Deviance*, ed. Jack D. Douglas. New York: Random House.
Balbus, Isaac. 1973. *The Dialectics of Legal Repression*. New York: Russell Sage.
Barak, Gregg L. 1974. "In Defense of the Poor: The Emergence of the Public Defender System in the United States (1900–1920)." Ph.D. dissertation, University of California, Berkeley.
———. 1975. "In Defense of the Rich: The Emergence of the Public Defender," *Crime and Social Justice* 3:2–14.
Becker, Howard S. 1973. *Outsiders: Studies in the Sociology of Deviance*. New ed. New York: Free Press. (Originally published 1963.)
Bierne, Piers. 1979. "Empiricism and the Critique of Marxism on Law and Crime," *Social Problems* 26:373–85.
Bottomore, Tom. 1975. *Marxist Sociology*. London: Macmillan.
Carter, Timothy, and Donald Clelland. 1979. "A Neo-marxian Critique, Formulation and Test of Juvenile Dispositions as a Function of Social Class," *Social Problems* 27:96–108.
Center for Research on Criminal Justice. 1977. *The Iron Fist and the Velvet Glove*. 2d. ed. Berkeley, Cal.: Center for Research on Criminal Justice. (Originally published 1975.)
Chambliss, William J. 1974. "The State, the Law, and the Definition of Behavior as Criminal or Delinquent." In *Handbook of Criminology*, ed. Daniel Glaser. Chicago: Rand McNally.
———. 1975. "The Political Economy of Crime: A Comparative Study of Nigeria and the USA." In Ian Taylor, Walton, and Young (1975).
———. 1976. "Functional and Conflict Theories of Crime." In *Whose Law, What Order?*, ed. W. J. Chambliss and M. Mankoff. New York: John Wiley.
———. 1978. *On the Take*. Bloomington: Indiana University Press.
Chambliss, William, and Robert B. Seidman. 1971. *Law, Order and Power*. New York: McGraw-Hill.
Clarke, Dean H. 1978. "Marxism, Justice and the Justice Model," *Contemporary Crises* 2:27–62.
Clarke, J., C. Crichter, S. Hall, T. Jefferson, and B. Roberts. 1978. *Policing the Crisis*. London: Macmillan.

Cohen, Stanley, ed. 1971. *Images of Deviance*. Harmondsworth, Middlesex: Penguin Books.

Cohen, Stanley. 1979. "Guilt, Justice and Tolerance: Some Old Concepts for a New Criminology." In Downes and Rock (1979).

Coser, Lewis. 1956. *The Functions of Social Conflict*. New York: Free Press.

Currie, Elliott. 1974. Review of *The New Criminology*, in *Crime and Social Justice* 2:109–13.

——. 1975. "Managing the Minds of Men: The Reformatory Movement, 1865–1920." Ph.D. dissertation, University of California, Berkeley.

Dahrendorf, Ralf. 1959. *Class and Class Conflict in Industrial Society*. Stanford: Stanford University Press.

Downes, David, and Paul Rock, eds. 1979. *Deviant Interpretations: Problems in Criminological Theory*. New York: Barnes and Noble Books.

Foucault, Michel. 1975. *Surveiller et Punir: Naissance de la prison*. Paris: Gallimard. (Also published as *Discipline and Punish: the Birth of the Prison*. New York: Vintage Books, 1979.)

Genovese, Eugene D. 1965. *The Political Economy of Slavery: Studies in the Economy and Society of the Slave South*. New York: Pantheon.

——. 1971. *In Red and Black: Marxian Explorations in Southern and Afro-American History*. New York: Pantheon.

——. 1974. *Roll, Jordan, Roll: The World the Slaves Made*. New York: Pantheon.

Genovese, Eugene D., ed. 1973. *The Slave Economies*. New York: John Wiley,

Gouldner, Alvin W. 1962. "Anti-minotaur: the Myth of a Value-free Sociology," *Social Problems* 9:199–213.

——. 1968. "The Sociologist as Partisan: Sociology and the Welfare State." *The American Sociologist*, 1968, pp. 103–16.

Greenberg, David F. 1976. "On One-dimensional Marxist Criminology," *Theory and Society* 3:611–21.

——. 1977a. "Socio-economic Status and Criminal Sentences: Is There an Association?" *American Sociological Review* 42:174–75.

——. 1977b. "Delinquency and the Age Structure of Society," *Contemporary Crises* 1:189–223.

——. 1979. *Mathematical Criminology*. New Brunswick, N.J.: Rutgers University Press.

——. 1980. *Crime and Capitalism: Readings in Marxian Criminology*. Palo Alto, Cal.: Mayfield Publishing Co.

Greenberg, David F., and Drew Humphries. 1980. "The Co-optation of Fixed Sentencing Reform," *Crime and Delinquency* 26:206–25.

Hagan, John, and Ilene Bernstein. 1979. "Conflict in Context: The Sanctioning of Draft Resisters," *Social Problems* 27:109–22.

Hagan, John, and Jeffrey Leon. 1977. "Rediscovering Delinquency: Social History, Political Ideology and the Sociology of Law," *American Sociological Review* 42:587–98.

Harring, Sidney L. 1976. "The Development of the Police Institution in the United States," *Crime and Social Justice* 5:54–9.

——. 1977. "Class Conflict and the Suppression of Tramps in Buffalo, 1892–94," *Law and Society Review* 11:873–911.

——. 1980. "Policing a Class Society: Late Nineteenth and Early Twentieth Century Expansion of the Urban Police." In Greenberg (1980).

Harring, Sidney L., and Lorraine M. McMullin. 1975. "The Buffalo Police 1872–1900: Labor Unrest, Political Power and the Creation of the Police Institution," *Crime and Social Justice* 4:5–14.

Hay, Douglas. 1975a. "Property, Authority and the Criminal Law." In Hay et al. (1975).

——. 1975b. "Poaching and the Game Laws on Cannock Chase." In Hay et al. (1975).

Hay, Douglas, Peter Linebaugh, John G. Rule, E. P. Thompson, and Cal Winslow. 1975. *Albion's Fatal Tree: Crime and Society in Eighteenth-Century England*. New York: Pantheon.

Hepburn, John R. 1977. "Social Control and the Legal Order: Legitimated Repression in a Capitalist Society," *Contemporary Crises* 1:77–90.

Hirst, Paul Q. 1975. "Marx and Engels on Law, Crime and Morality." In Taylor, Walton, and Young (1975).

Hobsbawm, Eric J. 1959. *Primitive Rebels*. New York: Norton.

Horowitz, Irving L., and Martin L. Liebowitz. 1968. "Social Deviance and Political Marginality: Toward a Redefinition of the Relation between Sociology and Politics," *Social Problems* 15:280–96.

Humphries, Drew, and David F. Greenberg. 1979. "Historical Change in Social Control." Paper presented at the 1979 meeting of the American Sociological Association.

Ignatieff, Michael. 1978. *A Just Measure of Pain: The Penitentiary in the Industrial Revolution, 1750–1850*. New York: Pantheon.

Inciardi, James A., ed. 1980. *Radical Criminology: The Coming Crises*. Beverly Hills: Sage Publications.

Jacobs, David, and David Britt. 1979. "Inequality and Police Use of Deadly Force: An Empirical Assessment of a Conflict Hypothesis," *Social Problems* 26:403–12.

Jankovic, Ivan. 1977. "Labor Market and Imprisonment," *Crime and Social Justice* 8:17–31.

——. 1978. "Social Class and Criminal Sentencing," *Crime and Social Justice* 10:9–16.

Klockars, Carl B. 1979. "The Contemporary Crises of Marxist Criminology," *Criminology* 16:477–515.

Krisberg, Barry. 1975. *Crime and Privilege: Toward a New Criminology*. Englewood Cliffs, N.J.: Prentice-Hall.

Liazos, Alexander. 1972. "The Poverty of the Sociology of Deviance: Nuts, Sluts and Perverts," *Social Problems* 20:103–20.

Linebaugh, Peter. 1976. "Karl Marx, The Theft of Wood, and Working Class Composition: A Contribution to the Current Debate," *Crime and Social Justice* 6:5–16.

Lizotte, Alan J. 1978. "Extra-legal Factors in Chicago's Criminal Courts: Testing the Conflict Model of Criminal Justice," *Social Problems* 25:564–80.

Mankoff, Milton. 1978. "On the Responsibility of Marxist Criminologists: A Reply to Quinney," *Contemporary Crises* 2:293–301.

Mann, Michael. 1970. "The Social Cohesion of Liberal Democracy," *American Sociological Review* 35:423–39.

Mannheim, Hermann. 1960. *Pioneers in Criminology*. 2d ed. London: Stevens.

Marx, Karl, and Frederick Engels. 1968. *Selected Works*. Moscow: Progress Publishers.

Matza, David. 1969. *Becoming Deviant*. Englewood Cliffs, N.J.: Prentice-Hall.

Meier, Robert F. 1977. "The New Criminology: Continuity in Criminological Theory," *Journal of Criminal Law and Criminology* 67:461–9.

Miliband, Ralph. 1969. *The State in Capitalist Society*. New York: Basic Books.

Mills, C. Wright. 1959. *The Power Elite*. New York: Oxford University Press.

Moorhouse, H. F., and C. W. Chamberlain. 1974. "Lower-class Attitudes to Property: Aspects of the Counter-ideology," *Sociology* 8:387–405.

Morris, Norval. 1974. *The Future of Imprisonment*. Chicago: University of Chicago Press.

Pearce, Frank. 1976. *Crimes of the Powerful*. London: Pluto Press.

Pearson, Geoffrey. 1978. "Goths and Vandals—Crime in History," *Contemporary Crises* 2:119–39.

Platt, Anthony M. 1974. "The Triumph of Benevolence: The Origins of the Juvenile Justice System in the United States." In *Crime and Justice in America: A Critical Understanding*. Boston: Little, Brown.

———. 1975. "Prospects for a Radical Criminology in the United States." In Taylor, Walton, and Young (1975). (Originally published 1974 in *Crime and Social Justice* 1:2–10.)

———. 1977. *The Child Savers: The Invention of Delinquency*. 2d ed. Chicago: University of Chicago Press. (Originally published 1969.)

Plummer, Ken. 1979. "Misunderstanding Labeling Perspectives." In Downes and Rock (1979).

Quinney, Richard. 1970. *The Social Reality of Crime*. Boston: Little, Brown.

———. 1975a. *Criminology: Analysis and Critique of Crime in America*. Boston: Little, Brown.

———. 1975b. "Crime Control in Capitalist Society: A Critical Philosophy of Legal Order." In Taylor, Walton, and Young (1975).

———. 1977. *Class, State and Crime: On the Theory and Practice of Criminal Justice*. New York: David McKay Co.

———. 1978. "The Production of a Marxist Criminology," *Contemporary Crises* 2:277–92.

Radzinowicz, Leon. 1966. *Ideology and Crime: A Study of Crime in Its Social and Historical Context*. London: Heinemann.

Ramsey, Frank P. 1931. "Universals." In *The Foundations of Mathematics*, by Frank P. Ramsey. London: Routledge & Kegan Paul, 1931.

Reppetto, Thomas. 1974. *Residential Crime*. Cambridge, Mass.: Ballinger.

Rock, Paul. 1979. "The Sociology of Crime, Symbolic Interactionism and Some Problematic Qualities of Radical Criminology." In Downes and Rock (1979).

Rock, Paul, and Mary McIntosh, eds. 1974. *Deviance and Social Control*. London: Tavistock.

Rudé, George. 1964. *The Crowd in History: A Study in Popular Disturbances in France and England, 1730–1848*. New York: Wiley.

Rusche, Georg, and Otto Kirchheimer. 1939. *Punishment and Social Structure*. New York: Columbia University Press. (Reprinted 1968. New York: Russell & Russell.)

Schauffler, Richard. 1974a. "Criminology at Berkeley: Resisting Academic Repression," *Crime and Social Justice* 1:58–61.

——. 1974b. "Criminology at Berkeley: Resisting Academic Repression, Part II," *Crime and Social Justice* 2:42–45.

Schwendinger, Herman, and Julia Schwendinger. 1970. "Defenders of Order or Guardians of Human Rights?" *Issues in Criminology* 5:123–57. Also in *Critical Criminology*, ed. I. Taylor, P. Walton, and J. Young. London: Routledge & Kegan Paul, 1975.

——. 1976. "Delinquency and the Collective Varieties of Youth," *Crime and Social Justice* 5:7–25.

——. 1977. "Social Class and the Definition of Crime," *Crime and Social Justice* 7:4–13.

Sellin, Thorsten. 1976. *Slavery and the Penal System*. New York: Elsevier.

Singer, Peter. 1979. "On Your Marx." *New York Review of Books* 26(2):44–47.

Sparks, Richard F., Hazel G. Genn, and David J. Dodd. 1977. *Surveying Victims: A Study of the Measurement of Criminal Victimization, Perception of Crime and Attitudes to Criminal Justice*. New York: Wiley.

Speiglman, Richard. 1977. "Prison Psychiatrists and Drugs: A Case Study," *Crime and Social Justice* 7:23–39.

Spitzer, Stephen. 1975. "Toward a Marxian Theory of Deviance," *Social Problems* 22:638–51.

Steinert, Heinz. 1978. "Can Socialism be Advanced by Radical Rhetoric and Sloppy Data? Some Remarks on Richard Quinney's Latest Output," *Contemporary Crises* 2:303–13.

Sutherland, Edwin H. 1940. "White Collar Criminality," *American Sociological Review* 5:1–12.

——. 1941. "Crime and Business," *Annals of the American Academy of Political and Social Science* 217:112–18.

——. 1949. *White Collar Crime*. New York: Dryden Press.

Takagi, Paul. 1975. "The Walnut Street Jail," *Federal Probation* 39:18–26.

Taylor, Ian, and Laurie Taylor, eds. 1973. *Politics and Deviance*. Harmondsworth: Penguin Books.

Taylor, Ian, Paul Walton, and Jock Young. 1973. *The New Criminology: For a Social Theory of Deviance*. London: Routledge & Kegan Paul.

Taylor, Ian, Paul Walton, and Jock Young, eds. 1975. *Critical Criminology*. London: Routledge & Kegan Paul.

Thompson, E. P. 1975. *Whigs and Hunters: The Origin of the Black Act*. New York: Pantheon.

Tigar, Michael E., and Madeleine R. Levy. 1977. *Law and the Rise of Capitalism*. New York and London: Monthly Review Press.

Tilly, Charles, ed. 1978. *Historical Studies of Changing Fertility*. Princeton: Princeton University Press.

Turk, Austin T. 1966. "Conflict and Criminality," *American Sociological Review* 31:338–52.

———. 1969. *Criminality and Legal Order*. Chicago: Rand McNally.

———. 1979. "Analyzing Official Deviance: For Nonpartisan Conflict Analyses in Criminology," *Criminology* 16:459–76.

Van den Haag, Ernest. 1975. *Punishing Criminals*. New York: Basic Books.

Vold, George. 1958. *Theoretical Criminology*. New York: Oxford University Press.

Von Hirsch, Andrew. 1976. *Doing Justice: The Choice of Punishments*. New York: Hill & Wang.

Weinberg, Martin S. 1966. "Becoming a Nudist," *Psychiatry* 29:15–24.

———. 1970. "The Nudist Management of Respectability: Strategy for, and Consequences of, the Construction of a Situated Morality." In *Deviance and Respectability*, ed. Jack D. Douglas. New York: Basic Books.

Weis, Joseph. 1976. "Liberation and Crime: The Invention of the New Female Criminal," *Crime and Social Justice* 6:17–27.

Werkentin, Falco J., Michael Hofferbert, and Michael Bauermann. 1974. "Criminology as Police Science, or: 'How Old is the New Criminology?'" *Crime and Social Justice* 2:24–41.

Wheeler, Stanton. 1976. "Trends and Problems in the Sociological Study of Crime," *Social Problems* 23:525–34.

Wilson, Edward O. 1978. *On Human Nature*. Cambridge, Mass.: Harvard University Press.

Wilson, James Q. 1975. *Thinking about Crime*. New York: Basic Books.

Young, Jock. 1975. "Working Class Criminology." In Taylor, Walton, and Young (1975).

Philip J. Cook

Research in Criminal Deterrence: Laying the Groundwork for the Second Decade

ABSTRACT

Deterrence theory has been developed primarily by economists, who have viewed potential criminals as rational decision-makers faced with an array of illicit opportunities characterized by costs (time, possible adverse legal consequences, and so forth) and payoffs. The crime decision is thus characterized in a way that fits the well-developed theoretical framework of decision-making under uncertainty. Herbert Simon and others have questioned the descriptive accuracy of this theory, and are beginning to uncover systematic patterns in decision-making that violate the predictions of the economic theory: this work could usefully be incorporated into the crime choice framework. One of the most important issues for further research in this area is the way in which potential criminals acquire information about criminal opportunities and the effectiveness of the criminal justice system. A simple "realistic" model of threat communication can be outlined that yields deterrence-like effects, even though no one is well informed concerning the true effectiveness of the system. Three other questions that have been of great interest to deterrence theorists are discussed: (1) what factors influence the rate at which active criminals commit crimes; (2) which dimension of the threat of punishment has a greater deterrent effect—likelihood or severity; and (3) what effect does the threat of punishment for one type of crime have on involvement in other criminal activities?

Philip J. Cook is Associate Professor of Public Policy Studies and Economics, Duke University.

Much of the recent empirical work on deterrence has used a fundamentally flawed approach to estimating the responsiveness of crime rates to sanction probability and severity. The flaw is that the measures of "probability of punishment" used in these studies reflect the choices made by criminals as well as the intrinsic effectiveness of the criminal justice system. Therefore, these measures do not serve as appropriate indices of criminal justice system effectiveness. The empirical approach that appears most productive is the evaluation of discrete changes in law and policy—"natural experiments," that can tell us a good deal about the deterrence process.

The core concern of deterrence research has been to develop a scientific understanding of the relationship between the crime rate and the threat of punishment generated by the criminal justice system. A decade ago, criminologists tended to view deterrence as an archaic theoretical construct associated with Bentham, Beccaria, and other somewhat naive scholars from the distant past. Deterrence research has enjoyed a revival during the 1970s, but so far has produced little more than a frame of reference, a variety of hypotheses and suppositions, and a scattering of empirical observations which are more anecdotal than systematic.

This essay serves in part as an introduction to modern research in criminal deterrence. My main concerns are to present a clear statement of the questions that have motivated social scientists working in this area, and a critical discussion of the methods used to answer these questions. This literature has already been summarized and critiqued by a number of scholars (e.g., Brier and Fienberg 1978; Carroll forthcoming; Chaiken 1978; Cook 1977; Ehrlich 1979; Gibbs 1975; Nagin 1978; Walker 1979; Zimring and Hawkins 1973). The most notable contribution of this sort is the recent report of the National Academy of Sciences Panel on Deterrence and Incapacitation (Blumstein, Cohen, and Nagin 1978), which offers a very well-documented assessment of the empirical literature. While this essay inevitably covers some of the same ground, it is more a complement than a substitute for the panel report; for example, I devote considerably more attention to discussing the theory of criminal choice, and organize my discussion of the empirical literature in a way that I believe offers important new insights into the problems and prospects of this work.

For those who have not already acquired a taste for the theoretical and empirical investigation of criminal deterrence, some initial attempt to motivate the reader may be helpful. When criminologists assemble to exchange thoughts on crime control, a common observation is that the criminal justice system has little impact on crime rates; the big effects, so it is said, come from "root causes" such as demographic patterns, the influence of family and neighborhood, and the distribution of legitimate opportunities. Yet consider the likely consequences if we disbanded the police and rewrote the criminal codes to eliminate sanctions; there would surely be a crime wave of unprecedented proportions. Evidence from police strikes and related incidents supports this prediction.[1] Furthermore, the inevitable response to mushrooming crime rates would be the widespread development of private alternatives to the criminal justice system—vigilante groups and vastly increased efforts at private protection.[2] My assessment is that the criminal justice system, ineffective though it may seem in many areas, has an overall crime deterrent effect of great magnitude, and would quickly be reinvented in some form by the private sector if government got out of the business of issuing threats of punishment to would-be criminals. If this assessment is correct, it would be fair to say that the deterrents generated by the justice system have a large civilizing influence which is by no means minor in comparison to the influence of "root causes" of crime.

The everyday debates in the criminal justice policy arena are

[1] Police strikes in Liverpool (1919) and Montreal (1956) and the mass arrest of the Copenhagen police force by the Nazis in 1944 are discussed by Johannes Andenaes (1974). The huge increase in crime rates that followed each of these events is persuasive evidence that the threat of punishment has a substantial inhibiting effect on crime.

[2] Current private expenditures on protection against crime probably exceed total public expenditures on the criminal justice system. Bartel (1975) gives some empirical results on the demand for private protection, and both she and Clotfelter (1977) discuss the degree of substitutability between public and private expenditures.

not, of course, concerned with whether to stop punishing criminals entirely, but rather with questions of degree: how many tax dollars should be devoted to apprehending and punishing criminals, how severe a punishment is appropriate for each crime type, and so forth. The evaluation of these issues hinges in part on our assessment of the *marginal* deterrent effects of changes in the certainty and severity of punishment, a more problematic issue than assessing the overall deterrent effect of current threat levels. It is quite possible that mild penalties are almost as effective as severe penalties, or that a 50 percent change either way in the size of the typical big-city police department would have a much less than proportionate effect on crime. If there are sharply decreasing returns to scale in criminal justice system activities, then there is no contradiction between my assessment that the overall deterrent effect of the system is enormous, while the effect at the margin tends to be small or perhaps even zero in some instances. Estimating the magnitudes of marginal deterrent effects stemming from various criminal justice system activities is the ultimate task facing scholars in this area.

What is actually known about these magnitudes? The answer is "not much," if we exclude theoretical speculation, laboratory experiments, and results derived from badly flawed data and statistical methods. What is left is a collection of anecdotes—case studies—that suggest only one generalization: a wide range of criminal activity is subject to the influence of legal threats. A sample of recent findings supports this generalization. (1) Large increases in police patrol activity were effective in reducing robberies in New York City subways (Chaiken, Lawless, and Stevenson 1974) and outdoor felonies in the Twentieth Precinct of New York (Press 1971). (2) The increase in the perceived probability and severity of punishment for drunk driving resulting from the British Road Safety Act was initially very effective in reducing this crime and alcohol-related accident rates (Ross 1973, 1977). A reduction in the legal minimum drinking age from twenty-one to eighteen in Michigan, Wisconsin, and Ontario caused a small increase in alcohol-related accidents for this age group (Williams et al. 1975). (3) Draft evasion rates during the Vietnam war era were responsive to conviction rates (Nagin and Blumstein 1977). (4) The increase in the likelihood of arrest for attempted airline hijacking that resulted from the airport security measures adopted in 1973 virtually eliminated this crime (Landes 1978). (5) The increase in the statutory punishment for carrying a gun illegally in Massachusetts (the Bartley-Fox Amendment) apparently reduced the use of guns in violent crime (Pierce and Bowers 1979).

These studies suggest that there exist feasible actions on the part of the criminal justice system that may be effective in deterring crimes committed by drunks (driving under the influence) and desperate men (hijacking); crimes that are widespread and not considered immoral (carrying a concealed weapon, underage drinking); crimes that are, for some at least, a matter of conscience (draft evasion); and common crimes of theft and violence. These studies do *not* demonstrate that all types of crimes are potentially deterrable, and certainly they provide little help in predicting the effects of any specific governmental action.

What about the various hypotheses and suppositions that constitute the conventional wisdom concerning deterrence? Are crime rates more responsive to changes in the probability of punishment than to equivalent changes in the severity of punishment? Are juveniles less deterrable than adults? Are "crimes of passion" deterrable at all? These and related questions may be answered by "common sense" or theoretical considerations, but relevant empirical evidence is weak or nonexistent. The first decade of social science research in criminal deterrence has generated many interesting questions but few answers.

This essay is organized as follows. Section I explains the model of individual rational choice, which is the centerpiece of deterrence theory, with an eye to answering the objections of those who find the model silly or implausible. I include a discussion of three questions of great interest to deterrence theorists. (1) What factors determine the rate at which an active criminal commits crimes? (2) Which dimension of the threat of criminal punishment has a greater deterrent effect—probability or severity? (3) What effect does the threat of punishment for one type of crime have on involvement in other criminal activities? Section II describes, analyzes, and rejects the "Ehrlich paradigm," the approach to estimating the deterrence effects that has dominated the literature during the last decade. Section III then summarizes and assesses the policy evaluation literature, with greater focus on technique than on specific findings. The final section proposes a partial research agenda for deterrence research in the 1980s.

I. The Crime Decision: Theoretical Perspectives on the Deterrence Process

The role of theory in the study of criminal deterrence, as in other scientific inquiries, is to generate interesting, testable hypotheses and provide a framework for interpreting empirical observations. A "good" theory explains known facts in a parsimonious way and generates accurate predictions. There are two main issues to be considered in a complete theory of criminal deterrence: first, the influence of the threat of criminal sanctions on the choices made by individuals regarding their participation in criminal activity; and second, the effectiveness of various criminal justice system activities in producing threats. This section is limited to the first issue; the threat production process is discussed briefly in section II.

A. The Rational Potential Criminal

An increase in the probability or severity of punishment for a particular type of crime, or both, will reduce the rate at which that crime is committed, other things being equal. This assertion is not an assumption but, rather, is derived from a theoretical argument, developed primarily by economists in recent years.[3] Observed crime rates are viewed as the aggregate result of choices made by rational individuals. Potential criminals weigh the possible consequences of their actions, both positive and negative, and take advantage of a criminal opportunity only if

[3] See Heineke (1978a) for a recent review. Gary Becker (1968) gave the first statement of this theory in modern times; his work was extended by Ehrlich (1973), Block and Lind (1975), Block and Heineke (1975), and others.

it is in their self-interest to do so. Jeremy Bentham expressed the point this way: "[T]he profit of the crime is the force which urges a man to delinquency: the pain of the punishment is the force employed to restrain him from it. If the first of these forces is the greater the crime will be committed: if the second, the crime will not be committed" (quoted in Zimring and Hawkins 1973, p. 75).

A satisfactory characterization of the "rational potential criminal" must elaborate on Bentham's proposition to take into account the subjectivity of "profit" and "pain," as well as individual differences in objective circumstances. Individuals respond differently to equivalent criminal opportunities, for reasons that include the following:

1. Individuals differ in their willingness to accept risks. The consequences of committing a crime are uncertain. Arrest and conviction are always less than certain, and for some common crimes the probabilities are small indeed. The consequences of conviction are also uncertain, given the wide discretionary power of judges in sentencing. Potential criminals will differ in their assessment of the probability of "losing" the gamble offered by a particular criminal opportunity, and also differ in the degree to which they are risk-averse.

2. Individuals differ with respect to "honesty preference"— the strength of their preference for behaving in a law-abiding manner. How much net "profit" is required to persuade an individual to overcome his ethical concern for staying within the law? Furthermore, for crimes that are *malum in se*, the individual's ethical concern may extend to the criminal act itself.

3. Individuals differ with respect to their evaluation of the "profit" to be gained from a crime. These differences are largest for crimes for which the payoff is not money (which most everyone values) but rather is "in kind"—consider, for example, crimes of violence, vandalism, draft evasion, and double parking.

4. Individuals differ in their objective circumstances: their income, the value they place on their time, their skills in committing crimes successfully and evading capture, and their reputation in the community. An arrest for shoplifting, followed by a

dismissal of charges, may be of little consequence for an unemployed teenager but may ruin the life of a college professor. An individual's circumstances also influence the nature of criminal opportunities available to him—few of us are in a position to embezzle money, fix prices, or commit treason.

Thus, the "profit" and "pain" associated with equivalent criminal opportunities will be evaluated differently by different individuals. Some may find it very worthwhile, others will be close to indifferent, while a third group will view it as highly unattractive. The key point is that a change in either the probability or average severity of punishment will cause some people to change their minds about whether the opportunity is, on balance, attractive, and thereby change their behavior. A small change will affect only those who were previously close to indifference (perceived "profit" and "pain" about equal); changing the behavior of others will require a larger change in probability or severity.

Most discussions of the deterrence mechanism distinguish between "general" and "special" deterrence. The latter concept refers to the deterrent effect of punishment on those who have been punished. This notion is a bit vague (Walker 1979). It is possible that those who have suffered a criminal sanction once will be more likely to be deterred by the threat of punishment thereafter, but there is no evidence to support this notion.

The threat of punishment may play a grander role than simply acting as a debit in the potential criminal's cost-benefit analysis of a crime opportunity. Cook (1977) discusses its role as a socializing and moralizing force.

Punishment in the form of incarceration reduces crime by incapacitating inmates (Cohen 1978). Correctional treatments may also reduce crime by rehabilitating some convicts, although existing programs appear to be largely ineffective (Lipton, Martinson, and Wilks 1975).

B. Objections to the Theory

The economists' theory of criminal deterrence, as characterized above, has been useful in developing the implications of a long neglected notion in the criminology literature—that criminals can be viewed as rational decision makers intent on furthering their personal welfare in an environment that provides crime opportunities coupled with sanction threats. However, some critics find this assumption of rationality in the decision to commit a crime highly implausible and inconsistent with descriptive evidence on criminal behavior. Herbert Jacob (1979) succinctly states the two major objections with that assumption:

> (a) It implies that people who contemplate committing a crime have a realistic perception of the probabilities of being sanctioned and of the severity of the sanction. The little evidence we have on perceptions of legal sanctions by the general public indicates that these perceptions are incorrect and variable. . . . (b) It implies that people who commit crimes act after rational calculation rather than on impulse. We have much reason to believe that many crimes are committed on impulse, either under the influence of alcohol or simply as the result of opportunity and need intersecting. (p. 584)

Jacob's arguments are persuasive, and lead many criminologists to conclude that common appropriative crimes and much violence are not very responsive to the threat of punishment. But this conclusion does not follow from his argument. The existence of a strong deterrent effect does not require that potential criminals be fully informed or fully rational in their crime decisions. A theoretical model which postulates full rationality on the part of criminals is clearly "unrealistic" but may nonetheless generate valid predictions because it contains essential elements of truth. The assumptions of a rational choice/full information model can be relaxed without undermining the prediction that an increase in the threat of punishment will reduce crime. I deal with Jacob's objections in reverse order, since the second point is more fundamental.

1. Limits on rational calculation. It may be true, as Jacob suggests, that many criminals do not consider the consequences of their acts, other than those consequences which are obvious, certain, and immediate. This impulsiveness is often thought to be particularly characteristic of youths and of people who are intoxicated, in a state of high emotional arousal, deviant, or emotionally disturbed. These groups constitute a large percentage of the perpetrators of some types of crime. Are these crimes deterrable? Two affirmative arguments are worth mentioning.

Deterrence theory is concerned with making predictions about aggregate behavior. The accuracy of such predictions does not require that every individual act predictably. The prediction that crime is deterrable follows just as readily from an assumption that 10 percent of criminals are capable of rational decision-making, as from an assumption that *all* potential criminals have this ability; assuming, that is, that the remaining 90 percent do not respond to a change in the threat level in a systematically perverse fashion.

The deterrence mechanism does not require that each crime opportunity be evaluated separately or fully. Herbert Simon (1957) and his followers (Payne 1980) have developed the notion of "limited rationality" as a descriptively more accurate alternative to the "full rationality" notion propounded by economic theorists (see Carroll 1978 for a discussion of this issue in the context of the crime decision). Limited rationality models of decision-making incorporate observed limitations on people's capacity to acquire and process information. In particular, it is thought that people tend to economize on this scarce capacity by adopting rules of thumb, or "standing decisions," which eliminate the need completely to analyze every new decision. A person whose judgment is impaired by emotion or inebriation may still be guided by his personal standing decisions, which in turn may reflect concern with the threat of punishment. Most of us have long ago adopted standing decisions to refrain from robbery and assault, no matter what the circumstances. An increase in the threat of punishment may have the effect of persuading more people to adopt such decisions, thus inhibiting them from acting "on impulse" when next an attractive crime opportunity arises.[4]

---

[4] John Conklin's interviews (1972) with convicted robbers in Boston yield some anecdotal evidence on impulse control: "A few offenders stated that they could not trust themselves with loaded firearms, fearing that in a confrontation with a resisting victim they might 'lose their head' and shoot" (p. 111). Conklin reported that these robbers carried unloaded or partially unloaded guns.

This defense of the rational choice model is not entirely satisfactory. The remaining concern is that those potential criminals who are sufficiently thoughtful and aware to respond to changes in the threat of punishment will, under some circumstances, violate the norms of rational decision-making in some systematic and predictable fashion. If so, then it would be possible to gain improved predictive power from a theory which took these systematic deviations from rationality into account. For example, extensive experimentation by psychologists using human subjects demonstrates that people tend to make certain predictable errors in decision-making tasks involving choices between lotteries.[5] An example is the tendency of experimental subjects to ignore low-probability events entirely—a tendency which is confirmed by the failure of most residents of flood plains to buy heavily subsidized flood insurance policies (Kunreuther and Slovic 1978). In circumstances where people do take low-probability events into account (e.g., shark attack), there is a tendency to place an inappropriately large weight on these low-probability outcomes. Most of this experimental work has not employed criminal choice problems, although the analogy should be clear. An exception is Carroll's recent report (1978) of experimental findings involving crime choice with convicted criminals as subjects, which may prove the entering wedge to further research of this sort. Carroll's perspective is worth quoting: "The proposed approach thus offers a new model of how the person decides about crime opportunities. He or she is not viewed as the 'economic person' making exhaustive and complex calculations leading to an optimal choice. Rather, it is the 'psychological person,' who makes a few simple and concrete examinations of his or her opportunities and

[5] Two interpretative summaries of this literature are provided by Kahneman and Tversky (forthcoming) and Tversky and Kahneman (1974).

Some crimes, such as robbery, are usually committed by two or more perpetrators working together. The crime decision in this case must involve some sort of group process. Social psychologists have studied group decision-making in the face of risky choices, and documented a fascinating effect known as "risky shift"; the reference is to the tendency of a group discussion to shift the preferences of members of the group toward more risky choices than they would have selected before the discussion. This effect is observed only if the individuals who make up the group are already inclined to a relatively risky choice before the discussion. See Myers and Lamm (1976) for a review of this and other "group polarization" effects.

makes guesses that can be far short of optimal" (p. 1513). The challenge to deterrence theorists is to find predictable ways in which the "psychological person" deviates from the "economic person."

2. *Threat communication.* Jacob's first objection to the rational choice model of criminal behavior concerns the reliability of the threat communication process. Rational choice models provide a framework for analyzing the effect of the individual's *perception* of the legal sanction threat on his participation in illegal activities. This relationship is of theoretical interest but is not directly policy relevant: what policy-makers need is information on the effect of *actual* (rather than perceived) criminal justice system activities on crime rates. If perceptions were sufficiently accurate, there would be no need to distinguish between, say, the actual probability of arrest for a particular criminal act and this probability as perceived by various potential criminals. If the link between actual and perceived is weak, then one can question the claim that increased enforcement efforts will deter crime. A third possibility is that public perceptions are not accurate, but do tend to be systematically related to criminal justice system activities. This possibility serves as the basis for a response to Jacob's first criticism of rational choice models of criminal behavior.

What are the important channels by which information on the certainty and severity of punishment is communicated to potential criminals? Three channels are discussed below: the media, visible presence of enforcers, and personal experience and observation. Although these channels do not provide potential criminals with accurate information, the information they do provide is systematically related to the truth. That systematic relationship is sufficient to generate predicted deterrent effects.

The media. The threats generated by criminal justice system activities are "advertised" in the media, primarily through news reporting of legislative actions, newsworthy crimes and criminal court cases, introduction of new programs and policies, etc. Occasionally, officials will launch an effort to publicize a particular law enforcement effort, such as a crackdown on speeding. A dramatic example of the possibilities for a media "advertising" campaign is the intensive publicity given the British Road Safety Act of 1967—most of the British public was aware of the provisions of this act by the time it was implemented (Ross 1973).[6] But such success is surely rare.

Verbal messages concerning specific provisions of the law, the likelihood of being caught, or both, are communicated through a variety of other means: bumper strips remind us of the 55 mph speed limit; roadside signs inform us that there are penalties for littering, that the local traffic enforcement unit employs radar, and that a residential area is protected by a neighborhood watch organization; official documents announce the legal penalties for supplying false information; and residences and stores post warning signs—"Shoplifters will be prosecuted," "Operation Identification," and so on.

The use of such official verbal communications is like other forms of advertising. The effectiveness of such messages might well be enhanced by a systematic application of the technology of using the media to inform and persuade, but Madison Avenue has not yet entered the crime control business.

Visible presence of enforcers. The proximity of police emits a potent signal that the probability of arrest for a crime committed in the immediate vicinity is high. A police cruiser eliminates driving infractions in its immediate area—an effect which is extended by CB radio communication. Private guards in stores, airports, and other public locations produce an analogous signal for would-be robbers, hijackers, and shoplifters.

The resources devoted to routine patrol activity by police would presumably be hard to justify unless this visible police presence had an effect beyond the immediate vicinity. If the police are seen frequently in an area, potential criminals may be persuaded that there is a high likelihood of arrest in that area due to presumed low police response time and the chance that

[6] The British Road Safety Act creates a precise scientific standard by which to judge whether a driver is legally "under the influence" of alcohol (viz., blood alcohol content in excess of .08 percent) and it establishes a mandatory one-year suspension of driving privileges for drivers who are convicted of violating this standard.

they will happen on the scene while the crime is in progress. While the relation between police visibility and public perceptions of their effectiveness has not been studied directly, there are a number of studies of the deterrence effect of the density of police patrol. These studies are reviewed in section IV.

Personal experience and observation. Active criminals accumulate personal experience during the course of their criminal careers; this experience surely has a powerful effect on perceptions of criminal justice system effectiveness among the group which is of greatest importance in the crime picture. If active criminals find that they are rarely arrested, unlikely to be convicted if arrested, and unlikely to be sentenced to prison terms if convicted, then they may acquire a justified sense of invulnerability. The effect of arrest and subsequent proceedings on the criminal's perception of the system's effectiveness is the key issue in the study of "special deterrence"—the deterrent effect of the punishment threat on an individual who has been convicted. An arrest can push the criminal's overall perception of the risk of punishment for crime up or down, depending on whether the consequences of arrest are more or less unpleasant than he expected. Probation and parole dispositions are interesting in this context when viewed as an effort to persuade the convict that he will be closely watched and is very likely to be imprisoned if rearrested.

Victims, witnesses, and jurors also acquire personal experience with the effectiveness of the system, and this experience may influence their perception of whether "crime pays." Furthermore, an active criminal's friends and associates may be somewhat aware of his criminal activities and their legal consequences. Thus, each arrest, court proceeding, and sentence may have a large influence on the perceptions of a relatively few people. On the other hand, the public at large is not likely to know about or be influenced by any one case, unless it is highly newsworthy.

This communication mechanism suggests that the deterrence process may often operate in a strikingly different fashion than is typically assumed in the rational choice models of criminal behavior. These models implicitly assume that each potential criminal in some fashion monitors the overall probability of apprehension and punishment for each crime type. By this assumption, each arrest and criminal disposition has some marginal (infinitesimal) effect on the perceptions of all potential criminals. This assumption seems highly unrealistic, given that even criminologists working with volumes of statistics have difficulty in measuring changes in these probabilities accurately (although the first two communication channels discussed above may provide potential criminals with some vague sense of the overall performance of the system). The alternative possibility, suggested here, can be stated as follows:

> Each arrest and disposition has a relatively large effect on the perceptions of a small number of potential criminals (including the arrestee himself), and goes essentially unnoticed by all others.

I have developed a model (Cook 1979d) which simulates the criminal behavior of a population of robbers, incorporating this assumption. The main features of this model are:

(a) At any time, a robber's perception of arrest and punishment is influenced by his own recent experience and that of a few "friends." Perceptions differ widely among robbers, because each observes only a small fraction of the actions taken by the system.

(b) Even if the true effectiveness of the system remains constant, there is considerable turnover among active robbers: robbers are deterred and "undeterred" according to their own experiences and those of their friends.

(c) An increase in the true effectiveness of the system results in a corresponding increase in the mean of robbers' perceptions of effectiveness, and an increase in the number of robbers who are deterred. These changes do not occur because the robbers observe that the system has become more effective, but rather because the likelihood that a robber will observe one or more friends apprehended is increased when the overall effectiveness of the system increases.

This model is abstract, and can be criticized for its simple, mechanistic assumptions concerning the complex phenomena of perception, communication, and criminal behavior. It does serve to demonstrate, however, that the deterrence process does not require that criminals' perceptions of the risk of punishment be accurate or that they be derived from observations of the overall performance of the criminal justice system. It may also serve the useful purpose of provoking further research into the communications processes which link official activity to individual perceptions of the threat of punishment.

The three communication channels discussed above do not exhaust the possibilities. In some instances, direct word-of-mouth communication among criminals with similar interests may be important; rumors concerning police and judicial activities circulate and at times have considerable potency. Another possibility is that potential criminals make judgments on the basis of direct observation of the extent of criminal activity in the area: if "everyone" is doing it, it must pay. A familiar example to many of us is the judgment of how much it is "safe" to exceed the speed limit; if the traffic is averaging 70 mph, then it seems safe to assume that the probability of being ticketed for driving 70 is very low.

In general, it is reasonable to assume that the relative importance of each of the several channels of information on criminal justice system effectiveness differs with the type of crime, the degree to which the potential criminal associates with criminally active people, and other factors. The link between official activities and the public's perception of them constitutes half of the deterrence story. Better understanding of this link could be exploited to the advantage of crime control efforts. Two examples are worth noting:

> The initial publicity given the British Road Safety Act apparently succeeded in giving the British public a greatly exaggerated impression of the true likelihood of being caught. While this impression evidently was corrected

after several years of experience, many lives were saved in the interim (Ross 1973).

Intensive police manning of the New York subways during high crime hours of the day initially caused a deterrent effect not only during these times but also during the rest of the day (when police manning levels were not changed). It has been suggested that this "phantom effect" could have been sustained by random changes in police assignments (Chaiken, Lawless, and Stevenson 1974).

Jacob's observations that potential criminals are poorly informed, and in some cases act impulsively, are valid but not sufficient to negate the predictions of deterrence theory. These predictions do not depend on every criminal being fully informed and rational. Limited rationality on the part of some fraction of potential criminals, combined with an information transmission mechanism that is systematic if not completely accurate, is sufficient to generate deterrent effects. Indeed, there is a great deal of evidence that criminals, like other people, respond to objective changes in their opportunities as if they were rational. It would be unfortunate to reject the claims of deterrence theory on the a priori grounds of implausibility.

On the other hand, careful descriptive studies and laboratory experiments to investigate the way in which individuals acquire information and evaluate opportunities may well yield some insights into criminal decision-making, insights that will help refine the predictions of rational choice models and even suggest means of increasing the effectiveness of the system in deterring crime.

The preceding discussion developed a basic perspective on the deterrence process, focusing on information processing and decision-making by the potential criminal. Three specific issues are discussed below from this perspective: the determinants of the extent to which an individual participates in criminal activity; the relative importance of the probability and severity of punishment in deterring crime; and the influence of sanction threats for one type of crime on the relative attractiveness of other types of crime.

C. Degree of Involvement in Crime

Previous sections have discussed the deterrence phenomenon as if criminal activity were an all-or-nothing decision. Yet criminals differ widely in their degree of involvement in crime. The number of, say, robberies committed in a year is the product of the number of active robbers and the average number of robberies committed by each. The deterrence process may influence both factors: the *rate* at which active robbers commit crimes, as well as the decision whether to "enter" the robbery "business" at all.

The basic question with respect to intensity of criminal activity is this: what limits are there on the extent of participation in illicit activity of a potential criminal who decides that it is worthwhile to commit his first offense? The discussion focuses on property crimes and three mechanisms that may act to limit the activity level of an active burglar, robber, shoplifter, or other economic criminal.

I suspect that a large proportion of the population is "opportunistic" with respect to property crimes. Without special effort, many people occasionally encounter an extraordinarily good opportunity to steal, and take advantage of it. Examples include taking towels from a hotel, walking out of a shop without paying because the checkout lines are momentarily left unattended, and so forth. We can imagine each person having a standard rule of thumb by which he judges whether such opportunities are worthwhile; the more stringent one's standards (in terms of legal risks and payoff), the less frequently will one encounter suitable opportunities in the normal course of daily activities. An increase in the effectiveness of the criminal justice system or in the severity of punishment will reduce the number of suitable opportunities for those who are opportunists, with a resulting reduction in their individual theft rates.

A more active involvement in theft would be characteristic of people we ordinarily would think of as "robbers," "burglars," "shoplifters," etc. Instead of a series of yes-or-no decisions on opportunities supplied by the individual's environment, more active thieves would be concerned with searching out and developing opportunities, and would make explicit decisions about the intensity of their illicit activity. Two limiting factors for such people are the opportunity cost of time, and the effects of increased income on the willingness to take risks.

The latter effect seems relevant to understanding employee theft and embezzlement, income tax evasion, and other economic crimes for which time is not an important input (see Allingham and Sandmo 1972 for a formal model of this sort). Given that the magnitude of the offense is positively correlated with the risk of detection and punishment (and also the severity of punishment, perhaps) the miscreant can be viewed as choosing a risk-payoff combination from a continuum of possibilities. An increase in the effectiveness of the system for detecting and punishing criminals in these cases will make this type of crime less attractive and persuade some to "drop out" completely. For those who remain active, it is not obvious whether the augmented risk of punishment will cause an increase or decrease in the rate of offending. A perverse result of increased effectiveness may occur, for example, if the increase in effectiveness is concentrated at the low end of the theft spectrum; those who do not drop out may move up the continuum, given that the difference in risk for large and small thefts has been reduced.

For crimes which require a substantial time input, such as fencing, running numbers, and prostitution, the opportunity cost of time may be an important limiting factor in the extent of involvement. The legitimate wage rate would then influence both the entry decision and the decision with respect to degree of involvement. (Ehrlich 1973 develops a model of this sort, which is criticized by Heinecke 1978a. See also Block and Heinecke 1975.) Once again there is a theoretical possibility that an increased probability of apprehension will *increase* criminal activity levels for those who do not drop out. For example, if police start arresting prostitutes more frequently, some may increase their efforts in order to maintain their standard of living while meeting the additional costs of bail, legal fees, and fines. This result is analogous to the theoretical possibility of a "backward bending labor supply curve"; there is nothing intrinsically irrational about people choosing to work harder in response to a reduction in the net rate of return to their efforts.

While these models of participation in illicit economic activities permit a theoretical possibility that an increase in the likelihood of detection will increase the overall crime rate, the actual importance of this possibility is doubtful. It seems more plausible that if more effective measures are taken against a particular type of criminal activity, the dominant effect will be to cause criminals to act with greater caution or to switch into other illicit or licit activities.

D. Certainty versus Severity of Punishment

One of the more intriguing issues in the deterrence literature is whether crime rates are more responsive to changes in the likelihood or the severity of punishment. The importance of this issue is suggested by two relevant policy dilemmas. First, sentencing authorities must allocate scarce prison capacity among felony convicts; one consideration is whether prison sentences should be relatively common but short, or relatively uncommon but long. Second, prosecutors have to decide whether to use their scarce resources to produce a high conviction rate with relatively low-quality convictions (through generous offers in plea bargaining), or to concentrate their resources on gaining high-quality convictions of a relatively few defendants while dismissing the remaining cases. The first alternative in each case is compatible with the commonly held view that the likelihood of punishment has a greater deterrent impact on crime rates than does the severity of punishment.

A precise illustrative statement of this hypothesis can be expressed as follows:

> A 10 percent increase in the average severity of punishment for a crime will have a smaller deterrent effect than a 10 percent increase in the likelihood of punishment.

For example, if the only form of punishment for convicted robbers is imprisonment, an increase in average sentence from three years to 3.3 years will have less deterrent effect than an increase in likelihood of imprisonment from .050 to .055.

The usual assumptions made in economic analysis of decision-making under uncertainty support this claim when the punishment is in the form of imprisonment, but support the opposite conclusion when the punishment is a fine. The argument behind these conclusions can be illustrated by the following two "lotteries" involving prison sentences. In the first lottery, there is a 10 percent chance of receiving a one-year prison sentence; the second lottery offers a 5 percent chance of a two-year prison sentence. These two lotteries have the same expected value (one-tenth of a year in prison), but most people would not view them as equally threatening; if two years in prison is not viewed as being twice as bad as one year, then the second lottery would be preferred. If so, then the first lottery would have a greater deterrent value. In general, we expect that increases in the probability of imprisonment, coupled with proportionate reductions in the prison term, will increase the deterrent value of the threat of punishment.

The second example involves punishment in the form of a fine. Suppose now that the prison terms in the two lotteries specified above are replaced with fines of $1,000 and $2,000 respectively. Once again the two lotteries have the same expected value ($100). If people are risk-averse, a common assumption in economic theory, they will prefer the first lottery (a $2,000 loss is subjectively more than twice as bad as a $1,000 loss to a risk-averse person). However, Tversky and Kahneman (1974) report that in laboratory experiments most subjects are *not* risk-averse with respect to financial losses, and would in fact choose the smaller probability of a proportionately larger fine. Once again, then, the first lottery should have greater deterrent value, and the conventional wisdom (among criminologists, not necessarily economists), regarding certainty and severity of punishment is reaffirmed. While this sort of theoretical analysis and laboratory experimentation seems rather remote from criminal behavior, it is interesting to observe that this type of evidence does support the conventional wisdom.

The claim that certain punishment is a more effective deterrent than severe punishment is often buttressed by an assertion that crime rates are unresponsive to variations in severity. If true, the sentencing authorities could reduce average sentences a great deal without noticeable effect on the crime rate. The most compelling issue, and the one given the greatest scholarly attention, is whether capital punishment is a greater deterrent to murder than a long prison term. At the other end of the spectrum are questions concerning the potential loss of deterrent effect resulting from the increased use of diversion programs, suspended sentences, and fines in the place of incarceration.

It is commonly acknowledged that the threat of a more severe penalty will cause defendants to put more effort and resources into their defense. Indeed, one of the social costs of capital punishment, mandatory sentencing provisions, and related efforts to increase the severity of punishment is that these cases take up an increased portion of court resources through appeals and other defense efforts to resist conviction. It seems implausible that the severity of punishment should be highly salient to the criminal after arrest but not before.

While we would expect a rational criminal to respond in some degree to increases in the severity of punishment, it is certainly plausible that the marginal deterrent effect of increasing prison sentences declines rapidly as the length of the sentence increases, due to the tendency of people to discount the future. A simple mathematical model may be helpful in illustrating this point.[7] Suppose that an individual assigns one unit of "disutility" to a

---

[7] The model postulates that the individual's subjective evaluation of the prison terms is equal to the sum of the disutilities discounted to the present. If the disutility of one year in prison is denoted d, and the discounted present value of n years in prison is denoted D_n, then

$$D_n = \sum_{t=1}^{n} d \left(\frac{1}{1.15}\right)^{t-1}.$$

The value chosen for d does not influence the value of the ratios reported in the text, and was set equal to 1.

year in prison, and has a time discount rate of 15 percent per annum. It would then be true, in present value terms, that a two-year prison term has about 87 percent greater disutility than a one-year term. However, under these assumptions a twenty-year term has only 25 percent greater disutility than a ten-year term. It is plausible, then, that increasing the severity of punishment when punishment is mild may have a much greater deterrent effect (even proportionately speaking) than increasing severity when punishment is already severe.

E. Substitutes and Complements

Establishing a rational sentencing policy, and appropriate priorities in prosecution and police investigation, is complicated by the possibility that variations in the threat of punishment for one type of crime may affect the incidence of other crime types, via two mechanisms. First, given limited police, court, and corrections resources, increasing the priority given to one type of crime necessarily entails a reduction in the priority given one or more other crime types. Second, in deciding whether to commit one type of crime, criminals will be influenced by the legal threat not only to that crime type but also to related types of crime. The latter mechanism must be given consideration in any complete characterization of the deterrence process. An analogy from the economic theory of consumer demand provides insight and useful terminology for discussing this mechanism. Suppose the price of gasoline increases 50 percent due to a change in policy by the OPEC cartel. The primary effect would be to reduce the quantity of gasoline purchased. Secondary effects include an increase in the demands for public transportation, fuel-efficient autos, and central city housing, and a decrease in demand for luxury autos and suburban housing. Commodities which become more desirable when the price of gasoline increases are known as "substitutes" for gasoline; those which become less desirable are "complements." While the analogy is by no means perfect, I will use these terms to discuss the secondary effects of a change in the threat level to a particular type of crime.

1. *Substitutes.* Various types of property crime are presumably

substitutes for each other. Recidivism data demonstrate that there is a great deal of crime switching among active criminals; for example, 22 percent of men arrested for burglary in the District of Columbia in 1973 were subsequently arrested for robbery within three years (compared with 33 percent who were rearrested for burglary) (Cook and Nagin 1979). The Rand study of self-reported crime by a sample of forty-nine incarcerated robbers found that they admitted having collectively committed 1,492 auto thefts, 2,331 burglaries, 855 robberies, and 1,018 other serious thefts during their criminal careers (Petersilia, Greenwood, and Lavin 1978). Given this sort of versatility, one would expect that an increase in the relative law enforcement effectiveness against robbery would result in an increase in other types of theft crimes. Variations in other sorts of crime-specific deterrents would be predicted to have the same effect: if shopkeepers arm themselves, then thieves may switch from commercial robbery to commercial burglary; increased use of burglar alarms would have the opposite effect.

A second dimension to the substitution phenomenon is geographic displacement. A large increase in the number of police assigned to one precinct in a city may result in some increase in crimes committed in neighboring precincts. A houseowner who posts an Operation Identification sticker increases the burglary risk to his stickerless neighbor. Intensive police manning of the subway system may cause an increase in taxicab and bus robberies. Exact fare systems on buses may increase the robbery risk to convenience stores. I know of no studies of crime displacement across state lines or between distant metropolitan areas, but it is likely that some buyers of illicit merchandise (drugs, machine guns, stolen goods) travel some distance in order to take advantage of more lax enforcement in another jurisdiction. Organized crime operations would be expected to locate their activities so as to minimize legal risks, to the extent that other considerations permit; an example in this context would be the decision of where to land illicit drug shipments smuggled in from South America or Mexico.

A very important aspect of the substitution phenomenon frequently arises in the design of criminal sentencing policy. It is thought that the structure of criminal sentences must include a strong marginal deterrent to the use of threat or violence to reduce the likelihood of violent resistance to arrest. If the typical sentence for robbery without violence is a long term of imprisonment, robbers may be more inclined to kill their victims and other witnesses. Defendants who are faced with the likelihood of conviction and severe punishment will be more tempted than others to jump bail and intimidate witnesses, knowing that even if they are caught there is little more that the system can do to them; this is, of course, the reasoning behind denying defendants the right to bail in capital cases.

Zimring and Hawkins (1973) discuss this aspect of sentencing policy in terms of the "fortress" and the "stepladder." The "fortress" approach is to erect a high and more or less uniform "barrier" around the domain of criminal activity. The "stepladder" approach adjusts the punishment to the seriousness of the crime, in the hope that if the potential criminal *does* decide to act, the penal code will provide an adequate incentive to limit the seriousness of his crimes. If the preceding discussion of the deterrent effect of changes in the length of prison term is correct, the bottom "rungs" of the stepladder must be kept low in order to allow "room" for effective differences in sentencing between robbery, robbery with victim injury, and robbery murder; the usual sentence for robbery should not be more than a year or two in prison. This type of policy must be evaluated in the context of priority-setting by police and prosecutors—if sentences are relatively uniform, then a greater burden is placed on officials to create a stepladder effect through gradations in the likelihood of arrest and conviction.

2. Complements. Complementarity arguments have been extremely important in motivating criminal justice policy in the area of heroin and handguns. A key argument for vigorous law enforcement efforts to interdict the flow of heroin and other illicit drugs is that an increase in the "effective price"[8] of such drugs resulting from law enforcement efforts will reduce the

[8] A term coined by Mark Moore (1973), and discussed in his article.

incidence of property crimes. Similarly, the crimes of illegal acquisition, possession, and carrying of handguns are thought to be complementary to robbery and murder. Both these claims of complementarity are highly controversial, of course, and even if there is such a relation it must be demonstrated that these roundabout techniques for reducing property crimes or murder are the most effective use of resources against these crimes.

There are some very interesting sorts of interrelations within market-oriented complexes of criminal activity. Typically illegal commodities markets will involve suppliers, middlemen, and customers. In prostitution, they are, respectively, the prostitutes, pimps, and johns; in heroin, they are the poppy growers and heroin processors, the importers and retailers, and the users; in burglary they are the burglars, the fences, and the purchasers of stolen merchandise. In each case, we would expect that law enforcement efforts directed at any one of the three types of actors would reduce the amount of criminal activity by the other two types of actors. For example, a crackdown on fencing would lower the price that fences pay to burglars and make fences generally more cautious in dealing with both burglars and customers. The result would be to reduce the rate of return to burglary, thereby causing a reduction in the number of burglaries and ultimately a reduction in the illegal purchase of stolen merchandise.[9]

The question for law enforcement officials is what strategy will be most effective in disrupting the market which supports each of these activities. In the case of burglary, for example, prosecutors can bargain with burglary defendants to gain convictions of fences, or vice versa. Undercover police can pose as fences to identify and collect evidence against burglars, or al-

---

[9] Strictly speaking, burglary and fencing are not "complementary" activities in the sense this term is used in economic theory. An increased legal threat to fencing does not *directly* cause a reduction in burglary, as would be true if they were complementary crimes. The reduction in burglary is an indirect effect of the crackdown on fencing, the direct cause being the reduction in the price paid by the fence.

Recent literature on prospects for combating fencing include Blakey and Goldsmith (1976) and Walsh (1976). Klockars (1974) provides a fascinating description of fencing activities.

ternatively pose as burglars to facilitate arrests against fences. Similar strategic choices are available in illicit drugs and prostitution. The correct strategy should be dictated by the consideration of which of the roles in these illicit markets are most vulnerable to available techniques of law enforcement.

II. Empirical Study of the Deterrence Process

The discussion of theoretical issues in deterrence research presented above suggests a wide-ranging agenda for empirical work, including basic research on decision-making under uncertainty, on communications processes, and on the structure of illicit markets. The great bulk of the empirical deterrence literature, however, has been concerned with deriving estimates of the impact of criminal justice system activities on crime rates, and it is this body of applied research that I review here and in section III.

Measuring deterrence effects outside of the laboratory requires data on criminal opportunities and criminal behavior for a number of units of observation. Almost all studies have used some geographic entity as the unit of observation—precincts, cities, states, or the entire nation. The empirical study of deterrence has thus been concerned with aggregate rather than individual behavior. Practical problems of collecting data on individuals have prevented field studies of microbehavior.

There are two basic approaches to the empirical study of the deterrence process, which I label "criminal opportunity" and "policy impact." This distinction can be explained with the aid of a simple diagram:

$$\text{actions (policy)} \xrightarrow{\ \ A\ \ } \text{criminal opportunities} \xrightarrow{\ \ B\ \ } \text{crime rates}$$

In the diagram, the causal connection between crime rates and crime control policy (broadly construed to include the criminal law, resource levels, priorities, and so forth) is broken down into two links. Link A represents the effect of policy on the quality of criminal opportunities; this can be viewed as a production process in which criminal justice system inputs "produce" threats of punishment. The probability and severity of punishment associated with each criminal opportunity thus constitute the vector of outputs of the system. Link B represents the deterrence effect of threats of punishment on crime rates. The criminal opportunity studies attempt to estimate the strength of this deterrence relationship for a variety of crime types. In many cases these studies also include a separate estimate of the production relationship (link A), so that it is possible by combining the two relationships to derive an estimate of policy on crime. Policy impact studies, on the other hand, estimate the effect of policy on crime directly, without considering the intervening variables characterizing the quality of criminal opportunities.

It would seem that the criminal opportunity studies are the more informative of the two categories, especially if the objective is to learn about the deterrence process rather than about policy impacts. However, these studies, unlike the policy impact studies, require the use of an index of the quality of criminal opportunities, or "threat level." I argue below that the measures of threat level actually used in these studies are not valid, and furthermore that the data necessary to calculate a valid measure are not usually available. In short, this approach appears to be a dead end, in spite of the numerous studies of this sort which have appeared in the economics and sociology literature during the last decade. Before justifying this rather extreme claim, I first give a more complete description of the approach and its intellectual history. A review of the policy impact literature is left for section III.

A. A Decade of "Criminal Opportunity" Studies

Jack Gibbs published the first article reporting a statistical analysis of this sort in 1968. Gibbs simply related (by a contingency table method) the murder rate with a variable intended to measure the probability of punishment—namely, the number of convicts sent to prison for murder divided by the number of murders—using cross-section data by state for 1959–61. He also related the state murder rates with the average prison terms served by incarcerated murder convicts in each state. He interpreted his results as evidence that murder is indeed deterrable.

Gibbs's technique was very primitive by reigning standards for the statistical analysis of nonexperimental data, since it did not attempt to control for other variables which influence murder, and took no account of the possibility that the causal relation between crime and punishment may go in both directions. The first state-of-the-art study was incorporated in Isaac Ehrlich's thesis in 1970, subsequently published in 1973—the same year as Sjoquist, and Carr-Hill and Stern, published very similar studies. These studies, while much more sophisticated than Gibbs's, used measures of the probability and severity of punishment similar to his. A paradigm was established by this work which has been employed since by a number of economists and sociologists. These studies have employed a variety of data sets, including state-level data for recent census years, data on large cities, data on precincts of New York and counties in California, and similar data sets for Canada and the United Kingdom.[10] The results of these studies have for the most part been favorable to the deterrence doctrine, seemingly documenting a statistically significant and often rather large effect of the "probability of punishment" as measured on each of the seven FBI index crimes. The results for the deterrent effect of punishment severity have generally been weaker and less consistently significant. However, Ehrlich's (1975) subsequent and highly sophisticated study of the marginal deterrent effect of capital punishment on murder estimated a deterrent effect so large that only the most confirmed abolitionist could claim it to be irrelevant—one way of summarizing his result is that each execution saves eight lives. This study received widespread attention, and was submitted to the Supreme Court as part of the solicitor general's brief in *Gregg v. Georgia*, 428 U.S. 153 (1976).[11]

The great potential importance of this work, and particularly the intense controversy engendered by Ehrlich's study of capital punishment, culminated in the formation of the National Research Council's Panel on Research on Deterrent and Incapacitative Effects. This panel performed a thorough review of all the

[10] Nagin (1978) includes a very useful table which summarizes these studies.
[11] Bailey (1978) has a brief history of the use of this and other such studies.

major reports published at that time, including replications of Ehrlich's work and a highly technical critique of the problems with the econometric paradigm employed in this literature. The panel's conclusion was decidedly negative: "The major challenge for future research is to estimate the magnitude of the effects of different sanctions on various crime types, an issue on which none of the evidence available thus far provides very useful guidance" (Blumstein, Cohen, and Nagin 1978, p. 7). The panel did not choose to reject the basic approach, however, but instead encouraged scholars to develop better data sets and seek methods for eliminating certain biases which they consider damaging to the validity of the results (pp. 46–50).

It is easy to criticize any nonexperimental statistical technique which employs error-ridden data to assess some aspect of a complex and poorly understood process. Much more difficult is to judge whether the criticisms are sufficiently important and damaging to warrant rejection of available findings, or even abandonment of the entire approach. If there is no practical alternative for studying the phenomenon, the relevant question is whether the statistical technique in question can generate results which are more reliable than intuition alone. In this case I accept the panel's conclusion as cited, but would go even farther than they in discouraging future use of the Ehrlich paradigm. My conclusion is influenced by the numerous problems discussed in the panel report and elsewhere,[12] but stems primarily from apparently insuperable difficulties with measuring the quality of criminal opportunities.

B. Measuring the Quality of Criminal Opportunities

Since the primary motivation for criminal opportunity studies is to estimate the response of crime rates to the probability and

[12] Studies of the deterrent effect that use cross-section or times series data on jurisdictions, such as those that fit the Ehrlich paradigm, suffer from a variety of statistical problems, including: (1) the poor quality of the data on crime; (2) the difficulty of distinguishing between the effect of punishment on crime rates, and the effect of crime rates on the likelihood and severity of punishment; (3) the difficulty in controlling for the variety of factors that influence crime rates. These problems are discussed below in section III, and are developed in detail in Blumstein, Cohen, and Nagin (1978), Cook (1977), and Brier and Fienberg (1978) among other places.

severity of punishment, obtaining valid measures of these variables is crucial to the whole enterprise. In practice, the measure of probability used in this literature is some type of clearance rate, most commonly the arrest rate or the ratio of prison admissions to crimes reported to the police. While these clearance rates may *look* like probability measures (they usually lie between zero and one), they cannot be literally interpreted as such. After all, the individual crimes reflected in these measures are not homogeneous but, rather, differ widely with respect to a number of factors. For example, the 1960 ratio of prison admissions for murder to murders committed in New York was .54 (see Vandaele 1978a, p. 331), but the probabilities of punishment for the hundreds of murders reflected in this ratio ranged from near zero (in the case of some skillfully planned gangland executions) to near one (for, say, murders of family members). If the clearance rate is not a measure of a single probability of punishment, then what does it measure? At best, it can be viewed as a measure of the *average* probability of punishment for crimes committed.[13] Is it appropriate to use the average probability as a sort of index of the overall effectiveness of the criminal justice system?

In fact, the clearance rate fails even as an index of overall effectiveness, because the clearance rate reflects not only criminal justice system activities but also the many factors (including the system's effectiveness) which influence the care and judgment exercised by criminals. (The argument here was first made in Cook 1979a and elaborated in Cook 1979c.) For example, robbers would be expected to adapt to an increase in the potential effectiveness of the system in solving robbery cases and gaining convictions of robbery defendants; if, under the new more effective regime, robbers tend to be more selective in choosing vic-

---

[13] The major source of inaccuracy in the clearance rate is in the denominator —the number of crimes. Cook (1977, p. 189) compares clearance rates for burglary using two measures of the number of burglaries committed: the "burglaries known to the police" in the Uniform Crime Reports, and the burglary rate estimates derived from the crime surveys in twenty-six cities sponsored by the Law Enforcement Assistance Administration. The differences tend to be large and variable.

tims and more cautious in their modus operandi, the observed change in the clearance rate may be misleadingly small.

Consider the following artificial example. Suppose that Crime City makes arrests and convictions in 10 percent of its street robberies and 20 percent of its commercial robberies in 1980. In 1981, the Crime City police organize a hidden camera program to combat commercial robberies, which is successful in increasing the probability of arrest and conviction for such robberies to 30 percent. This increase in effectiveness has a strong deterrent effect on commercial robberies, with some displacement effect to street robberies. Suppose the relevant numbers look like the data in table 1.

Usually the available data would not be detailed enough to permit separate analysis of commercial and street robbery. A statistician may therefore conclude that the hidden camera program had no effect—after all, the overall clearance rate did not change. The problem here is not that the clearance rate is inaccurately measured (although that too is usually a problem in practice)—the problem is that the clearance rate is not a valid index of the true effectiveness of the criminal justice system. In this example, the true increase in effectiveness had no effect on the clearance rate. If other numbers had been used, the observed clearance rate could have gone up—or even down.

Economists have studied this type of index number problem rather extensively (Fisher and Shell 1972). One conceptually simple solution is to construct a Laspeyres index. The Consumer Price Index is of this sort. In my numerical example, a Laspeyres

TABLE 1

	1980		1981	
	# of Robberies	Clearance Rate	# of Robberies	Clearance Rate
Commercial............	100	.20	50	.30
Street................	100	.10	135	.10
Total.................	200	.15	185	.15

index for the clearance rate would use the 1980 mix of crimes as weights in calculating clearance indexes for both 1980 and 1981. This index would be .15 in 1980 and .20 in 1981, the increase reflecting the actual increase in the effectiveness of the police. But there is little hope for the forseeable future that the detailed data necessary to construct such an index will become available.[14]

The only promising prospect for criminal opportunity studies that I can see involves "target-specific" analyses of victimization rates. We can imagine a study of bank robbery within a jurisdiction, for example, which characterized the robbery opportunities provided by each bank in terms of an assortment of attributes including presence of a guard, ease of escaping from the scene, use of hidden cameras, and average amount of loot available from cashiers. The extent to which these variables explain differences in victimization rates is a measure of the deterrent effect of these dimensions of the quality of bank robbery opportunities. Similar studies could be conducted of robbery and burglary victimization rates for other types of commercial targets, of shoplifting where the quality and display of the merchandise were the key measures, and of location-specific traffic violations as a function of the characteristics of the location. Such studies would yield useful information on the deterrence process.

III. Lessons from Policy Innovations

Major changes in criminal law and policy, if properly evaluated, can serve as object lessons concerning criminal behavior and the performance of the system. In particular, policy innovations which are intended to change the threat level can teach us about the process of threat production and the responsiveness of criminals to changes in the threat level. A number of such evaluations have been published during the last decade. These studies represent the beginnings of an empirical basis for deterrence-oriented policy formation.

Policy innovations which have been evaluated in terms of their

---

[14] A more complete discussion of the "endogeneity" problem in the use of the clearance rate is in Cook (1979a). Manski (1978) discusses some closely related technical issues.

deterrent effects include changes in the substantive law (legalization of abortions, change in the speed limit, reduction of legal drinking age), changes in resource allocation (increased preventive patrol, career criminals prosecution units), and changes in the severity of criminal sentencing provisions. (Zimring 1978 provides a summary of several of these studies.) Evaluations of these innovations have much in common with evaluations of innovations in other areas of social policy, and my review draws on this larger context to some extent.

A. Comparison with the Criminal Opportunity Studies

The main objective of the criminal opportunity studies, the deterrence research fitting the Ehrlich paradigm, is to isolate and measure the effect of the threat level on crime rates. Absent a valid index of the threat level, this objective is beyond reach. The alternative, incorporated in the policy impact studies, is to analyze the deterrence effects of factors which are thought to determine the threat level—the criminal code, the quality and quantity of committed resources, the organization of these resources, the quality of civilian cooperation, and so on. Whatever deterrent effect is generated by changes in these factors can be assumed to stem from the induced change in the threat level, but the magnitude of this change is unknown.

An example serves to illustrate this limitation of the policy impact evaluations. In 1966, the New York Police Department increased the number of patrolmen assigned to the Twentieth Precinct by about 40 percent. S. J. Press (1971) conducted a thorough and sophisticated evaluation of the impact of this increase, and concluded that it reduced "inside" felonies (those which are invisible from the street) by 5 percent and outside felonies 36 percent during the year following the change. These estimates are certainly interesting and relevant to evaluating the worth of the increase in police manpower. However, there is no way of measuring the change in the threat levels to inside and outside felonies, so it is not possible to derive an estimate of the responsiveness of crime to the threat level from this report. (Press does report the changes in the arrest rates for inside and outside felonies, but, as explained above, the arrest rate is not a valid indicator for the threat level.) Given the large reduction in the number of outside felonies, we can conclude that the extra police were very productive in terms of augmenting the threat level, that the outside felony rate is highly responsive to changes in the threat level, or some combination of the two. This ambiguity frustrates the search for evidence on the degree to which crime is deterrable in the abstract sense formulated in the Ehrlich paradigm.

B. Three Approaches to Policy Evaluation

Three basic approaches to policy evaluation are distinguished by the type of data being used: (1) cross-section comparisons of jurisdictions which differ with respect to some dimension of criminal justice policy (e.g., police per capita, use of capital punishment for murder); (2) time series analysis of crime in a single jurisdiction before and after the adoption of some policy innovation; and (3) analysis of experimental field trials, involving random assignment of units to different "treatments" to test the efficacy of some policy innovation. Not all evaluations fit neatly into one of these three categories, but this partition is an adequate framework for discussing the relevant methodological issues.

The cross-section analyses involve correlating crime rates with "input" levels across jurisdictions. Several studies have analyzed interstate differences in crime rates as a function of the number of police per capita and other factors in order to measure the marginal deterrent effect of additional policy resources (see, e.g., Greenwood and Wadycki 1973 and Swimmer 1974). Several other studies have attempted to measure the impact of particular criminal code provisions (e.g., gun control ordinances, capital punishment) by systematic comparison of jurisdictions governed by these provisions with those which lack them (see, e.g., Maggadino n.d. on gun control).

The most frequently used approach is the "before and after" analysis of a policy innovation in a single jurisdiction. A partial listing of such studies published since 1970 is given in table 2. Some of these innovations were adopted as an experiment, in-

TABLE 2
Policy Impact Studies

Source	Intervention	Process Measures	Outcome Measures	Controls	Evidence of Deterrent Effect?
Williams et al. (1975)	Reduction in legal minimum drinking age from 21 to 18 in Michigan, Wisconsin, and Ontario.	None.	Drivers under 21 involved in fatal motor vehicle crashes: total; night time only; single-vehicle crash only.	Corresponding numbers for neighboring states.	Yes, but small.
Ross (1973)	The British Road Safety Act of 1967: creates "scientific" measures of drunkenness (.08% alcohol in blood) and mandates that suspect drivers submit to breathalyzer tests. Massive publicity campaign preceded implementation. Sanctions for conviction include a one year mandatory license suspension.	1. Survey of public knowledge of new law. 2. Number of breath tests administered. 3. Number of drivers charged under this and related laws. 4. Alcoholic beverage sales.	1. Total road casualties and fatalities. 2. Fatalities and serious injuries during peak drinking hours. 3. Fraction of drivers killed in accidents who were drunk.	1. Time series prior to enactment. 2. (a) Time series prior to enactment on same measure. (b) Fatalities and serious injuries for other times of the week. 3. Average for same measure prior to enactment.	Yes, strong initially.

TABLE 2 (*Continued*)

Source	Intervention	Process Measures	Outcome Measures	Controls	Evidence of Deterrent Effect?
Ross (1977)	Chief constable's order for stricter enforcement of British Road Safety Act in Cheshire, September 1975.	Number of breath-alyzer tests.	1. Fatalities and serious injuries. 2. Total crashes during drinking hours.	1. Time series before and after intervention. 2. (a) Time series before and after intervention. (b) Time series on total crashes during other times.	Yes.
Robertson, Rich, and Ross (1973)	Supervising judge's order to Chicago magistrates to sentence drunk drivers to 7-day jail terms, December 1970 to June 1971.	1. Numbers of arrests for DWI. 2. Conviction rates for DWI. 3. Number of 7-day jail sentences for all traffic-related offenses.	1. Auto fatality rate by month. 2. Pedestrian fatality rate.	1. Time series on both Chicago and Milwaukee. 2. Time series on both Chicago and Milwaukee.	No.
Landes (1978)	Mandatory pre-board screening of airline passengers and carry-on luggage in U.S., 1973.	Proportion of offenders apprehended within 12 months.	Number of domestic hijackings.	1. Time series of domestic hijackings. 2. Hijackings in other countries.	Yes.

TABLE 2 (*Continued*)

Source	Intervention	Process Measures	Outcome Measures	Controls	Evidence of Deterrent Effect?
Chaiken, Lawless, and Stevenson (1974)	Tripling of N.Y.C. Transit Police force in 1975, with the additional men placed in stations and on trains from 8 pm to 4 am.	1. Police manning levels. 2. Arrest rates.	1. Total felonies, total robberies, etc. 2. Felonies, robberies during 8 pm to 4 am period.	1. Time series prior to intervention. 2. Felonies, robberies during 4 am to 8 pm period.	Yes.
Beha (1977)	The Bartley-Fox Amendment creating a mandatory one year minimum prison sentence for carrying a firearm without a permit in Massachusetts. Implemented April 1975.	Various measures of arrests and dispositions of gun-related cases.	1. Number of FID cards and carrying licenses issued. 2. Fractions of aggravated assaults, homicides, and robberies involving firearms.	1. Time series prior to amendment. 2. Time series prior to amendment.	Yes.
Joint Committee on New York Drug Law Evaluation (1978)	The "Rockefeller" Drug Laws 1973, lengthening prescribed minimum prison sentences and creating a one year mandatory minimum sentence for heroin dealers.	Various measures of arrests and dispositions of heroin-related offenses in New York City.	1. Serum hepatitis cases and narcotics related deaths, N.Y.C. 2. Admissions to detoxification program and methadone maintenance in N.Y.C.	1. Time series, and corresponding series for Baltimore, Washington, D.C., and Philadelphia. 2. Time series.	No.

TABLE 2 (*Continued*)

Source	Intervention	Process Measures	Outcome Measures	Controls	Evidence of Deterrent Effect?
Press (1971)	Experimental increase of police manpower in New York City's 20th Precinct by 40 percent in October 1966.	Arrests for felonies and misdemeanors.	The differences in reported number of crimes between a previous "low man-power" and a "high power" period, weekly average seasonally adjusted. Calculated for 10 crime categories.	Corresponding differences calculated for groups of similar precincts. The pre-cincts included in the control groups differ according to crime category.	Yes, for outdoor crimes.
Zimring (1972)	Decriminalization of abortion in Hawaii, 1970.	Number of legal abortions and ratio of abortions to live births, 1970–71.	1. Change in number of live births between 1969 and 1970. 2. Change in ratio of illegitimate to legitimate births, 1969 to 1970. 3. Change in number of live births by ethnic group.	1. Corresponding change in Oregon and California.	No.
Schwartz and Clarren (1977)	Experimental adoption of team policing in one district of Cincinnati, 1973.	Arrest data, measures of police-community relations.	1. Crime rates, mea-sured by survey and by crimes reported by police.	1. Time series. 2. Crime rates in other districts of Cincinnati.	Yes, for burglary only.

cluding the team policing study in Cincinnati (Schwartz and Clarren 1977), the field interrogation study in San Diego (Boydstun 1975), and the increase in the Twentieth Precinct police force in New York (Press 1971). But these "experiments" lack most of the features of a complete experimental design, which would have to involve many geographic units sorted randomly between an experimental group (in which the policy innovation is implemented) and a control group.

A controlled experimental design with random assignment is generally viewed as the most reliable source of information about the effects of social innovations, and has been used on a large scale on subjects as diverse as the Salk vaccine tests and the negative income tax experiments. The use of this technique in criminal justice research has largely been limited to correctional programming studies, focused on rehabilitation effects. A partial (and famous) exception in the deterrence research is the Kansas City Preventive Patrol experiment (Kelling and Pate 1974).

C. Methodological Issues

The three approaches to policy impact evaluation share certain methodological concerns. A discussion of these issues serves as a more useful review of this literature than a summary of results, because policy impact evaluation has more promise than past. My discussion here focuses on problems of measurement and causation.

1. *Measurement of outcomes.* The first and often most difficult problem in outcomes measurement is obtaining *reliable* measures of target variables. The outcomes measures in the evaluation of a deterrence-oriented policy innovation are usually crime rates of some sort. A majority of relatively serious common law crimes are reported to the police, and these crime reports ordinarily are the most readily available data for measuring the impact of policy innovation. Problems arise with reliance on reported crime as a measure because reporting rates differ across jurisdictions and over time, and because the crime count is subject to manipulation by officials. For example, Chaiken (1978) discovered that the official records on subway crime in New York were

counterfeit to some extent, due to a police official's zeal to demonstrate the effectiveness of intensive police manning in reducing
subway crime. Even without conscious manipulation of the data,
large changes in police presence in an area may cause systematic
biases in the data, due to the possibility that police visibility may
influence reporting rates by citizens. For this reason some of the
more careful studies have supplemented police data with victimization surveys (e.g., Schwartz and Clarren's 1977 report on the
Cincinnati Team Policing Experiment; see table 2).

Victimless crimes pose a still greater measurement problem
because they only become known to authorities by accident or
by dint of police undercover work. A number of the studies
listed in table 2 have resolved this problem by using available
data on proxy variables thought to be highly correlated with the
incidence of the crime in question. The three studies of drunk
driving crackdowns and the study of changes in the minimum
legal drinking age all used readily available data on traffic accidents and casualties. Beha's study (1977) of the Bartley-Fox
Amendment employed robbery, assault, and murder data; he
argues that if the crime defined in the amendment (carrying a gun
without a license) were reduced by the harsh penalties it stipulated, the rate of violent crime would also be reduced. Zimring's
study (1972) of the legalization of abortion in Hawaii employed
data on the live birth rate as the basis for inferring the number
of illegal abortions before legalization.

These proxies are plausible indirect measures of the victimless
crimes targeted by these policy innovations. The real virtue of
these proxies, however, is that they are of direct policy interest
in themselves. Indeed, preventing serious traffic accidents is the
raison d'être of drunk driving statutes, and preventing violent
crimes was certainly the main purpose of the Bartley-Fox Amendment.

A second important issue in the measurement of outcomes is
specificity. The usual categories in which crimes are counted are
often too crude to provide sensitive indicators of policy impact.
Several important examples come to mind. First, a change in statutory sentencing severity, as in the Rockefeller drug laws or

the Bartley-Fox Amendment, usually exempts juveniles. The measure of severity used in most studies fitting the Ehrlich paradigm, average prison sentence, is applicable only to adults and the rare juvenile defendant who is waived to adult court. Given that a large percentage of serious crimes is committed by juveniles, an outcome measure which does not distinguish between juveniles and adults will tend to be an insensitive and "noisy" indicator of the effect of the policy.

Studies of the deterrent effect of capital punishment[15] almost always use some aggregate criminal homicide measure as the indicator of impact, even though the capital sanction is ordinarily reserved for felony murderers and other relatively small subsets of homicide defendants, and would not be expected to deter the sorts of homicide which constitute the majority in these statistics.

The importance of using as specific a crime measure as possible is that most policy innovations have a small effect at best,[16] and this effect can easily be submerged and lost in the normal fluctuations of an insensitive indicator. Part of the persuasiveness of Ross's evaluation (1973) of the British Road Safety Act results from his use of highly sensitive indicators. Instead of limiting his study to the gross accident rate, he distinguishes between fatalities, casualties, and minor accidents (accidents associated with drunk driving are more serious on the average than others); further, he distinguishes between accident rates during common drinking hours and accident rates on weekdays. Press (1971) expected (correctly) that the increase in police manning of the Twentieth Precinct would have a greater effect on outdoor, visible felonies than on indoor felonies, and analyzed these two crime types separately. Zimring (1972) distinguishes between illegitimate and legitimate birth rates in his study of abortion. Beha (1977) missed a good bet in failing to distinguish between firearms assaults committed at home, and those committed away from home. The latter necessitated carrying a gun in violation

---

[15] Sellin's studies of capital punishment are critiqued in Ehrlich (1975), Cook (1977), and Klein, Forst, and Filatov (1978).

[16] This generalization is documented and discussed in Gilbert, Light, and Mosteller (1975).

of Bartley-Fox, and so the rate of such assaults should be the more sensitive to the new law.

The third important issue in outcomes measurement is *inclusiveness*. A complete evaluation of a policy innovation requires inclusion of all likely outcomes which are of concern to deterrence theorists or policy makers. The most common issue here is displacement—a policy innovation targeted on one geographic area or one type of crime will, in addition to a possible deterrent effect, displace criminals to other areas or crime types. Press studied crime rates in precincts bordering the twentieth; Williams et al. (1975) studied accident rates for youthful drivers in regions bordering states which had lowered their legal minimum drinking age; Chaiken, Lawless, and Stevenson (1974) studied the effects of nighttime intensive police manning on the New York subways on daytime subway crime rates and on robbery rates for buses and taxis. Obvious substitution possibilities resulting from Bartley-Fox include an increase in nongun violent crime, a substitution of more vulnerable targets for commercial targets in robbery, and a substitution of burglary for robbery. In general, predicting the sorts of displacement effects that are worth studying requires insight into criminal behavior and criminal opportunities.

2. Measurement of inputs. A change in law or policy, however important it looks in theory, may be undermined or transformed during its implementation. It is important to study the implementation of a policy innovation to facilitate interpretation of measured outcomes. In some cases a careful analysis of implementation has revealed that the criminal justice system has absorbed an apparently important innovation with hardly a trace, thus explaining the lack of effect on crime.

The Kansas City Preventive Patrol Experiment (Kelling and Pate 1974) is a case in point. In this experiment, fifteen contiguous beats were divided into three groups; five beats were to receive intensive preventive patrol, in five a normal level of preventive patrol prevailed, and in the remaining five preventive patrol was eliminated. While this experimental design suggests that visible police presence would differ widely among the three groups of beats, Larson (1975) has argued that this was not so in practice. Police made it a point to patrol the perimeter of the "no patrol" beats, and to respond to calls in a highly visible fashion in these beats. A further indication of the lack of effect is that police response time to calls did not differ among the three experimental groups.

The Rockefeller drug laws, which increased statutory penalties for dealing in heroin and other drugs, had little effect on actual sentencing: the percentage of such defendants convicted and sentenced as felons was the same (11 percent) in 1976 as in 1973. Despite considerable advance advertising to the contrary, the British Road Safety Act of 1967 had little effect on the propensity of police to make arrests or issue citations in drunk driving cases. Similarly, the crackdown on drunk driving in Chicago, studied by Robertson, Rich, and Ross (1973), found there had been no significant change in arrest or conviction rates for drunk driving.

Of course, the innovation does not always get lost during implementation. Beha (1977) was impressed by the degree to which prosecutors and judges were carrying out the intent of the Bartley-Fox Amendment to impose one year minimum prison sentences on those guilty of carrying a gun without a license. None could argue that airport security measures introduced in 1973 were undermined during implementation—indeed, Landes (1978) reports that all hijackers since that time in the United States have been either killed or imprisoned. The team policing experiment in Cincinnati was successfully implemented for the first eighteen months, but undermined later by changes in policy. In any event, it is not safe to take any new policy at face value, and an investigation of its actual effects on the behavior of officials is an important feature of a complete evaluation.

In cross-section studies involving analysis of crime in jurisdictions which differ according to criminal code provisions or input levels, a common failing is to ignore differences in enforcement intensity. Maggadino (undated) compares states which differ with respect to gun control ordinances without analyzing enforcement procedures for these ordinances. A variety of studies

of the deterrent effect of capital punishment have simply compared murder rates of retentionist and abolitionist states, without
considering the *frequency* of executions in retentionist states.
Wilson and Boland (1976) argue persuasively that the number
of police employed in a city is not a good measure of police
activity, since police departments differ widely with respect to
prevention programs and to the percentage of the force which
is actually on the streets at any one time. Much of the information we would like to obtain from a policy innovation is lost if
implementation of the policy is ignored. While it may not be
possible to measure the change in the threat level, it is usually
possible to obtain some empirical notion of the degree to which
the new policy influenced activity levels and decision-making.
Such information aids in interpretation of findings on the crime
impact of the policy. In particular, if the innovation is found
to have no significant effect on crime, input measures may help
distinguish between two very different interpretations: "this type
of crime is not deterrable" versus "this crime was not deterred
because the actual performance of the system changed little or
not at all."

   3. Causation and control. Specifying the causal process which
generated nonexperimental data requires that assumptions be
made about how the different parts of the system being studied
fit together. These assumptions are usually controversial and
sometimes wrong. Indeed, Gilbert, Light, and Mosteller (1975)
find in their wide-ranging review of social policy innovation
studies that nonexperimental studies have reported misleading
findings on a number of occasions, as demonstrated later by a
controlled experiment. The two major challenges to the validity
of a nonexperimental finding are the possibility of reverse causation, and the possibility that factors other than the policy innovation caused the observed effect.

   In checking for the possibility of reverse causation, the key
question is why the innovation was adopted at a particular place
and time. The innovation may have been motivated by some
feature of the level or trend in crime in that jurisdiction. For
example, an unusual increase in traffic fatalities may motivate a

crackdown on speeding, which in turn is followed by a natural "regression" in fatality rates to the trend line.[17] The reduction in fatalities follows the crackdown but is not caused by it.[18]

Cross-section studies are particularly vulnerable to the reverse causation problem. Anyone who has correlated the number of police per capita with crime rates across cities understands this problem. This correlation is positive for most samples, simply because whatever deterrent effect extra police may yield is swamped by the reverse process: relatively high crime rates "cause" relatively large police forces, presumably due to the effect of crime on the public's demand for police protection. (See Cook 1977 for a discussion and display of these data.) The same effect must be expected in studies of interstate differences in gun control ordinances, capital punishment provisions, minimum legal drinking age provisions, and so forth—these laws are not adopted in a vacuum but, rather, are influenced by the public's concern with crime.

The reverse causation problem is not insurmountable. At least in principle, statistical techniques are available which permit estimation of a model that specifies equations characterizing both the deterrent effect of policy and the influence of crime on policy. The technical difficulties with these statistical techniques are a major topic of the National Academy of Sciences Panel's report (see Fisher and Nagin 1978).

Other than the problem of causal ordering, the most important challenge to the validity of a finding is the difficulty in controlling for factors, other than the policy innovation, which also influence crime rates. There are two basic approaches to controlling for other criminogenic factors. The first is to develop a model which explicitly specifies these other factors and uses a multivariate statistical technique which accounts for a number

[17] A regression effect of this sort was documented by Campbell and Ross (1968).

[18] The beauty of the imposition of the national 55 mile per hour speed limit in 1974, from an evaluator's viewpoint, is that it was clearly motivated by a consideration (the oil embargo) which had nothing to do with traffic safety. The unusually large reduction in fatalities in 1974 can be safely interpreted as a result of the new speed limit.

of these variables simultaneously. The second approach involves comparison of the crime trends for the group directly influenced by the policy innovation, with corresponding trends for similar groups not subject to the innovations. In either case, the objective is to predict what the crime rate *would have been* in the absence of the innovation, as a basis for comparison with the actual crime rate. The difference is, of course, a measure of the policy's impact on crime.

The multivariate approach is most often used in cross-section comparison studies. Crime rates differ among jurisdictions because of differences in criminal opportunities and the demographic, cultural, and socioeconomic characteristics of the populations. Only after accounting for these factors is it possible to partial out the specific effects of interjurisdiction differences in enforcement policy. One of the most important underlying differences among geographic units may be a complex of attitudes which can be labeled "public-spiritedness" or perhaps "respect for authority." In neighborhoods or cities characterized by a high degree of respect for authority, the crime rate will be relatively low due to effective citizen cooperation with police and prosecutors. (See Bayley 1976; Cook and Fischer 1976.) This attitude is also likely to be reflected in official policy, resulting in a systematic relationship between policy and crime rates across jurisdictions which adds to the direct effects of differences in policy. The difficulty in controlling for this complex of attitudes is in knowing exactly how it should be defined and measured. However, short-term policy impact studies in a single jurisdiction are immune to this problem if, as seems reasonable, attitudes toward authority change slowly.

Evaluations of individual policy innovations must control for criminogenic variables which tend to fluctuate over the period under consideration. Crime varies with the time of day, the day of the week, the season of the year, and a host of other factors. Controlling for these variables can be attempted through a multivariate model, estimated from historical data for the jurisdiction. More commonly, evaluation studies have used interrupted time series analysis or comparisons with trends in crime rates for groups similar to the group that is directly affected by the innovation. The interrupted time series analysis is most persuasive when the implementation of the policy has an immediate "slam bang" effect on crime—a change in the crime rate which is much larger than would be expected from historical fluctuations in the crime rate. Ross (1973), for example, reported a 60 percent drop in the "drinking hours" auto fatality rate immediately after implementation of the British Road Safety Act. Landes (1978) reports that there was only one domestic airline hijacking during the first year of intensive airport security measures, compared with twenty-seven the preceding year. The possibility of documenting a large effect of this sort is enhanced by use of a specific and sensitive measure of crime, but slam bang effects are rare. Gilbert, Light, and Mosteller (1975) document this point for policy interventions generally; crime is no exception.

The choice of control groups for a nonexperimental innovation is more an art than a science. The criterion is that crime rates in the control groups should be subject to the same influences (except for the innovation itself), and respond to them in roughly the same fashion, as the target group. Zimring (1972) chose California and Oregon as controls in his abortion legalization study in Hawaii; Williams et al. (1975) also used neighboring states in their study of the minimum drinking age. Proximity as a basis for choice of controls is not limited to geography: Ross (1973) used auto fatality rates during nondrinking hours, and Chaiken, Lawless, and Stevenson (1974) used subway crime rates during daytime hours. In some cases different age groups can serve as a basis of comparison—Williams et al., for example, could have used the auto fatality rate for drivers aged 21–24 as a control for his study of underage drinking.

An alternative to proximity as the basis for choice of control group is similarity. Press (1971) did not use precincts neighboring the twentieth as his controls, but rather chose groups of precincts (different for each crime type) which were similar to the twentieth in terms of population and crime rate. Beha (1977) compared violent crime in Boston with other large cities in the Northeast in his study of Bartley-Fox.[19]

4. Generalizations. Valid generalizations from the policy impact studies are few, and leave us far short of being able to answer the many questions posed by the theoretical discussion of deterrence in section I. Perhaps the only general statements worth making are: (1) a wide variety of crimes are deterrable, and there are no types of crime which have been demonstrated to be undeterrable; (2) the criminal justice system has considerable inertia, with seemingly large policy innovations often resulting in small change in the behavior of officials; and (3) given the difficulty of evaluating policy impacts, the fine points of deterrence theory will have to be checked out in the laboratory rather than the field. But the gradual accumulation of data from the field will certainly enhance our feeling for what works, and under what circumstances.

IV. Notes on a Research Agenda

Research relevant to understanding and managing the criminal deterrence process includes a wide range of topics and research methods. The five topics discussed below strike me as deserving greater attention by criminologists and research funding agencies than they have received in the recent past.

1. Comparative studies of risky decision-making. Laboratory experiments in decision-making under uncertainty can provide information on how decisions are influenced by the threat of adverse consequences of varying probability and severity. Extrapolating from the artificial laboratory setting to the "real world" is difficult, of course, but some questions are hard to investigate in a natural setting. One such question is the extent to which such factors as age, emotional arousal, and inebriation are related to "deterrability." One illustrative issue here is whether people tend to be more willing to risk adverse consequences when drunk

[19] Whatever the reasoning behind the choice of controls, it is important to validate the choice by correlating the crime rate for the control units with that of the target unit, preferably over a substantial period of time prior to the innovation. Omission of this validity check is a common failing of this literature.

than sober; a more important issue is whether this willingness to risk adverse consequences is less responsive to changes in the threat level when the subject is drunk than sober.

2. *Threat communication.* The extent to which the threat of punishment deters crime depends to some extent on how this threat is "marketed." Several lines of research may prove useful in this regard:

—An analysis of research findings on commercial advertising, dissemination of information on new products, etc., as a source of hypotheses concerning threat communication.

—Interviews with active and potential criminals to determine what sorts of information they regularly acquire on the effectiveness of law enforcement activities.

—Studies of the criminal's response to specific environmental cues related to the likelihood of arrest and punishment, including visible police patrol, signs posted to warn would-be violators ("shoplifters will be prosecuted"), and so forth.

3. *Complements and substitutes.* As explained in section IE above, the incidence of one type of crime will be influenced by the effectiveness of law enforcement efforts against closely related types of crime. A crackdown on fencing may reduce the burglary rate; a crackdown on carrying concealed weapons may reduce the rates of armed assault and robbery; an increase in the severity of sentencing for selling heroin may increase the rates at which defendants jump bail and attempt to intimidate witnesses before trial. Research on such interconnections among crime types should aid in targetting law enforcement resources.

4. *Private protection activities.* Expenditures on private protection against crime have been growing faster than public expenditures, and the total private and public expenditures are now of the same order of magnitude. Some types of investments in private security—guards, burglar alarms, hidden cameras—increase the probability of arrest and conviction for crimes against targets that are so protected. We would expect private efforts to enhance the overall effectiveness of the system, while at the same

time increasing the victimization rate of targets that remain unprotected. These effects may be quite large, and should be given
greater attention by social scientists.

5. *Other preventive effects of punishment.* Deterrence effects
have almost been ignored in discussions of the other preventive
effects of punishment. This sort of compartmentalized thinking
is dangerous for policy prescription and costly to the scientific
development of criminology. If the threat level influences the *rate*
at which active criminals commit crimes, as well as the *number*
of criminals who are active, then the measurement of incapacitation effects cannot ignore the deterrence phenomenon (Cook
1979d). Similarly, the outcome measures almost always used
in studies of correctional rehabilitation—some sort of recidivism
rate—will be influenced via deterrence by the threat environment
facing the released convict. A related concern is the possibility
that a correctional program will have a large enough effect on
the severity of punishment to undermine the deterrent effect of
punishment—a finding of reduced recidivism is insufficient to
demonstrate that the rehabilitation program reduced crime.

Together, these five research topics would substantially expand the range of deterrence research, and they by no means
exhaust the list of interesting possibilities. But to an important
extent, productive research projects cannot be identified deduc-
tively—there should be a large element of opportunism in the
choice of projects. The richest source of the "raw material" for
deterrence research has always been dramatic changes in criminal
justice policy in state and local jurisdictions, and that will continue to be true. The keys to exploiting this raw material are
early involvement and special data collection efforts.

Franklin Zimring (1978) has written an excellent analysis of
the research implications of recent policy experiments in deterrence. He concludes that a great deal of useful information which
could have been extracted from recent innovations was lost because of poor planning. A full evaluation of an innovation usually requires special data collection efforts. Measuring sensitive outcome variables and controls, and gathering information on implementation, require careful planning, an early start, and access

to official records—all of which have frequently been lacking with respect to major policy innovations. The problems in evaluating policy impacts for deterrence effects have much in common with policy evaluations in other areas of social policy. The greatest challenges to any such evaluation are measuring what are often small (but possibly important) effects, and measuring long-term effects.

The first decade of deterrence research has had some false starts and some successes. The successes in empirical field research have, for the most part, involved careful studies of specific policy changes. The major false start has been what I have called the "Ehrlich paradigm," though Isaac Ehrlich is only one of many who have utilized this approach. The appeal of this approach lies in the seeming generality of its empirical results. I believe there is a moral here: the quest for a single set of universally applicable estimates of deterrence effects is hopeless, given the nature of available data and the complexity of the underlying process which generates crime rates and sanction threats. It may pay deterrence researchers of the next decade to be modest. Sound generalizations will gradually emerge from the accumulation of carefully tested evidence on the deterrence process.

REFERENCES

Allingham, Michael G., and Agnar Sandmo. 1972. "Income Tax Evasion: A Theoretical Analysis," *Journal of Public Economics* 1:323–38.

Andenaes, Johannes. 1974. *Punishment and Deterrence.* Ann Arbor: University of Michigan Press.

Bailey, William C. 1978. *Deterrence and the Celerity of the Death Penalty: A Neglected Question in Deterrence Research.* Madison: Institute for Research on Poverty, University of Wisconsin.

Bartel, Ann. 1975. "An Analysis of Firm Demand for Protection Against Crime," *Journal of Legal Studies* 4:443–78.

Bayley, David H. 1976. "Learning About Crime—the Japanese Experience," *The Public Interest* 44:55–68.

Becker, G. 1968. "Crime and Punishment: An Economic Approach," *Journal of Political Economy* 78:526–36.

Beha, James A., II. 1977. "And *Nobody* Can Get You Out," *Boston University Law Review* 57:96–146 and 289–333.

Beyleveld, D. 1978. *The Effectiveness of General Deterrents against Crime: An Annotated Bibliography of Evaluative Research.* Cambridge, England: Institute of Criminology (in microfiche).

Blakey, G. Robert, and Michael Goldsmith. 1976. "Criminal Redistribution of Stolen Property: The Need for Law Reform," *Michigan Law Review* 74:1512–1626.

Block, Michael K., and John M. Heineke. 1975. "A Labor Theoretic Analysis of the Criminal Choice," *American Economic Review* 65:314–25.

Block, Michael K., and Robert C. Lind. 1975. "An Economic Analysis of Crimes Punishable by Imprisonment," *Journal of Legal Studies* 4:479–92.

Blumstein, Alfred, Jacquelin Cohen, and Daniel Nagin, eds. 1978. *Deterrence and Incapacitation: Estimating the Effects of Criminal Sanctions on Crime Rates.* Washington, D.C.: National Academy of Sciences.

Blumstein, Alfred, and Daniel Nagin. 1977. "The Deterrent Effect of Legal Sanctions on Draft Evasion," *Stanford Law Review* 28:241–75.

Boydstun, J. E. 1975. *San Diego Field Interrogation: Final Report.* Washington, D.C.: Police Foundation.

Brier, Stephen S., and Stephen E. Fienberg. 1978. *Recent Econometric Modelling of Crime and Punishment: Support for the Deterrence Hypothesis?* School of Statistics, University of Minnesota.

Campbell, Donald T., and H. Laurence Ross. 1968. "The Connecticut Crackdown on Speeding," *Law and Society Review* 3:33–53.

Carr-Hill, R. A., and N. H. Stern. 1973. "An Econometric Model of the Supply and Control of Recorded Offences in England and Wales," *Journal of Public Economics* 2:289–318.

Carroll, John S. 1978. "A Psychological Approach to Deterrence: The Evaluation of Crime Opportunities," *Journal of Personality and Social Psychology* 36:1512–20.

———. (forthcoming). "Committing a Crime: The Offender's Decision." In *Social-Psychological Analysis of Legal Processes*, ed. V. J. Konecni and E. G. Ebbesen. San Francisco: Freeman.

Chaiken, Jan M. 1978. "What Is Known about Deterrent Effects of Police Activities." In *Preventing Crime*, ed. James A. Cramer. Beverly Hills: Sage Publications.

Chaiken, Jan M., Michael W. Lawless, and Keith A. Stevenson. 1974. "The Impact of Police Activity on Subway Crime," *Urban Analysis* 3:173–205.

Clotfelter, Charles. 1977. "Public Services, Private Substitutes, and the Demand for Protection against Crime," *American Economic Review* 67:867–77.

Cohen, Jacquelin. 1978. "The Incapacitating Effect of Imprisonment: A Critical Review of the Literature." In Blumstein, Cohen, and Nagin (1978).

Conklin, J. 1972. *Robbery and the Criminal Justice System.* New York: Lippincott.

Cook, Philip J. 1977. "Punishment and Crime: A Critique of Current Findings Concerning the Preventive Effects of Punishment," *Law and Contemporary Problems* 41:164–204.

———. 1979a. "The Clearance Rate as a Measure of Criminal Justice System Effectiveness," *Journal of Public Economics* 11:135–42.

———. 1979b. "The Effect of Gun Availability on Robbery and Robbery Murder." In *Policy Studies Review Annual*, Vol. 3, ed. R. H. Haveman and B. B. Zellner. Beverly Hills: Sage Publications.

———. 1979c. "The Implications of Deterrence and Incapacitation Research for Policy Evaluation." In *An Anatomy of Criminal Justice*, ed. Cleon Foust and D. Robert Webster. Lexington, Mass.: Lexington Books.

———. 1979d. "A Unified Treatment of Deterrence, Incapacitation, and Rehabilitation: A Simulation Study." Durham, N.C.: Institute of Policy Sciences and Public Affairs, Duke University.

———. 1980. "Reducing Injury and Death Rates in Robbery," *Policy Analysis* 6:21–45.

Cook, P. J., and Gregory W. Fischer. 1976. "Citizen Cooperation with the Criminal Justice System." Durham, N.C.: Institute of Policy Sciences and Public Affairs, Duke University.

Cook, P. J., and Daniel Nagin. 1979. *Does the Weapon Matter?* Washington, D.C.: Institute for Law and Social Research.

Ehrlich, Isaac. 1970. *Participation in Illegitimate Activities: An Economic Analysis.* Ph.D. dissertation, Columbia University.

———. 1972. "The Deterrent Effect of Criminal Law Enforcement," *Journal of Legal Studies* 1:259–76.

———. 1973. "Participation in Illegitimate Activities: A Theoretical and Empirical Investigation," *Journal of Political Economy* 81:521–65.

———. 1975. "The Deterrent Effect of Capital Punishment: A Question of Life and Death," *American Economic Review* 65:397–417.

———. 1979. "The Economic Approach to Crime: A Preliminary Assessment." In *Criminology Review Yearbook*, ed. Sheldon Messinger and Egon Bittner. Beverly Hills: Sage Publications.

Ehrlich, Isaac, and Mark Randall. 1977. "Fear of Deterrence: A Critical Evaluation of the 'Report of the Panel on Research on Deterrent and Incapacitative Effects,'" *Journal of Legal Studies* 6:293–316.

Erickson, Maynard L., and Jack P. Gibbs. 1979. "On the Perceived Severity of Legal Penalties," *Journal of Criminal Law and Criminology* 70:102–16.

Fisher, Franklin M., and Karl Shell. 1972. *The Economic Theory of Price Indices*. New York: Academic Press.

Fisher, Franklin M., and Daniel Nagin. 1978. "On the Feasibility of Identifying the Crime Function in a Simultaneous Model of Crime Rates and Sanction Levels." In Blumstein, Cohen, and Nagin (1978).

Forst, Brian. 1976. "Participation in Illegitimate Activities: Further Empirical Findings," *Policy Analysis* 2:477–92.

Friedland, Nehemia, John Thibaut, and Laurens Walker. 1973. "Some Determinants of the Violation of Rules," *Journal of Applied Social Psychology* 3:103–18.

Geerken, Michael R., and Walter R. Gove. 1975. "Deterrence: Some Theoretical Considerations," *Law and Society Review* 9:497–513.

Gibbs, Jack P. 1968. "Crime, Punishment, and Deterrence," *Southwestern Social Science Quarterly* 48:515–30.

———. 1975. *Crime, Punishment, and Deterrence*. New York: Elsevier.

Gilbert, John P., Richard J. Light, and Frederick Mosteller. 1975. "Assessing Social Innovations: An Empirical Base for Policy." In *Benefit-Cost and Policy Analysis, 1974*. Chicago: Aldine.

Greenwood, Michael J., and W. J. Wadycki. 1973. "Crime Rates and Public Expenditures for Police Protection: Their Interaction," *Review of Social Economy* 31:138–51.

Heineke, John M. 1978a. "Economic Models of Criminal Behavior: An Overview." In *Economic Models of Criminal Behavior*, ed. J. M. Heineke. New York: North-Holland Publishing Company.

———. 1978b. "Substitution among Crime and the Question of Deterrence: An Indirect Utility Function Approach to the Supply of Legal and Illegal Activity." In *Economic Models of Criminal Behavior*, ed. J. M. Heineke. New York: North-Holland Publishing Company.

Jacob, Herbert. 1979. "Rationality and Criminality," *Social Science Quarterly* 59:584–85.

Johnston, James M. 1972. "Punishment of Human Behavior," *American Psychologist* 27:1033–54.

Joint Committee on New York Drug Law Enforcement. 1978. *The Nation's Toughest Drug Law: Evaluating the New York Experience.* Washington, D.C.: U.S. Government Printing Office.

Kahneman, Daniel, and Amos Tversky (forthcoming). "Prospect Theory: An Analysis of Decision under Risk," *Econometrica.*

Kelling, G., and A. Pate. 1974. *The Kansas City Preventive Patrol Experiment.* Washington, D.C.: The Police Foundation.

Klein, Lawrence R., Brian Forst, and Victor Filatov. 1978. "The Deterrent Effect of Capital Punishment: An Assessment of the Evidence." In Blumstein, Cohen, and Nagin (1978).

Klockars, Carl B. 1974. *The Professional Fence.* New York: Free Press.

Kunreuther, Howard, and Paul Slovic. 1978. "Economics, Psychology, and Protective Behavior," *American Economic Review* 68:64–69.

Landes, William M. 1978. "An Economic Study of U.S. Aircraft Hijacking, 1961–1976," *The Journal of Law and Economics* 21:1–32.

Larson, Richard C. 1975. "What Happened to Patrol Operations in Kansas City? A Review of the Kansas City Preventive Patrol Experiment," *Journal of Criminal Justice* 3:267–97.

Lipton, D., R. Martinson, and J. Wilks. 1975. *The Effectiveness of Correctional Treatment: A Survey of Treatment Evaluation Studies.* New York: Praeger.

Maggadino, J. P. n.d. "Towards an Economic Evaluation of State Gun Control Laws." Long Beach, Calif.: California State University.

Manski, Charles. 1978. "Prospects for Inference on Deterrence through Empirical Analysis of Individual Criminal Behavior." In Blumstein, Cohen, and Nagin (1978).

Moore, Mark. 1973. "Policies to Achieve Discrimination on the Effective Price of Heroin," *American Economic Review* 63:270–77.

Myers, David G., and Helmut Lamm. 1976. "The Group Polarization Phenomenon," *Psychological Bulletin* 83:602–27.

Nagin, Daniel. 1978. "General Deterrence: A Review of the Empirical Evidence." In Blumstein, Cohen, and Nagin (1978).

Packer, Herbert L. 1968. *The Limits of the Criminal Sanction.* Stanford: Stanford University Press.

Payne, John. 1980. "Information Processing Theory: Some Concepts and Methods Applied to Decision Research." In *Cognitive Processes in Choice and Decision Behavior,* ed. T. Wallsten. Hillsdale, N.J.: Lawrence Erlbaum.

Petersilia, Joan, Peter W. Greenwood, and M. Lavin. 1978. *Criminal*

Careers of Habitual Felons. Santa Monica, Calif.: Rand Corporation.

Pierce, Glenn, and William Bowers. 1979. "The Impact of the Bartley-Fox Gun Law on Crime in Massachusetts." Boston: Center for Applied Social Research, Northeastern University.

Plattner, Mark F. 1976. "The Rehabilitation of Punishment," *The Public Interest* 44:104–14.

Press, S. James. 1971. *Some Effects of an Increase in Police Manpower in the 20th Precinct of New York City.* New York: Rand Institute.

Robertson, Leon, Robert F. Rich, and H. Laurence Ross. 1973. "Jail Sentences for Driving While Intoxicated in Chicago: A Judicial Policy That Failed," *Law and Society Review* 8:55–68.

Ross, H. Laurence. 1973. "Law, Science, and Accidents: The British Road Safety Act of 1967," *Journal of Legal Studies* 2:1–78.

———. 1977. "Deterrence Regained: The Cheshire Constabulary's 'Breathalyser Blitz,' " *Journal of Legal Studies* 6:241–92.

Schwartz, Alfred I., and Sumner Clarren. 1977. *The Cincinnati Team Policing Experiment: A Summary Report.* Washington, D.C.: Police Foundation.

Sellin, T., ed. 1967. *Capital Punishment.* New York: Harper & Row.

Simon, Herbert A. 1957. *Models of Man.* New York: Wiley.

Sjoquist, D. 1973. "Property Crime and Economic Behavior: Some Empirical Results," *American Economic Review* 63:439–46.

Swimmer, E. 1974. "Measurement of the Effectiveness of Urban Law Enforcement: A Simultaneous Approach," *Southern Economic Review* 40:618–30.

Tullock, Gordon. 1974. "Does Punishment Deter Crime?," *The Public Interest* 36:103–11.

Tversky, Amos, and Daniel Kahneman. 1974. "Judgment under Uncertainty: Heuristics and Biases," *Science* 185:1124–31.

Vandaele, Walter. 1978a. "Participation in Illegitimate Activities: Ehrlich Revisited." In Blumstein, Cohen, and Nagin (1978).

———. 1978b. "An Econometric Model of Auto Theft in the United States." In *Economic Models of Criminal Behavior*, ed. J. Heineke. New York: North Holland Publishing Company.

von Hirsch, Andrew. 1976. *Doing Justice.* New York: Hill and Wang.

Walker, Nigel. 1979. "The Efficacy and Morality of Deterrents," *Criminal Law Review*, pp. 129–44.

Walsh, Marilyn. 1976. *Strategies for Combatting the Criminal Re-*

ceiver (Fence) of Stolen Goods. Washington, D.C.: U.S. Government Printing Office.

Williams, Allan F., et al. 1975. "The Legal Minimum Drinking Age and Fatal Motor Vehicle Crashes," *Journal of Legal Studies* 4:219–39.

Wilson, James Q., and Barbara Boland. 1976. "Crime." In *The Urban Predicament*, ed. W. Gorham and N. Glazer. Washington, D.C.: The Urban Institute.

Witte, Ann. 1980. "Estimating the Economic Model of Crime with Individual Data," *Quarterly Journal of Economics* 97:57–84.

Zimring, Franklin E. 1972. "Of Doctors, Deterrence, and the Dark Figure of Crime—A Note on Abortion in Hawaii," *University of Chicago Law Review* 39:699–721.

———. 1978. "Policy Experiments in General Deterrence: 1970–1975." In Blumstein, Cohen, and Nagin (1978).

Zimring, Franklin E., and Gordon J. Hawkins. 1973. *Deterrence.* Chicago: University of Chicago Press.

John Baldwin and Michael McConville

Criminal Juries

ABSTRACT

The jury represents the very cornerstone of the Anglo-American
legal system, and a massive literature has built up over the course
of this century as testimony to this fact. Three important sets
of empirical questions can be isolated: whether the jury is a
competent fact finder, able to assess evidence, understand legal
instructions, and reach appropriate results; whether juries are
representative of the communities from which they come and,
where not, whether juries of representative composition would
achieve significantly different verdicts; whether non-unanimous
juries and juries smaller than twelve are inferior to traditional
twelve-member juries. Findings on all these questions are
inconsistent and in dispute. All of the empirical research is
flawed by severe methodological limitations, but faulty
interpretation of research results is a more important problem.
A critical evaluation of the empirical research casts doubt on
many of the claims made by researchers about the working
of the jury. Part of the confusion results from different notions
of the jury's role. The authors argue that research on the jury
should be redirected toward methods which would make
for a fuller appreciation of the jury's political function.

One of the most striking features of trial by jury is that so little
is known about it. Its origins are obscure, and the ways in which
it has evolved to its present form are not fully understood. The
great English jurist Sir William Blackstone (1830) believed
that juries derived their standing from the provision in clause 39
of Magna Carta relating to judgment by one's peers, but this view

John Baldwin is Lecturer in Judicial Administration, University of Birmingham. Michael McConville is Lecturer in Law, University of Birmingham.

is now discredited (see Frankfurter and Corcoran 1926; Cornish 1968, pp. 11-12). Early in its history, the jury performed a function quite different from that of today: jurors were men drawn from a local neighborhood, likely to know both the accused and the facts of the case, and bound by their oath to decide between the disputants. Juries gradually changed their character and began to determine cases upon the evidence, but it was not until the eighteenth century that the rule was established that a juror should not act upon his own knowledge of a case. By the end of the nineteenth century, after a series of constitutional battles,[1] the jury was held to be the trier of fact, and trial by jury was firmly established as a cornerstone of the legal systems of England and the United States.

Although knowledge of the history of jury trial may be imperfect, one thing is certain: the jury has always attracted praise and scorn from writers to a degree unparalleled by any other legal institution. To some, the jury represents the very hallmark of democracy and the essential guarantor of freedom; to others, the notion that twelve people, unversed in the law and chosen at random from the community, should pronounce upon the lives and liberty of those charged with criminal offenses is anathema to any rational approach to decision-making. Blackstone (1830), for example, thought that trial by jury "ever has been, and I trust ever will be, looked upon as the glory of the English law. . . . The liberties of England cannot but subsist, so long as this palladium remains sacred and inviolate" (iii. 379, iv. 350). Jury skeptics are not persuaded by such grandiloquence, how-

[1] An early discussion of the issues is found in *Bushell's Case* (1670) Vaughan 135, 124 English Reports 1006, but the main debates in England surrounded criminal libel. In libel cases, judges repeatedly ruled that the only questions for the jury were the fact of publication and the truth of the innuendoes. By reserving to themselves the issue whether the expressions amounted to libel, the judges effectively disabled the jury from returning a general verdict: *R. v. Francklin* (1731) 17 St.Tr. 625; *R. v. Owen* (1752) 18 St.Tr. 1203; *R. v. Almon* (1770) 20 St.Tr. 803; *R. v. Miller* (1770) 20 St.Tr. 870; *R. v. Woodfall* (1770) 20 St.Tr. 895. Opposition to this practice grew and came to the forefront in *R. v. Shipley* (1783) 21 St.Tr. 847. The dispute eventually led to the passing of Fox's Libel Act (1792), which gave to the jury the right to give a general verdict on the whole issue. The landmark decision in the United States was *Sparf and Hansen v. United States*, 156 U.S. 51, 102 (1895). The preferred view is that the jury's right to decide the law (which still exists in Maryland and Indiana) is simply an uncontrollable power to acquit: see Henderson (1966).

ever, and Jerome Frank (1949), an American judge who is perhaps the most often quoted of all skeptics, delivered the following searing rejoinder: "When I hear the jury praised as the 'palladium of our liberties,' I keep thinking that, while a palladium . . . means something on which the safety of a nation or an institution depends, it is also the name of a chemical element which, in the spongy state, 'has the remarkable quality of absorbing up to nearly 1,000 times its own volume in hydrogen gas' " (p. 108).

These quotations must not be taken to reflect differing English and American attitudes toward the jury: disputes about the jury know no geographical limits, and critics and supporters abound in England as in the United States and the Commonwealth. Although the arguments shift from time to time and place to place, underlying the debate is a dispute about the proper role and function of the jury. On one view, the jury serves a political function, whereas on another, it is simply a body constituted to find the facts. The arguments may be charted by examining each of these roles in turn.

On the political view, the jury is seen as an independent and necessary element in the proper enforcement of the criminal law. By bringing the citizen into the judicial system, decisions on liability become more acceptable; participation of the ordinary citizen in the administration of the law assists in the education of the community and reduces the dominance of specialists or experts; and the jury provides a forum in which the harshness of the law may be tempered and the rights of individuals against oppressive or unfair state pressures protected and upheld. The general argument was well put by the Australian judge John Hale (1973):[2] "[The jury] enhances respect for and trust in the operation of the criminal courts: a jury is a microcosm of the community, their verdict is a verdict of the community and if they err the error is an error by people representing the man-in-the-street and not by a judge who, however impartial he is,

[2] Similar sentiments have been expressed by Holmes (1889); Wigmore (1929); Tocqueville (1960); Devlin (1956, 1979); Dashwood (1973); and Mungham and Bankowski (1976). Good reviews of the literature are to be found in Abraham (1968); Becker (1970); and Erlanger (1970).

nevertheless was appointed by the Executive Government which through one of its departments does the prosecuting" (pp. 102–3). While many critics of the jury are prepared to accept this general argument, the contention that the jury system helps to educate citizens in government and gives them greater confidence in democracy has been regarded by many writers at best as unsupported conjecture, at worst as downright absurdity (see, e.g., Frank 1949, p. 135; Steuer 1975).

The main battles, however, have concerned what some see as the heart of the jury's political function—the power of the jury to nullify harsh or unpopular laws. This capacity of the jury to apply a measure of equity to the cold application of legal principle has been seen by defenders of the jury as its central virtue (see, e.g., Holmes 1889; Curtis 1952; Shawcross 1947; Kadish and Kadish 1971; Knittel and Seiler 1972). Roscoe Pound (1910), for instance, states: "Jury lawlessness is the great corrective of law in its actual administration. The will of the state at large imposed on a reluctant community, the will of a majority imposed on a vigorous and determined minority, find the same obstacle in the local jury that formerly confronted kings and ministers" (p. 18). There is certainly some evidence that juries have from time to time acted as a restraint upon oppressive laws. The refusal of juries to convict in cases of criminal libel, the "pious perjury" they welcomed in order to avoid conviction on a capital offense, the indulgence shown toward "mercy killings," and the nullification of the Prohibition laws during the 1920s are simply the most famous examples of this exercise of discretion.[3] But the significance of these examples and the more general belief in the desirability of jury lawlessness is fiercely contested by jury critics. Thus, one of the leading English authorities, Glanville Williams (1963), while conceding that the jury has sometimes avoided the strict application of the law, maintained that "most of the great pronouncements on constitutional liberty, from the eighteenth century onwards, have been the work of judges. . . . The assumption that political liberty at the present day depends upon the institution of the jury . . . is

[3] Social historians have documented both individual incidents and general patterns of refusals by eighteenth- and nineteenth-century juries to convict "legally guilty" defendants. See, e.g., Ignatieff (1978) and essays in Hay et al. (1975).

in truth merely folklore" (pp. 259–60). Critics have also pointed out that, though proponents of jury trial assume the contrary,[4] jury lawlessness does not operate in one direction only and may even be used improperly to convict the unpopular or unattractive defendant or members of minority groups.[5]

A different approach to consideration of the jury—and it is the approach most researchers have adopted—is to set aside questions about the political functions of the jury and to concentrate upon how well it performs its formal fact-finding tasks. From this perspective the jury can be assessed in terms of how it ascertains the facts and applies them to the law as given in the judge's instructions. This raises three related questions: whether juries are able to understand legal instructions and are competent fact finders; whether the composition of the jury panels is appropriate to the tasks assigned it; and finally whether jury verdicts are affected by the size of the jury (six, twelve, or some other number) or by rules permitting conviction on the basis of non-unanimous votes. The bulk of this essay will be addressed to these questions, and we shall examine in subsequent parts of the essay the great volume of relevant research which has been conducted throughout the course of the present century. Before we turn to the empirical evidence, however, we must examine the general propositions that have been advanced.

As to the first question, bearing upon the ability of juries to understand legal rules, Frank (1949) had no doubt that those

---

[4] Knittel and Seiler (1972), for instance, in commenting upon the ability of the jury to bypass the law, write: "This happens chiefly in two groups of cases. There are those in which the juries acquit in mercy to the accused (as where they give an indulgent width to a plea of self-defence). And there are those in which a conviction in the eyes of the jury would lead to an unreasonably harsh punishment (e.g. driving offences)" (p. 317).
See also Pound (1910); Kadish and Kadish (1971); and Dashwood (1973).

[5] Brooks and Doob (1975) put the point well in the following passage: "But . . . law dispensing by the jury appears to cut both ways. The fact that minority groups have historically been unfairly subjected to jury lawlessness cannot be doubted. Furthermore many people would argue that the fact that the accused is a nice fellow, a good looking woman, a cripple, or employed, or that his or her victim is insufferable, should not affect the disposition of the case" (p. 180). Also relevant here are Jennings (1959); *Yale Law Journal* (1970); and Becker (1970). It should be noted that, in theory at least, the extent of jury lawlessness is limited by the power of the judge to withdraw the issue from the jury if he feels there is insufficient evidence to support a conviction. The available evidence, however, does not support the view that this power is used consistently by judges. On this, see McCabe and Purves (1972) and Zander (1974).

without training cannot understand what the judge tells them about legal rules.[6] Jurors, he said, are as unlikely to comprehend the meaning of the words in the judge's charge "as if they were spoken in Chinese, Sanskrit, or Choctaw" (p. 116). Some proponents of jury trial do not concede that the law is often misunderstood by jurors and, indeed, implicit in the general argument that jurors consciously correct the application of the law is the assumption that the law has first been understood. On a more general level, there has also been great dispute about whether juries are efficient fact finders. Experienced judges have often asserted that juries are not only skilled at finding the facts but that they are better at it than are judges. Lord du Parcq (1948), for example, said that, when questions of fact have to be decided, "there is no tribunal to equal a jury, directed by the cold impartial judge" (p. 10).[7] Critics have retorted that juries cannot recollect with accuracy the relevant evidence, that they fail to follow complex trials, that they get confused in cases involving multiple defendants, and that they are easily swayed by irrelevant considerations, prejudice, or emotion.[8] The counterargument to

[6] This may tell more about the legal rules than about the competence of the jury, and one of the arguments in favor of trial by jury has been that it is a necessary device for keeping the criminal law in touch with the ordinary man. See, for example, Devlin (1979, p. 147).

[7] This general conclusion has been supported on the basis that the way in which the jury deliberates is likely to reduce error. Thus, Joiner (1962) said: "The jury is a deliberative body. It does discuss, argue, and exchange ideas before it can report a decision. Therefore, it is not unfair to assume that the decision which it reaches may have fewer mistakes and fewer biases involved in it than would such a decision made by a single person" (p. 26).

[8] The charge of failure to recollect evidence is not necessarily an indictment of the abilities of individual jurors; often it is made with reference to the inadequate facilities for note taking given to juries. See, for example, Williams (1963, p. 278). Alleged failure to follow complex trials is discussed in Cornish (1968, pp. 179–83). It is only rarely that confusion in multiple-defendant cases becomes apparent, as in an English conspiracy case in which the Court of Criminal Appeal said of one defendant: "We think that he is really a typical example of a man who was sunk by means of a mass of evidence about frauds of different kinds, with the great majority of which he had no connection either direct or indirect, and in which he took no part whatever, and in which his name was never even mentioned" (R. v. Dawson and Wenlock [1960] 1 All E.R. 558, 563). As to emotions, Newman (1955), for example, writes: "In the light of the fact that the average juror is swayed by the emotion and prejudice of his heredity, background, training, (and how often, his breakfast?) there is often little hope that the objectivity desired in a trial will be obtained by recourse to the judgment of a panel of laymen" (p. 517).

this line of attack has been that, even if juries do occasionally blunder, this is preferable to a system under which a bad judge, unchecked by a jury, can make mistakes throughout the whole of his judicial career.

Another question as to the fact finding ability of juries is whether the composition of the jury panel is suitable for the task assigned to a tribunal of fact, a concern that cuts across the arguments for and against jury trial. Although proponents of trial by jury have made great play of the jury as a microcosm of the community, critics have contended that juries are not as a rule representative of the community at all. In both England and the United States, it has been said that the unrepresentative character of juries has resulted in the perpetuation of bias, particularly against women and racial minorities.[9]

Finally, one must recognize the challenge that has been posed to the jury system in recent years by moves to reduce the size of the panel (usually to six members) and to allow verdicts to be given on a majority vote. Though it must immediately be conceded that there is nothing inherently sacred about the traditional requirement that juries of twelve members reach unanimous verdicts (and a glance at the jury systems of other jurisdictions reveals variations in terms of jury size, composition, and unanimity requirements), these two changes have nevertheless been viewed by many writers as representing dangerous erosions of the jury's function and even as presenting a serious threat to its very continuance.

This brief review of the central arguments in the jury debate readily shows the passions that juries arouse and the lack of any clear pathway through the tangle of opinion, conjecture, and thinly disguised prejudice. This is not to imply that ignorance about the workings of juries should cause surprise. On the contrary, the single most noteworthy feature of the jury system is the secrecy that surrounds it. In the United States, the celebrated

[9] See generally Oppenheimer (1937); and Williams (1963). On biases against women, see the Morris Committee (1965) and Levine and Schweber-Koren (1976); and on the possibility of racial imbalance, see Broeder (1965b); Rhine (1969); *Yale Law Journal* (1970); Dashwood (1972); Van Amburg (1974); and Alker, Hosticka, and Mitchell (1976).

occasion for upholding the secrecy of the jury followed the attempt by Kalven and Zeisel (1966) to record the actual deliberations of juries. Although this was done with the consent of the trial judge and counsel, the jurors concerned were not informed and, once details of the investigation became public, there was, in the words of the researchers, a "national scandal." (For the background to this scandal in Wichita, Kansas, see Kalven and Zeisel 1966, preface, and Vaughan 1967.) As a direct consequence, many states made it a criminal offense to record deliberations or in any way interfere with jurors before verdict. There has been no comparable attempt in England to breach the veil of secrecy, but judges have made clear their objections to publishing accounts of interviews with jurors after the conclusion of a trial, and there have been suggestions that this would amount to a contempt of court.[10] At the time of writing, however, this issue has blown up in England with the publication of a lengthy article in the periodical the *New Statesman* (27 July 1979), concerned with the prosecution of the former leader of the Liberal party, Jeremy Thorpe, for conspiracy to murder. The trial in question had ended some five weeks earlier in the acquittal of Mr. Thorpe and his codefendants. In the article, there were several extracts from an interview with an unnamed juror in the trial including his account of parts of the jury's deliberations. As a result of the article, the attorney-general applied for an order of contempt of court against the publishers. It was held that an order could be issued if such disclosure imperiled the finality of jury verdicts or adversely affected the attitude of future jurors and the quality of their deliberations, but, on the facts of this case, the application was refused ([1980] 1 All E.R. 644). It follows that revelations about English juries can amount to contempt of court.

[10] In *R. v. Armstrong* (1922) 2 K.B. 555, Lord Hewart C.J. adverted to the fact that a juror had given an interview about what happened in the jury room to a newspaper and said that "nothing could be more improper, deplorable and dangerous" (p. 568). Earlier, in *Ellis* v. *Deheer* [1922] 2 K.B. 113, the Court of Appeal thought it unnecessary to say whether such action amounted to a contempt, and simply restated the importance of maintaining the rule as to the secrecy of jury deliberations.

I. The Methods Used to Study the Workings of Juries
Since few institutions are as well protected from outside scrutiny,[11] empirical inquiry into the workings of the jury is an almost uniquely difficult research undertaking. Yet such is the fascination of the jury that researchers have attempted throughout the course of this century to challenge the inscrutability of its decisions. In consequence, the vast body of research material that has been generated has yielded results that are often confused and contradictory.

Before we examine the empirical literature on juries, we shall attempt a critical appraisal of the methods that have been employed to shed light on jury verdicts and the ways they are reached. The most important point to bear in mind throughout this discussion is that all the methods used have been indirect and therefore imperfect. With the single unhappy exception in Wichita mentioned above (see Kalven and Zeisel 1966), no observer has gained access to the jury room itself, which after all holds the key to the questions researchers have posed. Furthermore, one cannot assume that researchers themselves are unbiased or neutral observers of the system. Often unstated, but readily apparent, biases (particularly in favor of jury trial) can be seen to color the interpretation of results. (These difficulties are discussed further in Baldwin and McConville 1979a, pp. 6–15.) Given these problems of access and interpretation, it is fairly easy to cast doubt on much of the research that has been done—and a degree of skepticism is by no means always misplaced—but we shall attempt (as jury researchers ourselves) a more constructive overview.

One may identify five main ways in which researchers and other commentators have attempted to uncover some of the

[11] One influential critic of the mystery that surrounds jury trial in England asserts that "the public's confidence in our present system of trial by jury is essentially a matter of faith. It is based on practically no evidence whatever . . . because no one is allowed to listen to the discussions in the Jury Room. Lawyers obviously believe that public confidence in the jury would be undermined if this were allowed to happen. . . . I cannot think of any other social institution which is protected from rational enquiry because investigation might show that it wasn't doing its job" (Mark 1973, p. 8).

mysteries of jury trial,[12] and it is worthwhile dealing briefly with each approach. The methods are as follows: (1) the impressionistic, autobiographical accounts written by individual jurors; (2) the observations of practitioners, notably judges, based upon their experiences of jury trial; (3) the systematic collection by researchers of jurors' opinions about their experiences of sitting on the jury; (4) the adoption of various forms of simulated jury panel designed to reconstruct or parallel the deliberations of the real jury; and (5) the attempt to assess the performance of the jury with reference to the views of other participants in the trial. The following examination of research methods will be primarily concerned with the last two approaches as these are the ones upon which most research effort, both in England and the United States, has been expended and upon which an evaluation of jury performance must presently depend. It is, however, worthwhile briefly dealing with the other approaches, as these are not without merit.

Turning first to the autobiographical accounts of jurors themselves, one is here confronted by a disparate collection of personal experiences, many of which are to be found in the pages of the popular press. Though these recollections often provide fascinating insights into the inner workings of particular juries, they are nonetheless inevitably partial and idiosyncratic. Indeed, were the experiences not so idiosyncratic, their authors would probably not have been moved to set them down in this way. Many of the issues to which such authors have addressed themselves (such as an almost obsessive concern with waiting in court corridors), though doubtless of considerable interest to court administrators, tell us little about how verdicts are reached. As one might expect, a whole spectrum of views on the deliberative process is obtained from examining these accounts of jury service. One reads writers like Head (1969), who felt that the juries on

12 Much work has recently been carried out on another approach—that of jury "modeling." We have chosen not to discuss this method here since it has been used primarily in relation to the question of jury size, rather than to illuminate the deliberative process as such. Good examples of this approach are given in Zeisel (1971); Davis (1973); Gelfand and Solomon (1973, 1974); Nagel and Neef (1975, 1977); and Kerr et al. (1976).

which she had served had had "no difficulty cutting through the
fatty tissue of the case to reach the marrow of the bone of right
and wrong" (p. 334), or Kennebeck (1975), whose service gave
him "a tremendous respect for this part of the system" (p. 249),
whereas Devons (1965) was so appalled by his experiences that
he felt moved to write that "if the jury is to remain part of the
English legal system, it is just as well that its proceedings should
remain secret" (p. 570). Between these extremes, there is a range
of opinions from which any one of a number of quite incompatible conclusions about the performance of juries might be drawn.
(For further accounts of this kind, see Connelly 1971 and the
collection compiled by Barber and Gordon 1976.)

The second source of information, derived from the publicly
expressed views of judges and other legal practitioners, provides
a much less equivocal picture. Judges have, with very few exceptions, been united in virtual adulation of the jury. To take
one typical example, Lord Justice Salmon said of the hundreds
of criminal trials over which he had presided in England: "There
were not more . . . than about half a dozen cases in which the
jury acquitted when I considered that they ought to have convicted—and, on reflection, when I looked back on them, I came
to the conclusion that at any rate as far as some of them were
concerned there was a good deal to be said for the jury's point
of view. A 1 or 2 per cent wrongful acquittal of guilty men is
surely a small price to ensure that the innocent should go free.
In any event, those acquittals never bothered me, but I should
not have slept in my bed if any innocent man had been convicted by the jury. Fortunately, that never happened." (*House
of Lords Debates*, 14 February 1973: cols. 1605–6. For other
examples, see Halsbury 1903; Devlin 1956, 1973; Clarke 1974;
Emmet 1974; and Joiner 1975.) Observations of this kind, sometimes no more than high-minded assertion, have to be treated
with caution since they are inevitably colored by all manner
of personal biases and prejudices. Such material, based upon
narrow personal experience and knowledge, does not allow generalizations to be safely made (except about those who have

advanced the testimony), but the bulk of it points in one direction—a belief that juries are extremely competent triers of fact.[13] The same may be said with almost equal force of the views expressed by members of the legal profession (see, e.g., Nizer 1946; Napley 1966; Friloux 1975; Corboy 1975). In the United States, as in England, one would have difficulty in finding serious criticisms of juries from these ranks.

A similar picture emerges when one examines the small number of more systematic observations that some judges and trial lawyers have made of their experiences of jury trials over a period of years. One judge in the United States, for instance, kept a private record of his views on the outcomes of some five hundred contested trials over which he had presided in a twelve-year period, and two English defense lawyers have more recently attempted the same kind of limited evaluation.[14] Although such records consist of the opinions of single observers, when taken together they must be regarded as evidence, if largely impressionistic, that the jury enjoys the confidence not only of the overwhelming majority of American and English judges but of the legal profession as well.

The empirical studies, based on systematic collection by researchers of jurors' opinions about their jury experience, have all been conducted in the United States. As we noted above, such exercises in England might well amount to contempt of court.[15] The outcome of the studies in the United States has, however, been disappointing, and a confused picture has emerged. Such limited attitude surveys may help us understand how in-

[13] A national poll of over a thousand trial judges in the United States by Kalven (1964) showed clearly that confidence in jury trial was extremely high. Further discussion of the question of judicial confidence in trial by jury is given in Baldwin and McConville (1979a, pp. 2–5).

[14] The American judge felt that the verdicts returned were "unquestionably right" in more than 85 per cent of all cases; see Hartshorne (1949). The English lawyers' inquiry was concerned with the narrower question of whether acquittal rates in criminal trials were excessive; see Elgrod and Lew (1973, 1975).

[15] Cornish (1968) interviewed a considerable number of jurors in England, though he does not give details of how this was carried out or of the extent to which the court authorities cooperated. It may be that they were simply unaware that the interviews were being conducted.

dividual jurors approach their task, but it is dangerous to assume, as many writers have, that such surveys amount to an assessment of the performance of the jury as a whole. To take one illustration of this error, one may cite several studies (e.g. Hunter 1935; Wanamaker 1937; Hervey 1947; Hoffman and Brodley 1952; Broeder 1965a) which show that individual jurors had obviously misunderstood the relevant legal concepts and rules or else had not applied them properly. But it cannot be inferred from this that the reasoning of the jury as a whole was similarly flawed. Since the verdict of a jury is in essence a complex amalgam of the views of individual jurors, it may be seriously misleading to draw inferences about juries' verdicts on the basis of misunderstandings, or even absurdities, as revealed to a researcher by individuals in an interview conducted some time after the trial. The really critical question—whether such misunderstandings had any direct bearing upon the final verdict returned—is one that cannot be answered by this kind of limited survey.

Some of these problems can be more satisfactorily examined, if not overcome, by means of the fourth method of inquiry—that based upon simulated panels. This method has the enormous advantage that the deliberations of a simulated or mock panel, unlike those of a real jury, can be recorded, dissected, and analyzed. Furthermore, the details in each mock trial can be controlled, and the experiments can then be replicated before large numbers of different panels. Well over fifty experiments have been conducted along these lines since the early years of this century.[16] The broad procedure generally adopted consists of presenting to a mock jury a reconstruction of a real trial (based usually upon a tape-recording of actors reading from the trial transcript) and then observing how the members of the mock jury react to the evidence and how they reach their verdict.

[16] The massive Chicago Jury Project, which has produced more published material on jury trial than any other, incorporated the "mock" jury approach into the project; see particularly Strodtbeck and Mann (1956); Strodtbeck, James, and Hawkins (1957); James (1959a, 1959b); and Simon (1967). One member of that team, in a review of the project as a whole, saw the use of such experimental juries as "the most important facet of the project" (Broeder 1959).

There are numerous variations of detail, described in a vast literature on the subject, but most of the research corresponds to this procedure. One important development has been introduced by researchers in recent years—that of the "shadow" jury—and this has been used imaginatively by McCabe and Purves (1974) in England and by Diamond and Zeisel (1974) in the United States. Shadow juries were put into courtrooms, as it were, alongside the real jury and listened to the same evidence and received the same instructions as to the law. The researchers then recorded their deliberations on the assumption that these recordings would give some indication of how real juries reacted to, say, the defendant and the evidence of different kinds of witness, and of how they reached their verdict. This assumption may, however, be called into question, since the verdicts that the shadow juries reached were not always consistent with those of the real jury. In the study by McCabe and Purves, as many as a quarter of the verdicts of the shadow juries were different from those of the real jury. In other words, one must doubt the degree of correspondence between the deliberations of the two panels if even the verdicts were at variance in certain cases.[17]

This brings us to what is certainly the greatest problem with all simulated jury experiments—that the mock or shadow jury is not determining the fate of the defendant in question. The effect of this factor on the deliberations of mock panels is impossible to determine. It may mean that they are less conscientious and careful in their deliberations than the real jury would be, since no one's liberty actually hinges upon their decision. But it is equally possible that the mock jury will behave more rationally

[17] The authors take an optimistic, if speculative, view of such disagreements: "The evidence of the 'shadow' jury discussions in cases where there was disagreement between real and 'shadow' jury verdicts allows no more than speculation about the different course of the real jury's reasoning. Where real and 'shadow' juries agreed it is tempting to say that we have a good idea how the real jury reached its decision. Although this might be going too far, our observation of the consistency in the discussions of each of the experimental groups, in their address to the evidence, their need for convincing proof, and their awareness of the criminal nexus in some of the more difficult cases, encourages us to think that this may be what juries are like" (McCabe and Purves 1974, p. 31).

than its real counterpart because it would be pointless to exercise its equitable jurisdiction to acquit a defendant whom it believes to be technically guilty in the broader interests of what it takes to be "justice" in that case. (Good discussions of jury "equity" are given in Broeder 1954; Newman 1955; Van Dyke 1970; and Brooks and Doob 1975.) We do not know which tendency is the more likely to be encountered, but neither will the researcher concerned. Some distortion will inevitably be introduced into the experiment, but it will be all but impossible to control for it and, we suspect, in most cases even to identify it. This distortion seems to us to call into question the whole approach based upon simulated jury panels. Furthermore, it is simply not possible to reproduce the atmosphere of a trial in a laboratory, and the mere act of recording or observing the deliberations of the mock jury is likely further to distort the nature of the discussion. (These difficulties are discussed in some detail in Bermant et al. 1974; Sealy 1974; and Kessler 1975.) To compound these serious problems, many researchers have contented themselves with samples of jurors composed exclusively of students,[18] who, though readily accessible to the psychologist in his laboratory, do not even approximate the social mix which would characterize virtually any real jury. Many students would, indeed, be ineligible for jury service. For these reasons, it is probably safer to regard this body of literature as tentative and exploratory in nature. It may be of value in helping us understand something of the dynamics of small-group decision-making, but it does not tell us much about how juries reach their verdicts.

The final method by which researchers have attempted to assess the performance of the jury has been to pit its verdict against the views of other participants in the trial. A considerable amount of research based upon this approach has been carried out over the years both in the United States and in England, and it is the method that we ourselves adopted in studying the outcome of

[18] Examples of this kind are to be found in the work of Becker, Hildum, and Bateman (1965); Boehm (1968); Landy and Aronson (1969); Nemeth and Sosis (1973); Hendrick and Shaffer (1975); and Goldman, Maitland, and Norton (1975).

jury trials in England (Baldwin and McConville 1979a). Kalven and Zeisel (1966), whose book *The American Jury* is the most often cited of any book written about juries, pioneered this approach. They sought the opinions of trial judges who had presided at no fewer than 3,576 criminal trials heard throughout the United States, in order to ascertain whether they agreed with the juries' verdict and, if they did not agree, the ways in which they differed. Three studies carried out more recently in England have formed part of the same tradition. McCabe and Purves (1972), whose study was conceived as an exploratory pilot exercise, sent questionnaires to counsel, solicitors, and sometimes to the trial judge, in 115 jury cases that had ended in the acquittal of the defendant.[19] Zander (1974) based his study (which was also confined to acquittals[20]) upon the opinions expressed by defense and prosecution barristers in a consecutive series of two hundred acquittals in London. He was particularly concerned to test the hypothesis that serious, professional criminals were the ones most likely to gain perverse acquittals.[21] In our own study (Baldwin and McConville 1979a) we sought the opinions of four groups—defense and prosecuting solicitors, po-

[19] McCabe and Purves (1972) are somewhat vague about the procedures they adopted and about the responses they received from those whose views they sought. On this point, see Baldwin and McConville (1979a, pp. 8–10).

[20] The preoccupation with acquittals on the part of English researchers very much reflects the political context within which the debate concerned with jury trial has been conducted in recent years. The question whether juries are unduly lenient toward defendants was raised forcibly by Sir Robert Mark, then commissioner of the Metropolitan Police Force, in a provocative and well-publicized lecture delivered in 1973. Indeed, it would not be going too far to say that Mark's views on jury trial have been more influential in setting the political framework for discussion than those of any other writer. Particularly important was his statement that "the proportion of those acquittals relating to those whom experienced police officers believe to be guilty is too high to be acceptable. . . . I wouldn't deny that sometimes common sense and humanity produce an acquittal which could not be justified in law, but this kind of case is much rarer than you might suppose. Much more frequent are the cases in which the defects and uncertainties of the system are ruthlessly exploited by the knowledgeable criminal and by his advisers" (Mark 1973, p. 10). This statement has stimulated a good deal of research, particularly concerned with the extent to which "professional" criminals are successful in gaining unjustified acquittals in the courts. See on this Zander (1974); Mack (1976); and Baldwin and McConville (1978; 1979a, pp. 106–24).

[21] We have been critical of the methodology adopted by Zander and of his interpretation of the results: see Baldwin and McConville (1974).

lice officers, and the trial judge—in an effort to build up a rounded view of several hundred jury verdicts.[22]

We take the view that this method, though obviously imperfect, is the most illuminating. The judge's opinion is particularly valuable in such an assessment since he, like the jury, is in court throughout the trial and is required to pay close attention to the evidence. Where his opinion can be pitted against the views of others involved in the trial, we would argue that a reasonably secure basis on which to assess the likely accuracy of verdicts can be established. It does not follow that juries *ought* to decide cases in the way that trial judges, lawyers, or other professionals would, and researchers who have made, implicitly or explicitly, the contrary assumption have been rightly criticized by Mungham and Bankowski (1976): "When the effort is made to test 'efficiency' or 'competence' it is assumed that we all know and agree upon a definition of what constitutes the 'good juror.' We would argue that no such consensus exists. . . . It would seem that . . . [often] the idea of the 'good juror' is he who knows the law as a lawyer; one who accepts the prevailing courtroom norms of legal rationality and who is willingly incorporated into the social order of the courtroom and the trial. This is a view that would seem to be at least tacitly accepted by most jury researchers" (p. 209). The criticism clearly goes to the very heart of the jury debate—deciding upon the jury's proper function. Is it the function of the jury faithfully to follow the legal rules and deliver a true verdict according to the evidence? Is it actually to challenge lawyers' notions of justice? Or is it simply to apply the law to the facts in a structural setting which allows the jury sometimes to reach a result not contemplated by the

22 We received generous funding from the Home Office to facilitate our own inquiry (1979a). We spent virtually a year in negotiations with the different bodies we wished to involve in our research. Though we were successful in persuading members of the judiciary, the police, and prosecution and defense solicitors, the ruling body of the Bar instructed members in the Birmingham area (who had already agreed to cooperate) not to participate in any aspect of the inquiry. For further details of our negotiations, see Baldwin and McConville (1979a, pp. 21-26). It goes without saying that any views expressed in this article are ours alone and are not to be taken as those of the Home Office or of our respondents.

formal rules? It is a recurrent theme of this paper that this question is ideological not empirical, although answers to it have a direct bearing upon the sense that is made of the findings of empirical researchers. In short, we would argue that the workings of the jury cannot be evaluated independently of its role definition. (Further discussion of the jury's function is given in Baldwin and McConville 1979b, pp. 886–89.)

II. Research Results

Having reviewed the principal methods that have been used by researchers to uncover the mysteries of the jury room, we now consider the fruits of their work. We shall examine the most important social scientific evidence—and there is a vast amount of it—under three broad headings: the performance of juries—including their competence as fact finders and their ability to understand legal instructions; the composition of juries; and the use of six-member juries and majority verdicts.

A. The Performance of Juries

Although jury research has taken many forms and focused on a variety of questions, the preoccupation of researchers has been with the actual performance of the jury. Do juries decide cases strictly in accordance with the weight of the evidence, or are their verdicts influenced by emotion, bias, or other legally irrelevant factors? The sheer weight of empirical evidence has tempted some reviewers (e.g. Simon and Marshall 1972) to jump to the conclusion, in our view misguidedly, that the jury is an extremely competent body, making its decisions overwhelmingly on the basis of evidence presented in open court.[23] Some writers have gone further and argued that, even in those cases in which the jury departs from the evidence, it does so in a direction which

[23] There are several reviews of the literature on juries, and this is the conclusion most authors have drawn. In their review of major empirical studies of jury behavior in the United States, Simon and Marshall (1972) concluded: "In the last two decades lawyers and social scientists have joined together in large-scale efforts to evaluate the jury system in more objective and scientific terms than had been done at any previous time. . . . By and large what has been reported indicates that the jury system works well, that the participants perform their task with intelligence and interest, and that the juries' verdicts are consistent with those that experts, i.e. judges, claim they would have reached" (pp. 229–30).

enhances, rather than undermines, the interests of justice. There is indeed a good deal of empirical evidence to support this general conclusion. To take the most often quoted example, Kalven and Zeisel (1966) discovered that judges were in general agreement with the verdicts of juries in about three-quarters of all the cases in their sample and that, where they differed, most verdicts were nonetheless eminently defensible. "The jury thus represents a uniquely subtle distribution of official power, an unusual arrangement of checks and balances. It represents also an impressive way of building discretion, equity, and flexibility into a legal system. Not the least of the advantages is that the jury, relieved of the burdens of creating precedent, can bend the law without breaking it" (p. 498).

Those who have attempted to study the jury system by means of simulated jury experiments have reached a similar, if more restrained, conclusion. Mock juries, it seems, base their deliberations largely upon the evidence, and only exceptionally are swayed by other factors. McCabe and Purves (1974), in what is arguably the most painstaking and realistic of the exercises so far conducted, summarize their results as follows:

> The members of every jury swear or affirm that they will bring in a verdict according to the evidence which has been presented to them in the course of the trial. . . . There can be little doubt that this requirement seems to be in the front of the collective mind of the jury as it leaves the court, and it is thereafter not usually displaced by any other consideration. . . . Time and time again, in our "shadow" jury discussions we found that even the most errant excursus, the most uncontrolled discussion, or the most imaginative reconstruction of events, were brought to an end by a reference to what was taken to be the evidence brought out in the court room (pp. 31–32).

Despite these confident assertions, we would urge caution in the interpretation of much of this research. We noted earlier a tendency on the part of some researchers to be sympathetically disposed toward juries, which devalues the findings in question.

For when researchers, under the guise of scientific objectivity, assume the role of advocates for the system, the reader must beware. Even the most eminent researchers in this field—Harry Kalven and Hans Zeisel of the University of Chicago—have been accused of this on several occasions.[24] One writer has referred, for instance, to their "thinly disguised reverence for juries" and to their "marked tendency . . . to interpret ambiguous data in favor of the jury" (Becker 1970, p. 329). Sympathy toward jury trial is apparent in much of their writing, as it is in the work of others, and if one scratches beneath the surface of the authors' own interpretation, certain disconcerting findings about juries are revealed. There are other clear instances (sometimes overlooked by the researchers concerned) of crucial misunderstandings and misconceptions about standards of proof, particularly in the literature on mock juries, that severely dent the image of the jury as a competent fact finder. For example, James (1959b) offers clear evidence that, although the testimony of experts is not rejected out of hand in the jury room, jurors misinterpret legal instructions or even on occasions disregard them. A more serious problem concerns the ability of jurors to understand technical instructions, a question examined by Arens, Granfield, and Susman (1965). They found that jurors' comprehension of judges' instructions was "dramatically low," with no more than a third of the jurors in their sample able accurately to recall the judge's instructions on the law of insanity once they reached the jury room.[25] But, "far more shocking than the morass of ignorance respecting mental disease and defect is the operative presumption of the defendant's guilt. . . . The low comprehen-

[24] Several trenchant critiques have been leveled at Kalven and Zeisel's methods and the inferences they draw from the material they collected. Apart from the difficulties raised by the unrepresentative nature of the samples of judges, cases, and types of offense, serious misgivings have been expressed about the inferences drawn by Kalven and Zeisel about judge-jury disagreements from answers to essentially descriptive questions. Indeed, in 10 percent of the cases, the reasons for such disagreements were supplied by Kalven and Zeisel and not by the judges. Moreover, their conclusion that the jury does not misunderstand the case is simply unsupported by their evidence. For a full discussion of these and other shortcomings, see Griew (1967); MacKenna (1967); Walsh (1969); Becker (1970); and Bottoms and Walker (1972).

[25] This finding was not paralleled in the Chicago jury experiments: see James (1959b) and Simon (1967).

sion characterizing the assessment of the insanity defense is fully matched by the low comprehension governing the assessment of the burden of proof. This finding is particularly ominous" (p. 26). This apparent failure of the jury adequately to grasp the meaning of proof beyond reasonable doubt strikes at the heart of the jury's function. The traditional safeguard supposedly enshrined in jury trial becomes no more than empty rhetoric. Yet the jury's failure in this regard has been noted by several researchers in addition to Arens, Granfield, and Susman.[26]

The problem became apparent to us when we were examining the outcome of some seven hundred jury cases in Birmingham and London. In that study, we were struck by the unexpected volume of criticism of juries' verdicts expressed by judges, defense and prosecuting lawyers, and police officers.[27] Particularly surprising was the criticism by members of the judiciary. One judge, for example, in answer to a question seeking his opinion of the factors that might have produced an acquittal in a particular case, replied, "God knows!" Other judges merely wrote on the questionnaire the single word "Perverse." Still others replied at length, stating why they had disagreed with a particular verdict. (For lengthy verbatim quotes from judges and other respondents in our sample, see Baldwin and McConville 1979a, pp. 34–83.) Our methodology aimed to achieve a rounded view of verdicts by collating the opinions of different groups of respondents about individual cases. When we did this for all cases that had ended as acquittals, we found that only about a third

[26] The most prominent writers are Hoffman and Brodley (1952); Simon (1970); Simon and Mahan (1971); and Cornish and Sealy (1973). Although, as we have already indicated, there are weaknesses in the mock jury approach, the method is more useful in uncovering the extent to which laymen can recall and comprehend legal instruction than in illuminating the way in which questions of guilt are determined.

[27] The basic approach that we adopted in this research was simple and pragmatic. Since we could not eavesdrop on the jury and were not allowed to contact any jurors after trial, we decided to tap the views of other participants in the trial to find out what they had made of the jury's verdict. This was, of course, very much a second-best procedure, but we were confident that, given the high response rates achieved and the frankness of the opinions expressed about each verdict by respondents, a rigorous evaluation of jury verdicts could be made. Further discussion of the methods adopted in this research, and of its limitations is given in Baldwin and McConville (1979a, pp. 20–36; 1979b, pp. 863–67).

were regarded as justified by all of the respondents we contacted, and as many as a quarter were doubted by at least three groups.[28] Furthermore, only in a few of these cases did respondents attribute the acquittal to the jury's having placed equitable considerations above the cold application of legal principle. Much more common was a belief that there was simply no reasonable explanation for the acquittal.

But criticisms of verdicts were not confined to acquittals. Indeed, the most disturbing finding to emerge concerned certain convictions in the sample. As we noted earlier, researchers in England (and to a lesser extent in the United States as well) have tended to overlook the possibility that juries might convict the innocent. We found that, in about 6 percent of all cases that had resulted in convictions, doubts about the outcome were expressed by two or more respondents.[29] It is interesting to note that over half the questionable convictions in our sample were doubted by trial judges,[30] and over 90 percent by police officers (who are temperamentally and professionally unlikely to adopt this position without good reason).

Much has been written about the sort of factors likely to endanger the innocent (such as the risks surrounding evidence of identification, or unsatisfactory police evidence), but none of

[28] This is the more remarkable because we classified a response as critical of the verdict only when the criticism was made explicitly and unambiguously; uncertainty or surprise at a particular verdict was not treated as disagreement with it. The result was totally unexpected because earlier research on jury acquittals in England (particularly that of McCabe and Purves 1972 and Zander 1974) had produced an opposite conclusion. We have been critical of the methods used by these researchers and view the interpretation of their findings as suspect: see Baldwin and McConville (1974; 1979a, pp. 8–11).

[29] We adopted a less exacting standard in classifying questionable convictions than that used in relation to questionable acquittals, because in law a defendant is entitled to an acquittal if there is any reasonable doubt, whereas he or she cannot be convicted unless there is proof beyond reasonable doubt.

[30] If a judge allows the case to go to the jury, it does not follow that in a bench trial he would have come to the same conclusion as the jury. The most that can be inferred (if the judge has acted properly) is that there is some evidence on which a jury could convict. To upset a conviction by jury in England, it is not sufficient to show that the judge doubted its correctness, that the case against the defendant was weak or, indeed, that the verdict was against the weight of the evidence. For these and other reasons, current English appeals procedures are wholly ineffective in remedying potential miscarriages of justice of this kind: see Williams (1963) and Baldwin and McConville (1979b, pp. 882–86).

these appeared to be relevant to an understanding of how these cases of questionable conviction arose. Other factors seemed much more important, principally the difficulties juries may have experienced in appreciating the high standard of proof required in criminal cases, precisely the same difficulty noted by earlier researchers discussed above. Some respondents questioned whether, in particular cases, the jury had grasped the subtleties of "reasonable doubt"; others felt that a defendant had been entitled to the benefit of the doubt in a finely balanced case; and others contended that the jury had misapplied the concept or failed to follow the instructions that the judge had given. These considerations raised in our minds a possibility that certain juries may have been too easily convinced of a defendant's guilt, a possibility ignored by many earlier researchers. We would not argue that this is the jury's general inclination. Indeed, our own results relating to acquittals suggest the opposite tendency. But it seems likely that the legal standard of proof is an exceptionally difficult one for laymen to apply, and it is therefore to be expected that different juries will interpret the standard in different ways.

On the evidence of our research, we concluded that jury trial was an unpredictable method of discriminating between the guilty and the innocent, and we considered that the reverence accorded the jury by other researchers was misplaced or excessive. We can only speculate on why our results and conclusions are at variance with those of most other researchers, although a few points can be made with confidence. All are agreed that juries reach sensible verdicts in the great majority of cases, but this in itself tells us very little about how well the jury is functioning. This is not merely because the criteria used in the assessment of what is "sensible" are imperfect. It is rather because one needs to know a good deal about the kind of cases in which juries appear to err. If it were discovered, for example, that juries returned questionable verdicts in only 5 percent of all cases, this could not be taken per se as a demonstration of the efficacy of jury trial. More detailed examination might reveal, say, that the 5 percent of cases involved the questionable conviction of members of minority groups, or the questionable acquittal of all murderers and armed robbers.

We were struck by the serious nature of many of the offenses that we classified in our own research as questionable convictions,[31] and we reemphasize the point that it is cases within this category that raise in our minds the most disturbing questions about the efficacy of trial by jury. Yet some researchers have so structured their inquiries that the question whether juries wrongfully convict defendants is not even raised.[32] Others have simply minimized the importance of uncomfortable findings. Kalven and Zeisel (1966), for instance, seem to have been untroubled by the possibility that in some cases the jury may have been unduly harsh on defendants. Citing the cases of black defendants which appear to fall within this category, they euphemistically refer to the jury's "negative sympathy index" (p. 210) toward black defendants—a disingenuous expression which does not disguise the real concern that such a finding should surely have aroused in the authors. Their finding that trial judges would have acquitted entirely or convicted only on a lesser charge in 3 percent of all cases did not appear to weaken their faith in jury trial—a finding which led one critic sternly to observe: "If it were to be found by research in England that this difference occurred with equal frequency, it is to be hoped that the situation would not be accepted with equanimity, but that further investigation of the reasons why juries convict in such cases would be set in motion immediately" (Cornish 1968, p. 173).

The problems surrounding the interpretation of findings of this kind are of much more than academic importance. For the conclusions of research may be used by the courts in treating juries' verdicts as inviolable, or they may be cited by legislatures introducing modifications to existing procedures. This has indeed already happened on a number of occasions in the United States. The question is whether we should grant to jury verdicts—which

[31] These cases included murders, rapes, and robberies as well as other serious violent and property offenses. For further details, see Baldwin and McConville (1979a, pp. 68–87).

[32] This applies particularly to the English studies concerned solely with acquittals by jury, especially those by McCabe and Purves (1972) and Zander (1974).

may on occasion spring from misunderstanding, ignorance, or prejudice—a degree of sanctity which effectively preempts adequate review. Perhaps in human terms the jury reaches a just determination as often as can be expected, and alternative forms of tribunal, if subjected to the same detailed scrutiny, would display similar imperfections.[33] The important point is that there are as many dangers in minimizing the jury's imperfections as in exaggerating them.

B. The Composition of Juries

In the United States and in England, the principle that juries must be impartial is deeply entrenched and is given expression in the general requirement that juries form a representative cross section of the community. The Supreme Court's statement of principle in *Thiel* v. *Southern Railway Co.*, 382 U.S. 217,220 (1946) could equally well apply to England:[34]

> The American tradition of trial by jury, considered in
> connection with either criminal or civil proceedings,
> necessarily contemplates an impartial jury drawn from a
> cross-section of the community. . . . This does not mean,
> of course, that every jury must contain representatives of
> all the economic, social, religious, racial, political and
> geographical groups of the community; frequently such
> complete representation would be impossible. But it
> does mean that prospective jurors shall be selected by
> court officials without systematic and intentional
> exclusion of any of these groups.

[33] Whether the jury is working well or badly depends largely upon the standard against which its performance is being measured. One may posit some perfect standard and test the jury's performance against that, but this is a spurious method of comparison. Alternatively, it would be possible to measure the jury's performance against that of other tribunals, such as judges, lay magistrates or other assessors, or other systems of dispute resolution, such as plea bargaining. The material for a comparative study of this kind is, however, lacking and our theoretical understanding of other systems imperfect.

[34] In England, the Morris Committee (1965), upon whose recommendations the present law relating to juries is principally based, stated that "it is . . . inherent in the very idea of a jury that it should be as far as possible a genuine cross-section of the adult community" (para. 50). A Practice Direction issued by the Lord Chief Justice in 1973 reemphasized that it is "contrary to established practice for jurors to be excused on more general grounds such as race, religion, or political beliefs or occupation" [1973] 1 All E.R. 240.

Although arguments have been increasingly advanced that representative juries of this kind are ill-suited to sit in judgment in trials involving members of minority groups, the traditional view has been that the goal of selection should be a jury that is a microcosm of the wider community.[35]

It is equally clear, however, that in both jurisdictions the actual composition of juries is in important respects at variance with this stated ideal. In the United States, Mills (1962), for example, found that, although there was no exclusion of any major occupational group, the selection procedure was such as to give a much greater chance of selection to eligible members of professional and managerial groups than to craftsmen, operatives, service workers, and laborers. This finding was strikingly confirmed in his later study (Mills 1969). Others have commented upon selection procedures which operate to underrepresent certain groups.[36] The general conclusion is summed up by Van Dyke (1977): "In most courts in the United States significant segments of the population are still not included on juries as often as they would be in a completely random system aimed at impaneling a representative cross-section. Blue-collar workers, non-whites, the young, the elderly, and women are the groups most widely underrepresented on juries, and in many jurisdictions, the underrepresentation of these groups is substantial and dramatic" (p. 24). In England, until recently, there has been no comparable body of empirical evidence to indicate how rep-

[35] See *Yale Law Journal* (1970), where it is argued that the jury system "must be structured to produce a substantial number of blacks on juries trying cases directly affecting the interests of black litigants or of the black community" (p. 537). The arguments for all-black juries are reviewed by Dashwood (1972), who, while conceding that there are good reasons for ensuring that at least some of the jurors come from the racial or cultural minority to which the accused belongs, concludes that the "divisive" step of having all-black juries is not justified in Britain.

[36] Robinson (1950) showed that lower occupational and economic groups were systematically excluded from federal grand juries in the Southern District of California. On exclusion of the young, see *Journal of Criminal Law and Criminology* (1975) and Van Dyke (1977). On women, see particularly Levine and Schweber-Koren (1976) and Alker, Hosticka, and Mitchell (1976). On blacks see e.g. *Yale Law Journal* (1963, 1965); Van Amburg (1974); and Van Dyke (1977). See also Robinson (1950); Vanderzell (1966); Buckhout (1973); and De Cani (1974). Beiser (1973) concludes that jury venires are "disproportionately male, middle-aged, educated, and employed" (p. 199).

resentative juries are. There is no doubt, however, that Devlin's (1956) characterization of English juries as "predominantly male, middle-aged, middle-minded and middle-class" held good at least until 1974, when legislative changes brought an end to the traditional requirement (which had existed since 1825) that all jurors be property owners. Thus, in 1965, the Morris Committee, which had been appointed specifically to examine qualifications for jury service, discovered that women formed only 11 percent of the total number of eligible jurors, a direct result of restrictions imposed by the property qualification. In what was the first study of its kind conducted in England, we were able to use information on the background of juries specifically gathered for us by the Lord Chancellor's Department. Using this material, we noted that juries were in certain respects reasonably representative of the wider community but much less so in others (for a full account of our findings, see Baldwin and McConville 1979a, pp. 88–105). We examined the composition of all juries in the Birmingham Crown Court over a twenty-one-month period in 1975 and 1976, and found that, in terms of age and occupational structure, they bore a close correspondence to the Birmingham population as a whole. In two respects, however, juries were markedly unrepresentative. Although women constituted one-half of those eligible for jury service, almost three-quarters of jurors were male. Members of ethnic minorities were similarly underrepresented. It is apparent, therefore, that in the United States and England, the ideal of a representative jury has yet to be attained.

It is true of course that juries can never be fully representative, if only because the rules relating to eligibility directly or indirectly exclude certain groups. Among groups affected by such rules in both jurisdictions have been women and the young (see e.g. Cornish 1973; *Journal of Criminal Law and Criminology* 1973; Levine and Schweber-Koren 1973). But the major causes of unrepresentative juries lie not in the rules relating to eligibility but in the way in which jurors are selected from the eligible pool. Three factors in particular account for the distortions. In the first place, the way in which names are drawn from the eligible pool has the effect of discriminating against certain groups. In both countries, there is a heavy reliance on voter registration lists and these lists notoriously underrepresent the young and blacks (see Alker, Hosticka, and Mitchell 1976; Van Dyke 1977). Linked to this is a wide administrative discretion which is as a rule vested in court clerks to grant excusals to those called to serve. The exercise of this discretion has often had the effect of greatly reducing the numbers of certain groups (particularly women, blacks, and the highly educated) in the jury pool. The second source of distortion arises from discriminatory practices at the initial selection stage. Such practices are hard to uncover but in both countries researchers have noted that some court clerks have adopted an informal system under which fewer women than men are called.[37] The final and perhaps most controversial influence over jury composition is the voir dire procedure adopted in the United States by virtue of which potential jurors may be removed with or without cause from the jury pool.[38] The rationale behind this procedure is to ensure the integrity of the jury by eliminating those who may be prejudiced about the defendant, the prosecution, or some aspect of the case. In the United States, jurors may be challenged for cause (that is, on some specific and legally recognized basis of partiality) or peremptorily (that is, without any reasons being given). The number of challenges for cause is generally unlimited, but, before a juror can be removed, the judge must be convinced that

[37] In England, the Morris Committee (1965) adverted to the fact that many women have family commitments which make it difficult for them to spare the time for jury service. In order to meet this difficulty, they endorsed a "generous use of the summoning officer's power to excuse." A similarly liberal granting of excuses to women operates in the United States: see Alker, Hosticka, and Mitchell (1976) and Van Dyke (1977, pp. 121–23).

Levine and Schweber-Koren (1976) reported that in Erie County court clerks, under instruction or at their own volition, pursued a policy of calling fewer women than men, apparently on the basis that women would be more likely than men to claim exemptions. In our research, we discovered that there was an unofficial policy operating in Birmingham under which twice as many men as women were summoned: Baldwin and McConville (1979c).

[38] Discussions of the voir dire procedure are given by Emerson (1968); Hare (1968); Rhine (1969); Mackoff (1971); Schulman et al. (1973); Van Amburg (1974); Padawer-Singer, Singer, and Singer (1974); Fried, Kaplan, and Klein (1975); Saks (1976); Blunk and Sales (1977); and Van Dyke (1977).

the juror is prejudiced. The number of peremptory challenges is limited, and the number allowable varies between jurisdictions. In England, where there is no real equivalent of the *voir dire*, each defendant is permitted three peremptory challenges[39] and an unlimited number of challenges where reasonable cause is shown. The prosecution may also challenge for cause and may, without giving reasons, require a juror to "stand by," whereupon that juror is excluded from the panel. The evidence appears to show that, in the United States, the use of the peremptory challenge (particularly to strike out blacks)[40] and the introduction of social-scientific techniques in jury selection (as used in the trial of the Harrisburg Seven in the early 1970s) has occasionally had an important influence on the final composition of the jury. In England, on the other hand, the system of challenging has not developed to anything like the same degree. English lawyers have traditionally been denied any information of importance on the background of jurors, and English judges have rarely permitted detailed cross-examination of those on the panel. Our own research in Birmingham confirmed that the right to challenge is used sparingly by both defense and prosecution lawyers.[41] Indeed, no more than 101 challenges were made throughout the whole period of the study, and, of these, only thirteen were made by the prosecution. We found no real evidence of any concerted attempt to affect the composition of more than a handful of juries—still less of such attempts bringing about

[39] Criminal Law Act, 1977. Prior to this act, each defendant was entitled to exercise up to seven peremptory challenges. The law was changed because of allegations that the power was being abused, especially in trials involving several defendants.

[40] See, for example, Van Amburg (1974) who found that, although the sworn jury panels represented a fair cross section of the community with respect to the black population, the use of the peremptory challenge by the prosecution virtually eliminated black representation. According to Van Dyke (1977), challenges for cause are not a major distorting factor since they are used on few occasions in most trials.

[41] Until 1973, jury lists contained the names, addresses and occupations of those called for service, but since then lawyers have even been denied information on occupation. On Birmingham, see Baldwin and McConville (1979a, chap. 6). Earlier the Morris Committee (1965) had noted that "only in a relatively small minority of cases" was any use made of the right of peremptory challenge.

the desired result. Since there was seldom more than a single challenge by either side in a case, the juries impaneled in Birmingham were scarcely affected by the challenge procedure.[42]

Though the question of the representativeness of juries is important in terms of the basic rights of groups and individuals, the central issue in the present context is whether the composition of a jury has any bearing upon the verdict. The emphasis that many lawyers, particularly in the United States, place upon the screening of jurors implies that the composition of a jury can have a decisive influence over the verdict it returns. A smattering of research evidence lends weight to this view. This evidence, drawn from both simulated jury experiments and field studies, indicates that verdicts may be influenced by a variety of factors, including the representation on juries of those of different sex, socioeconomic status, age, and race.[43] We shall say a little about each of these variables, but it is important to note at the outset that much of the research evidence is weak and contradictory.

Turning first to the relation between the verdict and the number of females on juries, there is some evidence to suggest that women jurors decide cases in different ways from men. Thus, for instance, Simon (1967) in her simulated jury experiments discovered that, in housebreaking offenses, women were more sympathetic toward the defendant than were men, although, in incest cases, housewives were more punitive than any other group. Contrary to her own earlier study (James 1959a) and to the findings of Strodtbeck and Mann (1956) and

[42] Recently, however, a storm of controversy has arisen over the disclosure by the attorney-general that in certain "exceptional types of case" (cases with strong political motives, or involving terrorists and persons believed to be professional criminals), it has been the practice of the prosecution to investigate jury pools prior to trial in order to decide whether any juror should be challenged: see Harman and Griffith (1979).

[43] This list by no means exhausts the possible variables. Researchers have examined, for example, the personality characteristics of individual jurors and the influence of the foreman (Bevan et al. 1958; Boehm 1968; and Mitchell and Byrne 1973); the order of presentation of defense and prosecution evidence (Lawson 1968); the influence of jurors' values (Becker, Hildum, and Bateman 1965); cognitive and memory processes (Calder, Insko, and Yandell 1974); the attractiveness of the defendant (Landy and Aronson 1969; Nemeth and Sosis 1973). For discussions of these and related phenomena, see Hawkins (1962); Gordon and Temerlin (1969); and Goldman, Maitland, and Norton (1975).

of Strodtbeck, James, and Hawkins (1957), she did not find differential rates of participation in jury discussions between males and females. In England, Sealy and Cornish (1973), in their mock jury study, found no association between the sex composition of the jury and verdict although there was a slight tendency in rape cases for women to be readier to convict. The evidence from these studies does not, therefore, point to any specific or clear relation between sex and verdict. Other studies have produced similarly confusing evidence (see e.g. Nagel and Weitzman 1972; Snyder 1971).

Much the same can be said of the socioeconomic composition of juries. The studies conducted by Simon (1967) and Adler (1973) suggest that juries of higher socioeconomic status are less likely to acquit than lower-status juries; and both Broeder (1965c) and Hermann (1970) found the occupational background of jurors had some bearing upon verdict. These results are not, however, confirmed in the study of Sealy and Cornish (1973). The only consistent link that Sealy and Cornish found was that between the age composition of juries and their verdicts. Their data indicated a slight tendency for young jurors to be less likely to convict, but, in a similar mock jury study, Simon (1967) concluded that age did not affect the verdict. Finally, as to race, there is some evidence to show that blacks are more likely to acquit than are whites, but other relations are unclear.[44]

It was against this background of research that we set out to examine the extent to which the verdicts of real juries in England were influenced by the social characteristics of the jurors. Altogether, 326 different juries sat in Birmingham in the period of study, and we obtained detailed information on the backgrounds of all 3,912 jurors concerned. The principal findings were that the age, sex, and occupational composition of the jury were not significantly related to the verdicts returned. It was not possible, however, to make generalizations with respect to

[44] Both Broeder (1959, 1965b) and Simon (1967) found that blacks had a greater tendency to acquit, but, whereas Broeder noted that those of British background were more likely to favor the prosecution, Simon found them to be more likely to favor acquittal than all other groups apart from blacks.

race, since so few members of minority ethnic groups were called to serve.[45] We concluded, as Simon (1967) had done in the United States, that individual attitudes and prejudices probably exerted greater influences on the final verdict than did any general social characteristics of the jury as a whole.

C. Research on Six-Member Juries and Majority Verdicts

Whatever view one takes of the merits of trial by jury in the Anglo-American legal system, one consideration is inescapable: it is an extremely expensive method of resolving issues of guilt and responsibility. Alternative procedures are administratively simpler and cheaper to operate, and it is not surprising that, despite the rhetoric surrounding judgment by one's peers and formal adversarial proceedings, the great majority of criminal cases are settled either by a guilty plea or by a bench trial. Although it is important to note that intense pressures of various kinds exist to reduce the cases tried by jury,[46] we shall confine ourselves here to two recent innovations—the introduction, in the United States, of six-member juries and, in both jurisdictions, of verdicts delivered by less-than-unanimous juries.[47] Such in-

[45] An earlier survey (Home Office Statistical Department 1975) had similarly concluded that, with respect to age, changes in the composition of the jury following a reduction in the age qualification for jury service had no discernible effect upon outcome. In another study concerned with changes in composition, Brown (1979) concluded that alterations in the occupational makeup of juries produced no change in the acquittal rate.

We also looked at the characteristics of the foreman and found that, although foremen were disproportionately drawn from males of higher socioeconomic status, this was not associated with the verdicts returned.

[46] These pressures are highly effective in minimizing the number of jury trials. In both jurisdictions, some 90 percent of all defendants plead guilty. See generally on this, Newman (1966); Blumberg (1970); Heberling (1973); and Baldwin and McConville (1977).

[47] The U.S. Supreme Court held in *Williams* v. *Florida*, 399 U.S. 78 (1970) that juries as small as six in number were constitutionally acceptable. Some states have adopted six-member juries, others have not. It was held in *Burch* v. *Louisiana*, 99 S.Ct.1623 (1979), that verdicts must be unanimous in six-member juries.

In *Johnson* v. *Louisiana*, 406 U.S. 356 (1972), and *Apodaca* v. *Oregon*, 406 U.S. 404 (1972), the United States Supreme Court held that unanimity of juries was not required under the Constitution and a majority of nine out of twelve jurors was sufficient. In England, the Criminal Justice Act 1967 abolished the requirement that juries be unanimous, and introduced majority verdicts of ten out of twelve jurors if the jury had failed to produce a unanimous verdict after deliberating for at least two hours.

novations have been seen by many writers as representing serious erosions of the fundamental principles of jury trial (see e.g. Kirkpatrick 1968; Zeisel 1971; Saari 1973; Ashman and McConnell 1973; Harman and Griffith 1979). As one writer put it, "In the four years from 1968 to 1972, the bottom has fallen out of the jury system" (Saari 1973, p. 12). Others have argued that these changes undermine the principle that guilt be established beyond reasonable doubt, for the requirement of a unanimous verdict by twelve may be a guarantee that, no matter how difficult questions of proof are, conviction is unlikely if the defendant's guilt is at all doubtful.

It is interesting to note that the question of juries of fewer than twelve members is scarcely even discussed in England, though it has stimulated lengthy and acrimonious debate in the United States. However, the introduction of majority verdicts in England, which was accompanied by a vigorous public debate, can be seen as in effect another way of reducing the size of juries. Indeed, as Zeisel (1971, p. 722) observes, in terms of nullifying minority viewpoints, it is a "reduction with a vengeance" and far more effective to this end than a simple reduction in jury size.[48]

Despite the bitterness of the controversy and the importance of the issues involved, the effects of such changes have proved exceedingly difficult to evaluate. Much of the empirical evidence upon which legislatures relied to justify the changes proposed has been of very questionable quality,[49] and more recent endeavors by researchers have produced little improvement. Some have conducted field surveys, comparing panels of different sizes, to determine whether the verdicts of smaller juries are (as many critics have supposed) less consistent in character and less favorable to the defense than twelve-member juries. Though the results of different studies are somewhat contradictory on this

[48] Juries in Scotland (which consist of fifteen members) can deliver verdicts on the basis of a simple majority (i.e. eight votes only are sufficient to ensure conviction). This has never, to our knowledge, provoked much debate in Scotland.

[49] There are several critiques in the literature of this misuse and distortion by the legislatures of social scientific evidence. See, in particular, Zeisel (1971); Zeisel and Diamond (1974); Zeisel (1975); Lempert (1975); and Saks (1977).

point, there is at least some evidence (notably from Beiser and Varrin 1975) which supports this position. The problem is, however, that there can be no guarantee that the nature of the cases tried by each panel is identical—indeed, in several cases the researchers concerned have been forced to concede that they are not. What is required is systematic monitoring over a lengthy period in which both types of jury hear the same trial, or else some kind of random allocation of trials; for legal and moral reasons, an exercise of this nature is not possible.

Psychologists have been eager to employ their own method of evaluation, based upon simulated jury trials, to overcome these problems. We noted earlier that experiments of this kind have to be treated with the greatest caution because of the element of artificiality which inevitably weakens them. In the study of juries of different sizes, this difficulty is equally relevant and is again compounded by the fact that very few of the studies are based upon samples that even approximate real jurors, most researchers contenting themselves with student subjects.[50] The studies are, in short, inevitably limited and open to differences of interpretation. On the little evidence available, one might risk the tentative assertion that, though some researchers have found differences in the length of deliberations and the way that evidence is considered by six-member juries, there is only one study (that of Valenti and Downing 1975) in which significant differences in the types of verdict returned by six- and twelve-member juries have been noted.[51] But even this limited statement would

[50] This criticism applies to the studies conducted by Kessler (1973); Valenti and Downing (1975); Davis et al. (1975); and Snortum, Klein, and Sherman (1976), among others. It is not difficult to accept the assessment offered by Saks (1977) that "the lesson for social scientists is that such a relatively simple question, so obviously within their research paradigms to answer, was nevertheless thoroughly bungled by the studies conducted post *Williams*" (p. 48).

[51] Nagel and Neef (1977) argue that there is no satisfactory way of testing the impact of six- and twelve-member juries other than by applying the principles of deductive logic based upon known facts and reasonable assumptions. Using information taken from Kalven and Zeisel (1966) on the proportion of defendants convicted by jury, they calculate that reducing the size of juries to six members would increase the probability of conviction by 2 per cent (from 64 percent to 66 percent). They deduce, on the same basis, that introducing nonunanimous verdicts (of ten out of twelve jurors) would increase the probability of conviction overall by 4 percent (from 64 percent to 68 percent).

be imprudent for, as many of the researchers concerned acknowledge, their studies are flawed by inherent methodological weaknesses and by the small size of the samples used.

It is true that some findings have emerged in these comparisons
which might lead one to conclude that the verdicts of twelve-
member juries are indeed to be preferred to those of smaller
panels. For instance, there is considerable evidence to show that
the length of deliberation is less for smaller juries (see particularly Valenti and Downing 1975; Davis et al. 1975; Padawer-Singer,
Singer, and Singer 1977; Saks 1977). Zeisel (1971) has demonstrated very effectively that smaller juries cannot possibly be as
representative of the wider community as twelve-member juries.
Minority viewpoints are less likely to be represented and, even
if they are, less likely to be heard. In this sense, the six-member
jury is much less of a cross-section of the community than is a
larger panel. Since there seem to be only very small savings in
terms of time and cost by employing six-member juries, the
arguments in favor of preserving the traditional twelve-member
jury—which certainly commands great public confidence—seem
much stronger.[52]

A similar conclusion can be drawn about unanimous verdicts
as opposed to majority or quorum verdicts. Although the os-
tensible reason for introducing majority verdicts was the fear
that jurors might be bribed or intimidated or that an unreasonably
stubborn juror might be able to thwart the will of the majority
(for a balanced discussion of these factors, see Ryan 1967), it
is important to remember that this situation would lead only to
a hung jury (and a retrial) rather than to an outright acquittal.
Somewhat surprisingly, accurate figures on majority verdicts are
difficult to obtain. In England, the questions that are put to foremen at the conclusion of each trial are framed so as not to reveal

[52] There is some evidence that minority viewpoints, if forcibly expressed,
can hold greater sway on smaller jury panels, and there are obvious dangers
in this. See Snortum, Klein, and Sherman (1976). On insignificant cost and time
saving, see Pabst (1972, 1973) and Beiser and Varrin (1975). Pabst (1973),
basing his conclusion upon examination of District of Columbia courts, stated
that the court records showed "virtually no difference in voir dire or trial
time, and only from 12 to 20 percent difference in overall juror manpower
requirements" (p. 6).

whether an acquitted defendant has been acquitted by a majority decision. In consequence, the available figures (given in the *Judicial Statistics* published annually by the Lord Chancellor's Department) relate only to convictions. Calculated on this basis, majority verdicts are returned in about 12 percent of trials—a rate which seems to vary little over time or between different geographical areas. Comparable figures are more difficult to obtain for the United States, where majority verdicts have been introduced in some states only (for some comparative estimates, see Kalven and Zeisel 1967).

There is some evidence to suggest that, once juries are allowed to return majority verdicts, they begin to use them in cases that earlier would have led to unanimous decisions and not to hung juries. The reason for this seems to be that, as Kalven and Zeisel (1967) note, juries often cease their deliberations once they reach the required majority, rather than persevering in overcoming the intransigence of one of their number. This observation is supported to some extent by the results of psychological experiments with simulated jury trials (particularly that conducted by Davis et al. 1975). Kalven and Zeisel estimate that in only 2 percent of all trials would hung juries be transformed into majority verdicts. In the light of these estimates, one may conclude that the introduction of majority verdicts, as with six-member juries, have produced paltry savings in costs and time, and that these savings may only have been achieved at the price of reducing public confidence in the jury by an inevitable lowering of the standard of proof.

III. Conclusions and Implications

On any fair appraisal of the literature on juries, it has to be said that a confusing picture emerges. One indication of this is that the massive body of research evidence has been signally unsuccessful in shifting ideological commitments of both critics and apologists. It is not simply because, for some individuals, prejudices will always be stronger than the facts; rather, it is because the facts are unclear or, where clear, too weak to dent the prejudices. It is difficult to point to any single finding of researchers which cannot be neutralized by one side or the other in the wider political debate. If, for example, juries are found to get certain cases wrong, that may be used to show that they get most cases right. If juries on occasion misunderstand the law, that may be the fault of the law or of the lawyers and not any shortcoming on the part of the jury. If juries defy certain laws, the laws in question may be criticized as unjust, oppressive, or inequitable. If juries are not representative of the wider community, the reply may be that impartiality is more important than representativeness. And if juries are representative, it may be objected that only the defendant's peer group can sufficiently understand his actions and give him a fair trial. These competing interpretations are possible both because the facts themselves are ambiguous and because proponents and critics of jury trial often approach the issues from entirely different standpoints. Much depends upon whether you begin or end with a conclusion. Nevertheless, it is possible to draw out of the morass of evidence and opinion a few important observations relating to the present position of the jury, its representativeness, the public's view of its role, and its general reliability as a tribunal of fact.

While the jury is not moribund, there is no doubt that for decades it has been in decline, and that it has been subjected to attacks which, though not mortal, have dealt severe blows to its health. In the United States, jury trial accounts for no more than 5 percent of all felony prosecutions; 85 to 90 percent of convictions are by guilty plea, usually following a plea bargain. Similarly in England, the overwhelming majority of criminal cases are now disposed of in the lower criminal courts without a jury, and of those cases which reach the higher courts, a majority end in the defendant pleading guilty, sometimes following negotiations over charge or sentence. How far this decline from its earlier preeminence is caused by the full and informed choice of defendants and how far it is caused by threats of heavier punishment or offers of inducements is a matter of dispute. What cannot be in doubt, however, is the nature and volume of more direct attacks on the structure of the jury itself. In both countries, the introduction of majority verdicts, administrative meddling with jury venire, and increasing attempts to handpick jurors, and, above all, the acceptance in the United States of juries of fewer than twelve members, strike at the heart of traditional notions about jury trial. If any trend can be discerned, it is that the jury, now effectively confined in criminal cases to a small proportion of relatively serious offenses, is undergoing changes which will fundamentally affect its character.

A second feature of the jury in both the United States and England is that it cannot be said to be a true cross-section of the community. A great number of studies have established that certain groups, particularly women and ethnic minorities, are heavily underrepresented on jury panels. In important respects juries today bear a much closer resemblance to the wider community than they did in times when wholesale discriminatory practices operated against large sections of society. Vestiges of such discrimination can still be seen to operate, however, in the bureaucratic interference with jury venires and in the selective use of strikes against specific groups. Moreover, the development of selection practices at the voir dire in the United States and of pretrial screening of jurors under English vetting procedures have an increasing influence on the final composition of the panel. Although the trend may be readily charted, it is far from clear what, if anything, should be done about it. The reason for this is that notions of jury composition conflict with demands for representative judgment, random judgment, impartial judgment, and judgment by equals. "A body may act fairly even if it is not independently appointed or constituted. Again, a body that is randomly chosen may not act fairly, and a representative body is not by its representativeness rendered impartial. Fairness or impartiality may not be a typical characteristic of the general community" (Marshall 1975, p. 5). The assumptions behind jury vetting, the voir dire, and calls for peer group juries are incompatible with selection based upon truly random procedures. At present, both jurisdictions sit uneasily between these conflicting demands, and no program for action can be laid down until the primary decision as to the sort of jury desired is settled.

Whatever misgivings there may be about the composition of juries, there is little doubt that trial by jury enjoys a high level of public confidence. One interesting question concerns the source of this confidence. It may be related not to what jurors actually do in discharging their duties, but to the mere fact that they participate in the process of government. Again, it may reflect a conscious appreciation of the process of jury trial itself, in which community sentiment applied to individual behavior is seen as a socially useful and equitable method of dispute resolution. Or it may spring from a wider-ranging evaluation of the whole criminal process in which the jury, whatever its defects, is preferred to the judgment of officials, professionals, or experts. These are all questions upon which empirical inquiry could be brought to bear. So, for example, if public confidence is based primarily upon the belief that trial by jury discriminates effectively between the guilty and the morally, factually, or legally innocent, the available evidence suggests that such confidence is not wholly justified. Or if it is based upon the value of citizen participation in government, there may be other more effective ways of achieving the same end. And if the value of trial by jury is believed to lie in the contribution that community sentiment can make to the practical application of the law, research strategies could be profitably redirected. As McCabe (1974, p. 279) put it:

> We need to know much more about the way juries actually function, about the relationship between jury function and community evaluation of wrong-doing, about the contribution to decisions of different kinds of jurors and the way in which effectively random rather than neighbourhood selection of jurors might affect the possibility of acquittal. In asking these kinds of questions researchers would move . . . to a more general reflection upon the kinds of tribunal that provide a decision that is appropriate and just in the eyes of the community as well as in the eyes of the defendant—and the definition of the 'community' in such a case would be a proper subject of research.

Research on such questions would be difficult to devise,[53] but it is our view that an attempt should be made to move away from undifferentiated generalization toward an examination of clearly enunciated hypotheses.

Related to this issue of public confidence is the question whether the jury is a reliable and accurate tribunal. As we have already pointed out, there has been an unfortunate tendency on the part of some researchers to allow biases in favor of jury trial to distort the interpretation of their results. When allowances are made for this, it would still be true to say that the empirical evidence, taken as a whole, suggests a high degree of jury reliability. But there remain disturbing doubts, and these doubts give rise to important theoretical concerns. In the first place, cases of questionable conviction have been identified in which juries, through inadvertence or prejudice, have failed to discharge their duties properly. The problem is serious because the unreasoned verdict, itself an integral feature of jury trial, makes effective appellate review almost impossible. The worries do not end here, however. Where the jury has acquitted on the basis of sentiment, sympathy, or equity, the readiness of researchers to grant approval to such decisions is very much open to question. This is not simply because the equity argument is double-edged (that tacit approval is thereby given to those decisions brought about by opposite sentiments), but because of the arbitrary treatment of defendants that this approach endorses. The assumption often made is that equitable considerations will be given effect by the jury whenever they are present,[54] but there is no evidence for

[53] A good start has been made by Casper (1978) on the narrower question of the perspective of defendants. One interesting finding to come out of his study concerned the sorts of demands that defendants make of the system. He writes: "Their judgments about the fairness of their treatment in the context of criminal courts are an amalgam of self-interest, notions of equity, and their sense of whether the process has been one in which they feel their interests have been adequately represented" (p. 162).

[54] The analysis of Kalven and Zeisel (1966) might appear to run counter to this, but their arguments are unconvincing. They argue that, where the evidence is close, the jury is "liberated" from the discipline of the evidence and thus is able to respond to issues of sentiment. There is no reason to suppose, however, that Kalven and Zeisel were able to distinguish "close" cases with any accuracy: their method simply allowed them to group as close all cases which the judge thought other than "very clear" (see Walsh 1969, p. 148). And judges themselves regarded 30 percent of jury verdicts which were at odds with their own evaluation as "without merit."

this. On the contrary, any objective evaluation demonstrates that such is not the case. There are many occasions on which defendants attract sympathy but are nevertheless convicted, and many others where, through no fault of the defendant, no sympathy factor appears. The concept of equal justice or even-handed treatment is usually confined to sentencing, but it is also relevant to situations in which some defendants, by chance or good fortune, obtain favorable verdicts whereas others, through accident or mischance, are deprived of such benefits. Moreover, it takes no imagination to imbue an otherwise questionable verdict with equitable qualities. Thus, it might be said that although a defendant is factually guilty, he should nevertheless be acquitted because (1) he comes from a good home background and has already suffered enough, or (2) he comes from a disadvantaged section of the community and we should expect less of him, or (3) he is unemployed and so should excite our sympathy, or (4) he is in good employment and a conviction would lead to the loss of his job, his pension and his social standing. When one adds to this scenario chance factors such as the attractiveness or unattractiveness of the defendant or his victim, the facile nature of the exercise becomes apparent. The short point is that there is no reason to think that juries always take into account, or give equal weight to, extralegal considerations of this kind, and, even if it is conceded that juries ought to be free to decide cases on such grounds, there is no evidence whatever to suggest that the jury is a reliable or predictable instrument for giving legitimacy to such notions. Indeed, as a working unit the jury changes its character from case to case, and these variations are crucial in understanding whether a chord of sympathy will strike an acceptable note. Idiosyncracy is in this sense inherent in our system of jury trial, and it would be unduly optimistic to suppose that different juries will deal with similar cases in the same way.

It is not the purpose of this essay to suggest that jury research has been unproductive or that it should come to an end. The legal rules and political conventions which prevent direct observation of jury deliberations render much of the evidence problematic, but the possibilities for future inquiry are not by any means exhausted. Nevertheless, jury research has in our view reached something of an impasse, and perseverance with existing approaches is not likely to be productive. What is now required is some attempt to confront more fundamental issues raised by jury trial and to examine juries within their social and political context. Apart from those already mentioned, the issues relevant here would include consideration of whether juries are capable of accurately discriminating between the factually innocent and the legally and factually guilty; whether juries consciously and routinely take into account equitable factors, and conversely whether they systematically ignore other considerations of a like nature; whether defendants prefer open-court adjudication to other methods of dispute resolution such as bench trial or plea bargaining; whether confidence in jury trial springs from a belief in its positive qualities or whether the jury gains its prestige by comparison with other tribunals used in the criminal process; and what specific qualities of jury trial are valued by defendants and the wider public. It is only when these questions are addressed that we can hope to move away from a debate characterized by superficial assertion and unstated ideology toward a fuller appreciation of the political functions performed by juries.

REFERENCES

Abraham, Henry J. 1975. *The Judicial Process*. 3d ed. New York: Oxford University Press.

Adler, Freda. 1973. "Socioeconomic Factors Influencing Jury Verdicts," *New York University Review of Law and Social Change* 3:1–10.

Alker, Hayward R., Carl Hosticka, and Michael Mitchell. 1976. "Jury Selection as a Biased Social Process," *Law and Society Review* 11:9–41.

Arens, Richard, Dom D. Granfield, and Jackwell Susman. 1965. "Jurors, Jury Charges and Insanity," *Catholic University of America Law Review* 14:1–29.

Ashman, Allan, and James McConnell. 1973. "Trial By Jury: The New Irrelevant Right?" *Southwestern Law Journal* 27:436–53.

Baldwin, John, and Michael McConville. 1974. "The Acquittal Rate of Professional Criminals: A Critical Note," *Modern Law Review* 37:439–43.

——. 1977. *Negotiated Justice*. London: Martin Robertson.

——. 1978. "Allegations against Lawyers: Some Evidence from Criminal Cases in London," *Criminal Law Review* 741–49.

——. 1979a. *Jury Trials*. London: Oxford University Press.

——. 1979b. "Trial by Jury: Some Empirical Evidence on Contested Criminal Cases in England," *Law and Society Review* 13:861–90.

——. 1979c. "The Representativeness of Juries," *New Law Journal* 129:284–86.

Barber, Dulan, and Giles Gordon, eds. 1976. *Members of the Jury*. London: Wildwood House.

Becker, Theodore L. 1970. *Comparative Judicial Politics*. Chicago: Rand McNally.

Becker, Theodore L., Donald C. Hildum, and Keith Bateman. 1965. "The Influence of Jurors' Values on their Verdicts: A Courts and Politics Experiment," *Southwestern Social Science Quarterly* 46:130–40.

Beiser, Edward N. 1973. "Are Juries Representative?" *Judicature* 57:194–99.

Beiser, Edward N., and René Varrin. 1975. "Six-member Juries in the Federal Courts," *Judicature* 58:424–33.

Bermant, Gordon, Mary McGuire, William McKinley, and Chris Salo. 1974. "The Logic of Simulation in Jury Research," *Criminal Justice and Behavior* 1:224–33.

Bevan, William, Robert S. Albert, Pierre R. Loiseaux, Peter N. Mayfield, and George Wright. 1958. "Jury Behavior as a Function of the Prestige of the Foreman and the Nature of his Leadership," *Journal of Public Law* 7:419–49.

Blackstone, Sir William. 1830. *Commentaries on the Laws of England* (4 vols.). Dublin.

Blumberg, Abraham S. 1967. *Criminal Justice*. Chicago: Quadrangle Books.

Blunk, Richard A., and Bruce D. Sales. 1977. "Persuasion During the Voir Dire." In *Psychology in the Legal Process*, ed. B. D. Sales. New York: Spectrum Publications.

Boehm, Virginia R. 1968. "Mr. Prejudice, Miss Sympathy, and the Authoritarian Personality: An Application of Psychological Measuring Techniques to the Problem of Jury Bias," *Wisconsin Law Review* 3:734–50.

Bottoms, Anthony E., and Monica Walker. 1972. "The American

Jury: A Critique," *Journal of the American Statistical Association* 67:773–79.

Broeder, Dale W. 1954. "The Functions of the Jury: Facts or Fictions?" *University of Chicago Law Review* 21:386–424.

———. 1959. "The University of Chicago Jury Project," *Nebraska Law Review* 38:744–60.

———. 1965a. "Plaintiff's Family Status as Affecting Juror Behavior: Some Tentative Insights," *Journal of Public Law* 14:131–41.

———. 1965b. "The Negro in Court," *Duke Law Journal* 19:19–31.

———. 1965c. "Occupational Expertise and Bias as Affecting Juror Behavior: A Preliminary Look," *New York University Law Review* 40:1079–1100.

Brooks, W. Neil, and Anthony N. Doob. 1975. "Justice and the Jury," *Journal of Social Issues* 31:171–82.

Brown, Don W. 1979. "Eliminating Exemptions from Jury Duty: What Impact Will It Have?" *Judicature* 62:436–48.

Buckhout, Robert. 1973. "Jury Without Peers: An Overview of Social Science Research on Juries in Criminal Trials." Mimeographed. New York: Center for Responsive Psychology.

Calder, Bobby J., Chester A. Insko, and Ben Yandell. 1974. "The Relation of Cognitive and Memorial Processes to Persuasion in a Simulated Jury Trial," *Journal of Applied Social Psychology* 4:62–93.

Casper, Jonathan D. 1978. *Criminal Courts: The Defendant's Perspective.* Washington, D.C.: U.S. Government Printing Office.

Clark, Tom C. 1966. "The American Jury: A Justification," *Valparaiso University Law Review* 1:1–7.

Clarke, Edward. 1974. "The Selection of Juries and in Particular Qualifications for Service and the Right of Challenge," In *The British Jury System*, ed. N. Walker. Cambridge: Institute of Criminology.

Connelly, Michael J. 1971. "Jury Duty—The Juror's View," *Judicature* 55:118–21.

Corboy, Philip H. 1975. "From the Bar." In Simon (1975).

Cornish, William R. 1968. *The Jury*. London: Allen Lane.

———. 1973. "Qualifications for Jury Service," *Criminal Law Review* 85–94.

Cornish, William R., and Philip A. Sealy. 1973. "Juries and the Rules of Evidence," *Criminal Law Review* 208–23.

Curtis, Charles P. 1952. "The Trial Judge and the Jury," *Vanderbilt Law Review* 5:150–66.

Dashwood, Alan. 1972. "Juries in a Multi-racial Society," *Criminal Law Review* 85–94.

———. 1973. "The Jury and the Angry Brigade," *University of Western Australia Law Review* 11:245–55.

Davis, James H. 1973. "Group Decision and Social Interaction: A Theory of Social Decision Schemes," *Psychological Review* 80: 97–125.

Davis, James H., Norbert L. Kerr, Robert S. Atkin, Robert Holt, and David Meek. 1975. "The Decision Processes of 6- and 12-Person Mock Juries Assigned Unanimous and Two-Thirds Majority Rules," *Journal of Personality and Social Psychology* 32:1–14.

De Cani, John S. 1974. "Statistical Evidence in Jury Discrimination Cases," *Journal of Criminal Law and Criminology* 65:234–38.

Devlin, Sir Patrick. 1956. *Trial by Jury*. London: Stevens.

———. 1973. "Should the Jury System Be Reformed?" In *Cases and Materials on the English Legal System*, ed. M. Zander. London: Weidenfeld and Nicolson.

———. 1979. *The Judge*. London: Oxford University Press.

Diamond, Shari, and Hans Zeisel. 1974. "A Courtroom Experiment on Juror Selection and Decision Making," *Personality and Social Psychology Bulletin* 1:276–77.

Devons, Ely. 1965. "Serving as a Juryman in Britain," *Modern Law Review* 28:561–70.

Du Parcq, Lord. 1948. *Aspects of Law*. Birmingham: University of Birmingham Holdsworth Club.

Elgrod, Stuart J., and Julian D. M. Lew. 1973. "Acquittals—a Statistical Exercise," *New Law Journal* 123:1104–6.

———. 1975. "Acquittals—Further Statistics," *New Law Journal* 125:45–46.

Emerson, David. 1968. "Personality Tests for Prospective Jurors," *Kentucky Law Journal* 56:832–54.

Emmet, Richard P. 1974. "The Need for a Scientific Study of the Jury's Deliberative Process," *Alabama Lawyer* 35:97–103.

Erlanger, Howard S. 1970. "Jury Research in America," *Law and Society Review* 4:345–70.

Frank, Jerome. 1949. *Courts on Trial*. Princeton: Princeton University Press.

Frankfurter, Felix, and Thomas G. Corcoran. 1926. "Petty Federal Offenses and the Constitutional Guaranty of Trial by Jury," *Harvard Law Review* 39:917–1019.

Fried, Michael, Kalman J. Kaplan, and Katherine W. Klein. 1975. "Juror Selection: An Analysis of Voir Dire." In Simon (1975).

Friloux, Anthony C. 1975. "Another View from the Bar." In Simon (1975).

Gelfand, Alan E., and Herbert Solomon. 1973. "A Study of Poisson's Models for Jury Verdicts in Criminal and Civil Trials," *Journal of the American Statistical Association* 68:271–78.

———. 1974. "Modelling Jury Verdicts in the American Legal System," *Journal of the American Statistical Association* 69:32–37.

Goldman, Jacquelin, Karen A. Maitland, and Pennie L. Norton. 1975. "Psychological Aspects of Jury Performance," *Journal of Psychiatry and Law* 3:367–80.

Gordon, Robert I., and Maurice K. Temerlin. 1969. "Forensic Psychology: The Judge and the Jury," *Judicature* 52:328–33.

Griew, Edward. 1967. "The Behaviour of the Jury—A Review of the American Evidence," *Criminal Law Review* 555–74.

Hale, John. 1973. "Juries: The West Australian Experience," *University of West Australian Law Review* 11:99–104.

Halsbury, Lord. 1903. "Trial by Jury," *Law Journal* 38:469–72.

Hare, Francis H. 1968. "Voir Dire and Jury Selection," *Alabama Lawyer* 29:160–75.

Harman, Harriet, and John Griffith. 1979. *Justice Deserted: The Subversion of the Jury*. London: National Council for Civil Liberties.

Hartshorne, Richard. 1949. "Jury Verdicts: A Study of Their Characteristics and Trends," *American Bar Association Journal* 35:113–17.

Hawkins, Charles H. 1962. "Interaction Rates of Jurors Aligned in Factions," *American Sociological Review* 27:689–91.

Hay, Douglas, Peter Linebaugh, and E. P. Thompson. 1975. *Albion's Fatal Tree: Crime and Society in Eighteenth-Century England*. New York: Pantheon.

Head, Mrs. Ben T. 1969. "Confessions of a Juror," *Federal Rules Decisions* 44:330–38.

Heberling, Jon L. 1973. "Conviction Without Trial," *Anglo-American Law Review* 2:428–72.

Henderson, Edith G. 1966. "The Background of the Seventh Amendment," *Harvard Law Review* 80:289–337.

Hendrick, Clyde, and David R. Shaffer. 1975. "Murder: Effects of Number of Killers and Victim Mutilation on Simulated Jurors' Judgments," *Bulletin of the Psychonomic Society* 6:313–16.

Hermann, Philip J. 1970. "Occupations of Jurors as an Influence on Their Verdict," *Forum* 5:150–55.

Hervey, John G. 1947. "The Jurors Look at our Judges," *Oklahoma Bar Journal* 1508–13.

Hoffman, Harold M., and Joseph Brodley. 1952. "Jurors on Trial," *Missouri Law Review* 17:235–51.

Holmes, Oliver Wendell. 1899. "Law in Science and Science in Law," *Harvard Law Review* 12:443–63.

Home Office Statistical Department. 1975. "Acquittal Rates at the Crown Court January–June 1974." In *The British Jury System*, ed. N. Walker. Cambridge: Institute of Criminology.

Hunter, Robert M. 1935. "Law in the Jury Room," *Ohio State University Law Journal* 2:1–19.

Ignatieff, Michael. 1978. *A Just Measure of Pain: The Penitentiary in the Industrial Revolution, 1750–1850*. London: Macmillan.

James, Rita M. 1959a. "Status and Competence of Jurors," *American Journal of Sociology* 64:563–70.

——. 1959b. "Jurors' Assessment of Criminal Responsibility," *Social Problems* 7:58–69.

Jennings, Sir Ivor. 1959. *The Law and the Constitution*. 5th ed. London: University of London Press.

Joiner, Charles W. 1962. *Civil Justice and the Jury*. Englewood Cliffs, N.J.: Prentice-Hall.

——. 1975. "From the Bench." In Simon (1975).

Journal of Criminal Law and Criminology, Note. 1975. "The Exclusion of Young Adults from Juries: A Threat to Jury Impartiality," *Journal of Criminal Law and Criminology* 66:150–64.

Kadish, Mortimer R., and Sanford H. Kadish. 1971. "The Institutionalization of Conflict: Jury Acquittals," *Journal of Social Issues* 27:199–217.

Kalven, Harry. 1964. "The Dignity of the Civil Jury," *Virginia Law Review* 50:1055–75.

Kalven, Harry, and Hans Zeisel. 1966. *The American Jury*. Boston: Little, Brown.

——. 1967. "The American Jury: Notes for an English Controversy," *Chicago Bar Record* 48:195–201.

Kennebeck, Edwin. 1975. "From the Jury Box." In Simon (1975).

Kerr, Norbert L., Robert S. Atkin, Garold Stasser, David Meek, Robert W. Holt, and James H. Davis. 1976. "Guilt Beyond a Reasonable Doubt: Effects of Concept Definition and Assigned Decision Rule on the Judgments of Mock Juries," *Journal of Personality and Social Psychology* 34:282–94.

Kessler, Joan B. 1973. "An Empirical Study of Six- and Twelve-Member Jury Decision-Making Processes," *University of Michigan Journal of Law Reform* 6:712–34.

——. 1975. "The Social Psychology of Jury Deliberation." In Simon (1975).

Kirkpatrick, Laird C. 1968. "Should Jury Verdicts Be Unanimous in Criminal Cases?" *Oregon Law Review* 47:417–29.

Knittel, Eberhard, and Dietmar Seiler. 1972. "The Merits of Trial by Jury," *Cambridge Law Journal*, pp. 316–25.

Kramer, Charles. 1970. "The Psychology of a Jury Trial," *Practical Lawyer* 16:61–72.

Landy, David, and Elliot Aronson. 1969. "The Influence of the Character of the Criminal and His Victim on the Decisions of Simulated Jurors," *Journal of Experimental Social Psychology* 5:141–52.

Lawson, Robert G. 1968. "Order of Presentation as a Factor in Jury Persuasion," *Kentucky Law Journal* 56:523–55.

Lempert, Richard O. 1975. "Uncovering 'Nondiscernible' Differences: Empirical Research and the Jury-Size Cases," *Michigan Law Review* 73:643–708.

Levine, Adeline G., and Claudine Schweber-Koren. 1976. "Jury Selection in Erie County: Changing a Sexist System," *Law and Society Review* 11:43–55.

Mack, John A. 1976. "Full-time Major Criminals and the Courts," *Modern Law Review* 39:241–67.

MacKenna, Sir Bernard. 1967. "The Behaviour of the Jury: A Comment," *Criminal Law Review* 581–86.

Mackoff, Benjamin S. 1971. "Jury Selection for the Seventies," *Judicature* 55:100–104.

Mark, Sir Robert. 1973. *Minority Verdict*. London: BBC Publications.

Marshall, Geoffrey. 1975. "The Judgment of One's Peers: Some Aims and Ideals of Jury Trial." In *The British Jury System*, ed. N. Walker. Cambridge: Institute of Criminology.

McCabe, Sarah. 1974. "Jury Research in England and the United States," *British Journal of Criminology* 14:276–79.

McCabe, Sarah, and Robert Purves. 1972. *The Jury at Work*. Oxford: Blackwell.

———. 1974. *The Shadow Jury at Work*. Oxford: Blackwell.

Mills, Edwin S. 1962. "A Statistical Study of Occupations of Jurors in a United States District Court," *Maryland Law Review* 22:205–14.

———. 1969. "A Statistical Profile of Jurors in a United States District Court," *Arizona State Law Journal* 329–39.

Mitchell, Herman E., and Donn Byrne. 1973. "The Defendant's Dilemma: Effects of Jurors' Attitudes and Authoritarianism on Judicial Decisions," *Journal of Personality and Social Psychology* 25:123–29.

Morris Committee. 1965. *Jury Service*. Cmnd.2627. London: Her Majesty's Stationery Office.

Mungham, Geoff, and Zenon Bankowski. 1976. "The Jury in the

Legal System." In *The Sociology of Law*, ed. P. Carlen. Keele: University of Keele.

Nagel, Stuart, and Lenore Weitzman. 1972. "Sex and the Unbiased Jury," *Judicature* 56:108–11.

Nagel, Stuart S., and Marian Neef. 1975. "Deductive Modeling to Determine an Optimum Jury Size and Fraction Required to Convict," *Washington University Law Quarterly* 4:933–78.

———. 1977. "Determining the Impact of Legal Policy Changes Before the Changes Occur." In *Public Law and Public Policy*, ed. J. A. Gardiner. New York: Praeger.

Napley, David. 1966. "The Jury System," *New Law Journal* 116:1620–21.

Nemeth, Charlan, and Ruth H. Sosis. 1973. "A Simulated Jury Study: Characteristics of the Defendant and the Jurors," *Journal of Social Psychology* 90:221–29.

Newman, Charles L. 1955. "Trial by Jury: An Outmoded Relic?" *Journal of Criminal Law, Criminology, and Police Science* 46:512–18.

Newman, Donald J. 1966. *Conviction: The Determination of Guilt or Innocence Without Trial.* Boston: Little, Brown.

Nizer, Louis. 1946. "The Art of Jury Trial," *Cornell Law Quarterly* 32:59–72.

Oppenheimer, Benton S. 1937. "Trial by Jury," *University of Cincinnati Law Review* 11:141–47.

Pabst, William R. 1972. "Statistical Studies of the Costs of Six-man Versus Twelve-man Juries," *William and Mary Law Review* 14:326–36.

———. 1973. "What Do Six-Member Juries Really Save?" *Judicature* 57:6–11.

Padawer-Singer, Alice M., Andrew N. Singer, and Rickie L. J. Singer. 1974. "Voir Dire by Two Lawyers—An Essential Safeguard," *Judicature* 57:386–91.

———. 1977. "An Experimental Study of Twelve vs Six Member Juries under Unanimous vs Nonunanimous Decisions." In *Psychology in the Legal Process*, ed. B. D. Sales. New York: Spectrum Publications.

Pound, Roscoe. 1910. "Law in Books and Law in Action," *American Law Review* 44:12–36.

Rhine, Jennie. 1969. "The Jury: A Reflection of the Prejudices of the Community," *Hastings Law Journal* 20:1417–45.

Robinson, W. S. 1950. "Bias, Probability, and Trial by Jury," *American Sociological Review* 15:73–78.

Ryan, John V. 1967. "Less than Unanimous Jury Verdicts in Criminal Trials," *Journal of Criminal Law and Criminology* 58:211–17.

Saari, David J. 1973. "The Criminal Jury Faces Future Shock," *Judicature* 57:12–17.

Saks, Michael J. 1976. "Social Scientists Can't Rig Juries," *Psychology Today* 9:48–57.

———. 1977. *Jury Verdicts*. Lexington: Lexington Books.

Schulman, Jay, Phillip Shaver, Robert Colman, Barbara Emrich, and Richard Christie. 1973. "Recipe for a Jury," *Psychology Today* 6:37–44.

Sealy, Philip A. 1974. "What Can Be Learned from the Analysis of Simulated Juries?" In *The British Jury System*, ed. N. Walker. Cambridge: Institute of Criminology.

Sealy, Philip A., and William R. Cornish. 1973. "Jurors and Their Verdicts," *Modern Law Review* 36:496–508.

Shawcross, Sir Hartley. 1947. "Address Delivered by the Attorney-General to French Judges and Lawyers," *Modern Law Review* 10:1–15.

Simon, Rita James. 1967. *The Jury and the Defense of Insanity*. Boston: Little, Brown.

———. 1970. "Beyond a Reasonable Doubt: An Experimental Attempt at Quantification," *Journal of Applied Behavioral Science* 6:203–9.

———, ed. 1975. *The Jury System in America*. Beverly Hills: Sage Publications.

Simon, Rita James, and Linda Mahan. 1971. "Quantifying Burdens of Proof: A View from the Bench, the Jury, and the Classroom," *Law and Society Review* 5:319–30.

Simon, Rita James, and Prentice Marshall. 1972. "The Jury System." In *The Rights of the Accused*, ed. S. S. Nagel. Beverly Hills: Sage Publications.

Snortum, John R., Jeff S. Klein, and Wynn A. Sherman. 1976. "The Impact of an Aggressive Juror in Six- and Twelve-Member Juries," *Criminal Justice and Behavior* 3:255–62.

Snyder, Eloise C. 1971. "Sex Role Differential and Juror Decisions," *Sociology and Social Research* 55:442–48.

Steuer, Aron. 1975. "The Case Against the Jury," *New York State Bar Journal* 47:101–46.

Strodtbeck, Fred L., and Richard D. Mann. 1956. "Sex Role Differentiation in Jury Deliberations," *Sociometry* 19:3–11.

Strodtbeck, Fred L., Rita M. James, and Charles Hawkins. 1957. "Social Status in Jury Deliberations," *American Sociological Review* 22:713–19.

Tocqueville, Alexis de. 1960. *Democracy in America*. New York: Vintage Books.

Valenti, Angelo C., and Leslie L. Downing. 1975. "Differential Effects of Jury Size on Verdicts Following Deliberation as a Function of the Apparent Guilt of a Defendant," *Journal of Personality and Social Psychology* 32:655–63.

Van Amburg, Lisa. 1974. "A Case Study of the Peremptory Challenge: A Subtle Strike at Equal Protection and Due Process," *Saint Louis University Law Journal* 18:662–83.

Vanderzell, John H. 1966. "The Jury as a Community Cross-section," *Western Political Quarterly* 19:136–49.

Van Dyke, Jon M. 1970. "The Jury as a Political Institution," *Catholic Lawyer* 16:224–41.

———. 1977. *Jury Selection Procedures*. Cambridge, Mass.: Ballinger.

Vaughan, Ted R. 1967. "Governmental Intervention in Social Research: Political and Ethical Dimensions in the Wichita Jury Recordings." In *Ethics, Politics, and Social Research*, ed. G. Sjoberg. Cambridge, Mass.: Schenkman.

Walsh, Michael H. 1969. "The American Jury: A Reassessment," *Yale Law Journal* 79:142–58.

Wanamaker, Walter B. 1937. "Trial by Jury," *University of Cincinnati Law Review* 11:191–200.

Wigmore, John H. 1929. "A Programme for the Trial of Jury Trial," *Journal of the American Judicature Society* 12:166–70.

Williams, Glanville. 1963. *The Proof of Guilt*. London: Stevens.

Yale Law Journal, Note. 1963. "Negro Defendants and Southern Lawyers: Review in Federal Habeas Corpus of Systematic Exclusion of Negroes from Juries," *Yale Law Journal* 72:559–73.

———. 1965. "The Defendant's Challenge to a Racial Criterion in Jury Selection: A Study in Standing, Due Process and Equal Protection," *Yale Law Journal* 74:919–41.

———. 1970. "The Case for Black Juries," *Yale Law Journal* 79:531–50.

Zander, Michael. 1974. "Are Too Many Professional Criminals Avoiding Conviction?—A Study in Britain's Two Busiest Courts," *Modern Law Review* 37:28–61.

Zeisel, Hans. 1971. ". . . And Then There Were None: The Diminution of the Federal Jury," *University of Chicago Law Review* 38:710–24.

———. 1975. "Jury Research in the United States." In *The British Jury System*, ed. N. Walker. Cambridge: Institute of Criminology.

Zeisel, Hans, and Shari S. Diamond. 1974. " 'Convincing Empirical Evidence' on the Six Member Jury," *University of Chicago Law Review* 41:281–95.

Joan Petersilia

Criminal Career Research:
A Review of Recent Evidence

ABSTRACT

A criminal career may consist of a single, undiscovered, venial
lapse or a high level of sustained involvement in serious crime.
Modern criminal career research derives largely from policy
concerns about the likely crime preventive effects of
incapacitative sanctions. Consequently, criminal career research
tends to be more concerned with sustained than with venial
criminal careers. If a small number of individuals commits a
disproportionate number of serious criminal acts and if they can
be identified and confined early in their careers, the argument
goes, significant numbers of serious criminal offenses could
be prevented. The leading criminal career research, much of
it unpublished, has produced useful results, but cannot give
much guidance on sanctions use to policy makers. Less than
15 percent of the general population will be arrested for
commission of a felony and about one-half of these will never
be arrested for another. Very roughly, only 5 percent of the
population will demonstrate the beginnings of a sustained
criminal career, but once three contacts with the police have
been recorded, the probability of another will be very high.
Criminal careers preponderantly begin early in life, commonly
between the ages of fourteen and seventeen and often for
expressive reasons. Serious criminal careers are often continued
for instrumental reasons. Repetitive offenders tend not to

Joan Petersilia is Research Associate in the Criminal Justice Program, the
Rand Corporation.
The author is indebted to the researchers who shared their unpublished and
draft materials, particularly Lyle Shannon, Marvin Wolfgang, James Collins,
Mark Peterson, and Alfred Blumstein. She also greatly benefited from discus-
sions with Peter Greenwood, Marvin Lavin, and Franklin E. Zimring.

specialize narrowly; the mix of offenses may shift from one stage of a sustained criminal career to the next, often increasing in seriousness, but not as a consistent rule. Offense rates depend on the offender's age, his criminal record, and the offense type committed. Arrest, conviction, and incarceration rates increase as the career advances, unlike offense rates, which tend to decline. Continuing criminal careers are not necessarily marked by a growth in sophistication and income or of geographic range. Although it is clear that a small portion of the universe of known offenders commits a disproportionate number of offenses, the data accumulated to date on criminal careers do not permit us, with acceptable confidence, to identify career criminals prospectively or to predict the crime reduction effects of alternative sentencing policies.

The study of criminal careers is concerned not with a few isolated deviant acts, but with criminality persisting over many years.[1] Criminal career research seeks to illuminate how such careers are initiated, how they progress, and why they are discontinued. The distinguishing characteristic of criminal career research is its concern with systematic changes in behavior over time or as a result of cumulative criminal justice system contacts. In focusing attention on persons who repeatedly engage in serious crime, it attempts to explain the relation between crime and the offender's interaction with criminal justice agencies. A better understanding of the characteristics of the criminal career should enable criminal justice policies to be designed to intervene in the career at an effective point, whether for crime control or rehabilitative purposes.

Research of this kind elicits interest in part because it may influence the allocation of resources to obtain maximum crime reduction. Knowledge of the extent and type of crime committed at various stages of a career is necessary if we are to identify and imprison offenders during their most criminally active years. Likewise, understanding the lengths of criminal ca-

---

[1] This characterization of an individual's criminal activity as a "career" is not meant to imply that offenders derive their livelihoods primarily from crime. Rather, the concept is intended to structure an offender's involvement in the criminal justice system over time. In this manner, the sequence of events can be studied as an integrated and bounded activity.

reers could assist in decisions about the appropriate duration of imprisonment.

The desirability of studying the criminal behavior of offenders throughout their criminal careers has long been recognized. In the early 1900s, Georg von Mayr (1917) argued that a "deeper insight into the statistics of criminality is made possible by the disclosure of developmental regularities in which criminality develops in the course of a human lifetime." Early studies usually concentrated on unique careers of individual offenders through biographical or autobiographical case studies (e.g., Sutherland 1937; Shaw 1930, 1931; Booth 1929; Martin 1952). While these studies were interesting and insightful, their subjects were probably not representative offenders. It is likely that they were chosen for their unique interest.

A more systematic attempt was made to investigate the criminal career in a series of studies by Sheldon and Eleanor Glueck, beginning in the early 1930s (Glueck and Glueck 1930, 1934a, 1934b, 1937, 1943a, 1943b, 1950). They were particularly interested in the correlates of delinquent and criminal behavior, the progression from delinquency to adult crime, career length, age of onset, and the effects of treatment on continued delinquency. Their research expanded knowledge of the criminal career and of criminality in general. However, the issues they examined were broad, the methodology was unsophisticated, and they dealt mostly with variables of the juvenile age range.

Only minor advances were made in the next few decades by sociologists and criminologists trying to develop theoretical explanations of persistent criminality. A major effort was made to develop a framework in which to view different career patterns (e.g., Gibbons 1968; Clinard and Quinney 1973).

In the early 1970s, criminal career research changed course and began to advance noticeably. Published results of empirical studies confirmed what many suspected: recidivists, who constitute a minority of all offenders, are responsible for a disproportionately large number of serious crimes. Marvin Wolfgang, Robert Figlio, and Thorsten Sellin (1972), in the most publicized of these reports, reported that more than half of all crimes and two-thirds of the violent crimes were committed by only 6% of the birth cohort they studied.

Other research disclosed that recidivists, even when arrested, are unlikely to be convicted and imprisoned. A study of sentencing practices in Los Angeles County showed that only 50% of defendants who had served a prior prison term received a prison sentence for a subsequent robbery conviction, and only 15% for a subsequent burglary conviction (Greenwood 1977). Recidivists were often spared stringent punishment by prosecutors willing to reduce charges for a guilty plea and by judges hopeful of rehabilitation. The fast return to the streets of some defendants, especially those sufficiently sophisticated to manipulate the criminal justice system to their advantage, followed by their resumption of crime and subsequent rearrest, created a dismaying image of "revolving door" justice. One implication of these results was that serious crime might be significantly lessened if recidivists were reliably identified, vigorously prosecuted, and consistently imprisoned.

There was, in the seventies, a growing disillusionment with rehabilitation programs, which once were viewed as a major justification of prisons. Lipton, Martinson, and Wilks (1975) suggested that rehabilitative treatment does not reduce an offender's propensity to commit future crime, and other surveys of correctional research pointed in the same direction (Bailey 1966; Kassebaum, Ward, and Wilner 1971; Robison and Smith 1971; Ward 1973).

If rehabilitation of offenders appeared an unpromising crime control strategy, an alternative was to focus on deterrence and incapacitation. Some research suggested an inverse relationship between the incidence of crime and the certainty and severity of punishment (Tittle 1969; Ehrlich 1973). And, because crime rates increased in the 1960s while incarceration rates and average sentence lengths decreased (Shinnar and Shinnar 1975), some argued that those phenomena were causally related and urged that sentences be made harsher (e.g., Wilson 1975). Even if the criminal justice system can not successfully rehabilitate criminals, the argument went, perhaps it can enhance public safety by removing persistent offenders from the streets and by deterring crime through the use of more certain and stringent punishment (Wilson 1975; van den Haag 1975).

The likely effects and the implications of such policies are not well understood. Deterrence research is at a rudimentary stage (see, e.g., Blumstein, Cohen, and Nagin 1978). Several recent publications report on efforts to estimate the crime reduction that might result if proportionately more offenders were imprisoned, if prison sentences were longer, or both. The estimates vary widely, depending on the assumptions made. For instance, Shinnar and Shinnar concluded that violent crime rates could be reduced by as much as 80% if every person convicted of a violent crime were imprisoned for five years (1975). However, a second study concluded that violent crime would be reduced by only 4% by increasing the imprisonment of convicted offenders (Van Dine, Conrad, and Dinitz 1977). Several others (Clarke 1974; Greenberg 1975; Ehrlich 1973) concluded that incapacitation effects are quite small. Finally a recent study found that the crime rate would be reduced 15%, and the prison population would eventually increase 50%, if every person convicted of a felony were imprisoned for one year (Petersilia and Greenwood 1978). Lack of data on various aspects of criminal careers hampers the assessment of these policies on crime and forestalls timely recognition of offenders.

Little is known about the extent and types of crime committed at different stages of criminal careers. Few reliable estimates have been made of the probabilities of arrest, conviction, and incarceration. How these probabilities vary over the career, among offenders, or among offense types, is not known. These questions are central to the assessment of criminal justice policies that aim to increase deterrent or incapacitative effects. If crime commission and arrest rates differ significantly among offenders and over the career, the effect of longer sentences on overall crime will depend greatly on who is incarcerated for how long.

Little is known about how and when the criminal career begins, or how long it is likely to last, why criminal careers persist, and why some persons abandon criminal careers early, others continue into adult crime, and still others begin crime careers late in life.

Research intended to overcome these gaps in our knowledge has gone largely unpublished. That which has been published has not been compared and synthesized. This essay reviews recent quantitative evidence on the criminal career. This review is selective and limited to the results of four major projects: two were launched partly in response to the policy concerns discussed above, and the other two are important longitudinal research projects. Section I describes the research projects discussed. Their objectives, methodologies, and the populations studied are summarized. Section II discusses methodologies identifying those best suited to the examination of specified criminal career issues. Section III, the bulk of the essay, summarizes and compares findings on each of several major issues. Section IV discusses policy implications and points to areas where further research is needed.

I. Overview of Criminal Career Research Projects

This overview is based on four active research programs: the Rand Corporation projects directed by Peter Greenwood; the Philadelphia birth cohort studies directed by Marvin Wolfgang; the Racine, Wisconsin, birth cohort studies directed by Lyle Shannon; and the Carnegie-Mellon incapacitation project directed by Alfred Blumstein. These projects differ in terms of the issues addressed, parts of the criminal career examined, sources of data analyzed, populations studied, and research designs employed.

A. The Rand Corporation Habitual Criminals Program (1974 to Present)

During the past four years, Rand has been conducting a number of studies designed to provide new insights and data concerning "serious habitual offenders"—adult criminals who engage in serious predatory or violent crimes over extended periods. The original objectives were to determine the magnitude of the habitual offender population, describe the characteristics of the offenders, and analyze their interactions with the criminal justice system. As the research proceeded, the focus has been influenced by a growing interest in incapacitation as a policy goal, and a concentration on career criminals as a specific means of crime reduction. To clarify or resolve issues raised by either of these policy initiatives requires more reliable information on individual crime commission rates, and the probability of arrest, conviction, and incarceration. Rand has increasingly turned its attention to the amount and types of crime committed by persons with various characteristics. A central concern is to estimate arrest, conviction, and incarceration probabilities—across offenders, offense types, and the criminal career.

Two projects within the Rand program are particularly relevant. The first, *Criminal Careers of Habitual Felons* (Petersilia, Greenwood, and Lavin 1978), focused on the criminal careers of forty-nine prison inmates, all armed robbers serving at least a second prison term. The data were gathered in lengthy personal interviews with the offenders and from their official criminal records.

The interview instrument was a highly structured questionnaire which asked the offenders to recall events in their criminal careers. The questionnaire was administered in three sections corresponding to juvenile, young adult, and adult career periods. Each section contained approximately 200 questions; most were repeated from one section to the next. Questions covered such areas as family relationships, school record, sources of income, frequency of criminal activity, arrests and convictions, criminal motivations, methods of planning criminal acts, involvement with drugs and alcohol, use of violence, and postrelease behavior patterns.

Official criminal justice records were obtained for each individual; these records were used to assess reactions of the system to the offender and to test the validity of the self-reported arrest and conviction information. When the interview responses were compared with data from official records, the results showed that respondents reported approximately 75% of their official arrests or convictions. Contrary to expectations, *less* validity was associated with the reporting of less serious offenses and with events occurring *closest* to the time of the interview (Petersilia 1978a).

A sample of 49 individuals is too small to permit reliable inferences about the larger offender populations. Because the sample was small and limited to incarcerated felons who met specified criteria, the findings do not necessarily apply to broader populations of offenders. However, because of the comprehensiveness and quality of the information, this study adds substantially to research on criminal careers.

The second Rand study, *Doing Crime: A Survey of California Inmates* (Peterson, Braiker, and Polich 1980), reports on a survey of 624 male inmates drawn from five California prisons. The survey was self-administered, and anonymous. The randomly sampled offenders were representative of all California prison inmates. The survey covered each offender's criminal activity; his arrests, convictions, and incarcerations; juvenile history and family background; employment; motives for committing crime; perceptions of the benefits and risks of crime; and attitudes toward the criminal justice system. The survey primarily concerned the three years prior to the current conviction.

The self-reported crime information was used to explore individual patterns of crime and to estimate the prevalence, offense rates, and arrest rates for major felonies—critical elements of models of the incapacitative effects of incarceration. The survey responses were also used to examine the characteristics of different types of career criminals, for instance, those who engage in specific types of crime, or have certain motivations.

Rand recently expanded and refined the survey instrument, and administered it to approximately 2,500 prison and jail inmates in California, Michigan, and Texas. The instrument design and sampling procedures have undergone substantial modification to improve the reliability of the offense rate data. The second survey was also self-administered, but was not anonymous; accordingly, the surveys can be matched with corresponding official record data. The supplementary data include criminal history items, diagnostic information, and measures of current prison adjustment. At the time of this writing, the data of the second survey have not yet been analyzed.

B. *The Philadelphia Birth Cohort Study (1972 to Present)*

Marvin Wolfgang and others at the University of Pennsylvania are engaged in a longitudinal birth cohort study. They are trying to learn about the ages of onset, the progression or cessation of delinquency, and the relation of these phenomena to delinquents' personal and social characteristics, and to make comparisons between delinquents and nondelinquents. In addition, they are examining the probabilities that offenders will switch from one crime to another, crime commission rates, and the relation between juvenile delinquency and adult crime.

The cohort consists of all males born in Philadelphia in 1945 who resided in the city at least from ages ten to eighteen. The cohort data have been collected in three stages. In the first phase, 9,945 such individuals were located using police, court, school, and selective service records. One goal was to estimate the probability that an individual would become an officially recorded delinquent, that is, to separate the cohort into delinquents and nondelinquents. Comparisons could then be made between delinquents and nondelinquents on the basis of social, economic, and personality variables. The first phase of the research (Wolfgang, Figlio, and Sellin 1972) examines the relations between such background variables as race, socioeconomic status, types of schools attended, residential moves, grade level, I.Q., and delinquency. Findings are also presented on the age of onset of delinquency, and on crime switch in the delinquent career.

In the second phase of the research, a sample of 971 (10%) of the original cohort was selected to be followed to age twenty-six and to be interviewed. Official police records were obtained for all members of the sample. The second phase permits a study of the relation between delinquency and adult crime. Although the researchers planned to interview the complete follow-up sample for more detailed information, many could not be located. Fifty-eight percent, or 567 persons, were located and interviewed. Unfortunately, the interviewed individuals differed in some respects from those not available for interviews; they tended to be less serious offenders, white, and of higher socio-economic status.

The interview lasted one to two hours; information was sought on educational, employment, military, and marital variables. Subjects were asked to report their involvement in thirty different kinds of illegal behavior, ranging in seriousness from homicide to public drunkenness. Crime rate information was obtained by asking each respondent how often he committed each offense before and after he reached age eighteen.

In the third phase, police, court, and prison records were used to complete official criminal histories on the 10% follow-up sample to age thirty. Only selected findings from the second and third phases have been published (Wolfgang 1973, 1977; Collins 1977).

C. The Racine, Wisconsin, Birth Cohort Studies
(1974 to Present)

Lyle Shannon and his associates at the Iowa Urban Community Research Center in Iowa City are conducting a longitudinal birth cohort study of crime in Racine, Wisconsin. Racine is a medium-sized industrial city of approximately 100,000 people. Various techniques are used to examine how individuals proceeded through various stages of what might be called developing, delinquent, and criminal careers. Some cohort members were offenders throughout the period studied. Others dropped out of their criminal careers at various stages, and still others avoided contact with the police—at least until later stages of their lives. Efforts were made to predict which categories of people are more likely to engage in delinquent behavior, to terminate delinquent behavior as they get older, or to continue into adult criminal activity.

The researchers followed three mixed-sex birth cohorts. The 1942 cohort consisted of 1,352 persons; the 1949 cohort, 2,099 persons; and the 1955 cohort, 2,676 persons. Data collection was cut off in 1974. The effective period during which the 1942 co-hort could accumulate a police contact record was the twenty-seven-year span between the ages of six and thirty-two; for the 1949 cohort, between six and twenty-five; and for the 1955 cohort, between six and twenty-one. The cohort members were initially identified from the files of the Racine (Wisconsin) Unified School District. These files identified persons in public, private, and parochial schools. Each cohort member's length of residence in Racine was determined from phone directories, city directories, and information from family and friends. Persons with continuous residence were defined as those missing no more than three years' residence between the age of six and the data collection cutoff date. In the 1942 cohort, 633 persons had continuous residence; in the 1949 cohort, 1,297 persons; and in the 1955 cohort, 2,149 persons. Depending on the type of analysis involved, either entire cohorts or only those persons with continuous residence were used. The possibility was examined that those without continuous residence in Racine differed from others, and it was determined that movers and stayers were not significantly different in their careers for the period for which comparison was possible. The movers and stayers were quite similar in terms of race, extent and seriousness of police contacts, and socioeconomic status, during the period in which both lived in the Racine area.

The name of each cohort member was checked against the files of the Racine Police Department to determine who among continuous residents of the city had a police contact. The "contacts" included Part I and Part II offenses of the Uniform Crime Reports,[2] as well as juvenile conditions (e.g., truancy). In addition, lengthy interviews were conducted with 333 persons from the 1942 cohort and with 556 from the 1949 cohort. Shannon asserts that the background and criminal histories of those interviewed were fairly representative of their respective cohorts (Shannon 1976, pp. 96–97). Information on sociodemographics, employment, family variables, attitudes, and peer associations was obtained in the interview.

[2] Part I offenses are criminal homicide, forcible rape, robbery, aggravated assault, burglary, larceny-theft, and motor vehicle theft. Part II offenses include almost all other crimes (except traffic law violations).

The complete results of the Racine cohort study have not been published; a book is expected to report major findings in 1980. However, a number of papers have appeared (see e.g., Olson 1977; Shannon 1978a, 1978b).

D. Carnegie-Mellon's Research Program on Incapacitation

The Carnegie-Mellon study examines adult careers only, using official record data. The objective of this series of studies, directed by Alfred Blumstein of Carnegie-Mellon University, is to understand individual criminal activity in terms of a criminal career, counting the beginning of a career as the first crime committed, and the end as the last crime committed. During a criminal career, the offender commits crimes, accumulates arrests, is convicted after some of these arrests, and in some cases is incarcerated. A criminal career can thus be characterized by a set of variables: the number of crimes committed per year per individual; the probabilities of arrest for a crime, of conviction after arrest, and of incarceration after conviction; and the length of the career.

These studies have relied principally on an FBI data tape containing the official criminal histories of all 5,364 adult offenders arrested at least once in 1973 in the District of Columbia for the crimes of homicide, rape, aggravated assault, robbery, burglary, grand theft, and auto theft. Records for all prior adult arrests and for those following arrests that occurred anywhere in the United States until October 1975 are on the tape. Using these data, the Blumstein group "models" the criminal career, and derives various career patterns.

II. Methodological Issues

The criminal career researcher must choose among a number of methodological options. The choices involve tradeoffs in terms of the strength of the inferences to be drawn from the research, its cost, and the time required. The options fall into three broad areas: the data sources; the research design; and the appropriate population for study.

A. Data Sources

Official records, and self-reports obtained through interviews or surveys, are particularly useful in criminal career research.

Official records include criminal histories, police reports, and court records. Depending upon their accessibility and the amount of effort required to locate and extract information, official records can provide extensive data on the crimes (and criminal proceedings) for which people have been arrested. However, official records vary greatly in completeness. In some jurisdictions, criminal histories will be available for each person arrested, listing the type and date of each prior arrest and possibly the case disposition. The coverage of criminal histories will depend on which agency maintains them. Local police files often include only local arrest information. Rap sheets maintained by a state bureau of criminal identification often include all arrests in the state. The Federal Bureau of Investigation attempts to provide national coverage. State or federal criminal histories are limited by their reliance on local law enforcement agencies for arrest information. Police sometimes fail to report arrests, particularly when the case is dropped without prosecution.

Information on specific arrests recorded on the rap sheet can be supplemented with data from police department offense reports or from court records. These sources can provide more detailed information, such as the offender's employment history and schooling. Rap sheets are often computerized or in easily codable formats; with other records there are substantial difficulties and costs in obtaining access to agency files, linking data across files, and devising coding schemes.

Information concerning recorded and unrecorded criminal activity of individuals can also be obtained by using structured interviews or questionnaires. The subjects are asked how frequently they committed each of a number of specific types of crime. The questions may limit the respondents' attention to specific periods, say during the preceding year, or they may be more inclusive, covering the full criminal career, or the period since age eighteen.

Depending on their purpose, self-report instruments may request specific information about each offense, such as how much money was obtained from a particular robbery, or they may ask for information of a more general nature, such as whether the offender was usually armed.

Research on any particular aspect of criminal careers can rely on official records, self-reports, or a combination of the two. Each method must be assessed in terms of its advantages and disadvantages.

Research that relies wholly on official records draws from only a part of each offender's criminal behavior: it is biased by variations in detection rates for different crimes, and by the unevenness of law enforcement with respect to certain racial and socioeconomic groups. One goal of the research is to estimate separately the rate at which individuals engage in different types of crime and the probability that a single crime will result in an arrest. (Both crime commission rates and arrest probabilities vary among offense types, offenders, and at different points in the criminal career.) An offender's arrest record will disclose only the product of the crime commission rate and the probability of arrest, his arrest rate over time. Data from self-report studies can be used to overcome these limitations and to estimate the frequency of commission of different crime types and the associated probability of arrest.

An additional advantage of self-reports is that they can provide much richer detail about offenses and the offender's background. They can provide information on the offender's motivation for committing a specific crime and the amount of pre-crime planning involved. The researcher using official records is limited to those data that have been collected and compiled; that data may not contain the variables of interest. Moreover, official records are limited by the coding formats of the data systems being used and by biases introduced when coding rules or data emphases change over time.

Principal disadvantages associated with self-reports are their reliance on subject cooperation, uncertainties in their validity, and their cost. Self-report research depends on access to research subjects; that may require assistance by parole or probation authorities to locate them or permission from correctional authorities to interview them and, finally, their personal consent. Both research ethics and recent human-subjects legislation require that the researcher inform his subjects of whatever risks they may incur by answering the questionnaire (see Gándara 1978).[3] Some subjects will refuse to cooperate, whatever the inducement. By comparison, official-record studies require no such subject cooperation, but the researcher must obtain access to the files of interest. Accordingly, self-report crime studies begin with what may be a biased sample—those who agree to participate.

Responses to crime rate questions are contaminated by problems of memory and definition, and by deliberate distortions of criminality. These validity problems are not well understood. Even when the researchers use reliability measures in their instruments—to detect and discard inconsistent and unreliable patterns of responses—they cannot measure the validity of crime rate responses if the subject provides plausible and consistent responses to interrelated questions. For instance, the researcher may ask the respondent essentially the same question, but in a different format. If the two responses are vastly different, the reliability of the response might be questioned. However, if the respondent answers both questions consistently, but falsifies the information, the researcher has no way to check its validity.

Official criminal histories, by contrast, are subject to some control by subsequent adjudication processes. Although arrest charges may not accurately reflect the individual's behavior, and some arrests may not be justified, relatively few arrest histories are seriously distorted by systematic "harassment" arrests or inflation of charges. Furthermore, each arrest entry is generated by a reasonably independent process, reducing the opportunity for selective bias against any one offender. This is not true of

[3] This is particularly germane to criminal career research, since inmates are asked to report committing crimes for which they were never arrested. Inmates may fear that their responses will be made available to law enforcement agencies. Information of this type is now immune from the legal process and cannot be admitted as evidence in any judicial proceeding without the subject's written consent (42 U.S. C. 3771[a]).

self-reports. An individual who desires to misrepresent his true criminality can systematically distort his response to draw a picture which, although plausible, errs seriously.

Cost is the final major difference between official records and self-reports. If official record studies are limited to computerized criminal history files, or even standardized rap sheets, their cost per subject is far less than that for studies based on self-reports. Self-reports from survey questionnaires cost less per subject than personal interviews, but still appreciably more than official record data. This cost difference is exacerbated by the data cleaning (e.g., coding open-ended responses, checking skip patterns, etc.) and reliability checks required to process self-report data responsibly.

In summary, self-reports can provide fuller and richer information than can official records but at a greater cost and with uncertain validity. Nevertheless, for criminal careers research, self-reports are indispensable for estimating the relations between crime rates and arrest probabilities, and the variation in crime rates over offense types among offenders, and over their criminal careers.

B. Research Design

Longitudinal and cross-sectional studies are the two leading designs for criminal career research. In longitudinal studies, data are collected at different times on a given set of subjects, and the researcher is able to report changes in descriptions and explanations. Cohort studies are the primary type of longitudinal design used in criminal career research. A cohort study collects data repeatedly from a specific population, although the successive samples may be different. Changes in the criminal career can then be established by measuring different attributes over time.

Most criminal career research is based on cross-sectional surveys. In a cross-sectional survey, data are collected at one time from a sample selected to represent some larger population at that time. Such a design serves not only for purposes of description but also for the discovery of relations existing between variables at the time of the study. A cross-sectional study might show that an 18-year-old in the selected population has a higher offense rate than a 30-year-old, but this result would not necessarily imply that offense rate declines with age. The current 18-year-olds may continue to commit crime at the same higher rate when they are 30. Nevertheless, a finding that the current 30-year-olds have a lower offense rate than the current 18-year-olds would aid in estimating the effects of alternative sentencing policies.

In principle, a longitudinal design is advantageous because many central issues involve change over time. In a longitudinal design, members of a birth cohort might be tracked until their deaths. Such a design is likelier than a cross-sectional study to identify valid causative factors—factors that can then be verified by experimental manipulation. Since causal processes work forward in time, time-dependent events can help eliminate otherwise plausible explanations of the data.

Longitudinal research is superior to cross-sectional if one is primarily interested in drawing causal inferences. Consider a study of the effect that criminal justice sanctions have on the continuation of the career. A cross-sectional design could involve two samples of persons convicted: those who went to prison and those who did not. The study would compare the subsequent offense rates of the two groups. But even if those who served a prison sentence committed more crime subsequently than those who did not, an inference that imprisonment helped to increase criminality would not necessarily be justified. The two samples may differ in aspects other than the term of imprisonment, and these other aspects may account for the difference in offense rates. A longitudinal design avoids this complication by allowing each individual to act as his own control, and by permitting analysis of each individual. If we found that a particular individual's criminality increased after a term of imprisonment, this would be a stronger basis for suggesting that prison has criminogenic effects. However, it still could not be concluded that prison *caused* greater crime, since other variables have also been introduced concurrently—aging, loss of family contacts, employment—and those variables, rather than imprisonment, may be responsible.

Longitudinal studies do have their problems. If cooperation is required from subjects and dropout rates are significant, progressive losses in the sample at each measurement point can substantially distort results. More important, a longitudinal cohort analysis is typically plagued by the confounding of "history" (that is, the changing of the external socioeconomic environment) with the maturation or aging of the cohort. It is difficult to know whether events that occurred in the year the cohort reached a certain age were characteristic of that age (and therefore likely to occur to other cohorts when they reached that age) or whether they were the result of a change that occurred in the world in that year (and therefore likely to have occurred to other age cohorts at the same time).

As society changes, each cohort encounters a unique set of social and environmental events. The life patterns of people in one cohort will differ in some respects from the patterns of any other cohort. Different cohorts age in different ways, and these differences cannot be measured from a longitudinal study of a single cohort. Data from several cohorts can provide a means to distinguish history effects.

By comparison, cross-sectional analyses focus on individuals of all ages in a particular year to see what they did in that year. Therefore, these analyses are particularly vulnerable to unique events that happened in that particular year. If there is no interaction of that event with age, however, the age-specific inferences will not be distorted.

Another problem in longitudinal research is the bias introduced when subjects are repeatedly contacted and interviewed. This "testing effect," however, can be measured and taken into account in the analysis, for instance, by not testing a matched subpopulation.

C. Study Population

The third methodological question, the appropriate population to study, presents three choices: cohorts; random samples of the general population; and groups of offenders identified at some point in the criminal justice system.

Birth cohorts or cohorts selected at an early point in the life cycle are of obvious interest for identifying early predictors of future criminality and for establishing probability estimates of future career progression. If they represent general populations in natural settings, they are the appropriate source of estimates of the prevalence of various forms of criminal careers in a general population. The principal problem for criminal career research is that most people do not commit serious offenses; if the cohort is to contain an adequate number of serious offenders, it must be extremely large, and correspondingly expensive. In the Racine birth cohort study, only about 8% of the 1942 cohort, 10% of the 1949 cohort, and 14% of the 1955 cohort had a police record that included a felony, and only 3–4% of each cohort was ever incarcerated (Shannon et al. 1980, chap. 17). A cohort design would be inappropriate if the research was primarily interested in persons who were repeatedly arrested, convicted, or incarcerated. Further, if one were interested in describing differences associated with race, sex, and crime types, the resulting samples would be too small for even simple comparisons of percentages at a reasonable level of confidence.

Another problem with birth cohorts is the timing of data collection. If data collection begins while the cohort is quite young, the research can proceed no faster than the aging of the cohort. If it begins when the cohort has already matured, there will be problems in locating appropriate records to trace the cohort's early years.

Studies based on a random sample of the general population suffer from some of the same difficulties as birth cohort studies, particularly the small percentage of subjects who will have serious criminal careers. Although cross-sectional studies involving the general population will provide more current data than a cohort study, they are more likely to underestimate the prevalence of criminality because more serious offenders tend to be difficult to locate and are less willing to be interviewed. The small fraction of serious offenders is likely to be grossly underrepresented in such a study.

Most criminal career research relies on samples of persons who have shown themselves to be criminals. Subjects have usually been arrested, convicted, or imprisoned.

The easiest offenders to identify and locate are those incarcerated. Information on their characteristics and prior criminal behavior is available from official records, and they are relatively responsive to interviews. A sample of nonincarcerated convicted persons is also easy to identify and is reasonably well described by court records. The difficulty with any group not confined lies in locating and interviewing a representative sample of its members (for a discussion of problems, see Buffum 1976). Samples of known offenders include those who have a higher-than-average probability of a serious criminal history. While such samples are inappropriate for predicting the onset of criminal behavior, or the prevalence of crime, they are appropriate for many studies of criminal justice policy in that they deal with the only population which the criminal justice system can directly affect—those offenders who are known to it.[4] They are also the only practical means to study the particular characteristics of a serious criminal career—variations in crimes committed, motivations, the extent of pre-crime planning, crime commission rates, arrest probabilities, and related questions.

The major shortcoming of this approach is that by sampling only persons who have shown themselves to be criminal, one fails to consider other persons who may have had similar experiences, but either did not become criminal at all, were so successful at crime that they were never arrested, or discontinued a criminal career before the sample was selected. Because only persons who are still involved in crime are being studied, one cannot make causal inferences. For example, if a large percentage of arrested males were found to have a history of alcohol use, it would not follow that alcohol use caused their criminal involvement. Persons who discontinued their careers earlier, or

---

[4] The system may indirectly affect unidentified offenders or potential offenders through deterrence. To date, the magnitude of this effect has not been established. See Blumstein, Cohen, and Nagin (1978) for a recent review of deterrence research.

even those who never became involved in crime, might have a similar incidence of alcohol use.

There is no single preferred research design or data collection procedure. The choice of design must depend on the questions to be studied. Competing considerations must be weighed. Appropriate criteria in designing new studies should be that these studies build on the methodological techniques developed in previous research and offer some clear advance over prior work. Advances in understanding of criminal career development are most likely to result from a process of triangulation, in which increasingly consistent findings derived by different research methods eventually narrow the range of uncertainty about key functional relationships and career characteristics.

III. Review of Findings

A. The Prevalence and Importance of Criminal Careers

The question of how to identify people who will have or are having criminal careers contains at least four subsidiary questions. (1) What percentage of the population will come into contact with the criminal justice system as offenders? (2) What percentage of the population will have repeated contacts with the criminal justice system? (3) How much crime can be attributed to repetitive offenders? (4) On what basis can we predict that a particular juvenile will become a repetitive offender?

1. Estimating the prevalence of offenders. It is reasonable to suppose that offenders who pursue a career of crime will sooner or later have an official contact with law enforcement, typically an arrest, possibly culminating in conviction and imprisonment. Career criminals can be viewed as those offenders with police records who are repeatedly arrested, convicted, and imprisoned. Estimating the prevalence of career criminals is a fundamental research task. Interpreting the estimates requires an appreciation of how many people have police records of some sort.

The Wolfgang and Shannon birth cohort studies have proved to be a feasible approach to the estimation of known offenders in the general population. These studies suggest that one-half to two-thirds of the general population will experience at least one officially recorded police contact before the age of thirty.[5] Wolfgang's study found that the probability that a male born in 1945 who lived in Philadelphia will have an officially recorded police contact for a nontraffic criminal offense is 47% by the age of thirty (Collins 1977, p. 20). In Shannon's cohorts, 69% of the males in the 1942 cohort had a nontraffic offense; 67% of the 1949 cohort; and 59% of the 1955 cohort.

The two studies used different definitions of a police contact and that may explain some differences in results (Wolfgang, Figlio, and Sellin 1972, p. 68; Shannon 1976, p. 15). Unlawful conduct of a very minor nature, such as disorderly conduct, was included in both. In the Shannon study, "police contacts" include traffic violations and juvenile status offenses such as incorrigibility and truancy.[6] Eliminating these minor contacts (and the female cohort members) from the Racine data markedly reduces differences in the incidences of police contacts reported by the two studies.

In the Philadelphia birth cohort, the variables of race and socioeconomic status were strongly related to whether individuals had an official contact.[7] Twenty-nine percent of the whites

[5] An "officially recorded police contact" is not synonymous with an arrest. An arrest can be defined as "taking a person into custody by authority of law, for the purpose of charging him with a criminal offense or for the purpose of initiating juvenile proceedings, terminating with the recording of a specific offense. Events which do not terminate with booking or other official registration of an offense are not regarded as arrests. Events commonly described as 'field interviews,' 'field interrogations,' or 'temporary detentions' in any location, whether or not the officer considers the person under arrest during some part of the episode, are not included in the definition of arrest" (*Directory of Criminal Justice Terminology* 1976, p. 15). Since both the Shannon and the Wolfgang studies record police contacts made in the course of investigations, and Shannon records all traffic offenses, they have, technically speaking, recorded more than arrests. This is particularly true with the Shannon cohort data; almost half of the recorded police contacts result from traffic violations or police investigations. Wolfgang did not record juvenile events or traffic violations, so that the recorded police contacts for his cohorts more closely resemble arrests.

[6] In the 1942 Racine cohort, 42% of all police contacts were for traffic offenses; 20% for disorderly conduct; and 20% for suspicion or investigation (Shannon 1979, p. 2).

[7] In both the Philadelphia and the Racine cohorts, socioeconomic status was determined using data supplied by the Bureau of Labor Statistics. This information reported the average income level of residents by census tract.

had a police contact and 50% of the nonwhites. Twenty-six percent of the boys from higher socioeconomic status (SES) backgrounds had a police record, compared with 45% of boys from
the lower SES classification (Wolfgang, Figlio, and Sellin 1972,
p. 245). Other factors related to having a police contact were
a high number of residential and school moves, and low school
grades and I.Q. level. Wolfgang and his associates also found
that nonwhites and boys from the lower SES classification tended
to have more serious and more frequent contacts throughout their
careers (Wolfgang, Figlio, and Sellin 1972, p. 89).

The Racine cohorts also show higher contact rates for minorities. Two-thirds of whites and nine out of ten blacks had
a police contact during their careers (Shannon 1978b, p. 7).
Shannon found that persons with at least one police contact were
a little more likely to have lived in a home with only one parent
present, have a negative attitude toward police, have close friends
who had been in trouble with the police during junior high
and high school, and have a slightly higher delinquent self-con-
cept (Shannon 1976, pp. 96–117). Regularity of employment
for the head of household, parents having been in trouble with
the law, and having a regular job during high school, were unrelated to the likelihood of an individual's having had an official
contact.

A more central concern to criminological research is the proportion of the general population that has a police record reflecting more serious criminal behavior. Data from the Racine
birth cohort permit its subjects to be classified in terms of the
most serious police contact experienced. The results are given in
table 1. This tabulation indicates that only 8–10% of the members of Racine cohorts had a police record involving a felony.
By comparison, results from the Philadelphia study revealed that
for Index or Part I offenses, 13% of that cohort possessed a police record prior to age 18 and 22% prior to age 30 (Wolfgang
1977, p. 9).

2. *Estimating the prevalence of criminal careers.* Some individuals have one police contact, but no more. The birth cohort
studies suggest that approximately one-third of those who had

one police contact do not have another. Conceivably, though it is unlikely, a career criminal might be arrested once, and then evade further arrests. More likely, if the career continues, so do the arrests. Both sources of cohort data indicate that if a second police contact occurs, the likelihood that the individual will have a third contact is quite high, around 70%. This conditional probability of still another contact tends to increase, so that at whatever age an offender has his fourth or fifth arrest, the probability that he will experience another is better than 80%; and the Philadelphia data show that, on the average, the next arrest will be an Index arrest a third of the time (Collins 1977, p. 20). Table 2, in presenting the estimates, indicates that a criminal career marked by many police contacts is relatively uncommon. In particular, if the entries in each column of table 2 are multiplied to produce the unconditional probabilities (males only) of six arrests, we obtain .05, .12, .15, .14, and .14 respectively. For fe-

TABLE 1

Most Serious Police Contacts of
Racine Birth Cohorts

| Cause of Contact | Birth Cohort | | |
	1942	1949	1955
Suspicion or investigation	19.4%	17.3%	11.4%
Juvenile condition[a]	1.4	1.8	4.0
Misdemeanor, minor[b]	31.1	29.5	20.6
Misdemeanor, major[c]	8.1	10.1	8.6
Felony, property[d]	4.7	5.8	5.7
Felony, person[e]	2.6	4.5	8.8
Contacts of any type	68.3%	69.0%	59.1%
(N)	(633)	(1297)	(2149)

Source: Recalculated from Shannon (1976, p. 60). Overlaps among the categories reflect disparities in classification by the police.
[a] Vagrancy, disorderly conduct, incorrigibility, truancy
[b] Obscene behavior, disorderly conduct, vagrancy, liquor, sex, traffic/moving vehicles, traffic/other, gambling, family-parent status, incorrigibility
[c] Escape, theft, narcotics and drugs, weapons, assault, fraud, violent property destruction, burglary, forgery
[d] Burglary, theft, auto theft, forgery, violent property destruction
[e] Robbery, assault, sex offenses, narcotics and drugs, homicide, traffic/moving vehicles, escape, suicide

males, the unconditional probability of six arrests is .02 for all three Racine cohorts. Yet, the likelihood that a criminal career continues, once begun, is substantial.

3. *Volume of crime attributable to career criminals.* Birth cohort studies provide estimates not only of the incidence of offenders in the general population and of career criminals among those offenders, but also of the proportion of recorded crime attributable to career criminals. The latter's crime contribution turns out to be disproportionately large.

In the 1942 Racine birth cohort, 1% of the males had four or more felony contacts, but this small group accounted for 29% of such contacts. In the 1949 cohort, the 3% who had four or more felony contacts accounted for nearly 50% of the contacts. And, finally, in the 1955 cohort, the 6% who had four or more felony contacts accounted for 70% (Shannon 1980, p. 4). Similarly, the 6% of the Philadelphia cohort with five or more

TABLE 2

Probability of First and Continuing Police Contacts for Males and Females from the Racine and Philadelphia Cohorts

| | Philadelphia | | Racine | | | | | |
| | Males | | Males | | | Females[d] | | |
Contacts[a]	Early[b]	Recent[c]	1942	1949	1955	1942	1949	1955
One	.394	.473	.573	.535	.478	.159	.232	.243
Two, given one	.538	.662	.868	.874	.833	.795	.806	.833
Three, given two	.651	.717	.661	.665	.653	.514	.433	.474
Four, given three	.716	.798	.726	.726	.800	.500	.733	.576
Five, given four	.722	.828	.824	.749	.810	.556	.697	.719
Six, given five	.742	.847	.771	.864	.819		.652	.634
.	.	.	.	.	.	.	.	.
.	.	.	.	.	.	.	.	.
.	.	.	.	.	.	.	.	.
Fourteen, given thirteen	.884	.955	.923	.905	.952			.833

[a] Traffic, status offenses, and contacts for suspicion, investigation, or information omitted to make Racine and Philadelphia data comparable.
[b] Wolfgang, Figlio, and Sellin (1972), p. 162.
[c] Wolfgang and Collins (1978), p. 19.
[d] Female continuity figures stop when fewer than 5 have continuing contacts.

official police contacts were responsible for 51% of all officially recorded police contacts in the juvenile years. When the cohort was followed up to age thirty, the chronic offenders (now 15% of the cohort) had been charged with 74% of all the official crime by cohort members, and accounted for 84% of the personal injury offenses and 82% of the serious property offenses (Collins 1977, p. 16).

The Rand inmate survey confirmed the existence of a group of chronic offenders who commit a disproportionate amount of crime. A relatively small group of offenders, appropriately described as career criminals, who share similar characteristics were found to have committed a substantial portion of crimes. They are offenders who reported that they have been engaged in crime for most of their lives, who regard themselves as professionals committed to a criminal career, who have certain psychological attributes that would dispose them toward committing crime, and who foresee a likely return to future crime. Inmates who held these and other identifiable characteristics reported committing a disproportionate amount of crime while on the street. The researchers classified 25% as career criminals, and found that this group reported committing about 60% of the armed robberies, burglaries, and auto thefts committed by the entire sample, and about one-half of the assaults and drug sales (Peterson, Braiker, and Polich 1980, p. 262).

4. *Juvenile criminality and criminal careers.* Most individuals who have contacts with the police do not become career criminals. Juvenile delinquency does not inevitably lead to a life of adult crime. A central issue for criminal careers research is the identification of factors that discriminate between people who do and people who do not continue criminal activity after their initial police contacts. Criminologists have long hypothesized that family background and education, early delinquency, drug and alcohol involvement, employment performance, and other socioeconomic factors will be associated with a sustained pattern of criminal activity.

The Philadelphia and Racine cohort studies and many other

studies[8] have found the characteristics of juvenile criminality to be the most reliable predictor of an adult criminal career. Those who engage in serious crime at an early age are the most likely to continue to commit crimes as adults. By contrast, when juvenile criminality is lacking, sporadic, or unserious, an adult criminal career is exceedingly uncommon.

For the Philadelphia cohort, the likelihood of having an arrest record between the ages of 19 and 26 years is about .43 for those who were juvenile offenders, but is only about .12 for those who were not (Wolfgang 1977, p. 8).[9] This is consistent with the Rand studies, which found that respondents who committed a serious crime before age 16 tended to report more adult crime, commit more types of crime, commit violent crimes at a higher rate, and hold professional criminal attitudes (Peterson, Braiker, and Polich 1980, p. 194).

Shannon and Olson distinguished three age periods in their study of the Racine birth cohorts: juvenile (6–17 years), intermediate (18–20 years), and adult (21 years and older). From information in official records (e.g., race, sex, age at first police contact, type of residential area, etc.) and from interviews (e.g., peer associations, employment, etc.), they tried to identify factors from an earlier age period that predict seriousness of officially recorded events in later periods (Olson 1977).

Although they found evidence that males, minority persons, and those from lower-status residential areas tend to be the more serious offenders within each age period, these factors alone poorly explain the variance in seriousness scores within each period.[10]

[8] In a review of biographical predictors of recidivism, Pritchard (1979) found in 77 out of the 95 studies that age at first arrest was related to whether an offender recidivated.

[9] In the Philadelphia cohort, the unconditional probability of being a juvenile offender was .35, and of having a police record by the age of twenty-six years was .43.

[10] The seriousness score for each age period was the product of the frequency of contact and the seriousness score assigned to each contact category. The contact categories were classified into one of six categories (scored in descending order of seriousness): felonies involving persons (6); felonies involving property (5); major misdemeanors (4); other misdemeanors (3); juvenile status offenses (2); and contacts for suspicion or investigation (1).

The overwhelming predictor of the seriousness of juvenile criminality was age at first police contact. Fifty-four percent of the 57% explained variance in juvenile seriousness scores in the 1942 Racine birth cohort was accounted for by the age of first police contact. This factor accounts for 31% of the 44% explained variance in these scores in the 1949 cohort.

Juvenile seriousness score instead of age at first contact was the most important predictor for the intermediate period. Of the variance in intermediate period seriousness scores of the 1942 cohort, 34% is explained with 31% being due to juvenile seriousness scores alone. In the 1949 cohort, this factor explains 28% of the variance of a total of 33% explained.

Intermediate seriousness score is the most important explanatory factor pertaining to the variance in adult seriousness scores. In the 1942 cohort, this factor explains 25% of a total of 38% explained variance. In the 1949 cohort, 58% of the total of 61% explained variance is attributed to this variable (Olson 1977, p. 16).

The Racine birth cohort study thus suggests that the age at which an offender has his first recorded contact with the police shapes his subsequent criminal career. The earlier the contact, the greater the likelihood that a relatively serious career will follow. Thus the question: what best explains the age at which the first police contact occurs?

Being male and having friends in trouble with the police are associated with lower age at first police contact. Olson (1978) performed a multiple regression analysis of personal interview data for a subset of the Racine birth cohorts. The initial regression model included these possible explanatory factors: employment during high school, amount of education, attitude toward school, age at leaving the family home, age at first job, age at marriage, number of siblings, sex, persons responsible for rearing, regularity of household head's employment, race, social area of residence, self-reported delinquency, aspirations to change, attitude toward police, degree of automobile use, extent of juvenile friends' trouble with law enforcement, and perceived police patrol activity. Only two of these factors—sex and having friends in trouble with the police—helped explain the variance in the age at which police contact first occurs.[11] However, the two together accounted for only 26% and 21% of this variance, respectively, in the 1942 and 1949 birth cohorts. Evidently the interviews did not sufficiently tap the most important determinants of age at first police contact.

Thus, while it has been learned that an early onset of juvenile contacts with police tends to be a precursor of a serious criminal career, the present state of knowledge does not tell us whether this early onset reflects mainly chance, an early onset of delinquent behavior, selectivity of law enforcement, or something else.

B. Characteristics of Criminal Careers

Among important questions explored are: (1) At what age do criminal careers most often begin? (2) What types of crime are committed at the start of the criminal career? (3) How does the seriousness of an offender's crime vary over time? (4) To what extent do offenders vary their crimes rather than specialize? (5) What is the probability that an offense will result in an arrest, conviction, and incarceration? (6) How long do criminal careers last?

1. Age of onset. There is considerable evidence that a majority of criminal careers begin in the early to mid teens. The Philadelphia cohort study found that there were more first arrests at age 17 than at any other age: 10% of all those arrested were first arrested at this age. The percentage of first arrests increased steadily from age 8 to age 17: 2% were first arrested at age 12 years, 8% at 16, 10% at 17. Thereafter first arrest rates decreased, becoming 2% at age 20, 1% at 22, and less thereafter (Wolfgang 1972, p. 411). Racine birth cohort data are consistent with these Philadelphia findings (Shannon 1976, p. 9). Moreover, these sources indicate that the earlier the first arrest, the

11 In the 1942 birth cohort alone, Shannon found that lower age at first police contact was associated with lower age at first full-time employment and with perceived heavy police patrol activity in the neighborhood. In the 1949 birth cohort alone, he found that lower age at first police contact was associated with higher level of automobile use, lower social status of area of residence, and more negative attitude toward police.

likelier it is that sustained serious criminal behavior will follow.

In the Philadelphia cohort, boys who were first arrested at age 13 were arrested more often than boys first arrested at any other age. The chronic offender in the Philadelphia cohort (defined to be one who had five or more juvenile arrests) experienced his first arrest at age 12–two years earlier, on average, than did the rest of the cohort (Wolfgang, Figlio, and Sellin 1972, p. 104).

Other studies using self-reported information and official records have obtained similar results. For example, Peterson, Braiker, and Polich (1980) found that 25% of their sample reported committing a first serious offense prior to age 14; 50% reported committing it prior to age 17; and 75% had committed it prior to age 21. In the sample of prison inmates analyzed in *Criminal Careers of Habitual Felons* (Petersilia, Greenwood, and Lavin 1978), age of first serious criminal activity typically began at about 13 or 14 years for those who became intensive offenders, with the first arrest occurring approximately one year later, by age 15.

2. *The initial type of crime.* Most criminal careers begin with minor misconduct, sometimes even status offenses. Self-report studies indicate that the most frequent pattern begins with truancy and incorrigibility, followed first by petty theft and auto theft and then by more serious property crimes. Nearly half of the inmates interviewed in the Rand criminal careers study reported that the first serious crime was auto theft; 30% revealed that it was burglary; and the remainder began with purse snatches, drug sales, and larceny (Petersilia, Greenwood, and Lavin 1978, p. 24).

The distribution of offense types giving rise to the first police contact in the Philadelphia and Racine birth cohorts is shown in table 3. The vast majority of first police contacts in all the cohorts involved relatively minor offenses, although first contacts were generally more serious in Philadelphia than in Racine.

There is evidence that the more serious the first police contact, the greater the likelihood that subsequent police contacts will occur. Those in the Philadelphia cohort who experienced a second police contact, for example, were more likely to have had a first contact that resulted from an incident involving bodily or property harm (Wolfgang 1972, p. 160).

3. Seriousness progression of crime types. It is natural to hypothesize that career criminals, as they gain experience and as their expectations increase, will undertake crimes of mounting seriousness. But how strong is the evidence to support this hypothesis? The answer is that the evidence is weak except that, as already noted, the beginning of a career at a young age tends to involve minor offenses. In the Racine cohort analysis, where six levels of seriousness were considered, the seriousness of the police contact did not systematically increase as the sequential number of the contact rose (Shannon 1978, p. 17). The Philadelphia cohort results are comparable. The probability of a police contact, when classified by seriousness—non-Index, injury, theft, damage—demonstrated no regular variation with respect to the sequential number of the contact (Wolfgang 1972, p. 248).

To some, this finding is unexpected. It suggests that the probability of committing specific types of offenses is largely independent of the number of prior offenses committed. The tenth

TABLE 3

First Police Contact by Reason for Contact
(Males Only)

Reason for First Contact	Phil-adelphia	Racine		
		1942	1949	1955
Non-Index offenses	65.0%	79.5%	75.3%	74.0%
Assault and personal injury	8.0	—	.5	1.7
Robbery, burglary, theft, and auto theft	14.0	20.1	23.8	23.6
Violent property damage	7.0	.4	.5	.4
Combinations of Index offenses	6.0	—	—	.4
Total	100.0	100.0	100.1	100.1

Source: Wolfgang, Figlio, and Sellin (1972, p. 160) and Shannon (1980). Categories for the Racine study have been modified to make them more comparable to the Philadelphia study by excluding traffic contacts, contacts for suspicion, investigation, or information from the non-Index category.

crime is no more likely to be an act of violence or a high-value property crime than is the fifth. This absence of seriousness progression is revealed in both cohort studies. There is, however, some contrary evidence. The offenders interviewed in the Rand criminal careers study did move from predominantly crimes of auto theft and burglary as juveniles to a greater proportion of robberies and forgeries in the adult years (Petersilia, Greenwood, and Lavin 1978, p. 18), but this sample was small and unrepresentative of offenders in general (all the offenders were serving their second prison term for a robbery conviction).

4. *Crime type specialization.* Do offenders tend to commit crimes of the same type or of different types? Evidence of a clear trend would facilitate the estimation of an offender's future risk to society, and would provide a better foundation for assessing the effects of criminal justice policy changes. Until recently, the study of this issue was based on official records. These records, however, may exaggerate the homogeneity of an offender's criminal activities; certain offenses have a higher probability of resulting in arrest. Thus, an offender who most often commits burglaries would be more likely to be arrested for one of his occasional robberies. Robberies are more easily solved and police tend to focus their limited resources on particular crime types.

Recent research on crime type specialization among persistent offenders has emphasized the use of self-reports to obtain a more representative picture of crime patterns. These newer studies suggest that offenders do not specialize even at the later stages of their careers. Offenders continue to engage in a variety of crime types throughout their careers. The mix may, however, shift from one stage to another.

Half of the inmates queried in the Rand inmate survey reported committing at least four different types of crimes during the three-year period preceding their current imprisonment. Only 10% of the entire sample could be regarded as specialists, that is, offenders who commit only one crime at a high rate. Drug sales and robbery were the most frequently reported specialty crimes. Of those who reported robbery as their main crime type, 11% were specialists in robbery; of those mainly committing cons, 9% were specialists; forgery, 5%; and drug sales, 15% (Peterson, Braiker, and Polich 1980, p. 52).

The criminal careers study also found nonspecialization. This sample of inmates had generally pursued their careers opportunistically, with the result that diversity rather than specialization was the norm. Whatever method of operation or target selection an offender developed (e.g., robbing small stores with female clerks) was usually a continuation of the most recent experience rather than a careful strategy (Petersilia, Greenwood, and Lavin 1978, p. 64).

The "lack of specialization" finding has several implications. Changes in arrest patterns of an offender may not denote changes in criminal behavior. Most offenders may be subject to arrest for any of a number of crimes; the specific crime for which they are arrested may be merely a matter of chance. The nonspecialization finding suggests changes for programs designed to reduce crime levels by concentrating on particular offender types. An example is the Career Criminal Prosecution Unit in San Diego County, initially funded by the Law Enforcement Assistance Administration. It concentrates on arrestees charged with robbery or robbery-related homicide. If career criminals commit many different kinds of offenses, many could be arrested for crimes other than robbery and thereby not receive the special attention appropriate to them. In general, nonspecialization means that the practice of attaching offense-type labels to particular offenders on the basis of arrests can be misleading. Few "robbers" specialize in robbery.

There are some patterns in commission rates for different offense types. Those who report high commission rates for one violent offense type tend to report high rates for other violent offense types. Property offenses are also subject to this pattern (Peterson, Braiker, and Polich 1980, p. 46). Williams observed that offenders arrested for felonies tended to be rearrested for felonies, but this was not a strict rule (Williams 1979, p. 86). Thus there is some empirical evidence that specialization occurs at least by broad classes of offense types, even though most criminal careers show diversity among specific crime types.

5. Offense, arrest, conviction, and incarceration rates. Criminologists have advanced various hypotheses about changes in the type and extent of criminal activity as a criminal career progresses. One is that the seriousness of the offenses increases over time, while the frequency declines. Another is that the offender ultimately "burns out" or matures out of crime in favor of lawful sources of income.

(i) Offense rates. The recent growth of interest in more certain and longer imprisonment of career criminals reflects a belief that career criminals contribute a disproportionate volume of crime and that their prolonged imprisonment would significantly reduce crime. Career criminals must be identified before they have reached the burnout stage of their career when they no longer pose an excessive risk to society. Otherwise, their incarceration will not prevent much crime.

Until recently, there were no satisfactory data on offense rates related to career stage. The National Academy of Sciences Panel on Deterrence and Incapacitation recommended that

> empirical investigations should be directed at estimating the parameters measuring the level of individual criminal activity, especially the individual crime rates . . . and career lengths (T). . . . Furthermore, since estimates of the incapacitative effect are sensitive to variations in these parameters, these estimates should not be restricted to highly aggregated population averages. They should be disaggregated by crime type and demographic group and should reflect the statistical distribution of the parameters (Blumstein, Cohen, and Nagin 1978, p. 80).

The most direct way to find out the rate at which an offender commits crimes is to ask him. The validity of this information perforce depends on the accuracy with which inmates report their crimes; undoubtedly, some offenses will be overlooked, concealed, or exaggerated. Because only limited verification is possible, such data must be used with extreme caution. The criminal careers study found that the inmate had recalled and disclosed about 75% of the items found on the official rap sheets (Petersilia 1978a, p. 45). To estimate offense rates, the researcher must use self-reports to supplement the official records, by themselves plainly incomplete and, for estimating purposes, biased.

The Rand studies are the most systematic recent efforts to estimate offense rates directly from data on individual offenders.[12] Others have used aggregated data on the number of offenses and arrests in a particular jurisdiction to infer average offense commission rates (usually for the purpose of estimating incapacitation effects). These estimates have ranged from less than one Index offense per year (Clarke 1974; Greenberg 1975), to between 1.4 and 2.8 (Greene 1977), to ten Index offenses per year (Shinnar and Shinnar 1975).[13]

Rand has used offender self-reports of the number of crimes committed during a specified "window period" prior to the current imprisonment, converting these to annual rates. Blumstein and Cohen (1978) have used official arrest histories to arrive at individual arrest rates which, when divided by the appropriate probability of arrest, yield individual offense rates. With either technique it is necessary to adjust for periods when the individual offender was incarcerated, because the aim is to calculate the rate at which an offender commits crime when free from restraint. Notwithstanding their differences, the self-report and the official record approach have generated estimates of offense rates that are reasonably close.

Table 4 shows estimated selected offense rates derived by use of the Rand self-report approach and Blumstein's arrest-history approach. The comparison is limited by differences in legal offense definitions in the two studies and because the offender populations were geographically widely separated (California versus Washington, D.C.), but the results are relatively consistent.

[12] Wolfgang and Collins interviewed a subsample of the Philadelphia cohort to estimate their crime rates before and after age eighteen. Over the offenders' careers, the combination of officially reported and self-reported offenses resulted in an annual mean for injury and property offenses of 1.1 for all offenders. Chronics had the highest self-reported offense rate of about 2.5 Index offenses a year over their careers (Collins 1977, p. 66).

[13] Differences in yearly rates obtained result from different assumptions, different data bases, and different jurisdictions. For a complete discussion, see Blumstein, Cohen, and Nagin (1978).

TABLE 4

Alternatively Derived Offense Rates

Offense Type	Annual Offense Rate Estimates	
	Self-Report Approach	Arrest-History Approach
Robbery[a]	1.97	3.41
Burglary	7.23	5.73
Aggravated assault[b]	2.38	1.72
Auto theft	3.48	2.98

Sources: Peterson, Braiker, and Polich (1980); Blumstein and Cohen (1978).

[a] The robbery offense rate from the self-report approach includes only armed robberies; from the arrest-history approach, robberies in general.

[b] Aggravated assault is defined differently in the two sets of data used.

The criminal careers study provided individual offense rates for a sample of forty-nine imprisoned serious offenders. They reported an average of two hundred crime commissions each over a typical career length of about twenty years. On average these career criminals had been imprisoned for about half of the period of their careers; the resulting estimate of their average offense rate is thus about twenty per year—four violent crimes and sixteen property crimes. These inmates, all serving at least a second prison term, were probably more active in crime than most career criminals, and their average offense rate probably exaggerates the rate to be found in a more inclusive population of repeat offenders.

Table 5 presents a summary of annual offense commission rates attributed to a representative cohort of incoming California prison inmates.[14] Column I shows the percentage distribution of these inmates by their most serious commitment offenses. (The entries do not total 100% because some offense types have not been included.) Column II shows the percentages of inmates who

[14] A cohort of incoming inmates is a better base for analysis of incapacitation effects than is a random sample of inmates; the latter is biased toward inmates with longer sentences. The characteristics of an incoming cohort can be estimated from those of a random inmate sample by means of a weighting scheme that reflects differences in sentence length (Chaiken 1978).

reported committing each specified crime type during the three-year period preceding the current incarceration. (The entries exceed 100% because most offenders committed crimes of more than one type during this period.) Column III gives the annual offense rate for those inmates who were active in a specified type of crime.

Finally, a few studies have investigated the important question of how self-report offense rates vary over the criminal career. The Rand criminal careers study found that offense rates varied significantly with age: criminality peaked early in the career. In the characteristic pattern, criminal activity begins at about age 14; the offense rate increases until the early 20s and tends to decline thereafter until age 30, when the majority of careers terminate. Offense rates among 14- to 21-year-old serious offenders averaged twenty to forty crimes per year; among 22- to 25-year-olds, about twelve crimes per year; and among 26- to 30-year-olds, seven per year. Even when the type of offense is

TABLE 5

Prevalence and Offense Rates for
Cohort of Incoming Prison Inmates

Offense Type	I Percentage Committed to Prison for this Offense	II Percentage Active in this Offense[a]	III Average Offense Rate for Actives[b]
Homicide	9	9	0.27
Rape	3	8	1.35
Robbery	34	37	4.61
Assault	7	59	4.47
Drug sales	10	48	155.00
Burglary	13	58	15.29
Auto theft	4	32	5.25
Forgery	4	40	5.56
"Cons"	—	63	9.45

Source: Peterson, Braiker, and Polich (1980, p. 41).
[a] An "active offender" reported committing at least one of the specified type of offense during the three-year period prior to his current imprisonment.
[b] Crimes per year of street time.

controlled for, there was still evidence of a decline of crime with age (Petersilia, Greenwood, and Lavin 1978, p. vii).

Collins found a similar pattern for chronic offenders in the Philadelphia age cohort. The chronic offenders had their highest self-reported offense rate during their younger years: between the ages of 14 and 17, they were committing more than four Index crimes per year; by age 22, they were committing only three per year (Collins 1977, p. 66).

Thus it appears that many offenders are persistent wrongdoers and that the teenage years are the period when the rate of wrong-doing is highest. If we could incapacitate substantial numbers of youthful offenders during their high crime years, we could—at least in absolute numbers—significantly decrease the numbers of offenses committed. The problem is, of course, and this is discussed below, we do not know which youthful offenders to lock up.

(*ii*) *Arrest rates.* The likelihood that a criminal act will lead to an arrest is one of the variables that helps characterize a criminal career. How this probability varies over the course of a career is a question of considerable interest. Many have speculated that older and more seasoned offenders become more adept at avoiding arrest.

Table 6 presents a set of arrest probabilities by offense type derived from the self-reported information obtained in the Rand inmate survey and pertaining to the population of all active California adult offenders. An arrest probability is calculated by dividing the number of crimes of a particular type that an offender reports committing, by the number of times he was arrested over the same time period for that type of crime. Blumstein and Cohen (1978) estimated the probability of arrest for any type of robbery to be .07; for assault, .11; and for burglary, .05. Their estimates are in reasonable accord with table 6.

Both estimation procedures undoubtedly involve errors, due, respectively, to self-report biases and assumptions about the arrest process. Nevertheless, when applied to completely independent samples the two procedures result in strikingly similar estimates of individual crime (table 4) and arrest rates (table 6).

It is relatively unlikely that the two substantially different procedures would produce the same wrong estimates. This suggests that the errors in both cases may not be unreasonable and lends some credibility to both sets of estimates (see Blumstein and Cohen 1978).

Efforts to relate systematic variations in arrest probabilities to offender characteristics have had only limited success. There is no persuasive evidence that the probability of arrest decreases with age and experience. To the contrary, offenders over thirty years old may have higher arrest probabilities than do younger offenders. Nor does the extent of the prior criminal record seem to explain variations in arrest probability (Peterson, Braiker, and Polich 1980, p. 80).

There do appear to be significant relations between arrest probability and juvenile criminality and between arrest probability and race. Offenders who reported serious juvenile criminal activity had substantially lower probabilities of arrest than those who did not. Black and Hispanic offenders appear to be more likely to be arrested than whites by a factor of two or three, a difference which some attribute to police tactics, but which has yet to be explored (Peterson, Braiker, and Polich 1980, p. ix).

The criminal careers study explored the possibility that differences in arrest probabilities result from the extensiveness of pre-crime planning by offenders. Although most of the inmate sample reported a low level of pre-crime planning and preparation, a few attempted to disguise their appearance or to choose

TABLE 6

Probability of Arrest
by Type of Offense

Offense Type	Probability of Arrest
Rape	.10
Armed robbery	.21
Assault	.10
Burglary	.07
Forgery	.06
Drug sales	.002

Source: Peterson, Braiker, and Polich (1980, p. 41).

an escape route. Unsurprisingly, those who engaged in greater planning efforts were less likely to be arrested for a criminal act. Offenders who reported some planning were five times less likely than those who did no planning to be arrested for any one crime (Petersilia, Greenwood, and Lavin 1978, p. 112). The propensity to plan did not increase with age. Those disposed toward planning appeared to manifest this characteristic as juveniles rather than as a result of later experience and associations.

Thus, while it appears that pre-crime planning does reduce the likelihood of arrest, planning seems not to be related to age and experience. Criminal careers research is in its early days, but—while the evidence is far from conclusive—it appears unlikely that the observed relation between declining arrests and age results from more skillful crimes by more seasoned criminals.

(*iii*) *Conviction and incarceration rates.* A criminal record has traditionally been considered an important factor in the decision whether to imprison a convicted offender. In some jurisdictions, some prior convictions may be specially alleged and, if proved, will justify or require a harsher sentence. Career criminals might be expected to have a higher probability of incarceration, once convicted, than do other offenders.

In the abstract, a defendant's prior record should not help determine whether he is convicted. Conviction should result from the strength of the evidence rather than from the defendant's criminal history. Most convictions, however, are the product of negotiated pleas, not trials. Plea negotiations are probably somewhat different when the defendant is a career criminal, and it is difficult to know whether the probability of conviction is affected. Nonetheless, for an arrest with marginal evidence or for a marginal crime, the likelihood that the case will be dropped by either the police or the prosecutor should be affected by the suspect's criminal record.

Rand examined a large body of California Offender Based Transactional Data (OBTS) on adult felony arrests.[15] The like-

---

[15] This data file consists of a random sample taken in four Southern California counties—Los Angeles, Orange, San Bernardino, and San Diego. The sample constitutes about 25% of the felony arrests in those four counties in 1973. This file contains arrest through disposition information for those 11,000 suspects arrested on a felony charge in 1973.

lihood of conviction, which averaged about .40 over the entire sample of felony arrests, did not appear to vary systematically with prior record. Cases against defendants with less serious records tended to drop out earlier in the criminal proceeding (Greenwood 1977, p. 20).

Following a conviction, the OBTS data indicated, the probability that a prison sentence would be imposed was strongly related to the defendant's prior record.[16] Seventy-two percent of convicted robbery defendants with prior prison records received a prison commitment, while only 16% of those with minor records went to prison. Almost no convicted burglars with a minor record were sentenced to prison; 23% with a prison record received a prison sentence.

The Rand criminal careers study throws some light on the relation between the likelihood of incarceration and the stages of a criminal career. About 50% of all early adult convictions resulted in incarceration, compared to 71% of later adult convictions (Petersilia, Greenwood, and Lavin 1978, p. 39).

The effect of this change in incarceration rate is embodied in another measure describing criminal careers, the "at risk" rate—the percentage of time the offender is on the street. The inmate sample in the criminal careers study had an "at-risk" rate of roughly 61% during the early adult career period (Petersilia, Greenwood, and Lavin 1978, p. 16).

Thus, viewed broadly, there is empirical evidence that career criminals are more likely to be convicted and imprisoned when arrested as their careers progress and that they spend a diminishing proportion of their time on the streets until their criminal activity abates.

6. Career length. Knowledge about the duration of criminal activity is required to estimate the impact of changes in sentencing policy on the volume of crime. Unfortunately, little empirical research on the lengths of criminal careers has been undertaken. A handful of studies have addressed the subject, but their

[16] Dungworth (1978) reports similar findings based on Prosecutor's Management Information System data applying to Washington, D.C. The average rate of prison commitment, given conviction, varied from 26% for offenders who had no prior record to over 60% for those who had at least one prior conviction and more than three prior arrests.

results are questionable because of methodological difficulties. The 1975 Uniform Crime Reports reported on 135,000 adult offenders who had at least two arrests and who had been arrested between 1970 and 1974. Using the time between the first and last arrests as a measure of criminal career length, the FBI concluded that the average career lasts five years and five months (FBI 1975).

This FBI figure is probably an underestimate. The first adult arrest was considered the initiation of the career, which is incompatible with much evidence that many adult offenders engage in juvenile crime. Moreover, treating the most recent arrest as the terminal point of the career is simply unsound. The most recent arrest indicates that the offender is still active, not that criminal activity has terminated.

Greene (1977) found that the lengths of adult criminal careers follow an exponential distribution with a mean between 10 and 15 years. He concluded that the mean adult career length is 11.9 years, but only on the questionable assumption that criminal careers begin at age 18. His results are consistent with those of the Uniform Crime Reports (FBI 1966, 1969), which show an average career length of ten years, and Collins (1977, p. 66), who concludes that the average career lasts approximately eight years.

C. *Other Aspects of Criminal Careers*

Some criminal careers research subjects have implications that transcend the organizational distinction between "incidence and prevalence" issues and career progression issues. However, the emphasis remains on how various factors change as a criminal career advances. Researchers have attempted to study criminal careers in terms of criminal motivation, criminal sophistication, drugs and alcohol involvement, and employment performance.

1. Criminal motivation. Some crimes are committed not simply for material gain, but for excitement, thrills, attention, and peer recognition. These nonmaterial motivations have been referred to as expressive needs (crimes committed to express emotion) rather than instrumental needs (crimes committed for what they yield) (Glaser 1974). Expressive purposes appear important in the initiation of a criminal career, but instrumental needs are a critical factor in its continuation. The Rand criminal careers study revealed the pattern shown in table 7.

The inmate sample in the Rand inmate survey was asked about the main reason for first becoming involved in crime. Those who reported the beginning of their serious crime between the ages of thirteen and fifteen years most often answered: "for excitement." Those who began their criminal careers between the ages of nineteen and twenty-one years most often gave the reasons "to get money for drugs—had a habit" or "to get money for day-to-day living—self or family support" (Peterson, Braiker, and Polich 1980, p. 195).

The inmate survey analysts were able to identify three statistically unrelated factors or scales that represented fifteen motivational items rated by the inmates as reasons for committing crimes. The most important of these three motivational factors was termed "economic distress," which included unemployment, indebtedness, and need for routine income; the second, "high

TABLE 7

Inmates' Self-Reported Main Reason
for Committing Crimes

Main Reason	Career Period		
	As a Juvenile	As a Young Adult	As an Older Adult
Hostility, revenge	9.5%	9.3%	9.8%
Thrills, attention, status	38.1	—	7.3
Peer influence	21.4	4.6	2.4
Total, expressive needs	69.0%	13.9%	19.5%
Money for rent, other self-support	19.0%	27.9%	22.0%
Money for family support	—	11.6	9.8
Total, support needs	19.0%	39.5%	31.8%
Money for drugs, alcohol	9.5%	30.2%	29.3%
Money for women	2.4	9.3	7.3
Total, high living	11.9%	39.5%	36.6%
No alternative/don't know	—	6.9%	12.2%
(N)	(42)	(43)	(41)

Source: Petersilia, Greenwood, and Lavin (1978, p. 76).

times"; and the third, "temper." Among inmates surveyed, 47% reported that economic distress was important to their crimes; 35%, high times; and 14%, temper. The different motivations explained differences in criminal activity. The greatest amount of crime was reported by those for whom high times were important and economic distress unimportant. Fewer violent crimes were committed by those who rated economic distress important. And while there were no significant differences in the amount of crime committed between those who rated temper important and those who did not, temper was positively associated with the commission of nonmonetary violent crimes, as might be expected (Peterson, Braiker, and Polich 1980, p. 136).

2. *Criminal sophistication.* Criminologists have long hypothesized that planning and preparation for crime will become more routine as the criminal career progresses (e.g., Gibbons 1968; Clinard and Quinney 1973). The notion is widespread that an impulsive juvenile offender matures into an adult professional criminal and, as an adult, pursues crime as a preferred occupation, continually developing skills, becoming ever more specialized, and steadily increasing his profits. Policy makers must be sensitive to whether career criminals do develop such sophistication. If criminal sophistication implies more adeptness in avoiding arrest and conviction, then prison populations should reflect a disproportionate presence of unsophisticated offenders, i.e., "losers." And if youthfulness implies a lack of sophistication, then the disproportionate number of young offenders may indicate naiveté rather than a greater incidence of crime committed by the young.

Published research does not support many of these traditional images of criminal development. It has already been noted that career criminals generally do not plan their crimes or specialize in crime types, even in later career stages. Another hallmark of sophistication might be the use of partners, informants, and fences in the execution of crimes. The criminal careers study found, at least for that sample of inmates, that the tendency to work alone becomes more pronounced as the career progresses. Experienced offenders who judged themselves competent at crime appeared unwilling to share profits or risk the chance that a partner might implicate them later (Petersilia, Greenwood, and Lavin 1978, p. 66).

Another attribute of criminal sophistication is thought to be the geographic range of criminal activity. A wider range denotes greater sophistication. The evidence here is mixed. Although the inmates in the criminal careers study moved beyond their immediate neighborhoods as they matured, most of them extended their criminal activities no farther than neighboring cities. Out-of-state excursions were exceptional. However, an FBI study reported that in one sample, 67% of those arrested for violent crime or burglary, with a record of at least two prior arrests, had been arrested in at least two states (FBI 1969).

The criminal careers study did not find that income from crime—a natural index of criminal sophistication—increased dramatically as criminal careers advanced. While monetary gain increased somewhat, the accumulation of adult criminal experience showed no clear payoff in richer returns. Criminal income was low under any circumstances, averaging only a few thousand dollars per year (Petersilia, Greenwood, and Lavin 1978, p. 70).

Whether a more representative sample of career criminals would show a significant correlation between criminal experience and monetary gain or, more generally, between criminal experience and criminal sophistication, remains an open question. These studies rely on data from offenders who are eventually arrested. Perhaps there are offenders who become sufficiently sophisticated that they consistently avoid arrest. Criminal sophistication and probability of arrest are probably inversely related. Consequently, prison samples probably underrepresent the offenders for whom crime is the most remunerative.

3. *Drugs and alcohol involvement.* Drugs and alcohol clearly play a prominent role in criminal careers, but the relations are exceedingly complex. The criminal careers study found that about half of the inmates studied had a history of drugs involvement by official records; by their own statements, about two-thirds had been heavy users of drugs, alcohol, or both. Over 60% reported being under the influence of alcohol or drugs

when committing crimes as adults. The desire for money to buy drugs and alcohol was the single most frequently cited reason for committing crimes (see table 7).

Both the Rand inmate survey and the criminal careers study investigated the influence of alcohol and drug use on the rates and types of crimes committed. The results suggest that offenders involved with alcohol alone committed crimes less frequently than other inmates; the crimes they committed were usually less serious. The inmates who had been involved with both alcohol and drugs tended to be the most serious offenders (Peterson, Braiker, and Polich 1980, p. xv; Petersilia, Greenwood, and Lavin 1978, p. 84). Inmates who reported frequent use of drugs also reported committing more property crimes than did non–drug users (Peterson, Braiker, and Polich 1980, p. xv). However, this association does not necessarily imply causation.

4. Employment performance. It is widely believed that unemployment and criminal careers are associated. Inability to locate a job or the loss of employment well may trigger the start of a criminal career. Once the career has begun, and an offender has developed a police record, the criminal record negatively affects his employment opportunities.

The criminal careers study and the Rand inmate survey explored the relation between employment and the development of the criminal career. Only one of the inmates interviewed in the criminal careers study reported that loss of employment triggered his criminal career, but several reported that employment problems contributed to their continued crime (Petersilia, Greenwood, and Lavin 1978, p. 88). Nearly 30% of the sample in the inmate survey said that inability to get a job was a very important motivating factor to their continued criminality (Peterson, Braiker, and Polich 1980, p. 129).

Both the criminal careers study and the inmate survey found that better employed offenders committed less crime overall than other offenders, and they also committed fewer crimes against persons (Petersilia, Greenwood, and Lavin 1978, p. 89; Peterson, Braiker, and Polich 1980, p. 136). These findings suggest that employment may not necessarily halt a criminal career, but it may dispose offenders to commit less serious and less frequent crimes.

The Racine cohort study examined the relation between employment and an official police record. Contrary to expectations, little direct relation was found between early full-time employment and the absence of a police record at lower seriousness scores. The tendency was in the opposite direction. The data suggest that those who worked during their teens or early twenties, particularly the males, had more police contacts and higher seriousness scores than those who were unemployed (Shannon 1980). The explanation may be that juveniles from lower socioeconomic-status homes begin work earlier; socioeconomic status is related to police contacts, and early employment may thus be indirectly correlated with police contacts.

D. The Effect of Criminal Justice Sanctions on the Criminal Career

Contacts with the criminal justice system are landmark events in a criminal career. Regrettably, available data suggest that sanctions may be counterproductive. Philadelphia cohort results show that a higher proportion of those who receive criminal sanctions continue to violate the law, committing more serious crimes with greater rapidity, than do those who were treated more leniently (Wolfgang, Figlio, and Sellin 1972, p. 231). Of course, this result may also imply that sanctioning tends to be selective. Sanctions are more likely to be applied against offenders who are correctly perceived as more serious.

The Racine birth cohort data indicate that the number of police contacts and the seriousness of the resulting sanctions prior to age 18 are related to the number of police contacts after age 18. Table 8 shows that males in the 1955 cohort tended toward greater involvement with the police after age 18 as the number of contacts and seriousness of sanctions before age 18 increased; similar results were obtained for the 1942 and 1949 cohorts.

The effect of criminal justice sanctions on the continuation of criminal careers is not adequately understood. It is reasonable to believe that more severe sanctions should inhibit the subse-

TABLE 8

Distribution of Number of Police Contacts
after Age Eighteen as a Function of the
Number of Contacts and Seriousness of
Sanctions Prior to Age Eighteen
(Males in 1955 Racine Cohort)

Number of Contacts Prior to Age 18	Seriousness of Sanctions Prior to Age 18	Number of Police Contacts after Age 18		
		None	1–4	5 or more
None	None	75%	24%	0.5%
1–4	None	56	40	4
1–4	Low	34	58	8
1–4	High	48	42	10
5 or more	None	38	35	26
5 or more	Low	17	51	31
5 or more	High	25	32	42
(N)		(598)	(399)	(117)

Source: Shannon (1980).

quent commission of crimes unless the probability of arrest and
conviction is so low that offenders disregard the risk of punishment. But it is also reasonable to view the jail or prison experience as itself fostering closer relations with other criminals, en-
gendering frustration with society, and exacerbating the difficulty
of obtaining legitimate employment after release. Consequently,
imprisonment may create pressures to continue a criminal career.
All that is known with certitude about how the opposing forces
are resolved is that the outcome varies from one offender to
another.

E. Summary of Conclusions

The following propositions recapitulate some of the major
findings on criminal careers that were presented above. They
are tentative, some being at best a majority view and others reflecting the results of a single investigation. They are best regarded as hypotheses to guide further efforts to achieve an understanding of criminal careers.

Less than 15% of the general population will be arrested
for the commission of a felony and, of these, perhaps 50%

will never be arrested for another. Very roughly, only 5%
of the population will demonstrate the beginnings of a
criminal career. But once three contacts with the police
have been recorded, the probability that still another
contact will be made is high.

Criminal careers preponderantly begin early in life,
commonly between the ages of fourteen and seventeen
years. The earlier criminal activities begin, the more likely
it is that sustained serious criminal conduct will ensue
in the adult years. Nevertheless, relatively few juvenile
delinquents become career criminals.

Criminal careers sometimes begin as youthful adventures,
for thrills and excitement and to achieve peer status. They may
then be continued for other reasons, e.g., for income.

Drugs and alcohol play significant roles in a majority of
criminal careers, and offenders who are involved with drugs
or with both drugs and alcohol generally commit more
crimes over the course of their careers than do others.

At every stage of his career, the offender will commit a
variety of offense types rather than specialize. The mixture
may shift from one stage to the next, often increasing
in seriousness, but not as a consistent rule. Crime targets
are more likely to be opportunistic than the results
of methodical planning.

Criminal careers markedly differ in offense rates. Some are
characterized by rates as low as 1–2 crimes committed per
year; others by 4–5 crimes per year; and those of highly
active offenders, by upwards of 20 per year.

Offense rates depend on the offender's age, his criminal
record, and the offense type committed. Self-reported rates
for those active in robbery are about 5 per year of such
offenses; in burglary, about 16 per year; and in drug sales,
about 155 per year. Cross-sectional studies disclose
that younger offenders have higher offense rates than
do older offenders, not only for crime as a whole but
generally also for individual offense types.

The probability of being arrested for an individual criminal act is no more than .10 on the average, but it varies widely over types of offense committed, from less than .01 for drug offenses to approximately .20 for robberies. Pre-crime planning and preparation, not commonplace among career criminals, lessen the likelihood of arrest.

Arrest, conviction, and incarceration rates increase as the criminal career advances, by contrast with offense rates, which tend to decline.

Prior criminal record has a powerful effect on the probability of incarceration and some effect on the probability of conviction. While criminal record gives an indication of an offender's propensity to commit further crimes, the predictive value of this information by itself is weak.

Criminal careers are not necessarily marked by a growth in criminal sophistication, in criminal income, or in the geographical range of activities.

No consistent effect on the termination of criminal careers as a result of criminal justice sanctions or treatment programs has been demonstrated. Some evidence, possibly biased because of the manner in which offender samples were selected, indicates that harsh punishment may help to extend criminal careers.

IV. Implications for Policy and Future Research

Much of the research discussed in this essay was undertaken in order to assess public policies directed at reducing crime by incapacitating a small number of career criminals. Thus the critical question—what policy implications do the findings suggest? First, there is a group of offenders who engage in large amounts of serious crime, most of which is never detected by the criminal justice system. Since these offenders appear to contribute disproportionately to crime, programs that successfully identified and incarcerated such persons might significantly reduce crime. Second, a number of offender characteristics are consistently correlated with high-rate criminality and should serve as hypotheses to be explored in future research. In current decision-making, these crime correlates can guide a judge in determining which of two offenders, with similar official criminal histories, is more likely to be engaged in high-rate criminal activities.

For an incapacitative crime control strategy to be effective, we need to know, first, whether there is a group of offenders who commit large numbers of offenses over a substantial period, and second, whether we can identify them. The first condition can be met. There is a small group of persistent offenders. Regrettably, however, we cannot reliably estimate the crime reduction effect of an incapacitative program for reasons discussed below. The second condition—ability to predict—cannot now be met.

Unfortunately, the data accumulated to date on criminal careers do not permit us, with acceptable confidence, to predict the effects of alternative sentencing policies on crime reduction. The data is not appropriate for that use for a number of reasons, the most important being the bias introduced by the particular samples of criminals studied. For the most part, estimates of the amount of crime offenders commit in an average year have been derived from studies of persons recently arrested or currently imprisoned. These persons have then been asked to recall their criminal activities over a recent time period. Any method of sampling based on an identification by the system results in an overestimation, or upward bias, of the estimated crime variables. To estimate the number of colds the average American gets in a given year, we would need to sample a random group of Americans. Suppose, however, that the researcher chose to sample only patients. The sample would be biased and, in all likelihood, hospital patients would have had more colds more often in the past year than the general population. Such a weighted sample of persons who have a higher probability of having a cold in the period of interest is ideal if one wants to make a more detailed study of persons who have had colds. However, using the "cold rate" of this group to determine the effects of a new medicine on the colds of the general population is clearly inappropriate. Studies based on samples of prison inmates are biased in a similar manner. The crime rates these offenders report are not typical of the general population. When the yearly crime rates reported by these inmates are used to estimate the number of crimes that would be prevented if every offender were sentenced to longer prison terms, the resulting crime reduction is grossly overestimated. We have no reliable empirical information on the relative distribution of crime rates between prison inmates and other offender populations. Research now being conducted by Rand includes jail populations, but sampling other offender groups is also necessary before we can estimate the reduction in crime that will be realized by alternative sentencing policies.

Although we are accumulating knowledge about criminal career patterns, we still cannot confidently identify career criminals. Criminal career research should continue to explore variations in offense rates and arrest probabilities as a function of age, prior record, and offense type. Findings to date generally suggest that crime commission rates decline with age, regardless of prior record. Policies that call for imprisonment of offenders early in their criminal careers might produce the greatest impact on crime, in contrast to present practice, in which offenders are imprisoned only after they have achieved significant criminal histories (see, e.g., Boland and Wilson 1978).

Incapacitation will be effective only if we can identify and imprison offenders at the most active stages of their careers. But an incapacitation policy is both unfair and costly if an undue number of inappropriate offenders receive extra stringent imprisonment. Thus, a critical issue for criminal career research is whether crime commission rates decline with age. Unfortunately, research to date focuses principally on "active" offenders who were recently arrested or are currently incarcerated. This occurs primarily because they are accessible study populations. As a result, we do not know whether persons who are no longer being arrested have actually terminated their criminal careers or have simply become more successful at crime, thereby avoiding arrest. If they have become more successful, then the findings concerning an age effect (older persons commit less crime) may be wrong. If this were true, tougher policies aimed at younger offenders may be misdirected.

Career termination is another area in which further research is needed. Little is known about the distinguishing characteristics of active criminals who shift completely into lawful pursuits. For occasional offenders this transition may not represent a significant event; but for active offenders it may represent a significant departure in attitude, behavior, and social contacts. Earlier research on career termination has relied mainly on general sociodemographic characteristics as discriminators (Olson 1977). The results have not been particularly enlightening.

Another related area calling for research is career relapse. Offender self-reports indicate that more than half of all prison inmates do not profess criminal attitudes, hold criminal identities, or believe crime pays, and engage in crime only sporadically (Peterson, Braiker, and Polich 1980; Petersilia, Greenwood, and Lavin 1978). There is little understanding of what motivates intermittent offenders to commit occasional crimes that are seemingly out of character.

Research should be pursued to identify the offender characteristics that are associated with high offense rates at any point in a career. Official arrest records are not a reliable indicator of high offense rates (Petersilia 1978a). Drug use, unemployment, marital status, and criminal sophistication appear to be correlates of high offense rates under certain conditions (Peterson, Braiker, and Polich 1980; Petersilia, Greenwood, and Lavin 1978). Knowledge about relations such as these could be helpful, for example, in guiding sentencing.

Most broadly, research is needed to enhance the predictability of criminal careers. Simply knowing that some offenders commit a disproportionate amount of crime is not helpful to policy formulation. As Blumstein (1979) recently noted:

Any stochastic sequence of events with a non-zero probability of termination after an event will inevitably result in a distribution of sequence lengths. In criminal-career terms, this implies that someone in a cohort has to have committed the most crimes in the cohort, and that person will, of necessity, account for a disproportionately large number of crimes. Or more generally, since every statistical distribution has to have a right-hand tail, the group of "chronic offenders" who comprise that right-hand tail will necessarily account for a disproportionately large number of offenses. The critical question is whether the members of that group are distinguishably different. Certainly they have different records in retrospect, but the same can be said of winners and losers in any chance process. The fundamental policy question, then, is whether the "chronic offenders" are identifiable in prospect, that is, during the period in which they accumulate a record, can one predict which individuals will turn out to be the ones with the longest sequence. Unless such discrimination can be made, any identification of "chronic offenders" can only be made retrospectively, and so is of little policy or operational value.

Thus far, the strongest predictors of adult criminal careers are thought to be the age at which serious juvenile criminality begins and the extent and seriousness of the juvenile criminal history. But what explains an early onset of juvenile crime? Is it peer and family relationships? Depending on what is shown by further research, what intervention might be feasible and productive? Improved predictability of criminal careers will generate a stream of such questions, but it is the key to countering these offenders.

Past experiences with a number of seemingly promising strategies should suggest that there are not likely to be any easy or universal answers to criminal behavior and the problems it poses for society. Nor is criminal career research likely to produce any panaceas. But it does offer a unique perspective, which can inform efforts to improve the criminal justice system.

REFERENCES

Avi-Itzhak, Benjamin, and Reuel Shinnar. 1973. "Quantitative Models in Crime Control," *Journal of Criminal Justice* 1:185–217.

Bailey, Walter C. 1966. "Correctional Outcome: An Evaluation of 100 Reports," *Journal of Criminal Law, Criminology, and Police Science* 57:153–160.

Belkin, Jacob, Alfred Blumstein, and William Glass. 1973. "Recidivism as a Feedback Process: An Analytical Model and Empirical Validation," *Journal of Criminal Justice* 1:7–26.

Blumstein, Alfred. 1979. "The Identification of 'Career Criminals' from 'Chronic Offenders' in a Cohort." Unpublished paper, Carnegie-Mellon University, Pittsburgh.

Blumstein, Alfred, and Jacqueline Cohen. 1978. "Estimation of Individual Crime Rates from Arrest Records." Working paper, Carnegie-Mellon University, Pittsburgh.

Blumstein, Alfred, Jacqueline Cohen, and Daniel Nagin, eds. 1978. *Deterrence and Incapacitation: Estimating the Effects of Criminal Sanctions on Crime Rates*. Washington, D.C.: National Academy of Sciences.

Boland, Barbara, and James Q. Wilson. 1978. "Age, Crime and Punishment," *Public Interest* 51:22–34.

Booth, Ernest. 1929. *Stealing Through Life*. New York: Knopf.

Buffum, Peter C. 1976. "Surveying Ex-Prisoners: Procedures and Pitfalls," *Prison Journal* 56(1):1–14.

Chaiken, Jan M. 1978. "Estimates of Offender Characteristics Derived from the Rand Prison Inmate Survey." Unpublished paper, The Rand Corporation, Santa Monica, Cal.

Clarke, Stevens H. 1974. "Getting 'Em Out of Circulation: Does Incarceration of Juvenile Offenders Reduce Crime?" *Journal of Criminal Law and Criminology* 65:528–35.

Clinard, Marshall, and Richard Quinney. 1973. *Criminal Behavior Systems: A Typology*. New York: Holt, Rinehart & Winston.

Collins, James J. 1977. "Offender Careers and Restraint: Probabilities and Policy Implications." Final draft report. Washington, D.C.: Law Enforcement Assistance Administration, U.S. Department of Justice.

Dungworth, Terence. 1978. *An Empirical Assessment of Sentencing Practice in the Superior Court of the District of Columbia*. Washington, D.C.: Institute for Law and Social Research.

Ehrlich, Isaac. 1973. "Participation in Illegitimate Activities: A Theoretical and Empirical Investigation," *Journal of Political Economy* 81:521–67.

Federal Bureau of Investigation, U.S. Department of Justice. 1967, 1970, 1975. *Crime in the United States—1966, . . . 1969, . . . 1974.* Washington, D.C.: U.S. Government Printing Office.

Gándara, Arturo. 1978. *Major Federal Regulations Governing Social Science Research.* Santa Monica, Cal.: The Rand Corporation.

Gibbons, Don C. 1968. *Society, Crime and Criminal Careers.* Englewood Cliffs, N. J.: Prentice-Hall.

Glaser, Daniel. 1974. "The Classification of Offenses and Offenders." In *The Handbook of Criminology*, ed. Daniel Glaser. Skokie, Ill.: Rand McNally.

Glueck, Sheldon, and Eleanor Glueck. 1930. *Five Hundred Criminal Careers.* New York: Knopf.

——. 1934a. *Five Hundred Delinquent Women.* New York: Knopf.

——. 1934b. *One Thousand Juvenile Delinquents.* Cambridge, Mass.: Harvard University Press.

——. 1937. *Later Criminal Careers.* New York: Commonwealth Fund.

——. 1943a. *Juvenile Delinquents Grown Up.* New York: Commonwealth Fund.

——. 1943b. *Criminal Careers in Retrospect.* New York: Commonwealth Fund.

——. 1950. *Unraveling Juvenile Delinquency.* Cambridge, Mass.: Harvard University Press.

Greenberg, David. 1975. "The Incapacitative Effect of Imprisonment: Some Estimates," *Law and Society Review* 4:541–80.

Greene, Michael. 1977. "The Incapacitative Effect of Imprisonment Policies on Crime." Doctoral dissertation, Carnegie-Mellon University, Pittsburgh.

Greenwood, Peter W. 1977. "The Disposition of Felony Arrests: Prosecution and Sentencing Policies in California, and Their Effects on Crime." Unpublished paper, The Rand Corporation, Santa Monica, Cal.

Greenwood, Peter, Sorrel Wildhorn, Eugene Poggio, Michael Sturmwasser, and Peter De Leon. 1977. *Prosecution of Adult Felony Defendants.* Lexington, Mass.: Lexington.

Greenwood, Peter, and Joan Petersilia. 1978. *The Rand Habitual Offender Project: A Summary of Research Findings to Date.* Santa Monica, Cal.: The Rand Corporation.

Kassebaum, Gene, D. A. Ward, and D. M. Wilner. 1971. *Prison Treatment and Parole Survival.* New York: John Wiley.

Law Enforcement Assistance Administration, U.S. Department of Justice. 1977. *LEAA Comprehensive Career Criminal Program An-*

nouncement. Washington, D.C.: Law Enforcement Assistance Administration, U. S. Department of Justice.

Lipton, Douglas, Robert Martinson, and Judith Wilks. 1975. *The Effectiveness of Correctional Treatment: A Survey of Treatment Evaluation Studies*. New York: Praeger.

Martin, John. 1952. *My Life in Crime: The Autobiography of a Professional Thief*. New York: Harper.

Martinson, Robert. 1974. "What Works? Questions and Answers about Prison Reform," *Public Interest* 35:22–54.

Morris, Norval. 1974. *The Future of Imprisonment*. Chicago: University of Chicago Press.

Mulvihill, Donald, and Melvin Tumin with Lynn Curtis. 1969. *Crimes of Violence: A Staff Report Submitted to The National Commission on the Causes and Prevention of Violence*. Washington, D.C.: U.S. Government Printing Office.

Olson, Michael R. 1977. "A Longitudinal Analysis of Official Criminal Careers." Doctoral dissertation, University of Iowa, Iowa City.

——. 1978. "Predicting Seriousness of Official Police Contact Careers: An Exploratory Analysis." Unpublished manuscript, University of Iowa, Iowa City.

Petersilia, Joan. 1978a. "The Validity of Criminality Data Derived from Personal Interviews." In *Quantitative Studies in Criminology*, ed. Charles Wellford. Beverly Hills, Cal.: Sage Publications.

——. 1978b. "The Prosecution of Career Criminals: An Idea Whose Time Has Come," *Prosecutor's Brief* 7:24–27.

Petersilia, Joan, and Peter W. Greenwood. 1978. "Mandatory Prison Sentences: Their Projected Effects on Crime and Prison Populations," *Journal of Criminal Law and Criminology* 69:604–15.

Petersilia, Joan, Peter W. Greenwood, and Marvin Lavin. 1978. *Criminal Careers of Habitual Felons*. Washington, D.C.: U.S. Government Printing Office.

Petersilia, Joan, and Marvin Lavin. 1978. *Targeting Career Criminals: A Developing Criminal Justice Strategy*. Santa Monica, Cal.: The Rand Corporation.

Peterson, Mark, Harriet Braiker, and Sue Polich. 1980. *Doing Crime: A Survey of California Inmates*. Santa Monica, Cal.: The Rand Corporation.

Pritchard, David. 1979. "Stable Predictors of Recidivism: A Summary," *Criminology* 17:15–21.

Reiss, Albert J. 1972. "Surveys of Self-Reported Delicts." Unpublished paper, Department of Sociology, Yale University.

Robison, James, and Gerald Smith. 1971. "The Effectiveness of Correctional Programs," *Crime and Delinquency* 17:67–80.

Shannon, Lyle W. 1976. "Predicting Adult Careers from Juvenile Careers." Unpublished paper, Iowa Urban Community Research Center, University of Iowa, Iowa City.

———. 1978a. "A Longitudinal Study of Delinquency and Crime." In *Quantitative Studies in Criminology*, ed. Charles Wellford. Beverly Hills, Cal.: Sage Publications.

———. 1978b. "A Cohort Study of the Relationship of Adult Criminal Careers and Juvenile Crime." Paper presented at the University of Stockholm, Sweden.

———. 1979. "Changing Trends in the Relationship of Juvenile Delinquency to Adult Crime." Paper presented to the Pacific Sociological Association, Anaheim, Cal.

———. 1980 (forthcoming). "Assessing the Relationship of Adult Criminal Careers to Juvenile Careers." Draft manuscript. Iowa Urban Community Research Center, University of Iowa, Iowa City.

Shaw, Clifford. 1930. *The Jack Roller: A Delinquent Boy's Own Story*. Chicago: University of Chicago Press.

———. 1931. *The Natural History of a Delinquent Career*. Chicago: University of Chicago Press.

Shinnar, Reuel, and S. Shinnar. 1975. "The Effects of the Criminal Justice System on the Control of Crime: A Quantitative Approach," *Law and Society Review* 9:581–611.

Skogan, Wesley G. 1975. "Measurement Problems in Official and Survey Crime Rates," *Journal of Criminal Justice* 3:17–32.

State Government News. 1979. The Council of State Governments, Lexington, Kentucky, Vol. 1.

Sutherland, Edwin. 1937. *The Professional Thief*. Chicago: University of Chicago Press.

Tittle, Charles R. 1969. "Crime Rates and Legal Sanctions," *Social Problems* 16:409–23.

Tittle, Charles R., and Allan R. Rowe. 1974. "Certainty of Arrests and Crime Rates: A Further Test of the Deterrence Hypothesis," *Social Forces* 52(4):455–62.

Tullock, Gordon. 1974. "Does Punishment Deter Crime?" *Public Interest* 36:103–11.

Twentieth Century Fund Task Force on Sentencing Policy toward Young Offenders. 1978. *Confronting Youth Crime*. New York: Holmes & Meier.

Van den Haag, Ernst. 1975. *Punishing Criminals: Concerning a Very Old and Painful Question*. New York: Basic Books.

Van Dine, Stephan, John Conrad, and Simon Dinitz. 1977. "The Incapacitation of the Dangerous Offender: A Statistical Experiment," *Journal of Research in Crime and Delinquency* 14:22–34.

Vera Institute of Justice. 1977. *Felony Arrests: Their Prosecution and Disposition in New York City's Courts.* New York: Vera Institute of Justice.

Von Mayr, Georg. 1917. "Statistics and Gesellschaftslehre," *Kriminalstatistik* 3:45 et seq.

Waldo, Gordon, and T. G. Chiricos. 1972. "Perceived Penal Sanction and Self-Reported Criminality: A Neglected Approach to Deterrence Research," *Social Problems* 19:522–40.

Ward, D. A. 1973. "Evaluative Research for Corrections." In *Prisoners in America*, ed. L. E. Ohlin. Englewood Cliffs, N.J.: Prentice-Hall.

Washington State Juvenile Code. 1978. Attorney General's Office, Seattle, Washington.

Williams, J. R., and Martin Gold. 1972. "From Delinquent Behavior to Official Delinquency," *Social Problems* 20:209–29.

Williams, Kristen M. 1979. *The Scope and Prediction of Recidivism.* Washington, D.C.: Institute for Law and Social Research.

Wilson, James Q. 1975. *Thinking about Crime.* New York: Basic Books.

Wolfgang, Marvin. 1973. "Crime in a Birth Cohort," *Proceedings of the American Philosophical Society* 117:404–11.

———. 1977. "From Boy to Man—from Delinquency to Crime." Paper prepared for National Symposium on the Serious Juvenile Offender, Department of Sociology, University of Pennsylvania.

Wolfgang, Marvin, Robert Figlio, and Thorsten Sellin. 1972. *Delinquency in a Birth Cohort.* Chicago: University of Chicago Press.

Zimring, Franklin E., and Gordon J. Hawkins. 1973. *Deterrence: The Legal Threat in Crime Control.* Chicago: University of Chicago Press.

Thomas Weigend

Continental Cures for American Ailments: European Criminal Procedure as a Model for Law Reform

ABSTRACT

As the gap widens between the ideal of adversary procedure and the practice of bargained justice, European ways of organizing the criminal process have gained attention. European criminal procedure, characterized by the dominating position of the judge before and at trial, appears to offer a workable alternative to the traditional adversary process. Although French and West German systems of pretrial investigation, prosecutorial discretion, and adjudication appear fundamentally different from American practice, only the last is substantially different in practice. American plea bargaining has no analogue in France or West Germany. Despite the existence of an investigating magistrate in France, French and German practices as to organization and control of pretrial investigation are not significantly different from American practice. Prosecutorial charging discretion is limited to less serious offenses in West Germany; however, neither in France nor in West Germany is prosecutorial decision-making effectively controlled with regard to the great majority of criminal cases. Disposition of cases by trial rather than by plea bargaining remains the prevalent method in both European countries. In order to profit from the advantages of the European system

Thomas Weigend is Research Assistant, Max Planck Institute for Foreign and International Law, Freiburg, West Germany.

The author is indebted to his colleague at the Max Planck Institute, Mr. Axel Dörken, for his faithful guidance through the intricacies of French law and to George Fletcher and Judge Marvin Frankel for their helpful comments on an earlier draft.

of providing brief, concise trials to all defendants, Americans may have to sacrifice revered common law institutions, like trial by jury and adversary presentation of the evidence.

When a legal system develops problems, remedies are first sought from within; when the domestic medicine chest has been emptied and the maladies persist, help must be sought elsewhere. The day of the comparativist has arrived. Comparative research has often been regarded as an irrelevant luxury indulged in by a few specialists who prefer traveling in time or space to dealing with the hard issues of the day. Lately, however, American writers and reformers have been looking to Europe for prescriptions for reform of the American criminal justice system. Comparative research is becoming an applied science, and comparativists are being sought after as the engineers of reform. Terms like *juge d'instruction*, *Legalitätsprinzip*, *correctionnalisation*, and *archiviazione*, which, only a few years ago, many American lawyers would have mistaken for the specialities of an ethnic restaurant, now punctuate reform discussions.

The United States has long prided itself on its ability to counter enormous problems with enormous powers to invent new solutions. Today, it seems imperative that new cures be found to heal the ailing American system of criminal justice. The system suffers from many wounds: a police preoccupied with the control of petty crime; prosecutors and public defenders with unmanageable caseloads; courts so overburdened that they can accord regular procedures only to a small fraction of defendants; bargained "justice" as the regular mode of dispositions; prisons in disarray, but without functioning alternatives; a parole system unable to prevent large-scale recidivism; the rule of law largely replaced by a rule of discretion.[1]

Despite heavy inoculations of money, personnel, and ideas, the

---

[1] It may be testament to American idealism (and lack of a sense of history) that each generation prophesies breakdown of the criminal justice system. See e.g. Greenberg (1976) and the reports of the Cleveland (Pound and Frankfurter 1922) and Chicago (Illinois Association for Criminal Justice 1929) crime surveys and the reports of the National Commission on Law Observance and Enforcement (e.g. 1931) and the President's Commission on Law Enforcement and Administration of Justice (1967a).

system as a whole seems to have lost its self-reformative power, its ability to adapt to new circumstances and to new problems. Beginning in the mid-70s, some American academics turned from the misery of their own country and went overseas for inspiration. They studied systems of criminal procedure which, in America, were generally labeled "inquisitorial" and were commonly pictured as secret, written proceedings in which the accused was presumed to be guilty and was stripped of procedural rights like those guaranteed by the United States Constitution. Americans seemed barely to have heard that torture had officially been abolished on the Continent.

Yet the American explorers, more or less to their surprise, discovered a system that seemed to work. They saw crimes being investigated in an orderly, professional fashion: prosecutors prosecuting instead of bargaining; judges conducting brief but complete trials whenever defendants wished to have them; courts basing their decisions on what actually happened, not on half-truths stipulated by the parties or developed in adversary proceedings. It could not even be said that defendants lacked basic procedural protections. To the contrary, less pressure was exerted on the accused to waive his rights than in the oligopolistic market of American plea bargaining, where, too often, the prosecutor offers a bargain too good to be refused. And, incredibly, the miraculous system was designed not only for small medieval towns or for rural societies remote from the problems of mass criminality; it operated also in modern, industrialized cities in countries like France, West Germany, and Italy. Even when confronted with critical questions, the agents of the inquisitorial system insisted that they were reasonably satisfied with it. While it could not be proved that it actually reduced the incidence of crime, at least it appeared to be able to distribute criminal justice reasonably fairly and even-handedly.

Professors John H. Langbein of the University of Chicago and Lloyd L. Weinreb from Harvard University, among other comparativists, have argued that Americans can learn much from European criminal procedures and have formulated models that

American jurisdictions might emulate. Weinreb devoted most of his efforts to the investigative stage of the criminal process (1977, chap. 6), while Langbein constructed an "inquisitorial" model for prosecution and trial (1974; 1977; 1978, pp. 21-22; Langbein and Weinreb 1978). While neither model was meant to be a ready-for-use device to turn a rotten procedural system into a perfect one, they were intended to point out the paths that sensible reform might follow.

Weinreb's model of the process of investigation, in its simplest form, looks like this: Police perform their original function of keeping peace and order in the community. When a crime has been reported, the police rush to the site, try to soothe the victim and to apprehend the culprit, and then turn matters over to an independent magistrate. The magistrate authorizes searches and arrests, decides about pretrial detention, hears witnesses, questions the suspect, appoints experts, gathers other evidence, and finally compiles the *dossier*, a file containing all the evidence which tends either to incriminate or to exculpate.

Under Langbein's model of nondiscretionary prosecution, the *dossier* is then turned over to the prosecutor, who, at least with respect to more serious offenses, is obliged to file an accusation against the suspect if the evidence appears to be sufficient for conviction.[2] The prosecutor lacks discretion as to what crimes to charge; he must accuse the defendant of the most serious offense that credible evidence can support. There is no room for bargaining among the parties. Guilty pleas remain possible, however, for cases in which the defendant sees no point in contesting the charges; yet the defendant who pleads guilty cannot expect sentencing concessions. If the defendant wants his day in court, a trial is held before a court composed of professional and lay judges sitting together. The presiding judge will have read the *dossier* in advance and can use it freely when he questions witnesses and the defendant. The latter, of course, may remain silent. Because the pretrial investigation has been conducted by a quali-

---

[2] Under Weinreb's model, the investigating magistrate would prepare the accusation and file it with the court; the prosecutor would assist in the preparation of the *dossier* and would later represent the state at the trial stage (Weinreb 1977, pp. 134–37).

fied magistrate, there is little need for the exclusion of evidence acquired in violation of legal rules. Complicated rules of evidence are unnecessary because the evidence is evaluated by lawyers and laymen sitting together. Anything that bears any reasonable relation to the issues of the case qualifies as admissible evidence. During the presentation of the evidence, counsel for the government and for the defense may suggest particular questions or lines of questioning to the court, but are prohibited from examining any witness themselves. When the court concludes that it has heard sufficient evidence, the defendant may address the court, and counsel for both sides sum up and make their final arguments to the court, which then adjourns to reach a verdict.

Neither model describes the actual criminal process in any particular European country, but both authors claim that they capture the spirit of Continental criminal procedure as it operates today. That claim is crucial for the success of the models. Both Weinreb and Langbein contend that their proposals are not millenarian ones, addressed to an ideal world, but are ideas that have been successfully applied in industrialized countries that share with the United States the principles of democracy and the rule of law.

Others have dismissed Langbein's and Weinreb's proposals as the celebration of form over substance (Goldstein and Marcus 1977, 1978). The reality, Goldstein and Marcus claim, is much closer to American practice than to the inquisitorial idea. The greater success of the European countries in providing justice and fairness must be attributed to factors other than the inquisitorial mode of proceeding. Goldstein and Marcus argue that, in France, Italy, and West Germany, unlike the Weinreb and Langbein models (but like the American experience), investigation of crime is almost completely dominated by the police (1977, pp. 246–64); short-cut proceedings are available for cases with cooperative defendants (pp. 264–69); and cooperation by the defendant is rewarded with leniency in sentencing (pp. 269–79). If Goldstein and Marcus are right, the inquisitorial model is not a functioning system of criminal justice for Americans to emulate, but instead dissolves into a *fata morgana*.

The crucial questions, then, are these. Does Continental practice actually apply legal rules radically different from the traditional American model of criminal justice? If so, is the European solution preferable? Can the European procedures be transplanted successfully into the United States? This essay attempts to answer these questions within the framework set by the controversy described above. However, the scope of the inquiry must be further limited. First, there is no such entity as "European criminal procedure"; rather, on that small continent, a multitude of procedural systems have grown and prospered independently of each other. The differences between them may be greater than their common features. Therefore, this essay discusses only the procedural systems of France and West Germany, those on which the current debate in America has focused. Second, a comparison of procedural systems in toto would require considerably more space, time, and knowledge than are available to me. This analysis concentrates on three contemporary problems in the United States: control of pretrial investigation; prosecutorial discretion; and plea bargaining. I intend to demonstrate two things. First, with respect to pretrial investigation and prosecutorial discretion, European practice differs slightly but not substantially from American patterns. Second, plea bargaining—the exchange of leniency for cooperation—is virtually nonexistent in France and West Germany, but a meaningful transfer of European know-how would require a drastic revision of principles of adjudication that are deeply engrained in Anglo-American legal thinking.

I. Control of Pretrial Investigation

There are few occasions when the interests of the individual and of the state are in such striking conflict as after the commission of a crime. The individual—especially if he was involved in the commission of the offense—wants to be left alone. The police, however, are obligated to intrude—to gather information about the incident from various sources and to record and store that information for further use. Neither legislation nor jurisprudence can adequately resolve that conflict. For while the system must, if liberal ideals are not to be sacrificed, protect the innocent individual against unwarranted intrusions into his privacy, it must find, arrest, and punish offenders lest the state's function of safeguarding vital interests of its citizens be put in jeopardy. That does not mean that there cannot, in a particular instance, be an equitable resolution of the tension. The respective values of protected interests, degrees of suspicion, and the relative intrusiveness of different measures of investigation must be carefully weighed—a task a council of philosophers or experienced judges might be equipped to do if given sufficient time to deliberate and to discuss the relevant issues. Unfortunately, in a criminal investigation, many critical questions must be answered on the spot: whether to stop and frisk a suspect, whether to search a car stopped for a traffic violation, whether to put someone under arrest, whether to continue questioning a suspect who is unwilling to talk but who may be close to changing his mind.

Once it is accepted that in a liberal state there can be no hard and fast rules as to what is permitted in a given situation of suspicion (a totalitarian state might solve the problem by simply permitting "everything"), the issue is whom to entrust with making the on-the-spot decision. The suspect could do it (in a super-liberal system which would require consent for every intrusion on privacy); so could the law enforcement agent of the state. Or it could be a neutral arbiter called to the scene of the investigation.

American law initially delegated authority to the police to strike the necessary balance between the interests of the state and those of the individual. The police were to combat crime in a manner consistent with constitutional guarantees of individual rights and liberties. It was with some hesitation that the practical effects of the built-in conflict were recognized: the exercise of police discretion did not gain much attention before the beginning of the '60s, when minority groups became more vocal in complaining about unequal treatment. It was only then that social scientists began to study police behavior (Wilson 1968; Skolnick 1966), and that lawyers began to explore the implications of the fact that police neither enforced nor respected all laws at all times (President's Commission 1967; Kadish 1962;

J. Goldstein 1960). In order to curb the perceived lawlessness of police, the U.S. Supreme Court prescribed a radical cure to the whole nation: beginning with the famous decision in *Mapp v. Ohio*, 367 U.S. 643 (1961), it handed down a series of decisions instructing the courts to exclude evidence gathered by the police in violation of constitutional mandates. One of the Court's primary goals was deterrence. If every policeman knew that disregard of the law would lead to the acquittal of the suspect or make his conviction more difficult, the theory went, he would think twice before resorting to illegal methods.

Whatever the logic of that proposition, it leads to a curious distribution of power in the investigative process. The policeman makes the decision, but its effectiveness is conditioned on its being approved much later by a neutral judge when the investigation has come to a close. It is that time lag which often leads to deplorable results: the citizen whose rights are violated here and now is neither protected nor necessarily consoled by procedural decisions made months later; yet greater damage than necessary is done to the interests of law enforcement. In Benjamin Cordozo's words:

> [H]ow far-reaching in its effect upon society the
> [exclusionary rule] would be. The pettiest peace officer
> would have it in his power, through overzeal or indiscretion,
> to confer immunity upon an offender for crimes the most
> flagitious. A room is searched against the law, and the
> body of a murdered man is found. . . . [The constable
> blunders], the privacy of the home has been infringed,
> and the murderer goes free. (*People* v. *Defore*, 150
> N.E. 585 [1926] at p. 588.)

A mistake made in the course of an ongoing investigation can be corrected if the unlawfulness of the act in question is detected early, but the removal of one stone from the completed building of evidence frequently makes conviction impossible. Moreover, the relation between the constable's blunder and the suspect's acquittal appears to be rather loose, even though the existence of such bonds has repeatedly been asserted on both psychological and ethical grounds (Allen 1961, pp. 251–52; Paulsen 1961, pp. 257–59; cf. Kaplan 1974, pp. 1029–35; Schrock and Welsh 1974, pp. 263–71; Oaks 1970). Even if the exclusionary rule does achieve its purpose—the protection of civil rights from overbearing by police—it does so in a clumsy and distorted way.

A. Pretrial Investigation in France

It is not surprising, therefore, that other ways of controlling pretrial investigation have long been sought. Among the European systems, French criminal procedure seems to offer the best example of an alternative model. French law formally takes control of the investigation out of the hands of the police and instead directs a neutral figure, the magistrate or *juge d'instruction*, to take charge of collecting the evidence. Article 81 of the French Code of Penal Procedure (CPP) provides that the *"juge d'instruction* shall undertake all acts of investigation he deems useful for establishing the truth." On its face, that provision prescribes the archetypal inquisitorial mode of criminal investigation—an independent magistrate, without personal or professional interest in the outcome, both seeks out the facts and protects the rights of the individual. Presumably, he conducts the investigation according to his own intuition and professional experience, relying on the parties for advice and on the police for minor ministerial functions, like summoning witnesses and executing arrest warrants. That model, which has prompted many of Professor Weinreb's reform proposals (cf. Weinreb 1977, pp. 119–34), is a very good one. It is too good to be true.

Pretrial procedure in France differs radically from the model the legislator may have had in mind.[3] When an offense is re-

[3] It is unclear, after amendments to the CPP in 1959, whether the *juge d'instruction* retained his role as the central figure of pretrial procedure. Two significant changes from prior law point in opposite directions. The authority to delegate investigations to the police suffered slight restrictions in Art. 81 para. 4 and Art. 151 para. 2 CPP. Yet the previously "officious" preliminary inquiry by the police received official recognition in Art. 75 CPP (Merle and Vitu 1973, p. 258).

ported, the police conduct the investigation—usually on their own, sometimes in cooperation with the prosecutor.[4] Articles 75–78 CPP give the police authority to conduct preliminary inquiries under the supervision of the prosecutor, presumably in order to enable the latter to make intelligent use of his discretionary power (Grebing 1979, p. 32; Krattinger 1964, p. 94). Only when the inquiry is concluded to the satisfaction of the police do they pass the file on to the prosecutor. The prosecutor then formally decides whether to dismiss the case, to charge the suspect with an offense of lesser seriousness (*délit*, punishable by imprisonment up to five years) in the *tribunal correctionnel*, or to ask the *juge d'instruction* to open a formal investigation (Grebing 1979, p. 30; Laroche-Flavin 1968, p. 32).

The *juge d'instruction*, like the prosecutor, has a formal role that far exceeds empirical reality. The *juge d'instruction* has to be involved when the suspect is to be accused of a serious felony (a *crime* punishable by imprisonment of more than five years) before the *cour d'assises* and when it is necessary to use some means of constraint (arrest, search, seizure, pretrial detention) in the course of the investigation. The second situation, use of constraint, might be expected to arise fairly often, thus involving the *juge d'instruction* in a substantial proportion of prosecutions. The statistics show the contrary: in 1974, of 513,176 *crimes* and *délits* processed and not dismissed by the prosecutor, only 14 percent were referred to the *juge d'instruction* (Ministère de la Justice 1977, 1: 16).[5] In the remaining 86 percent of cases, the police must have completed their investigation relying exclusively on voluntary cooperation. French legal literature indicates, however, that "voluntary" in form may be less than voluntary in practice. First, many people simply do not know that they

[4] The public prosecutor has formal authority to direct and supervise all police activities (Arts. 12, 13 CPP) and is authorized to open a preliminary investigation whenever he learns of an offense (Art. 75 CPP). In practice the prosecutor often does not learn of the crime until the police investigations are over, except in cases where the police need the prosecutor's consent in order to detain a suspect for more than twenty-four hours (cf. Art. 77 CPP).

[5] Under French law, a case can be sent to the *juge d'instruction* only by the prosecutor, not directly by the police. Since 1960, the absolute number of cases investigated by the *juge d'instruction* has remained almost stable; the *percentage* of judicial investigations has dropped from 24 percent to 14 percent (Ministère de la Justice 1977, 1:16).

need not accept a police "invitation" to appear for an interview
or to let an officer conduct a search (Krattinger 1964, p. 92).
Moreover, except for a requirement that written consent be obtained for searches (Art. 76 CPP), the police need not warn the
individual of his rights. Second, the innocent and the culpable
alike are hesitant to refuse to answer questions or otherwise
obstruct police investigations, lest they create or augment suspicion against themselves (Merle and Vitu 1973, p. 264). Third,
the police often convince a suspect that noncooperation will be
futile; the *juge d'instruction* will make him do later what he does
not want to do now (Merle and Vitu 1973, p. 260). Fourth, the
police possess one forceful tool, *garde à vue*, for achieving "voluntary" compliance: any person who presents himself at the
police station can be detained there, practically incommunicado,
for twenty-four hours, or for forty-eight hours if the prosecutor
consents (Arts. 63, 77, 78 CPP). *Garde à vue*[6] has often been
associated with interrogation methods known as *passage à tabac*
(not unlike the American "third degree") (Krattinger 1964, pp.
137–43; Garçon 1957, pp. 91–94); discreet allusion to the possibility of its imposition appears often to induce garrulity in
suspects and witnesses (Stefani and Levasseur 1977, p. 384; Merle
and Vitu 1973, p. 261).

Finally, the police have legal power to investigate *flagrants
délits* with even greater vigor. Literally, *flagrant délit* signifies
situations where the offender is caught while committing a crime.
Law and practice have, however, greatly enlarged the concept
so that it now encompasses situations in which a suspect is found
with objects indicating his involvement in the crime and also
cases of offenses committed within a house if the head of the
household asks the police to investigate (Art. 53 CPP; cf. Merle
and Vitu 1973, pp. 266–69). Whenever the flexible requirements
of *flagrant délit* are fulfilled, the police have enormous authority
over suspects and nonsuspects alike: they can prohibit anyone
from leaving the site of the alleged offense, arrest anyone in
order to establish his identity, arrest suspects, summon witnesses

---

[6] *Garde à vue* is a routine procedure with respect to suspects, comparable to
arrest in the United States. There is no evidence available to me, however, on
how often it is used with respect to witnesses.

to the police station for questioning (the *garde à vue* being available as a further means of facilitating the investigation), and conduct warrantless searches and seizures even on the property of nonsuspects (Arts. 56–63 CPP).

Investigation of a *flagrant délit* is especially favorable to the police because there is generally no right to counsel at that stage of the proceeding[7] (Roth 1963, p. 70). While some French writers clearly recognize the potential for abuse of the *flagrant délit* procedure and therefore demand its abolition (Laroche-Flavin 1968, p. 34), the assumption by the police of magisterial powers to investigate *flagrants délits* is an everyday occurrence (cf. Stefani and Lavasseur 1977, p. 273).

The considerable investigative powers of the police may explain the parsimonious use made of the *juge d'instruction*. Only if the suspect is to be taken into pretrial detention[8]—which, in 1974, happened in about 12 percent of all cases brought before the *cour d'assises* or the *tribunal correctionnel*[9] (Ministère de la

[7] Upon receiving a summons to appear and testify before the police, an individual can demand instead to be questioned by the prosecutor in the presence of a retained attorney (Art. 70 CPP).

[8] Pretrial detention (*détention provisoire*) can be ordered by the *juge d'instruction*, upon application of the *procureur*, if the defendant is suspected of a *crime* or of a *délit* punishable by more than two years imprisonment (Art. 144 §1, Art. 146 CPP). While the magistrate need not give reasons for his detention order in cases of *crimes*, he must find facts indicating the applicability of one of the following criteria if a *délit* suspect is to be detained: the protection of witnesses or of evidence from unlawful tampering; the prevention of fraudulent collusion between the suspect and his accomplices; the protection of the public order from disturbances caused by the offense; the protection of the suspect; preventing the suspect from repeating the offense; or the necessity of keeping the suspect at the disposal of the court (Art. 144 §§ 2, 3 CPP). Pretrial detention is generally limited to four months, but may be prolonged for another four months for any of the foregoing reasons (Art. 145 § 2 CPP). In the alternative, the *juge d'instruction* can place the suspect under judicial supervision (*contrôle judiciaire*) if he regards that measure as necessary for the pending investigation or for public safety in general (Arts. 137, 138 CPP). Judicial supervision implies a great variety of possible restrictions on the suspect's freedom; he can be required, for example, to post bond, to remain within a certain district, to refrain from seeing certain persons, to undergo medical treatment, or to turn in his driver's license. *Contrôle judiciaire* was introduced in 1970 as a desirable alternative to pretrial detention (Grebing 1974, pp. 220–53). In 1972, 12 percent of all suspects were placed under judicial supervision (Grebing 1974, p. 308).

[9] Of all cases (above the level of petty misdemeanors) tried in 1974, only 0.2 percent were brought before the *cour d'assises* (Ministère de la Justice 1977, 1:21). That court deals mainly with cases of intentional homicide (29 percent of its caseload) and of aggravated theft, including robbery (38 percent of its caseload) (Ministère de la Justice 1977, 2:6).

Justice 1977, 2: 358, 365)—or if the crime is exceptionally serious and beyond the jurisdiction of the *tribunal correctionnel*, must there be a judicial investigation.

But even the small percentage of cases that come before the *juge d'instruction* are often investigated by the police. Although he bears responsibility for establishing the facts and compiling the *dossier*, he has authority to delegate most of that job to other agencies (Arts. 151–55 CPP). The police, not surprisingly, receive most of those delegations, by means of a document named *commission rogatoire*. Frequently it consists only of a brief description of the offense and a mandate to the police officer to undertake the "necessary investigations" (Merle and Vitu 1973, pp. 354–59; Laroche-Flavin 1968, p. 65; Manke 1966, p. 32). The individual police officer must decide what measures are necessary and how to carry them out; he is entrusted with the full authority of a *juge d'instruction* except that he may not interrogate the suspect (Art. 152 CPP). Consequently, in many cases, the "investigating" magistrate does not investigate but waits for the police to bring him the fruits of their investigation. Far from assuming the active role provided for him by the Code, he remains passive and restricts himself to evaluating evidence gathered by others.

If the police, not the independent magistrates, conduct pretrial investigation, the same need for control arises as under the American system of police independence. Yet, possibly because of the "myth of judicial supervision" (Goldstein and Marcus 1977), controls are underdeveloped. The Code, to be sure, provides both for exclusion of tainted evidence (Arts. 170–74 CPP) and the imposition of disciplinary sanctions against offending police officers (Arts. 224–30 CPP), but in practice both means of control suffer from severe limitations.

Under the French exclusionary rule, the violation of certain rights of the accused in the course of the judicial investigation can lead to the striking in the *cour d'assises* of the tainted part of the *dossier* from the record. The exclusionary rule does not apply, however, to the preliminary inquiry conducted by the police before or instead of the judicial investigation (Merle and Vitu 1973, pp. 264–65). Thus, the *garde à vue*, warrantless searches, and other critical confrontations between the citizen and the executive are effectively exempt from the purview of the rule (Grebing 1974, pp. 50–51). Moreover, if the *juge d'instruction* does not recommend accusation of a *crime*, but sends the case, as he usually does, to the *tribunal correctionnel* for adjudication as a lesser offense, the corrective authority of that tribunal is very limited. It may strike parts of the *dossier* only if the rules concerning the interrogation of the accused were violated (Art. 174 CPP).[10] Finally, French law knows no equivalent of the "fruit-of-the-poisonous-tree" doctrine. If part of the record is stricken, the prosecution can easily be reinstituted and the tainted part of the investigation be repeated in accordance with the law. Thus, defendants do not gain much by a *nullification* and many don't bother to bring procedural mistakes to the attention of the court (Manke 1966, p. 41).

Administrative sanctions for police misconduct are inconsequential. The *chambre d'accusation*, a special panel at the *cour d'assises*, has supervisory power over all judicial law enforcement personnel (including the police) (Arts. 224–30 CPP). The chief prosecutor is empowered to bring charges against offending police officers, and the *chambre d'accusation* is authorized to suspend those found guilty of a violation. French observers state flatly, however, that the procedure has, during the 150 years of its existence, never been used (Laroche-Flavin 1968, p. 102). Blunders in the course of a criminal investigation do not even impair the career prospects of a police officer; even though he is formally part of a corps called "judicial police," his promotion is determined by the Ministry of the Interior, which employs criteria different from those of the judicial branch (Laroche-Flavin 1968, pp. 101–2). Lack of effective supervision may also be responsible for the high frequency of police brutality reported in the French press. If one is to believe the newspapers, the

10 French courts recognize the authority of the *tribunal correctionnel* to strike evidence if unlawful acts not covered by Art. 174 CPP were of such a nature as to "fundamentally vitiate" the search for and the establishment of the truth. Yet the two pertinent decisions of the *Cour de Cassation* (Supreme Court) uphold the acceptance of evidence by the *tribunal correctionnel* in cases where the conduct of the police clearly satisfied the "shock-the-conscience" standard (Cour de Cassation crim., Juris Classeur Périodique 1960 II, Nr. 11641; Cour de Cassation crim., Juris Classeur Périodique 1964 II, Nr. 13806).

passage à tabac is still a commonplace method in French police stations (cf. Marion 1979; Marcus and Deleplace 1979).

B. Pretrial Investigation in Germany

The formal structure of German pretrial procedure resembles its American counterpart closely, but the similarity is misleading. The public prosecutor is formally in charge of criminal investigations (§ 160 para. 1 German Code of Criminal Procedure [GCCP]). While French law still heavily relies on the *juge d'instruction*, German legislation in 1975 abolished its equivalent, the *Untersuchungsrichter*.

The German system is not a replica of the American. A "prosecutor" in Germany is not necessarily the same thing as a prosecutor in America. Neutral supervision of an investigation need not be the responsibility of an officer called "judge" or "magistrate" (Langbein and Weinreb 1978, p. 1558). And, indeed, according to German doctrine, the public prosecutor is not an adversary of the defendant but a neutral representative of the state, whose task it is to shed light on incidents brought to his attention and possibly involving criminal acts. Section 160 para. 2 GCCP requires the prosecutor to investigate not only facts inculpating the defendant but also circumstances exonerating him. Only if the prosecutor finds, after an impartial and independent investigation, that there is "sufficient cause for filing a public accusation" (§ 170 para. 1 GCCP) is he to bring charges against the suspect.

As in France, however, reality looks different. The police have primary control over pretrial investigations. While the Code empowers the prosecutor to ask the police for assistance, the police receive complaints and conduct most investigations on their own initiative, without substantive guidance and mostly without the prosecutor's knowledge. Even in cases of homicide, it is more often than not the police who interview witnesses and suspects, seize tangible objects, and visit the site of the crime, although prior consultations with the prosecutor's office are somewhat more frequent than in routine cases (Blankenburg, Sessar, and Steffen 1978, pp. 265–66).

The independence of German police is enhanced by their substantial coercive authority. A German police officer may arrest a suspect and detain him until the end of the following day (§§ 127, 128 GCCP). He may also, if there is danger in delay, order blood samples to be taken (§ 81a GCCP); search the body, belongings, and apartment of a suspect (§§ 102, 105 GCCP); and seize apparent evidence (§§ 94, 98 GCCP) or the means or the product of an offense (§§ 111c, 111e, 111f GCCP in connection with § 74 German Penal Code).

While only the prosecutor has power to subpoena witnesses or summon a suspect for questioning (§§ 161a, 163a para. 3 GCCP), most interrogations are actually conducted by the police, because, as in France, many witnesses cooperate voluntarily. In some cases, especially if critical testimony is to be preserved for later use at trial, interviews are conducted by a magistrate (*Ermittlungsrichter*), who can subpoena witnesses and receive sworn testimony (Roxin 1979, p. 52).

Some intrusions of gravity are entrusted exclusively to the magistrate: only he can order a suspect to be held in pretrial detention (§ 114 GCCP),[11] and only he can authorize wiretaps (§ 100b GCCP). But the magistrate has no independent investigative function; he acts only on motion of the prosecutor.

The police sometimes need the signature of the magistrate to be able to continue their operations, but they generally plan, organize, and carry out the investigation themselves. Only when the case is "solved" or "not solvable" (usually for lack of a known suspect) do they transmit the file to the prosecutor. If

---

[11] Under German law, a suspect can be placed in pretrial detention if the judge finds facts indicating his intention either to flee from justice or to tamper with the evidence. With respect to some offenses, such as sex crimes, aggravated theft, and assault, pretrial detention can also be ordered to prevent the suspect from repeating the crime before trial. Bail exists under German law as a means of lessening the danger of flight and thus of obviating the necessity of detention, but its practical importance is low. While general statistics are not available, the infrequent use made of bail can be demonstrated by 1969 figures from the state of North Rhine-Westphalia: of 8,578 pretrial detainees, only 35 were released on bail; similarly, only 29 of 6,712 Bavarian detainees were bailed in 1968 (Krümpelmann 1971, p. 92). The general frequency of pretrial detention in Germany is much lower than in France. Again, there are no reliable overall statistics, but from various independent sources it can be gathered that not more than 5–8 percent of those accused are held in jail before trial (cf. Blankenburg, Sessar, and Steffen 1978, p. 141; Kerner 1978, p. 553; Krümpelmann 1971, pp. 83–84).

the police indicate that the case cannot be solved or will be difficult to prove, the prosecutor usually dismisses it without further investigation. If the police regard the case as "solved," the prosecutor decides independently whether the evidence against the suspect is strong enough to make conviction at trial reasonably certain, whether the evidence gives him "sufficient cause" to file an accusation.[12] The decision is, in most cases, made solely on the basis of the written police file. A recent study shows that prosecutors personally undertake investigations only in 5 to 12 percent of all cases with a known suspect; and if they do, it is usually in order to improve the prosecution's position after the decision has been made to bring charges (Blankenburg, Sessar, and Steffen 1978, pp. 99–101).

By and large, there is a conspicuous absence in West Germany of direct judicial or quasi-judicial control of the investigative stage of criminal proceedings. Moreover, the German Code of Criminal Procedure contains but the vestiges of an exclusionary rule: § 136a GCCP prohibits the use of evidence extorted from the accused by means of physical abuse, drugs, torture, hypnosis, deceit, or unlawful threats or promises.[13] The courts have taken a small additional step by requiring exclusion of evidence in a limited number of situations where law enforcement officers had unlawfully intruded into the witness's most intimate sphere of privacy. Thus, the *Bundesgerichtshof* declared that neither a personal diary (19 Entscheidungen des Bundesgerichtshofes in Strafsachen 325 [1964]) nor the clandestine tape recording of a private conversation (14 Entscheidungen des Bundesgerichtshofes in Strafsachen 358 [1960]) can be used as evidence in a criminal

---

[12] Even in cases which the police regard as "cleared," the prosecutor often refuses to bring charges for lack of sufficient evidence. Dismissal rates of "solved" cases were shown in one study to vary between 17 percent (robbery) and 40 percent (embezzlement) (Blankenburg, Sessar, and Steffen 1978, p. 82).

[13] Writers on German criminal law are about evenly divided on the question of whether the equivalent of the fruit-of-the-poisonous-tree doctrine applies to violations of § 136a GCCP (see Meyer, in Löwe and Rosenberg 1978, § 136a, ns. 51 and 52). The courts have not yet decided that question. Another hotly debated issue is similar to the *Miranda* problem: can evidence of a confession be admitted although the police neglected their duty to advise the suspect of his right to remain silent? In 1968, the German Federal High Court of Appeals (*Bundesgerichtshof*) answered that question in the affirmative (22 Entscheidungen des Bundesgerichtshofes in Strafsachen 170).

trial unless the intrusion was justified as an act of self-defense (Roxin 1979, p. 124).

If these are the limits of judicial involvement in pretrial investigation, perhaps Goldstein and Marcus are right when they claim that "pre-trial investigation follows Code requirements only as much as the police choose to adhere to them" (1977, p. 262). Yet complaints about violations of rights by investigating police officers in Germany are rare. No single explanation why that should be so comes to mind. According to common stereotypes of "national character," one might expect German police to be more faithful to the letter of the law and less concerned with efficiency than their American colleagues. Yet empirical research shows that German police officers are as willing as their American counterparts to disregard laws and regulations if it appears necessary to "do the job" (Hinz 1975, p. 144; Hinz 1971, p. 141; cf. Spiegelberg 1977, pp. 92–96.[14] Nor can the difference be explained adequately by assuming that Germans hold law enforcement officers in greater respect than do Americans and therefore do not complain even if they believe that their rights have been violated. Empirical studies in both countries have shown that comparable percentages of people maintain a very good opinion of their local police and would give them more power than they already have (Stephan 1976, pp. 244–47; Biderman et al. 1967, p. 146).

It has been asserted that German police misconduct is uncommon because of the hierarchical organization of statewide police forces, merit promotion systems, and an elaborate system of internal discipline (Langbein and Weinreb 1978, p. 1560). That assertion is plausible but has not been adequately tested. Little is known empirically about the system of internal discipline in German police forces. American experiments with mixed review boards for citizen complaints of police misbehavior seem to have been somewhat less than successful (see Schlesinger 1977, pp. 72–76). Even so, the German experience suggests that further

---

[14] In one study no fewer than 65 percent of all officers agreed with the statement that police work cannot be done properly if each officer always adheres to the letter of the law (Hinz 1971, p. 141).

attempts at improving and extending departmental discipline should be encouraged (cf. Spiotto 1973, p. 277). However, the most perfect system of internal control is bound to fail if police attitudes silently or openly condone disregard of civil rights.

II. Prosecutorial Discretion

Much attention has been paid in recent years to the role and powers of the American prosecutor (Alschuler 1978; Davis 1976; Neubauer 1974; Rabin 1972; La Fave 1970; Davis 1969; Miller 1969). Criticisms have been made of the nearly absolute powers of the American prosecutor to dismiss provable cases and to accede to pleas to lesser charges without having to give reasons for those decisions (Alschuler 1978; Davis 1969, pp. 188–90). Those enormous powers create at least the potential for arbitrariness and for unequal treatment of offenders. Although recent attempts have been made to structure prosecutorial discretion by promulgating departmental guidelines (U.S. Department of Justice 1977; Kuh 1975; California District Attorneys Association 1974), as a practical matter compliance has been left largely to the good will and personal integrity of the individual prosecutor.

Yet it is quite possible to imagine a system in which charges must be pressed whenever the prosecutor deems the evidence sufficient for conviction. It is therefore advisable to concentrate on the question of whether the prosecutor should have authority not to prosecute when he believes conviction of the suspect to be likely. Use of the term "discretion" for *all* aspects of prosecutorial decision-making obscures isolation of that issue in much American writing. German scholars usually reserve the term "discretion" (*Ermessen*) for the decision whether to prosecute a "convictable" defendant. The question *what* to charge, while of great importance under American law, is of no consequence under German procedure, for reasons discussed in a later section of this essay, and is therefore not treated by German doctrine. Introduction of a special term for the prosecutor's evaluation of the evidence, such as "judgment" (Neubauer 1974, p. 503), would clarify analysis and center the discussion on the point worth discussing.

A. Prosecutorial Discretion in France

The French *procureurs* have prosecutorial powers not unlike those of American prosecutors, although crime victims can sometimes require that a prosecution be initiated. The *procureur* enjoys the same wide range of discretionary powers (Grebing 1979, pp. 43–45; Merle and Vitu 1973, p. 284; Vérin 1972, p. 923; Bouzat and Pinatel 1970, pp. 917–19). And, as in America, immense prosecutorial powers can produce arbitrary and inconsistent results (Arpaillange 1978). The *procureur* is neither obliged to prosecute every convictable offender known to him nor bound by standards for his decision to prosecute.

His power to drop cases is limited, however, by the institution of *action civile*. Under Article 2 CPP, the victim of a criminal act can initiate charges against the offender before a criminal court or ask the *juge d'instruction* to start an investigation. If the victim takes the initiative, the public prosecutor is legally bound to follow suit (Stefani and Levasseur 1977, pp. 136–37). This approach to limiting prosecutorial discretion, which certainly creates its own problems, has not been seriously considered in the United States (but see *Yale Law Journal* 1955). The notion that executive branch officials should have exclusive authority to initiate and control criminal prosecutions seems too firmly fixed in the American legal mind to permit such experiments.

B. Prosecutorial Discretion in Germany

The German prosecutor, although formally subject to considerable control, has effective powers comparable to those of his American counterpart. German law, as has repeatedly been described in American publications (Langbein 1977, pp. 87–111; Langbein 1974; Herrmann 1974; Davis 1969, pp. 191–95), gives private citizens virtually no role in setting the criminal process into motion.[15] But while the prosecutor alone has authority to initiate suits, German legislation has placed severe formal limits on his discretion. Under the original version of the Code, the

[15] There are minor exceptions. Private individuals may institute criminal proceedings for offenses such as libel, assault, and destruction of property (§ 374 GCCP).

prosecutor was under a legal duty to take a case to trial whenever he had "sufficient cause," that is, enough evidence, to do so (§§ 152, 170 GCCP). The prosecutor had to decide whether there was sufficient evidence to try the defendant; but even that decision, if it favored dismissal, could be appealed by the victim of the offense and reversed by a court (§§ 172–77 GCCP).[16]

In 1870, when the so-called *Legalitätsprinzip* (principle of mandatory prosecution) was codified, the drafters of the Code were motivated by distrust of the office of the public prosecutor or *Staatsanwalt*. That office had been introduced only in the first half of the nineteenth century, and it was feared that the prosecutor would, unless the statute kept a tight rein on him, be vulnerable to political and other pressures from the central government.

The strict mandate to bring charges whenever conviction is likely soon proved impractical, and over the years the original rule became encrusted with exceptions. Today, *Legalitätsprinzip* applies unequivocally only to the small number of felonies (*Verbrechen*) known in German criminal law.[17] For less serious offenses (*Vergehen*), the German prosecutor may decide whether

[16] Any victim whose complaint results in a finding that there is not "sufficient cause" for instituting charges may protest to the attorney general. If that official upholds the local prosecutor's decision, the victim can apply to the State Appellate Court for a judicial determination whether there is sufficient cause. If the court finds that there is sufficient evidence against an individual suspect, it orders the prosecutor to initiate charges. The private complainant has the right to join the prosecutor as a "supplementary prosecutor" (*Nebenkläger*) so that he can exercise some control over the conduct of the prosecution. In practice, motions for judicial determination of the sufficiency of evidence (*Klageerzwingungsverfahren*) are rarely made, and more rarely granted (Dahs 1977, p. 174). There were about one million criminal prosecutions (by trial or by penal order) in West Germany in 1978; only 1,692 *Klageerzwingungsverfahren* were instituted by private complainants (Statistisches Bundesamt 1979, p. 52). Yet the possibility of judicial review may discourage prosecutors from dropping cases too quickly as "unfounded."

[17] Only about 1 percent of all criminal offenses known to the police in 1978 were *Verbrechen* (Bundeskriminalamt 1979). *Verbrechen* is a narrower category of crimes than is "felony" in American law. The German Penal Code defines as *Verbrechen* any offense with a minimum penalty of one year of imprisonment. Representative crimes include murder, voluntary manslaughter, rape, robbery, mayhem, kidnaping, perjury, and arson. However, all theft offenses as well as (aggravated) assault, burglary, forgery, extortion, bribery, and most sex offenses are *Vergehen*. Translating that expression as "misdemeanor," as most authors do, may therefore lead an American reader to the incorrect equation *Vergehen* = misdemeanor = petty crime. In this essay, I use only the German terms.

to file charges or to drop the case (§ 153 GCCP).[18] If the defendant is suspected of having committed more than one offense, the prosecutor may charge him only with the most serious count and dismiss the others (§ 154 GCCP). Moreover, since 1975, the prosecutor no longer faces the polar choice between full prosecution and complete dismissal. He may, with respect to *Vergehen*, drop the case on the condition that the defendant pay a certain sum of money to the victim, to a charitable organization, or to the state (§ 153a GCCP).

It is important to note, however, that the prosecutor's discretion under German law is limited in various ways. First, he has statutory authority to dismiss a case only if the suspect's guilt appears to be minor and if prosecution is not required by the "public interest." Second, except in property offenses, any dismissal, conditional or unconditional, must be approved by the trial court; in practice the court rarely refuses to give its consent (Blankenburg, Sessar, and Steffen 1978, p. 113). Third, anyone aggrieved by the prosecutor's failure to file an accusation can complain to the individual prosecutor's superior, who will then examine the matter and may, if he agrees with the complainant, order that the prosecution be reopened.[19] Fourth, unlike the American prosecutor, the German *Staatsanwalt* is effectively precluded from overcharging as well as from undercharging. In an inquisitorial system such as the German, the parties' evaluation of the law is not binding upon the court. Thus, while the court must not investigate events other than those stated in the accusation (§ 264 para. 1 GCCP), it can convict the defendant (sub-

[18] Even with respect to felonies, the prosecutor may sometimes exercise unofficial and carefully hidden discretion. A recent study on the prosecution of homicide shows that the prosecutor often relabels offenses. Of all cases which the police had recorded as completed or attempted murders or manslaughters, the prosecutor redefined no fewer than 45 percent as less serious offenses such as negligent homicide, battery and coercion (Blankenburg, Sessar, and Steffen 1978, p. 262).

[19] Such complaints can be quite effective if employed in a systematic fashion. Some years ago, an organization of store owners distributed to its members complaint forms which could be sent to the chief prosecutor whenever charges against a shoplifter were dropped. That practice effectively resulted in a prosecutorial policy of never dismissing shoplifting cases (Gillig 1976, p. 206; Blankenburg, Sessar, and Steffen 1978, pp. 132–33). Today, many shoplifting cases are conditionally dismissed (§ 153a GCCP).

ject, of course, to timely notice) under any section of the Penal
Code even if the offense of conviction was neither charged nor
contemplated by the prosecutor (§§ 206, 264 para. 2 GCCP).
That provision prevents the prosecutor from indirectly influencing the sentencing decision through charging: once he files an
accusation, he cannot manipulate the seriousness of the charges
of which the defendant may be convicted.[20]

Notwithstanding the prosecutor's inability to control offenses
of conviction by his charging decisions, the discretionary power
of the German *Staatsanwalt* is comparable to that of the American prosecutor. An empirical study of property offenses strongly
supports that conclusion. Even when the police identified a suspect, the German prosecutor dismissed about half of the cases.
Of these dismissals, between 6 percent (aggravated theft) and
21 percent (embezzlement) were for "lack of public interest,"
while the remainder were based on a lack of evidence sufficient
for conviction (Blankenburg, Sessar, and Steffen 1978, p. 70; cf.
Ahrens 1978, p. 76). In recent years, there even seems to exist
a growing trend toward the new form of "conditional" dismissal
according to § 153a GCCP—the provision which stands for the
apex of the prosecutor's discretionary power under German
law.[21]

Germans have begun to look behind the protective veil of
Legalitätsprinzip and to appreciate that the prosecutor wields a
large amount of discretionary power. The myth of mandatory
prosecution has largely protected the *Staatsanwalt* from the development of effective controls. The judge routinely consents to
the prosecutor's decisions, the victim has little recourse outside
the prosecutorial hierarchy, and the Code lends no significant
guidance to the exercise of the prosecutor's discretion. Building
on American efforts to set guidelines for prosecutors, proposals
have recently been made to give content to the vague standards

---

[20] § 154a GCCP permits less important charges to be dropped even with respect to a single transaction. Thus, if a murderer makes his entry into the victim's house by breaking a window, the prosecutor can decide to charge him
only with murder and not with destruction of property. But the trial court
can, at any time and on its own motion, reintroduce the previously dropped
charge (§ 154a para. 3 GCCP).

[21] Conditional dismissals are discussed in section IIIB below.

("minor guilt" and "lack of public interest") provided by the Code and to give the prosecutor concrete and enforceable directions for the exercise of his discretionary power (Weigend 1978, chap. 7; Roxin 1976, pp. 20–21; Zipf 1974, pp. 501–2). The transfer of know-how seems to be going in a direction other than expected: rather than teaching Americans how to eliminate prosecutorial discretion, Germans are learning from them how to regulate it.

III. Plea Bargaining

Plea bargaining may be the most complex and intractable problem of modern American criminal justice. Although a vast literature has come into being in the last few years, plea bargaining remains a practice in search of a theory, and opinions are divided as to whether it constitutes an acceptable means of dispensing justice. To those who argue that it does not (e.g., Langbein 1978; Alschuler 1978), foreign systems, insofar as they manage to avoid the quid pro quo of speed for fairness, necessarily exert great attraction. Yet many American observers, accustomed to a system in which plea bargains typically dispose of 90 percent of cases, are skeptical. Do some European systems manage to handle their caseloads without resorting to plea bargains, or does bargaining simply take an unfamiliar form?

Before discussing whether plea bargaining is commonplace in France or Germany, it may be useful to define plea bargaining. That task is more difficult than it may seem; the practice is peculiarly American[22] and is closely related to particularities of American criminal procedure. Setting aside subtleties, the basic structure of plea bargaining can be described in terms of two models of case processing. The first, which I shall call the complicated model, is designed for defendants who claim to be innocent. The defendant is afforded a wide range of procedural rights and privileges and is entitled to a full development of the relevant facts; not surprisingly, the complicated model is costly

[22] A recent book by John Baldwin and Michael McConville (1977) argues, on the basis of close empirical studies of criminal courts in Birmingham and London, that defendants are sometimes offered inducements for guilty pleas. Their refutation of the conventional view that English lawyers and judges do not plea bargain provoked a furor.

in terms of time, labor, and money. The second, "simple," model can be used only if the defendant does not seriously contest the charges against him. The defendant waives most or all of his rights. Fact-finding is reduced to a minimum, and proceedings are swift, convenient, and inexpensive. Plea bargaining involves two elements: each defendant may choose between the complicated and the simple model; and, the system exerts pressure on all defendants to be "cooperative" and choose the simple model.

The American criminal process is the prototype of such a two-tier system. Jury trial (and to a lesser extent bench trial) is the complicated model. The guilty plea is the simple model. The American defendant is formally free to elect jury or bench trial, but is subject to powerful pressures to plead guilty. The prosecutor may offer to drop some charges or to recommend or not oppose a sentence less than the maximum to which the defendant is vulnerable. Even without a formal agreement, defense counsel may advise the defendant (soundly in most cases) that defendants who plead guilty receive less harsh sentences than defendants who are tried and found guilty. Whatever the prosecutor's coin, it is often enough to buy the defendant's guilty plea.

Description of American case processing in terms of the two models of jury trials and guilty pleas masks the rich variety of methods of handling individual cases. Trials before judges without juries permit somewhat less cumbersome application of evidentiary rules. Guilty pleas can be made and accepted at any stage of prosecution. Defendants can and do plead guilty at any time from initiation of proceedings until just before delivery of a verdict. The models may nonetheless be useful archetypes of American criminal procedure. A guilty plea at any time before the end of a trial will save time, bother, expense, and uncertainty for all concerned.

France and Germany can rightly be called "lands without plea bargaining" only if they manage to get by without at least one of the two crucial elements of the American system: it would have to be shown either that they do not have two different models of procedure, or that defendants are not pressured to choose the simple one.

A. Plea Bargaining in France

In the French system, it is easy to distinguish the simple from the complicated procedure. In the simple model, the case is investigated solely by the police, charges are brought by the prosecutor on the basis of the police *dossier* directly to the *tribunal correctionnel*, and that court adjudicates the matter swiftly, again on the basis of the *dossier*. An ordinary hearing before the *tribunal correctionnel* may last only a few minutes. The trial is conducted by the presiding judge,[23] who opens the proceedings by confronting the accused with the charges against him. The defendant responds with a brief statement, often a confession. If it appears necessary, the judge reads testimony of witnesses aloud from the *dossier*. After brief remarks by the prosecutor and the defense attorney, the verdict is announced and the sentence ordered (Laroche-Flavin 1973, pp. 75–78; Manke 1966, pp. 43–44; see also Hennion 1976).

The complicated model in France is as complicated as the simple model is simple. Criminal proceedings begin with a police inquiry, which consists only of collection of the evidence immediately available at and around the scene of the crime. The police present the case to the prosecutor, who asks the *juge d'instruction* to open an investigation. He gathers the necessary evidence. If he concludes that there is probable cause to bring the suspect to trial, he hands the *dossier* back to the prosecutor. The prosecutor, at that stage, has no choice but to forward the file to the *chambre d'accusation*. That judicial body reexamines the *dossier*, determines whether the investigation was proper, and whether there is probable cause to go to trial. If trial is warranted, the defendant is bound over to the *cour d'assises*, a mixed court consisting of three professional judges and nine lay persons (Art. 296 CPP). The trial is dominated by the presiding judge, who interrogates the defendant, questions witnesses, and receives any other evidence. It is his responsibility to establish all the necessary facts. After the attorneys have summed up the evidence, the

---

[23] The *tribunal correctionnel* consists of three professional judges (Art. 398 CPP). Only with respect to traffic offenses and a few other specified groups of minor misdemeanors can a single judge sitting alone adjudicate the matter (Art. 398–1 CPP).

court retires for deliberations. Eight votes are necessary to find the defendant guilty on any count. The full court also determines the sentence. Needless to say, proceedings before the *cour d'assises* last much longer than a trial at the *tribunal correctionnel*—sometimes several days, depending on the number of witnesses to be heard.

Thus France does have two different systems for handling criminal cases. The important questions are, accordingly, who receives the full trial, and why? Only if the dividing line lies between "cooperative" (for the simple model) and "noncooperative" (for the complicated model) defendants does the French system exhibit the stigmata of plea bargaining.

There is no evidence that confessions or other cooperation from defendants explain why some defendants are tried in the *cour d'assises* and others in the *tribunal correctionnel*. Technically, the division is simply one of seriousness of the offense: if the defendant is charged with a *crime* (which includes, among others, some aggravated forms of larceny, such as burglary), his case must follow the "complicated" course; otherwise the *tribunal correctionnel* is the competent court.

In practice, however, things are different. Many cases that could be tried as *crimes* are not. Prosecutors regard the complicated model as inappropriate, either because the punishment available for a *crime* (a minimum of five years imprisonment) is harsher than is warranted by the circumstances of the offense, or because the factual and legal issues involved simply do not justify the time and money associated with the complicated model.

Prosecutors avoid the full proceedings prescribed for *crimes* by use of a technique called *correctionnalisation* (Grebing 1979, pp. 73–74; Stefani and Levasseur 1977, pp. 374–77; Merle and Vitu 1973, pp. 560–64; see also Decheix 1970). It consists of a simple deceit to which all involved are parties. The prosecutor neglects to mention in the accusation those aggravating circumstances that distinguish a *délit* from a *crime*. *Délits* receive the simpler processing of the *tribunal correctionnel*.

Correctionnalisation bears strong resemblance to the partial dismissal of charges routinely engaged in by American prosecutors. The French court has an independent duty to inquire into the facts of the case and to deny relief if the case is outside its jurisdiction. Thus *correctionnalisation* works only if everyone (the defendant, the court, even the victim, who could bring an *action civile*) plays along. And in the great majority of cases, everyone does. The prosecutor initiates the practice because it saves him time without seriously compromising the social interest.[24] The court acquiesces because it knows that the *cour d'assises* cannot adjudicate all *crimes* actually committed. The defendant may spend less time in pretrial detention and can hope for a more lenient sentence if he is convicted of a *délit* rather than of a *crime*. Finally, the victim does not object, because he is more interested in a quick determination of his civil claim attached to the criminal proceedings than in relatively harsh punishment for the offender. The practice thus continues in spite of its undisputed illegality (Grebing 1979, p. 73; Merle and Vitu 1973, p. 564).

Despite strong surface similarities between plea bargaining and *correctionnalisation*, it does not appear that defendants are coerced into waiving their rights to more formal proceedings. What are the criteria which prosecutors apply when they "correctionalize"? Do they offer *correctionnalisation* as incentive or reward for a confession? Is the simple model reserved for cooperative defendants? Goldstein and Marcus (1977, p. 277; 1978, p. 1574 n. 15) assume that a tacit exchange of lesser charges for a confession necessarily takes place, albeit without explicit bargaining. But French literature (which tends to be anything but uncritical of its own system) lends no support to that assumption, nor do the French lawyers interviewed by Goldstein and Marcus.[25]

[24] Even though general sentence levels are higher for *crimes* than for *délits*, the actual sentences imposed by the *cour d'assises* may not be significantly higher than those handed out by the *tribunal correctionnel*. Probably because of the high five-year statutory minimum for all *crimes*, the *cour d'assises* often assumes the existence of extenuating circumstances, which lowers the minimum sentence to one year of imprisonment (Stefani and Levasseur 1978, p. 457; Merle and Vitu 1973, p. 561).

[25] French prosecutors interviewed by Goldstein and Marcus (1977, p. 277) indicated that they "leave considerations of mercy to the courts."

While French commentators deplore the arbitrariness with which *correctionnalisation* is handled by many prosecutors (Arpaillange 1978; Merle and Vitu 1973, p. 564; Vérin 1972, p. 953; Laroche-Flavin 1968, p. 76), none of them charges that the *procureur* systematically uses that device to induce or reward confessions.

It is unlikely that anything resembling a plea bargain takes place before the decision to "correctionalize" is made. First, most defendants do not have counsel during that early stage of the proceedings, so that the convergence of professional interests that characterizes bargaining in the United States is absent. Second, when the case reaches the prosecutor, the *dossier* usually contains all the evidence available to the police; if it does not include a confession, a prosecutor intent on saving time could be expected to forward the file to the *juge d'instruction* rather than reopen the preliminary inquiry and negotiate with the defendant. Finally, contrary to American law, a French defendant may withdraw a confession at any time before conviction. Thus, a prosecutor who rewarded a confession with *correctionnalisation* can never be sure that the defendant will not change his mind and present a full-scale defense before the *tribunal correctionnel*. While French prosecutors may, of course, bargain discreetly behind closed doors and be silent about it, it appears that they do not.

Correctionnalisation, then, appears primarily to be an effective device for reserving the complicated model for truly complicated or truly serious cases, and for channeling all others into the simple model.

B. Plea Bargaining in Germany

Germany also has different systems—of greatly different formality and complexity—for handling criminal cases. However, as in France, defendants are not coerced by promises of leniency into waiving their claims to more formal procedures.

The complicated model corresponds to the regular criminal procedure envisaged by the German Code. It works roughly like this. When an offense is committed, the police investigate and compile a file containing statements made by witnesses and suspects as well as other evidence. When the investigation is complete, the file is sent to the prosecutor, who decides whether to bring charges. If he thinks that conviction is likely and—with respect to *Vergehen*—that prosecution is in the public interest, he lodges an accusation with the appropriate court,[26] adding the police file, which has been augmented by the defendant's prior criminal record and by the results of any investigation the prosecutor himself may have undertaken. The court examines the file and the accusation, and formally determines whether the evidence is sufficient to warrant a trial (§§ 199, 203 GCCP). If it is, the court subpoenas witnesses and verifies that other necessary evidence is available.

Although the court relies on the prosecutor's file for pretrial preparations, no part of the file may be used as evidence. All evidence must be taken orally in open court. Only under very limited circumstances may prior testimony be read into the record (§§ 250–256, 264 GCCP). As in France, the trial is conducted by the presiding judge who questions witnesses and the defendant (unless the latter chooses to remain silent), and directs the taking of all other evidence. The parties need not be wholly passive. They may suggest additional evidence which the court can reject only for good cause (§§ 244 para. 3, 245 para. 2 GCCP), and they may question witnesses after the court has finished its interrogation (§ 240 para. 2 GCCP). When all the evidence is taken, the prosecutor and the defense attorney each sum up the evidence and argue to the court. Finally, the defendant may speak on his own behalf. Then the court retires for its deliberations on the verdict and on the sentence. A majority of two-thirds of all votes is needed for each decision unfavorable to the defendant (§ 263 GCCP).

Goldstein and Marcus argue that German practice has developed an abbreviated variant of the regular trial for "cooperative"

[26] The structure of German criminal courts is relatively complicated. Petty offenses are tried by a professional judge sitting alone. More serious charges are brought before the *Schöffengericht*, a court consisting of one professional judge and two laypersons sitting together; that court has authority to impose a maximum sentence of three years imprisonment (§ 24 para. 2 Court Organization Code). Cases of great importance, usually felonies, are decided by the *Grosse Strafkammer* consisting of three professional judges and two laypersons sitting together.

defendants. It "is more a selective verification of the file than the full and independent judicial inquiry promised by inquisitorial theory" (1977, pp. 266–67). They suggest that the dividing line between full and simplified procedures is the confession of the defendant. If the accused does not actively contest the charges, they say, the court conducts a brief trial with few witnesses, using the case file as its guide, and essentially asking witnesses to confirm what they had already told the police. Goldstein and Marcus rely heavily on a study of German criminal courts which found that the average trial time is roughly cut in half if the defendant makes a full confession (Casper and Zeisel 1972, p. 151). More recent data indicate that the difference between trials of "cooperative" and "non-cooperative" defendants may be much less dramatic: in a study of more than 400 lower court trials in Lower Saxony, Dölling found that the average trial of a confessing defendant took about 50 minutes, whereas trial time increased to about 70 minutes when there was no confession (Dölling 1978, p. 221).[27] It should be added, however, that most German courts consider a voluntary confession a mitigating factor in sentencing, although that practice is of dubious legality (Stree, in Schönke and Schröder 1978, § 46 ns. 41–42; Rudolphi et al. 1977, § 46 n. 75).[28]

And yet I would hesitate to draw a parallel between the simplified German trial of a confessing defendant and a plea bargain in an American court. Despite its relative brevity, the trial of a "cooperative" defendant remains a full and independent inquiry into the relevant facts, with none of the defendant's procedural rights curtailed or abrogated. A confession does not

[27] Dölling measured trial times for two different samples of judges. For the first sample, the amplitude was between 43 minutes (confession) and 65 minutes (no confession); for the second sample, average trial time ranged between 55 minutes (confession) and 73 minutes (no confession).

[28] The rationales for German judges' sentencing decisions are known, because written reasons must be provided for sentencing decisions. Almost invariably, a confession is cited as a reason for handing out more lenient punishment. Yet commentators point out that giving sentence credits to those who confess means imposing heavier sentences on those who do not—a practice which well may chill the defendant's right to remain silent. While it would clearly be impermissible, under German law, to pressure the defendant into a confession by threatening him with harsher punishment, the relevant statutory provision (§ 46 German Penal Code) expressly allows the court to take into account the offender's "conduct after the commission of the offense"—a clause sometimes interpreted to include conduct during investigation and trial.

necessarily amount to an admission of guilt; the accused may admit the facts and still claim that his conduct was legal or that he acted under an excusing misconception of fact or law.[29] Defense counsel can offer witnesses or other evidence for any purpose relevant to the issues of guilt or sentencing, and the court is bound to receive that evidence regardless of the defendant's confession.

Thus, the brevity of the trial is not second-class justice or a short cut to conviction. In most cases there is simply not much to prove or to discuss. If, for example, the defendant admits that he was at the scene of the crime when the offense was committed, there is no point in hearing alibi witnesses who would otherwise be of great importance; and if the defendant confesses that he hit his neighbor on the head, it would be an empty gesture to call five eyewitnesses. Even in confession cases, the court often calls witnesses to testify to matters on which the defendant has no information, such as the amount of damage done, or the level of the defendant's blood alcohol at the time of the offense. But such testimony usually can be heard within a few minutes. Thus, the myth of a simple procedure for uncontested cases is easily explained. The duty of a German court to fully investigate the facts does not exceed the bounds of reason. A credible confession dissolves reasonable doubt as to most issues of fact. Uncontested trials should require less time than do trials in which many contested facts have to be proved.

Another procedural device, the *Strafbefehl* (penal order), bears resemblance to plea bargaining. In 1977, almost half of all criminal cases which passed the stage of prosecutorial screening were disposed of by use of *Strafbefehl* (Statistisches Bundesamt 1978, pp. 22, 28, 30) One study found that 68 percent of simple larceny cases, 41 percent of embezzlements, 35 percent of criminal frauds, and 21 percent of aggravated theft cases, including burglary, were sanctioned by means of a penal order (Blankenburg, Sessar, and Steffen 1978, p. 70). *Strafbefehl* thus replaces

---

[29] German law is substantially more liberal than American law in recognizing claims of justification and excuse (cf. Fletcher 1974). In situations involving self-defense, necessity, or a necessary choice of evils, German law is reluctant to condemn the actor who finds himself in an extraordinary psychological situation.

disposition by trial in the majority of routine cases; it is typically employed in cases of shoplifting, minor theft, fraud, assault, drunken driving and hit-and-run accidents.[30] While the range of *Strafbefehl's* application technically extends to almost all cases of *Vergehen,* in practice it is restricted to cases of lesser seriousness, since the only sanctions which can be imposed by *Strafbefehl* are fines and the suspension of the defendant's driver's license (§ 407 GCCP).

When a defendant is suspected of having committed a *Vergehen,* the prosecutor can, instead of formally bringing charges against him, file with the court a written form containing a brief recitation of the relevant facts, an adjudication of guilt, and a proposed sentence. If the judge agrees with the suggested disposition and sentence (as he usually does), he signs the penal order, which is then delivered to the defendant. The defendant may accept or reject the *Strafbefehl.* If he accepts it, it operates as a valid penal judgment (§ 410 GCCP). The defendant may reject either the verdict or the sentence and obtain a full-fledged trial of the case. If the defendant is found guilty at the trial, the court is not bound by the sentence pronounced in the penal order (§ 411 para. 4 GCCP).

Strafbefehl has been called the "German guilty plea" (Langbein 1977, p. 96). Indeed, it bears all the traits characteristic of the simple model of criminal procedure. Little of the prosecutor's or the judge's time is required. The case can be resolved swiftly without a fact-finding process. The defendant's acquiescence and waiver of procedural rights and privileges are preconditions.

However, a simplified procedure that depends on guilty pleas is not necessarily the equivalent of plea bargaining. The essential feature of plea bargaining is that pressure is put on the defendant to make him choose the simpler system of adjudication. That element is absent from *Strafbefehl* practice. German prosecutors favor the penal order because it saves everyone involved (in-

---

30 *Strafbefehl,* while similar in operation to the traffic ticket in the United States, is not used in cases of traffic violations unless the driver was intoxicated or an accident with serious damage occurred. Minor traffic violations are regarded not as criminal offenses but as mere "violations of the public order," and are disposed of by way of a special administrative procedure. The ambit of *Strafbefehl* is further limited by the fact that it cannot be used against juvenile offenders.

cluding the accused) time and money. For defendants, it is a
discreet way to pay their dues to society without experiencing
the disgrace or bother of a public criminal trial.

In the normal case, neither side views the procedure as an
exchange of trial rights for a sentence discount. The penal order
is usually issued before the defendant or his counsel can approach
the prosecutor or the judge. Although instances of discussions
have been reported in which defense counsel indicates the willingness of his client not to appeal a *Strafbefehl* if the sentence
pronounced was below a certain limit (e.g. Herrmann 1974, p.
503), such modest attempts at "striking a deal" are still rare and
limited to exceptional situations in which high amounts of money
are at stake, as in major tax fraud cases. More important, even
if bargaining occurs, it lacks the oppressive elements which characterize American plea bargaining. The difference is crucial. The
German defendant is not punished for demanding trial (Felstiner
1979, p. 314). While he cannot be sure that the judge will impose the same or a lesser sentence after trial than that provided
by the penal order, the right to trial is still honored and its in-
vocation is not sanctioned by an increase in punishment. To the
contrary, judges often give a sentence discount to the defendant
who unsuccessfully appeals a penal order. The defendant may
persuade the court that his guilt is not as grave as it appeared
from the file. Or the judge may not have agreed with the prosecutor's original sentence suggestion but leaves it to the defendant
to take the initiative. Harsher punishment than that contemplated
by the penal order is imposed only if, in the course of the trial,
new facts are disclosed which let the defendant—or his act—
appear in a less favorable light.[31]

---

[31] Sometimes the questioning of the accused at trial establishes that he lives
in better economic conditions than the prosecutor earlier indicated. Under the
German day fine system, that fact, too, would lead to the imposition of a more
substantial fine. Goldstein and Marcus contend that penalties are frequently increased if penal orders are appealed without success (1978, p. 1575 n. 18). Their
evidence is weak. They do not cite any of the practitioners they interviewed
in Germany. They cite only a treatise on sentencing which refers back to a
single authority, the brief remarks of an Appellate Court judge, writing in
1952, on judgments which had to be reversed because of insufficient reasons
given for sentencing (Seibert 1952, p. 459). To my knowledge, no systematic
empirical study of the problem has yet been undertaken.

There are several reasons why German lawyers are unlikely to resort to informal bargaining (cf. Felstiner 1979, p. 321–22): first, the very idea of commercialized criminal justice is abhorrent (at best, exotic) to German legal tradition and theory; second, German defense lawyers, contrary to their American counterparts, have no financial interest in avoiding trial and in settling their cases; third, the courts have developed more or less strict sentence tariffs related to certain objective criteria of the offense (e.g., the value of the goods stolen, the level of blood alcohol) for most routine offenses eligible for disposition by *Strafbefehl*, and prosecutors, while not formally bound by them, are reluctant to deviate from the regular standard of punishment.

The German citizen—guilty or not—who receives a *Strafbefehl* need not meekly accept it for fear of incurring an additional penalty for using up the court's time. The rate of penal orders appealed and disposed of through regular criminal trials has increased from 20 percent in 1971 to 32 percent in 1978 (Statistisches Bundesamt 1971, pp. 78, 84; 1979, pp. 20, 26).[32] Thus, while the penal order does stand for the simple model in German criminal procedure, pressure is not placed on the defendant to give up the right to have guilt proved in a formal trial.

For the purposes of effective law enforcement, even *Strafbefehl* procedure may be too formal a way to deal with minor crime. In 1975, German legislation established "conditional dismissal," a way not only to impose sanctions without trial, but to do so without formal adjudication of guilt (§ 153a GCCP). Since its conception, conditional dismissal has steadily gained popularity with prosecutors. Conditional dismissal is possible if a person is suspected of having committed a *Vergehen* and if his guilt is determined to be minor. While § 153a GCCP theoretically applies to all *Vergehen*, the requirement of "minor guilt" limits its use to less serious cases. One study found that conditional

---

[32] The high appeal rate may indicate a tendency by prosecutors to propose a *Strafbefehl* even though they expect that the defendant will demand a trial (Schumann 1977, pp. 207–8). However, it is often difficult to foresee, on the basis of the police file alone, whether a defendant will accept a penal order. Many defendants—especially in traffic cases—have insurance for court costs and attorneys' fees and run no financial risk if they appeal a *Strafbefehl*; many therefore do appeal, even though the chances of winning an acquittal are slight.

dismissal was used fairly often—in 10 to 20 percent of all "convictable" cases—for minor offenses like negligent wounding (in the course of road traffic), assault, nonsupport of dependents, and criminal fraud (Ahrens 1978, p. 82). Another study found that increasing use of § 153a GCCP is made in cases of shoplifting and hit-and-run accidents (Felstiner 1979, p. 318).

Some cases are eligible both for conditional dismissal and *Strafbefehl*—a fact which underlines the importance of prosecutorial discretion in the area of petty crime. Conditional dismissal has, in many respects, the opposite effects of *Strafbefehl*. Under § 153a GCCP, the prosecutor offers, with the consent of the court, to refrain from seeking conviction by trial or by penal order if the defendant agrees to pay a certain sum of money to the state, to the victim, or to a charitable organization, or if he agrees regularly to support his dependents. If the defendant complies, the prosecutor is estopped from filing an accusation and the transaction is not entered into any official record. Otherwise regular procedures apply, and the case is disposed of by *Strafbefehl* or by trial.

Conditional dismissal satisfies all the requirements of a simple procedure, including the requirement that the defendant cooperate and acquiesce in the determination made by the prosecutor. But what about the second element of plea bargaining, the exertion of pressure on the defendant? The suspect's position is different from that of a citizen faced with a *Strafbefehl*. The prosecutor offers not only an expeditious way to resolve the charge but also substantive advantages. The payment required under § 153a GCCP is not only less onerous than a fine imposed by the court; "conditional dismissal" also precludes a finding of guilt and, consequently, a criminal record. Yet the very generosity of the offer makes it so devious. What defendant, once caught in the machinery of criminal justice, would not, even if innocent, happily buy his way out rather than fight a long battle and risk eventual conviction? The suspect is made an offer he cannot refuse. The implicit threat is there: "Go ahead and reject our offer, but don't expect any more concessions either from the prosecutor or from the court." That position does not hurt the suspect who is actually guilty; but it puts unbearable pressure on the innocent. Nor is the application of § 153a GCCP on innocent victims merely a theoretical possibility. The only published empirical study on the subject shows that in at least 23 percent of the conditional dismissals studied, the *Staatsanwalt* himself cited the "danger" of an acquittal as the reason for his consent to that disposition (Ahrens 1978, p. 130).[33]

Conditional dismissal has rightly been called the prosecutor's "emergency brake" to stop the procedure before it ends in an acquittal (Ahrens 1978, p. 47). The suspect can fall victim to his ignorance about the chances of reaching a favorable result. Much like the defendant in American plea bargaining, he faces a phalanx of seemingly benevolent lawyers (often including his own attorney), all of whom advise that it would be "best for him" if he paid the sum of money demanded by the prosecutor (Schmidhäuser 1973, pp. 533–34). Conditional dismissal requires a discretionary decision by the prosecutor and creates the additional risk that defendants will be treated unequally. It has been shown that affluent and educated defendants are disproportionately afforded the opportunity to avoid the stigma of conviction by paying "penance money" (Ahrens 1978, pp. 188, 202).

The parallels between plea bargaining and conditional dismissal are striking and should disturb German lawyers' self-complacency when they look bemusedly at the strange things happening in and around American court rooms. Yet there is one crucial difference: the "negotiated" guilty plea leads to a conviction, with its consequences of punishment and stigmatization; conditional dismissal results in payment of a sum of money —and nothing else. The name of an individual who receives a conditional dismissal is not recorded in any official register, and the law regards him as innocent of any wrongdoing.[34] The Ger-

---

33 Ahrens studied only conditional dismissals made after the beginning of the trial. These dismissals are officially pronounced by the court, with the consent of the prosecutor. Apart from that technical difference, however, they are comparable to conditional dismissals initiated by the prosecutor before charges are brought.

34 If any parallel must be drawn, it should therefore be between conditional dismissal and some forms of diversion. Americans have recognized that diversion presents psychological problems similar to those caused by plea bargaining (Nejelski 1976, p. 107; Morris 1974, pp. 10–11).

man suspect is not cleared of all charges, nor is he free from official sanctions, but, unlike the American defendant caught in the morass of plea bargaining, he does not forfeit his innocence. To some defendants, that difference may not appear to be all that important. Yet there is a fundamental distinction between pressuring a defendant to compromise and coercing complete submission.

IV. Conclusion

Where do we stand in the dispute between those who claim that there is nothing to learn from the old Continent, and those who contend that inquisitorial procedure is the key to improving the American criminal process? The result looks to be a stalemate. Some structural components of the criminal process seem to be universal and independent of procedural ideology: the investigative stage is dominated by the police, virtually to the exclusion of all other agencies; and public prosecutors exercise discretion in charging defendants even when that power is ostensibly denied them by applicable code provisions. Both phenomena are connected with equipment, training, and the self-images of the respective agencies. Only the police have sufficient personnel, skills, and technical equipment to investigate crime competently and coherently; they regard that activity as their legitimate task and develop techniques to diminish the force of outside controls. Prosecutors are trained, like judges, to make equitable and reasonable decisions on particular cases, not to apply narrowly drawn rules indiscriminately to all cases; they see themselves as arbiters rather than as ministerial employees. Further, they lack resources to prosecute fully more than a small fraction of all cases presented to them, so that the exercise of discretion becomes a functional necessity.

Plea bargaining seems to be less universal. It has no equivalent in France and, under the name of conditional dismissal, only a very feeble and underdeveloped analogue in Germany. Why? If the French and the Germans can do without plea bargaining, why not Americans? There appear to be a number of reasons why American plea bargaining has survived recurring attempts to "abolish" it. First, crime is a larger social problem in America than in Europe. American courts grapple with rapes, robberies, and murders; European judges are predominantly concerned with property offenses (see Langbein 1977, pp. 110–11). Table 1 shows crime rates of selected serious offenses in the United States and West Germany. The figures are taken from the official police statistics for the year 1977 (Bundeskriminalamt 1978, p. 10; FBI 1978, pp. 7, 13, 16, 20). The legal definitions of the offenses are somewhat different, but the variations are unlikely to change the overall picture. Sentences to long-term imprisonment are not extraordinary in an American criminal court; 82 percent of German defendants convicted of a criminal offense in 1974 were sentenced to pay a fine, and only 7 percent were sent to prison (Jescheck and Grebing 1978, p. 175). Those differences do not explain why plea bargaining is prevalent in America and not in Europe. They do, however, suggest difficulties that might be encountered if one tried to transfer procedural solutions developed in a more peaceful environment. Medicine that helps against the common cold may not be of much use in the fight against cancer (cf. Schlesinger 1977, pp. 107–8).

A second explanation for the prevalence of plea bargaining in America may be the relative rigidity and harshness of American substantive criminal law. When statutory penalties result more from popular demand and legislative caprice than from penological experience, conflicts inevitably arise between the

TABLE 1

Crime Rates in the United States and
West Germany, 1977
(number of crimes reported to the police
per 100,000 inhabitants)

Offense	United States	West Germany
Murder and non-negligent manslaughter	8.8	0.1
Rape	29.1	11.0
Robbery	187.1	34.6
Aggravated assault	241.5	85.7

maximum sanctions threatened by the substantive law and the need to impose sentences justified by the merits of the individual case. Such discrepancies create a need for prosecutorial discretion, and they prepare the ground for a "natural" system of bargaining—the defendant who would rather not risk being sentenced to an unusually long sentence is required to sacrifice his procedural options. That it is outrageous for an American judge to threaten to "throw the book" at a defendant leads this foreign observer to think that the book may be too heavy. Were it possible to reduce the range of the criminal law—especially in the area of victimless offenses—and to reduce the maximum authorized sanctions for most crimes, an important inducement (and justification) for bargaining would disappear.

There may be another, more specific reason why defendants must be induced in America to waive trial rights. France, Germany, and the United States all have at least one simple, as well as a complicated, model for disposing of criminal cases, but the gap between those types of procedure is nowhere as wide as in America. Trying a case before the French *cour d'assises* may take longer than trying it before the *tribunal correctionnel*, and holding a trial before the German *Strafrichter* may be more time-consuming than drafting and approving a *Strafbefehl* or negotiating a conditional dismissal, but in both countries, the cost involved in choosing the more complicated model is not prohibitive. Of course, both Continental systems would break down if every case was dealt with under the complicated procedure. Yet there is no reason to expect that will ever happen. There will always be many open-and-shut cases in which none of the participants has an interest in full formal processing. The choice becomes critical only in borderline cases. There, French and German prosecutors need not give much thought to how their choice would affect their and everyone else's workload, schedule, and monetary resources.

The situation is dramatically different in the United States. A jury trial requires not only that the lawyers spend an hour or a morning in court but often involves many of the following: finding, interviewing, and coaching witnesses; submitting briefs on, and arguing, pretrial motions to suppress evidence; fighting over discovery and inspection rights; devising tactics for questioning witnesses and generally for the conduct of the trial; analyzing and challenging the composition of the jury; preparing lengthy opening and closing arguments; presenting the evidence in a fashion understandable to uneducated and ignorant laypersons; arguing, again and again, about objections to particular lines of questioning and to the introduction of evidence; attacking the credibility of the opponent's witnesses; and preparing drafts of jury instructions.[35] That impressive list of tasks, which surely must induce lawyers to avoid trial by jury whenever possible, results from historical common law rules developed for jury trials (Frankel 1975, pp. 31–33).

The requirements of adversariness, of trial by jury, and of exclusion of irrelevant or unlawfully acquired evidence create numerous tasks for lawyers. Adherence to those principles no doubt enhances the likelihood that defendants receive fair trials —if they receive a trial at all. The admirable American preoccupation with safeguarding the individual's procedural rights has backfired. By affording the whole collection of procedural rights to a small minority of defendants, the system deprives the great majority of rights available to the accused in most civilized countries.

The reception of a guilty plea, by contrast, is simple. By means of plea bargaining, the complexities of a trial can be avoided by bringing power to bear on the individual who has none: the defendant.

Comparison seems to show, then, that it is the disproportion in America between the simple and the complicated models of adjudication which induces the American system to use coercion and deceit in order to reach the quick dispositions it has come to depend on for survival (cf. Langbein 1978, pp. 12–19).

Is there a remedy? If the diagnosis is correct, therapy should consist in narrowing the gap between the two models. In the

[35] This list describes aspects of jury trials. There are, in most jurisdictions, at least as many bench as jury trials. Bench trials are somewhat less complicated than jury trials. The important point is that 85–90 percent of all convictions result from no trial at all but from a plea of guilty.

abstract, it could be done either by simplifying the complicated procedure, or by complicating the simple procedure. American jurisdictions have made some effort to follow the second course. In some jurisdictions, including the federal system (e.g., Federal Rules of Criminal Procedure, Rule 11), the court is required to conduct something approaching a mini-trial when it is presented with a negotiated plea of guilty (see also Alschuler 1976, pp. 1146–48; *Yale Law Journal* 1972, pp. 299–304), to establish the factual circumstances of the offense and to reveal any conditions attached to the plea.

I see two dangers in the attempt to upgrade the simple procedure. Affording the defendant the semblance of a regular judicial hearing on the issue of his guilt may lend more legitimacy to plea bargaining than it deserves. However plea bargains are packaged, it remains true that the guilty plea is extracted from the defendant by the threat of an extra penalty for electing trial. The most elaborate process of judicial "confirmation" or "ratification" can only divert the public's and the defendant's attention from that fact, not change it. In any event, one should not underestimate the ingenuity of lawyers who seek ways to save time. If a serious reform of plea bargaining restored too many of the defendant's rights, and removed pressure to succumb to whatever the attorneys have "worked out," that practice would lose most of its attractiveness. Ways would be found to circumvent it and to replace legitimized but cumbersome plea negotiations with another form of dealing behind closed doors, thus creating a simple, simple procedure—the functioning of which one cannot imagine without trembling (cf. Parnas and Atkins 1978, pp. 110–12; Rosett and Cressey 1976, pp. 169–72).

There remains the other possible solution, a reform of trial procedures and rules. It would not be too difficult to find consensus on some modifications of current practice: simplify the rules on search and seizure in order to reduce the number of suppression hearings; cut back on the excesses of jury selection procedure; allow the judge to play a more active role in developing the evidence. But the limits of general agreement would be reached before much complexity was eliminated. For the elements which protract and complicate American jury trials are those components of criminal procedure which common law jurists have long revered as the most valuable assets of their legal tradition. For criminal procedure to be streamlined to make it available to cases of medium importance, some hallowed legal institutions would have to be reexamined. Among the institutions to be sacrificed: decision of the issue of guilt by laypersons sitting alone; ignorance by the trier of fact about the facts of the case before trial; separation of the functions of presenting evidence, deciding the facts, and presiding over the trial; and adversary presentation of evidence. Fortunately, I do not have to decide whether the benefits gained by reducing the role of plea bargaining would justify giving up any of these sacrosanct features of common law tradition. Still, if serious efforts are to be made to abolish or control plea bargaining in America, we must acknowledge the price to be paid.

REFERENCES

Ahrens, Wilfried. 1978. *Die Einstellung in der Hauptverhandlung gem. §§ 153 II, 153a II StPO: Eine empirische Analyse über neue Formen der Bekämpfung der Bagatellkriminalität.* Göttingen: Schwartz.

Allen, Francis A. 1961. "The Exclusionary Rule in the American Law of Search and Seizure," *Journal of Criminal Law, Criminology, and Police Science* 51:246–54.

Alschuler, Albert W. 1976. "The Trial Judge's Role in Plea Bargaining, Part I," *Columbia Law Review* 76:1059–1154.

———. 1978. "Sentencing Reform and Prosecutorial Power: A Critique of Recent Proposals for 'Fixed' and 'Presumptive' Sentencing," *University of Pennsylvania Law Review* 126:550–77.

Arpaillange, Pierre. 1978. "Rendre à la justice sa crédibilité: L'inégalité dans les poursuites," *Le Monde* 35 (21 September 1978), p. 16.

Baldwin, John, and Michael J. McConville. 1977. *Negotiated Justice.* London: Martin Robertson.

Biderman, Albert D., Louise A. Johnson, Jennie McIntyre, and Adrianne W. Weir. 1967. *Report on a Pilot Study in the District of Columbia on Victimization and Attitudes toward Law Enforcement.* Washington, D.C.: Bureau of Social Science Research.

Blankenburg, Erhard, Klaus Sessar, and Wiebke Steffen. 1978. *Die Staatsanwaltschaft im Prozess strafrechtlicher Sozialkontrolle.* Berlin: Duncker & Humblot.

Bouzat, Pierre, and Jean Pinatel. 1970. *Traité de droit pénal et de criminologie,* vol. 2. 2d ed. Paris: Dalloz.

Bundeskriminalamt. 1978. *Polizeiliche Kriminalstatistik 1977.* Wiesbaden: Bundeskriminalamt.

California District Attorneys Association. 1974. *Uniform Crime Charging Standards.* Los Angeles: Smith Pacific.

Casper, Gerhard, and Hans Zeisel. 1972. "Lay Judges in the German Criminal Courts," *Journal of Legal Studies* 1:135–91.

Dahs, Hans. 1977. *Handbuch des Strafverteidigers.* 4th ed. Köln: Otto Schmidt.

Davis, Kenneth C. 1969. *Discretionary Justice: A Preliminary Inquiry.* Baton Rouge, La.: Louisiana State University Press.

————. 1976. *Discretionary Justice in Europe and America.* Urbana and Chicago: University of Illinois Press.

Decheix, Pierre. 1970. "En finir avec l'hypocrisie de la correctionnalization," *Gazette du Palais* 1970, 2e semestre (doctrine), pp. 180–181.

Dölling, Dieter. 1978. *Die Zweiteilung der Hauptverhandlung: Eine Erprobung vor Einzelrichtern und Schöffengerichten.* Göttingen: Schwartz.

Federal Bureau of Investigation. 1978. *Uniform Crime Reports.* Washington, D.C.: U.S. Government Printing Office.

Felstiner, William L. F. 1979. "Plea Contracts in West Germany," *Law and Society Review* 13:309–25.

Fletcher, George P. 1974. "The Individualization of Excusing Conditions," *Southern California Law Review* 47:1269–1309.

Frankel, Marvin E. 1975. *The Search for Truth—An Umpireal View.* New York: Association of the Bar of the City of New York.

Garçon, Maurice. 1957. *Défense de la liberté individuelle.* Paris: Librairie Arthème Fayard.

Gillig, Volker Kurt. 1976. "Staatsanwaltschaftliche Ermittlungstätigkeit und staatsanwaltschaftliche Sanktionierungskriterien bei geringwertigen Ladendiebstahlsverfahren," *Kriminologisches Journal* 8:205–13.

Goebel, Julius, and T. Raymond Naughton. Repr., 1970. *Law Enforcement in Colonial New York.* Montclair, N.J.: Patterson Smith.

Goldstein, Abraham S., and Martin Marcus. 1977. "The Myth of

Judicial Supervision in Three 'Inquisitorial' Systems: France, Italy, and Germany," *Yale Law Journal* 87:240–82.

———. 1978. "Comment on Continental Criminal Procedure," *Yale Law Journal* 87:1570–77.

Goldstein, Joseph. 1960. "Police Discretion not to Invoke the Criminal Process: Low-Visibility Decisions in the Administration of Justice," *Yale Law Journal* 69:543–94.

Grebing, Gerhardt. 1974. *Die Untersuchungshaft in Frankreich: Entwicklung, Praxis, Reform.* Bonn: Röhrscheid.

———. 1979. "Staatsanwaltschaft und Strafverfolgungspraxis in Frankreich." In *Funktion und Tätigkeit der Anklagebehörde im ausländischen Recht,* ed. Hans-Heinrich Jescheck and Rudolf Leibinger. Baden-Baden: Nomos.

Greenberg, Douglas. 1976. *Crime and Law Enforcement in the Colony of New York.* Ithaca: Cornell University Press.

Hennion, Christian. 1976. *Chronique des flagrants délits.* Paris: Stock.

Herrmann, Joachim. 1974. "The Rule of Compulsory Prosecution and the Scope of Prosecutorial Discretion in Germany," *University of Chicago Law Review* 41:468–505.

Hinz, Lieselotte. 1971. "Zum Berufs- und Gesellschaftsbild von Polizisten." In *Die Polizei: Soziologische Studien und Forschungsberichte,* ed. Johannes Feest and Rüdiger Lautmann. Opladen: Westdeutscher Verlag.

———. 1975. "Soziale Determinanten des 'polizeilichen Betriebs.'" In *Die Polizei: Eine Institution öffentlicher Gewalt,* ed. Arbeitskreis Junger Kriminologen. Neuwied: Luchterhand.

Illinois Association for Criminal Justice. 1929. *The Illinois Crime Survey.* Chicago: Illinois Association for Criminal Justice.

Jescheck, Hans-Heinrich, and Gerhardt Grebing. 1978. *Die Geldstrafe im deutschen und ausländischen Recht.* Baden-Baden: Nomos.

Kadish, Sanford H. 1962. "Legal Norm and Discretion in the Police and Sentencing Process," *Harvard Law Review* 75:904–31.

Kaplan, John. 1974. "The Limits of the Exclusionary Rule," *Stanford Law Review* 26:1027–55.

Kerner, Hans-Jürgen. 1978. "Untersuchungshaft und Strafurteil." In *Gedächtnisschrift für Horst Schröder,* ed. Walter Stree, Theodor Lenckner, Peter Cramer, and Albin Eser. Munich: Beck.

Krattinger, Peter Georg. 1964. *Die Strafverteidigung im Vorverfahren im deutschen, französischen und englischen Strafprozess und ihre Reform.* Bonn: Röhrscheid.

Krümpelmann, Justus. 1971. "Statistische Angaben über die Untersuchungshaft in der Bundesrepublik." In *Die Untersuchungshaft im deutschen, ausländischen und internationalen Recht,* ed. Hans-Heinrich Jescheck and Justus Krümpelmann. Bonn: Röhrscheid.

Kuh, Richard H. 1975. "Plea Bargaining: Guidelines for the Manhattan District Attorney's Office," *Criminal Law Bulletin* 11:48–61.

LaFave, Wayne R. 1970. "The Prosecutor's Discretion in the United States," *American Journal of Comparative Law* 18:532–48.

Langbein, John H. 1974. "Controlling Prosecutorial Discretion in Germany," *University of Chicago Law Review* 41:439–67.

———. 1977. *Comparative Criminal Procedure: Germany.* St. Paul, Minn.: West.

———. 1978. "Torture and Plea Bargaining," *University of Chicago Law Review* 46:3–22.

Langbein, John H., and Lloyd L. Weinreb. 1978. "Continental Criminal Procedure: 'Myth' and Reality," *Yale Law Journal* 87: 1549–69.

Laroche-Flavin, Charles. 1968. *La machine judiciaire.* Paris: Editions du Seuil.

Löwe, Ewald, and Werner Rosenberg. 1978. *Die Strafprozessordnung und das Gerichtsverfassungsgesetz.* 23d ed. Vol. 2. Berlin: de Gruyter.

Manke, Klaus. 1966. "Die gerichtliche Voruntersuchung in Frankreich, Österreich, Italien und der Schweiz: Ein Vergleich im Hinblick auf die deutsche Strafprozessreform." J.S.D. dissertation, University of Freiburg.

Marcus, Michel, and Bernard Deleplace. 1979. "Bavures ordinaires," *Le Monde* 36 (11 October 1979), p. 14.

Marion, Georges. 1979. "Des policiers et des 'bavures,'" *Le Monde* 36 (6 September 1979), p. 1.

Merle, Roger, and André Vitu. 1973. *Traité de droit criminel.* Vol. 2. 2d ed. Paris: Editions Cujas.

Miller, Frank W. 1969. *Prosecution: The Decision to Charge a Suspect with a Crime.* Boston: Little, Brown.

Ministère de la Justice. 1977. *Compte Général 1974.* 2 vols. Paris: La Documentation Française.

Morris, Norval. 1974. *The Future of Imprisonment.* Chicago: University of Chicago Press.

National Commission on Law Observance and Enforcement. 1931. *Report on the Enforcement of the Prohibition Laws of the United States.* Washington, D.C.: U.S. Government Printing Office.

Nejelski, Paul. 1976. "Diversion: Unleashing the Hound of Heaven?" In *Pursuing Justice for Child,* ed. Margaret K. Rosenheim. Chicago: University of Chicago Press.

Neubauer, David W. 1974. "After the Arrest: The Charging Decision in Prairie City," *Law and Society Review* 8:495–517.

Oaks, Dallin H. 1970. "Studying the Exclusionary Rule in Search and Seizure," *University of Chicago Law Review* 37:665–757.

Parnas, Raymond I., and Riley J. Atkins. 1978. "Abolishing Plea Bargaining: A Proposal," *Criminal Law Bulletin* 14:101–22.

Paulsen, Monrad G. 1961. "The Exclusionary Rule and Misconduct by the Police," *Journal of Criminal Law, Criminology, and Police Science* 52:255–65.

Pound, Roscoe, and Felix Frankfurter, eds. 1922. *Criminal Justice in Cleveland*. Cleveland: The Cleveland Foundation.

President's Commission on Law Enforcement and Administration of Justice. 1967a. *The Challenge of Crime in a Free Society*. Washington, D.C.: U.S. Government Printing Office.

———. 1967b. *Task Force Report: The Police*. Washington, D.C.: U.S. Government Printing Office.

Rabin, Robert L. 1972. "Agency Criminal Referrals in the Federal System: An Empirical Study of Prosecutorial Discretion," *Stanford Law Review* 24:1036–91.

Rosett, Arthur, and Donald R. Cressey. 1976. *Justice by Consent: Plea Bargains in the American Courthouse*. Philadelphia: Lippincott.

Roth, Uta Margrit. 1963. "Das französische Strafverfahrensrecht und seine Reform." J.S.D. dissertation, University of Freiburg.

Roxin, Claus. 1976. "Recht und soziale Wirklichkeit im Strafverfahren." In *Kriminologie und Strafverfahren*, ed. Hans Göppinger and Günther Kaiser. Stuttgart: Enke.

———. 1979. *Strafverfahrensrecht: Ein Studienbuch*. 15th ed. Munich: Beck.

Rudolphi, Hans Joachim, Eckhard Horn, Erich Samson, and Hans-Ludwig Schreiber. 1977. *Systematischer Kommentar zum Strafgesetzbuch*. Vol. 1. 2d ed. Frankfurt: Metzner.

Schlesinger, Steven R. 1977. *Exclusionary Injustice: The Problem of Illegally Obtained Evidence*. New York and Basel: Dekker.

Schmidhäuser, Eberhard. 1973. "Freikaufverfahren mit Strafcharakter im Strafprozess?" *Juristenzeitung* 28:529–36.

Schönke, Adolf, and Horst Schröder. 1978. *Strafgesetzbuch: Kommentar*, 9th ed., ed. Theodor Lenckner, Peter Cramer, Albin Eser, and Walter Stree. Munich: Beck.

Schrock, Thomas S., and Robert C. Welsh. 1974. "Up from Calandra: The Exclusionary Rule as a Constitutional Requirement," *Minnesota Law Review* 59:251–383.

Schumann, Karl F. 1977. *Der Handel mit Gerechtigkeit: Funktions-*

probleme der Strafjustiz und ihre Lösungen—am Beispiel des amerikanischen plea bargaining. Frankfurt: Suhrkamp.

Seibert, Claus. 1952. "Fehler bei der Strafzumessung," *Monatsschrift für deutsches Recht* 6:457–60.

Skolnick, Jerome H. 1966. *Justice without Trial: Law Enforcement in Democratic Society.* New York: John Wiley & Sons.

Spiegelberg, Rüdiger. 1977. *Qualifikatorische Aspekte der Sozialisation in den Polizeiberuf—unter besonderer Berücksichtigung der Einstellungsänderungen gegenüber dem Publikum.* Frankfurt: Peter Lang.

Spiotto, James E. 1973. "Search and Seizure: An Empirical Study of the Exclusionary Rule and Its Alternatives," *Journal of Legal Studies* 2:243–78.

Statistisches Bundesamt. 1971. 1978. 1979. *Rechtspflege: Strafgerichte 1970, . . . 1977, . . . 1978.* Stuttgart and Mainz: Kohlhammer.

Stefani, Gaston, and Georges Levasseur. 1977. *Procédure Pénale.* 10th ed. Paris: Dalloz.

———. 1978. *Droit Pénal Général.* 10th ed. Paris: Dalloz.

Stephan, Egon. 1976. *Die Stuttgarter Opferbefragung: Eine kriminologisch-viktimologische Analyse zur Erforschung des Dunkelfeldes unter besonderer Berücksichtigung der Einstellung der Bevölkerung zur Kriminalität.* Wiesbaden: BKA-Forschungsreihe.

U.S. Department of Justice. 1977. "Materials Relating to Prosecutorial Discretion." Reprinted in *Criminal Law Reporter* 24:3001–8.

Vérin, Jacques. 1972. "Organisation judiciaire et indépendance de la magistrature (1)," *Revue de Science Criminelle et de Droit Pénal Comparé* 1972: 922–27.

Weigend, Thomas. 1978. *Anklagepflicht und Ermessen: Die Stellung des Staatsanwalts zwischen Legalitäts- und Opportunitätsprinzip nach deutschem und amerikanischem Recht.* Baden-Baden: Nomos.

Weinreb, Lloyd L. 1977. *Denial of Justice: Criminal Process in the United States.* New York: The Free Press.

Wilson, James Q. 1968. *Varieties of Police Behavior.* Cambridge, Mass.: Harvard University Press.

Yale Law Journal, Comment. 1955. "Private Prosecution: A Remedy for District Attorneys' Unwarranted Inaction," *Yale Law Journal* 65:209–34.

Yale Law Journal, Note. 1972. "Restructuring the Plea Bargain," *Yale Law Journal* 82:286–312.

Zipf, Heinz. 1974. "Kriminalpolitische Überlegungen zum Legalitätsprinzip." In *Einheit und Vielfalt des Strafrechts: Festschrift für Karl Peters zum 70. Geburtstag,* ed. Jürgen Baumann and Klaus Tiedemann. Tübingen: Mohr.

James B. Jacobs

The Prisoners' Rights Movement
and Its Impacts, 1960-80

ABSTRACT

Even as some prison officials and academics brand judicial
intervention in matters of prison policy and administration
as misguided and counterproductive, some prisoner advocates
despair of the capacity of law reform to produce meaningful
prison reform. The prisoners' rights movement should be seen
as a sociopolitical movement like the civil rights movement or
the women's movement. From this perspective, individual case
holdings that have dominated the attention of legal academics
are less significant than the capacity of law reform efforts to
shape and sustain a prisoners' rights movement with adherents
inside and outside of prison. It is also important not to adopt
too narrow a view of the impacts of the prisoners' rights
movement. Simple studies of compliance with judicial decrees
do not capture the complexity of changes occasioned by legal
activity. To appreciate fully the impacts of the prisoners' rights
movement on prisons and prisoners' lives, it is necessary
to consider such secondary effects as changes in prison
bureaucracies and personnel, public and political opinion,
and the self-esteem of prisoners and prison officials.

During the past two decades prisoners have besieged the federal courts with civil rights suits challenging every aspect of
prison programs and practices. It is as if the courts had become
a battlefield where prisoners and prison administrators, led by
their respective legal champions, engage in mortal combat. Although the war has dragged on for almost twenty years, and

James B. Jacobs is Associate Professor of Law and Sociology, Cornell University.

shows no sign of abating, strangely enough there seems to be
no agreement on which side is winning.

It frequently appears that both sides are trying to convince
the public and themselves that their own defeat is imminent.
Prison officials complain that the demands of litigation and court
orders have pressed their beleaguered staffs and limited resources
to the verge of collapse; they decry the naïveté of judges who
cannot see the deadly struggle for power which lies behind the
disingenuous facade of legal petitions which ask "only" for
"humane treatment" and "basic civil rights." Even worse, from
the perspective of prison officials, judges have not been content
merely to resolve limited conflicts, but have made Herculean
efforts, by use of structural injunctions (see Fiss 1978, 1979),
special masters (see e.g. Nathan 1979), and citizens' visiting
committees, to restructure and reorganize prisons according to
their own value preferences. Legal attacks and judicial interference have, according to some prison officials, fatally undermined their capacity to administer their institutions and to maintain basic order and discipline.

Activist prisoners and their advocates are equally despondent.
Each victory seems to accentuate how far their cause still has
to go to obtain its goals. And unfavorable court rulings, especially those of the Supreme Court, seem to harbinger the final demise
of all prisoners' rights. The latest decision to be heralded apoca-
lyptically is *Bell v. Wolfish*, 441 U.S. 520 (1979). The Supreme
Court, in an opinion by archvillain Justice William Rehnquist,
reversed a sweeping injunction condemning a multitude of conditions and practices at the Federal Bureau of Prisons' Metropolitan Correctional Center in New York City. The Court rejected
the Court of Appeals standard for review of jail conditions, under
which pretrial detainees could "be subjected to only those 'restrictions and privations' which inhere in their confinement itself or which are justified by compelling necessities of jail administration." Instead, the majority required only a showing
that jail practices are *reasonably related to a legitimate governmental objective*. Applying this less restrictive standard, the
Court upheld a prohibition on receiving books and magazines

from any source other than the publisher as well as a restriction on receipt of packages, double-bunking, unannounced cell searches, and mandatory visual inspection of body cavities.

With both sides claiming defeat, who is the real winner and who the real loser in the war over prisoners' rights? So put, the question is too simplistic to be useful. What is needed is a holistic understanding of the role of litigation and law reform in creating and sustaining a *prisoners' rights movement*, which includes prison reform efforts of all sorts, by prisoners and others.

Unfortunately, research has not been directed to this level of analysis. While the *Index to Legal Periodicals* lists more than 850 articles on prisoners' rights since 1963, most merely summarize recent legal developments or dissect judicial opinions. Strikingly absent are efforts to place the changing legal status of prisoners in a larger sociopolitical context, and empirical studies on the impact of legal change on prisons, prisoners' lives, and the drive for prison reform. The social science literature is even less helpful.

This essay seeks to chart a course for holistic analysis of the prisoners' rights movement. Section I sketches the origins and development of the movement and identifies the key actors, agencies, and institutions whose activities would have to be carefully studied and related to one another before the full story of the prisoners' rights movement could be told. Section II presents a critique of those who see the prisoners' rights movement as an example of judicial failure, and suggests a strategy for evaluating the impacts of the prisoners' rights movement.

I. Prisoners' Rights as a Sociopolitical Movement

In speaking of the *prisoners' rights movement* I refer to far more than the sum total of court decisions affecting prisoners. We are dealing with a broadscale effort to redefine the status (moral, political, economic, as well as legal) of prisoners in a democratic society. The prisoners' rights movement, like other social movements—the civil rights movement, the women's movement, the student movement—includes a variety of more or less organized groups and activities; there is also wide variation in the extent and intensity of individual participation. What is decisive, however, is a shared sense of grievance and the commitment to enhanced rights and entitlements for prisoners.

The prisoners' rights movement must be understood in the context of a "fundamental democratization" (Mannheim 1940) which has transformed American society since World War II, and particularly since 1960. Starting with the black civil rights movement in the mid-1950s, one marginal *group* after another—blacks, poor people, welfare mothers, mental patients, women, children, aliens, gays, and the handicapped—has pressed for admission into the societal mainstream. While each group has its own history and a special character, the general trend has been to extend citizenship rights to a greater proportion of the total population by recognizing the existence and legitimacy of *group* grievances.

Prisoners, a majority of whom are now black and poor, have identified themselves and their struggle with other "victimized minorities," and pressed their claims with vigor and not a little moral indignation. Various segments of the free society linked the prisoners' cause to the plight of other powerless groups. To a considerable extent the legal system, especially the federal district courts, accepted the legitimacy of prisoners' claims.

To recognize the prisoners' rights movement as part of a larger mosaic of social change is not to deny this movement's own sociopolitical history. The drive to extend citizenship rights to prisoners must be placed in the context of two hundred years of effort at prison reform. The issues being argued today in constitutional terms have previously been debated on religious, and utilitarian grounds (see e.g. Rothman 1980). Reformers of earlier generations did not pursue their objectives in the courts because, until recently, the courts were unreceptive to such complaints. The rule of law did not apply to prisoners; their status placed them "beyond the ken of the courts" (*Yale Law Journal* 1963).

Before the 1960s, prisoners were a legal caste whose status was poignantly captured in the expression "slaves of the state" (*Ruffin v. Commonwealth*, 62 Va. 790 [1871]). Like slaves, prisoners had no constitutional rights and no forum for presenting their grievances. But unlike slaves, prisoners were invisible, except perhaps for occasional riots, when they captured public attention.

Until the 1960s, the federal judiciary adhered to a "hands off" attitude toward prison cases out of concern for federalism and separation of powers and a fear that judicial review of administrative decisions would undermine prison security and discipline. A prisoner who complained about arbitrary, corrupt, brutal, or illegal treatment did so at his peril. Until recently, protest to the outside world was severely repressed (Hirschkop and Millemann 1969). Prisoners were, therefore, isolated from the rest of society; the possibility of forming alliances with groups outside prison was very limited. The precondition for the emergence of a prisoners' rights movement in the United States was the recognition by the federal courts that prisoners are *persons* with cognizable constitutional rights. Just by opening a forum in which prisoners' grievances could be heard, the federal courts destroyed the custodians' absolute power and the prisoners' isolation from the larger society (see Jacobs 1977). And the litigation in itself heightened prisoners' consciousness and politicized them.

The new era of prisoners' rights began in the early 1960s in the wake of the civil rights movement. In prisons, it was the Black Muslims who carried the torch of black protest. The Muslims succeeded with the assistance of jailhouse lawyers, and in turn provided an example for using law to challenge officialdom. A rights movement clearly had appeal for a generation of minority youth who had become highly conscious of their rights and entitlements. But the movement was not comprised solely of prisoners. It depended heavily on the involvement and efforts of free citizens, particularly lawyers and reinvigorated prison reform groups. Of course, the prisoners' rights movement would not have been possible without activism in the federal judiciary and some stamp of approval by the justices of the United States Supreme Court. Nor is prison reform the sole prerogative of courts; a complete sociopolitical history of the prisoners' rights movement would have to take federal and state legislative and administrative activity into account.

A. The Black Muslims and the Religious Freedom Controversy

A high priority for building a body of research on prisoners' rights is to document fully the activities of the Black Muslims in American prisons and jails. The Black Muslims filed lawsuits throughout the country in the early 1960s asserting denial of racial and religious equality. (By my count, there were sixty-six *reported federal court decisions* pertaining to the Muslims between 1961 and 1978.) The issues raised by the Muslims were timely and likely to appeal to federal judges. The legitimacy of demands by blacks for equal protection under the law in other contexts was becoming well established. The rights asserted—to read religious literature and to worship as one wishes— are fundamental in American values and constitutional history and difficult to deny. The only posture available to prison officials was to deny the Muslims' sincerity. Prison officials often disputed the Muslims' claim to religious legitimacy, but the result was to strengthen Muslim resolve and intensify their struggle (Jacobs 1979b).

The Supreme Court's first modern prisoners' rights case, *Cooper v. Pate*, 378 U.S. 546 (1964), was an appeal from a lower court ruling upholding the discretion of prison officials to refuse Muslim prisoners their Korans and all opportunities for worship. The Supreme Court's decision was narrow: the Muslim prisoners had standing to challenge religious discrimination under Section 1983 of the resurrected Civil Rights Act of 1871. But for the prisoners' movement it was not the breadth of the decision that mattered, but the Supreme Court's determination that prisoners have constitutional rights; prison officials were not free to do with prisoners as they pleased. And the federal courts were permitted, indeed obligated, to provide a forum where prisoners could challenge and confront prison officials. Whatever the outcome of such confrontations, they spelled the end of the authoritarian regime in American penology (see Jacobs 1977).

Once disputes between prisoners and prison officials were seen by outsiders to be religious controversies and not simply struggles for institutional control, the result was inevitable (Rothman 1973). The success of the Muslims on the constitutional issue of free exercise of religious rights brought the federal courts into the prisons. The abominable conditions in American prisons kept them there. Prisoners and their advocates presented their grievances in constitutional terms and federal courts became more deeply involved in disputes over prison practices, policies, and conditions.

The Black Muslims are undoubtedly the best organized and most solidary group to exist for any length of time in American prisons. They have set an example for other prisoners who soon began organizing themselves in groups and blocs, in contrast to the cliques of former times (Clemmer 1940; Irwin 1980). In place of the subcultural norm "do your own time," the Muslims introduced a new morality—group time (see Jacobs 1976). They showed how, through legal activism, prisoner groups could achieve solidarity and some tangible successes.

The issue of religious freedom was picked up by diverse prisoner groups, who saw the opportunity to formulate as a religious controversy their objections to prison life and their opposition to prison officials. The most dramatic example was the Church of the New Song, a "religion" begun by federal prisoners in Marion, Illinois, which soon spread to other federal and state facilities (see Jacobs 1979a, pp. 2–11). The church earned nationwide media attention; its leader proclaimed himself the Bishop of Tellus, prophesied in the Book of Revelations; its "liturgy" required porterhouse steaks and Harvey's Bristol Cream; its agenda called for the wholesale destruction of the American prison system. The status of the Church of the New Song was vigorously litigated in the Fifth and Eighth federal judicial circuits; the prisoners achieved several legal victories requiring correction departments to afford them the same opportunities and prerogatives as traditional religions.

B. Jailhouse Lawyers and Access to the Courts

The traditional role of the jailhouse lawyer had been to assist fellow prisoners in preparing postconviction petitions asserting defects in their prosecution or conviction. Prison officials often were hostile to jailhouse lawyers because of their status among, and influence over, fellow inmates (*Washington and Lee Law Review* 1968). There were also not unwarranted fears that jailhouse lawyers might abuse their power over other prisoners (Brierley 1971). It was not uncommon for prison rules to prohibit giving legal assistance of any kind; punishments could be very severe. Consequently, jailhouse lawyers often functioned "underground." Official hostility to jailhouse lawyers intensified as prisoners' rights actions succeeded, and as the jailhouse lawyers became judicially recognized adversaries.

The Supreme Court's decision in *Johnson v. Avery*, 393 U.S. 483 (1969), ushered in a new age in jailhouse lawyering (Wexler 1971). The court held that when prison officials are not providing prisoners with adequate legal services, prisoners can not be punished for providing legal assistance to one another. The decision marked another triumph for a class of prisoners whom the officials disliked and feared. More victories followed. In 1972, the Court held, in *Haines v. Kerner*, 404 U.S. 519 (1972), that prisoners' *in forma pauperis* petitions had to be treated in a manner most advantageous to prisoners; where there was a glimmer of a federal cause of action in the complaint the case could not be dismissed. *Wolff v. McDonnell*, 418 U.S. 539 (1974), extended the jailhouse lawyer's authority of representation to civil rights suits attacking institutional conditions and policies. The Court went even further in *Bounds v. Smith*, 430 U.S. 817 (1977), holding that the constitution imposed upon the states an affirmative obligation to provide prisoners with either adequate law libraries or adequate assistance from persons trained in the law. These decisions have established the jailhouse lawyer as an institutionalized adversary and have undoubtedly contributed to the popularity of litigation as a prisoner avocation.

C. Prisoners

By the late 1950s, and early 1960s, blacks constituted a majority of the prisoners in many northern prisons and in some states (Jacobs 1979b). Their consciousness aroused by the civil rights movement, it was only natural that this generation of minority prisoners would demand its rights even behind bars; it was not about to accept being invisible. By the late 1960s some black prisoners, such as Eldridge Cleaver, George Jackson, and Martin Sostre, had achieved extraordinary prominence. Their ties to outside groups, and to batteries of lawyers, could not be severed. And they may well have politicized their lawyers as much as their lawyers politicized them. Riots and law reform were paths to political change in the larger society during this period and the same phenomena became increasingly evident in the prisons.

D. The Prisoners' Rights Bar

A platoon, eventually a phalanx, of prisoners' rights lawyers, supported by federal and foundation funding, soon appeared and pressed other-than-religious constitutional claims. They initiated, and won, prisoners' rights cases that implicated every aspect of prison governance. In many cases the prisoners' attorneys were more dedicated and effective than the overburdened and inexperienced government attorneys who represented the prison officials (Bershad 1977, quoting Supreme Court Justice Lewis Powell).

Many of the leading prisoners' rights lawyers had earlier gained considerable experience working for black civil rights (Bronstein 1977). Herman Schwartz, a professor at the State University of New York at Buffalo, Alvin Bronstein of the American Civil Liberties Union's National Prison Project, William Bennett Turner and Stanley Bass of the NAACP Legal Defense Fund, and others brought both national perspective and some minimal coordination to the prisoners' rights litigation.

Notwithstanding the role played by a few national prisoners' rights groups and institutions, day-to-day advocacy has been carried on by hundreds of lawyers and paralegals on the state or local level. Many of these groups were founded and supported under the auspices of OEO Legal Services (see, e.g., Welch 1979). Prisoner Legal Services in Illinois, begun in the early 1970s by a nonlawyer activist, had nine full-time attorneys, several social workers, and a staff of forty by the mid-1970s, and was a potent force in the life of northern Illinois prisons (Jacobs 1977, chap. 5). Prison administrators viewed the organization as a powerful and omnipresent watchdog. Consideration of policy decisions always involved some attention to the likely reaction of the Legal Services staff. A number of prisoners' rights projects were established in law schools (Cardarelli and Finkelstein 1974) and contributed to the flow of outside legal actors into the closed prison world. A 1973 report by the Council on Legal Education for Professional Responsibility listed sixty-three law schools as providing some form of legal assistance to prisoners.

Many of these law students and prisoners' advocates identified strongly with the prisoners' interests, thereby building up the prisoners' hopes and encouraging their protests. In turn, the prisoners gave these legal personnel a "cause" and strong personal reinforcement. At times, legal services personnel went well beyond even far-reaching class actions and worked on such "political" tasks as establishing prisoner unions (e.g., *Jones v. North Carolina Prisoners' Union*, 433 U.S. 119 [1977]). Many lawyers began to see themselves no longer as technicians but instead as prisoners' rights advocates working for the reform or abolition of the prison system. The most extreme example was a small but influential group of radical lawyers and law collectives.

The American Bar Association gave the prisoners' movement the imprimatur of the established legal community. It created in 1970 the Commission on Correctional Facilities and Services for the purpose of advancing correctional reform. With Ford Foundation funding, the commission opened full-time offices in Washington. Its Resource Center for Correctional Law and Legal Services was a central clearinghouse for information and coordinated effort and resources among prisoners' rights groups and litigators. Legal periodicals on prisoners' rights were established, including one published for an ABA section. At least seven sections of the ABA later formed prisoners' rights committees, and, as of 1974, twenty-four state bar associations had special committees working on prison reform (American Bar Association, Commission on Correctional Facilities and Services 1975). The most active ABA Committee is the Joint Committee on the Legal Status of

Prisoners. Its recently completed *Tentative Draft of Standards Relating to the Legal Status of Prisoners* (1977) prescribes, among other things, a right to minimum wages for prisoner laborers, a right to form prisoner organizations, and a limited right to privacy. While not, at the time of writing, adopted by the ABA, that such standards are being seriously considered is an indication of the degree of legitimacy which the prisoners' rights movement has attained (see also U.S. Dept. of Justice 1978; National Council on Crime and Delinquency 1966, 1972).

Federal funding for prisoner legal services has lately become more difficult to obtain, in part because of the displacement of OEO Legal Services by the Legal Services Corporation. The ABA Resource Center for Correctional Law and Legal Services ran out of money in mid-1978. Illinois Prisoner Legal Services for all practical purposes went out of existence because of lack of funds at about the same time. Increasingly, those government grants which are available prohibit civil rights suits and class actions (American Bar Association, Resource Center on Correctional Law and Legal Services 1974, p. 407).

The luster of the prisoners' rights movement seems to be fading. The image of the prisoner as hero, revolutionary, and victim is disappearing. Other minority rights movements, such as that associated with the handicapped, are increasingly attracting resources and the energies of young attorneys. The pathbreaking prisoners' rights litigation is behind us. The nitty-gritty of more routine legal services may be less attractive to young lawyers with reformist aspirations. Whether a viable prisoners' rights movement at the grass roots level can survive funding cutbacks, judicial retrenchment, and other social change is unclear.

It would be wrong, however, to conclude that the prisoners' rights movement is dying. Increasing numbers of cases are filed each year; 11,195 prisoners' rights petitions were filed in federal district courts in the year ending 30 June 1979, a 451.5 percent increase since 1970 and a 15 percent increase over 1978 (U.S. Administrative Office of the United States Courts 1979; see also McCormack 1975). The vast majority of these cases are filed *pro se*, without legal representation. Most of the cases are dis-

missed at the pleading stage or on summary judgment (Turner 1979), but if only a small percentage survive, the number of litigated cases will continue to be substantial.

Fewer prisoners' rights lawyers are now available, but many of those are experienced and highly skilled. The ACLU's National Prison Project has only seven full-time attorneys, but carries on major litigation across the country, often supporting cases originally brought by a local ACLU chapter. The project effectively employs the services of a cadre of expert witnesses, including ex-correctional officials like David Fogel and John Conrad. The experience which this litigation team has accumulated over years in lawsuits around the country makes it a formidable opponent. The project's director, Alvin Bronstein, exerts influence in many ways besides litigation: for example by lobbying, accepting speaking engagements, and maintaining a high profile at national meetings and conferences.

It is possible that the U.S. Department of Justice will emerge as a crucial force in the reconstituted prisoners' movement of the 1980s. The Special Litigation Section has intervened in a number of important cases in the last few years, most notably a massive challenge to the Texas Department of Corrections. The Civil Rights of Institutionalized Persons Act, passed by Congress in 1980, clarifies and broadens the Justice Department's authority to represent prisoners in institutional litigation.

E. The Supreme Court

Any analysis of the prisoners' rights movement must acknowledge the crucial role of the United States Supreme Court. The prisoners' rights movement required at least the passive acquiescence of the Court. The movement also needed the symbolic shot in the arm that *Brown v. Board of Education* provided to the civil rights movement. The crucial prison case was *Cooper v. Pate*, 378 U.S. 546 (1964). Although a *per curiam* opinion, lacking the powerful language of *Brown v. Board of Education*, it left no doubt that prisoners have rights that must be respected.

Many legal victories followed after *Cooper v. Pate*. Each con-

tributed to the strength, self-confidence, and momentum of the prisoners' rights movement. A high water mark was reached in *Wolff v. McDonnell*, 418 U.S. 539 (1974), raising issues about the procedural protections to which prisoners are entitled at disciplinary hearings. The Supreme Court finally provided the kind of clarion statement that could serve as a rallying call for prisoners' rights advocates. Speaking for the Court, Justice White said:

> [The State of Nebraska] asserts that the procedure for disciplining prison inmates for serious misconduct is a matter of policy raising no constitutional issue. If the position implies that prisoners in state institutions are wholly without the protections of the Constitution and the Due Process Clause, it is plainly untenable. Lawful imprisonment necessarily makes unavailable many rights and privileges of the ordinary citizen, a 'retraction justified by the considerations underlying our penal system' [citations omitted]. But though his rights may be diminished by the needs and exigencies of the institutional environment, a prisoner is not wholly stripped of constitutional protections when he is imprisoned for crime. There is no iron curtain drawn between the Constitution and the prisons of this country.
> (418 U.S. 539 at 555 [1974])

Since *Wolff*, prisoners have won several important victories in the Supreme Court—e.g., *Estelle v. Gamble*, 429 U.S. 97 (1976) (deliberate indifference to serious medical needs constitutes cruel and unusual punishment), *Hutto v. Finney*, 437 U.S. 678 (1978) (approving a wide-ranging structural injunction against certain practices and conditions in the Arkansas prisons)—but none equals *Wolff* for eloquence.

I stress the symbolic importance of Supreme Court prisoners' rights decisions, not to belittle the holdings, but to emphasize that from a sociopolitical perspective what is crucial is the psychological impact of court decisions, the feeling of those in the field, in this case prisoners' advocates, prison officials, and their respective lawyers, that the Supreme Court and the Constitution are for them or against them. The negative impact of court decisions on morale is nicely captured in a case study of protracted litigation involving Louisiana's Jefferson Parish Prison (Harris and Spiller 1977, pp. 213–14):

> The one negative factor that unquestionably did flow from the suit involved the aggravation and adverse personal effects associated with it. Overall, it appears that the worst effects of the judicial intervention may have been psychological ones. It was psychologically very difficult for the defendants to accept that what they had been doing was wrong or inadequate when they believed that they were doing a decent job. It was psychologically very difficult for the defendants to accept that a federal judge who had never operated a correctional facility could dictate what would be done. It was psychologically very difficult for defendants to have their job performances criticized by persons who were not believed to understand their problems. It was psychologically very difficult for the defendants to accept blame for defects for which they saw others as being responsible. Acceptance of all of these things was made even more difficult by the fact that they were imposed publicly.

The positive impact of court decisions on movements such as the prisoners is more sharply grasped by Stuart Scheingold (1974, p. 131) than any other writer with whom I am familiar:

> Regardless of the problems of implementation, rights can be useful political tools. It is possible to capitalize on the perceptions of entitlement associated with rights to initiate and nurture political mobilization—a dual process of activating a quiescent citizenry and *organizing* groups into effective political units. Political mobilization can in its fashion build support for interests that have been excluded in existing allocations of values and thus promote a realignment of political forces. . . . [S]ince rights carry

with them connotations of entitlement, a declaration
of rights tends to politicize needs by changing the
way people think about their discontent.

The symbolic and psychological significance of being "vindi-
cated" or "repudiated" by a court explains wildly exaggerated
reactions to court decisions—exaggerated, that is, when viewed
through the lawyer's detached lens. But once the potential of
court decisions and even litigation itself to power a movement
or to demoralize its opposition is understood, then the relationship of courts to sociopolitical movements becomes much more
complicated than simply looking at the "holding" of each new
judicial decision.

It is hardly surprising that *Bell v. Wolfish*, 441 U.S. 520
(1979), is being heralded by prisoners' rights advocates as a
fatal blow to the movement and by prison officials as a vindication of their authority and competence. What makes *Wolfish*
more than just another case is Justice Rehnquist's rhetoric: for
example, his quip that the Constitution embodies no "one man,
one cell" principle and his repeated emphasis on the need for
judicial deference to prison officials.

The deplorable conditions and draconian restrictions of
our Nation's prisons are too well known to require recounting
here, and the federal courts rightly have condemned these
sordid aspects of our prison systems. But many of these same
courts have, in the name of the Constitution, become
increasingly enmeshed in the minutiae of prison operations.
Judges, after all, are human. They, no less than others in
our society, have a natural tendency to believe that their
individual solutions to often intractable problems are better
and more workable than those of the persons who are
actually charged with the running of the particular institution
under examination. But under the Constitution, the first
question to be answered is not whose plan is best, but in
what branch of the Government is lodged the authority to
initially devise the plan. This does not mean that constitutional

rights are not to be scrupulously observed. It does mean, however, that the inquiry of federal courts into prison management must be limited to the issue of whether a particular system violates any prohibition of the Constitution, or in the case of a federal prison, a statute. The wide range of "judgment calls" that meet constitutional and statutory requirements are confided to officials outside the Judiciary Branch of Government. (441 U.S. 520 at p. 562 [1979])

Neither prison officials nor prisoners' rights lawyers are much impressed by the facts that *Wolfish* is only one case, that it can be distinguished from many prison cases on its facts, that it is arguably applicable only to modern jails like the Metropolitan Correctional Center, or that an even more recent decision, *Vitek v. Jones*, 48 U.S.L.W. 4317 (1980), scores a victory for prisoners, by establishing a right to a hearing before transfer to a mental health facility.

This Supreme Court has demonstrated its concern that the prisoners' rights movement, or more specifically, the involvement of federal courts in matters of state prison administration, not go too far. In my view this does not mean a return to the "hands off" doctrine or a redefinition of prisoners as nonpersons. It does mean that prisoners' rights activists cannot in the foreseeable future expect highly dramatic decisions which will mobilize social and political energies on behalf of prisoners. If there is to be a stimulus for further momentum in the prisoners' rights movement it probably will not come from the Supreme Court. Having liberated prisoners from being slaves of the state, this Court seems unwilling to establish them as citizens behind bars.

F. The Lower Federal Courts

The significance of Supreme Court decisions notwithstanding, it would be a grave error, as Jerome Frank admonished three decades ago, to rely too heavily on appellate decisions as indicators of what lower courts are doing. Frank (1949) spoke of "the myth that upper courts are the heart of the courthouse government." Frank was right. Most legal analysts of the prisoners' rights movement are transfixed by Supreme Court decisions. Each new decision generates intense examination of the opinion's language, new doctrinal syntheses, and unending critiques of judicial logic. Hardly any attention is paid to *what the trial courts are doing* in prisoners' rights cases (but see Turner 1979).

Prisoners' rights cases are won and lost on the record. The Supreme Court has not effectively hemmed in activist federal judges (Frankel 1976). Most complaints deal with access to lawyers and legal materials, property loss or damage, brutality, censorship of mail, and medical care (Turner 1979). All of these fall within the ambit of recognized constitutional violations or are controlled by state law or previous consent decrees. Many prisoners' complaints can be redressed without breaking new ground.

A recent survey by the ACLU's National Prison Project shows sixteen states in which the prison system or the major institution is under a court decree on account of crowding or a "totality of conditions" which amounts to cruel and unusual punishment. In twelve other states, such suits are pending. Even *Bell v. Wolfish* has failed to prevent major judicial interventions into the operation of state prisons. Most notable, in recent months, is the decision of a federal district judge (*Ramos v. Lamm*, C.A. No. 77 K 1093 D. Col.) to shut down "old Max," Colorado's Canon Correctional Facility. And even a cursory glance through the *Criminal Law Reporter* will bolster the spirits of those who fear that prisoners' rights advocates will be stymied by *Bell v. Wolfish*. Consider *Morin v. Cooper*, 26 Crim. L. Rptr. 2365 (1979), a post-*Wolfish* decision by New York's highest court, holding that while *Wolfish* forecloses the argument by pretrial detainees that they have a federal constitutional right to "contact visits" with family and friends, such a right is guaranteed by the state constitution's due process clause.

Many prisoners' rights cases are not decided in the courts. Settlements are negotiated, sometimes with the approval and even the collusion of reform-minded administrators. These administrators are not averse to admitting that facilities are dilapidated and poorly maintained, or that medical care is inadequate; a court-approved consent decree on such matters may greatly improve their leverage in the executive budget competition and with the legislature (Schwartz 1972, p. 791; Harris and Spiller 1977, pp. 92–96). Furthermore, rules and practices can be liberalized and then blamed on the courts, thereby blunting criticism from rank and file guards.

G. Legislatures

The federal courts have been the most important redefiners of the legal status of marginal groups, with lawyers and federal judges the key implementers. However, to focus only on litigation would be too limited. Legislatures and executive agencies have also had key roles to play. Correctional politics is as much a legislative as a judicial game. Prisoners' rights advocates have frequently encountered intransigence and hostility among legislators, but they have also sometimes won support for important new programs. Increased legal activism by and on behalf of prisoners may have stimulated legislative support—if true, prisoners' rights litigation might be thought of as the legal counterpart of a riot, convincing recalcitrant legislators "that something must be done."

Some states moved to codify the basic requirements set forth in the landmark cases. The Illinois legislature, in 1973, enacted a comprehensive Unified Code of Corrections, addressing issues ranging from procedures for disciplinary action to availability of radios, televisions, and legal materials, and the treatment of prisoners with mental health problems (Illinois Ann. Stat. Ch. 38 § 1001-1-1 et seq. [1973]).

Other states, while continuing to delegate their rule-making authority for prisons to their correctional agencies, adopted strict rulemaking procedures, including provisions for public input and court review. California law, for example, until 1975 permitted the director of corrections to prescribe rules and regulations for the administration of the prison system and change them at his pleasure. Under the current statute he may promulgate new rules only in accordance with California's Government Code, which requires notice and public hearing prior to an exercise of rule-making authority. Furthermore, copies of proposed rules must be posted in the state's penal institutions (California Penal Code § 5058 [1970 and 1979 Supp.]). Until 1968, California Law (Penal Code § 2800) provided that a sentence to prison suspended an individual's civil rights. The section was amended in 1968 to provide what has come to be called an inmate bill of rights (*U.C.L.A. Law Review* 1973, p. 481).

In many states, legislation was necessary to establish halfway houses, work release programs, home furloughs, and grievance procedures (see, e.g., N.Y. Correction Law §§ 22-A, 22-B, 26, 139 [McKinney's Supp. 1978]). To take another example, the Minnesota legislature established an ombudsman for the department of corrections in 1973. The point is that a preoccupation with the courts should not blind us to the role of legislatures in both stimulating and impeding the goals of prisoners' rights advocates and their allies.

H. Departments of Corrections

When the federal courts began to involve themselves in prison disputes, some officials realized that written, uniform, and, most important, reasonable rules would reduce charges of unfairness, and reduce the chance of judicial intervention. Today, for example, due to a decision by a federal district judge, every rule of the Arizona Department of Corrections must be approved by the federal court (*Harris v. Cardwell*, C.A. No. 75–185 PHX–CAM, D. Ariz. 1977). The court-approved rules cover every aspect of prison operations.

Connecticut's rules and regulations run to more than four hundred pages. Some regulations track Supreme Court or lower federal court decisions, others go substantially beyond the courts. For example, prisoners are entitled to a hearing and an appeal in cases of disciplinary transfer from a minimum to a maximum security prison, despite a 1976 Supreme Court decision, *Meacham v. Fano*, 427 U.S. 215 (1976), holding that the Constitution does not require such procedures. And despite approval in *Bell v.*

Wolfish for rectal and genital searches whenever pretrial detainees meet visitors in person, Connecticut rules limit such searches to admissions from outside the institution and instances where officials have probable cause to believe that a prisoner is hiding contraband in a body cavity. *Bell v. Wolfish* itself noted that during the pendency of the case the Federal Bureau of Prisons liberalized one of the policies in dispute in the lawsuit, regarding receipt of books and magazines from sources other than the publisher. I suspect that litigation has frequently led to agency reconsideration and liberalization of policies and rules, even when not constitutionally compelled.

I. National Institute of Corrections; American Correctional Association

The National Institute of Corrections (NIC), a federal agency, has, in the past few years, played an increasingly important role in the prisoners' rights movement. NIC has sponsored research, conferences, and training programs of all sorts to institutionalize progressive legal reforms. For example, in conjunction with the Center for Community Justice, NIC provides training and technical assistance in the development and implementation of inmate grievance procedures. Recently it launched an ambitious project to train special masters to carry out more effectively their role of monitoring court decrees in prison cases.

It is not far-fetched to consider prison officials' key professional association, the American Correctional Association (ACA) as playing a role in the prisoners' rights movement, at least now. The ACA leadership and permanent staff are fully aware of legal developments, and through a variety of activities help to disseminate and clarify the legal requirements of prison officials. Since 1977, for example, with funding from the National Institute of Corrections, ACA has sponsored a Corrections Law Project, which exposes prison officials and state attorneys general from all over the United States to legal scholars and practicing attorneys who specialize in prisoners' rights. Perhaps even more important is the ACA's (see American Correctional Association 1978) substantial accreditation project, which attempts to hold state and local prisons and jails to comprehensive and progressive confinement conditions and practices.

II. Identifying and Evaluating the Impacts of the Prisoners' Rights Movement

The prisoners' rights movement is controversial. Some critics are deeply troubled by what they view as excessive judicial meddling in matters that would best be left to state legislatures and executive agencies (Glazer 1975). Other critics, or at least "doubters," are themselves prisoners' rights activists, but they judge reform through litigation to be torturously slow and often ineffective. In order to assess the validity of these criticisms, and to understand the intellectual and political milieu in which prisoners' rights activity is now being evaluated, it is necessary to sample the larger controversy over judicial involvement in reform of complex institutions like prisons, mental institutions, and school systems.

Some criticism of the role of courts in "institutional litigation" derives from objections rooted in political philosophy. Since the founding of the Republic there has been controversy over the proper role of the Supreme Court and the inferior federal courts. Those who favor majoritarian rule have always been troubled by the power of American courts to impose their value judgments on the society and to overrule other branches of government (see e.g. Bickel 1962). They have also opposed federal court "supervision" of state institutions on federalism grounds. Of course, a powerful case can and has been made for the opposite position (see e.g. Fiss 1979). My concern is not to debate political philosophy but merely to stress that the perceptions of various observers and commentators regarding the success of institutional litigation is colored by their underlying philosophical views.

Those who decry judicial activism as politically suspect are also likely to brand judicial efforts to resolve controversies in prison as misguided and counterproductive. Critics of judicial involvement in institutional litigation point to the inherent unsuitability of adjudication to resolve such controversies. Drawing upon Professor Fuller's classic (1978) article "The Forms and Limits of Adjudication," they may argue that the "social logic" of courts makes their primary role the adjudication of clear cut two-party disputes. The further courts stray from their traditional adjudicatory function, according to this view, the less effective they are. And this especially holds true for "polycentric" disputes, a category not clearly defined by Fuller, but undoubtedly embracing complicated institutional litigation involving multiple and interrelated interests and issues.

In what is sure to become a classic article, Owen Fiss (1979) directly challenges Fuller's contention that dispute resolution is the primary function of courts. While Fiss's argument is a systematic assault on Fuller's model, for my purposes it is enough to note that for Fiss "courts exist to give meaning to our public values." Thus, there is nothing odd, unusual, or parasitic (to use Fuller's term) about courts attempting to vindicate rights threatened by public bureaucracies. What has changed, in Fiss's view, is not the function of courts, but the form of adjudication. The emergence of a society dominated by large-scale organizations requires that courts shape their procedures to a new reality.

> The structural suit is one in which a judge, confronting a state bureaucracy over values of constitutional dimension, undertakes to restructure the organization to eliminate a threat to those values posed by the present institutional arrangement. The injunction is the means by which these reconstructive directives are transmitted. (Fiss 1979, p. 2)

The political or normative criticism of court intervention in institutional disputes is supplemented by an instrumental criticism—courts are not competent to adjudicate disputes involving complicated institutional policies, procedures, resources, and styles of administration. Perhaps the most sophisticated version of this criticism has been made by Donald Horowitz (1977). He argues that the following attributes of adjudication make it unsuitable for resolving complicated social problems: (1) adjudication is focused (the emphasis on rights implies disregard of costs); (2) adjudication is piecemeal; (3) courts must act when litigants call; (4) fact-finding in adjudication is ill adapted to the ascertainment of social facts; (5) adjudication makes no provision for policy review.

This is not the appropriate place for a rebuttal to Horowitz (but see Fiss 1979; Eisenberg and Yeazell 1980). Adjudication does have limitations in resolving certain kinds of controversies, but legislatures and administrative agencies, as he recognizes, also have their limitations. Their failures are easily as numerous as judicial failures. And despite their limitations, courts have certain institutional advantages in dealing with "public law litigation." Courts have some insulation from political pressures. They can tailor solutions to particular situations, involve parties who otherwise might be left out, and generate useful information which will not be filtered through the rigid structures and the preconceptions of bureaucracies. Courts provide an effective mechanism for registering and responding to grievances generated by the operation of public programs in a regulatory state and can fashion solutions flexibly, without a bureaucratic straightjacket (see Chayes 1976, p. 1308).

Not only those who oppose institutional litigation in principle and on the merits see courts as ineffective in institutional litigation. So vigorous a prison reform advocate as Leonard Orland (1975, p. 63) writes despairingly that "in the last analysis, the judicial struggle is an almost hopeless one; moreover, it carries enormous cost to prisoner, correctional administrator and court alike." And the director of the ACLU's National Prison Project concludes that "most prisons are so diseased and bankrupt that [litigation] achievements represent only the smallest and earliest steps of a very long journey" (Bronstein 1977). "Movement lawyers," even as they continue to struggle for prison reform in the courts, complain that judges are basically conservative and wedded to the status quo (e.g. Lottman 1976).

One can understand the frustration. Reform through litigation is time-consuming, frustrating, and often unsuccessful; of course, so are efforts to solve intractable social problems through comprehensive legislation or agency activism. Litigation moves slowly. Progress oft-times is measured in years. Judicial proceedings are expensive and time-consuming. Plaintiffs are paroled, or die, or lose interest. The career structures of prisoners' rights lawyers are unstable: funding is uncertain and career progressions are ambiguous. Lawyers for the state and for agency personnel come and go. Election outcomes bring new political regimes, and lawsuits can often be disrupted by the disappearance of prison administrators. When cases are resolved and injunctions are issued, compliance is not always obtained: sometimes because of willful obstructionism, sometimes because of bureaucratic incapacity to make changes, and sometimes because of political problems and inadequate resources.

Judicial decrees are not self-executing. Sometimes the persistent efforts of lawyers are needed to prevent the case from being only a hollow victory. Sometimes even those efforts are not enough. Although judges have the power to hold noncomplying administrators in contempt, they are reluctant to take such drastic remedial action. In complicated "totality of conditions" cases, federal judges have sometimes turned to special masters to help monitor compliance, gather information, and resolve ongoing disputes between the parties. But the special master is not an institutional panacea either. If the master lacks a full-time appointment and a staff, which is usually the case, he may simply not possess the capacity to see that a structural injunction is fully implemented (see *Yale Law Journal* 1975; *Harvard Law Review* 1977; Nathan 1979). Even under the best of circumstances, the special master or other court appointed monitor (i.e. citizens' committee) must depend upon the institution's staff for information as to whether a decree is being followed.

Notwithstanding these problems, I think it would be hard for anyone who studies America's prisons and jails not to conclude that enormous changes have occurred in the last two decades. For example, the editors of the *U.C.L.A. Law Review* (1973, p. 502), in their survey of judicial intervention in California prisons, found that "all of the administrators responding to the questionnaire agreed that some changes in correctional procedures, regulations, and facilities have come about specifically because administrators have anticipated what courts might do and have acted accordingly." Likewise, Professor Lawrence Bershad, former legal adviser to the District of Columbia Department of Corrections, observes (1977, p. 60) that "agency heads in most of the large cities and states find themselves having to anticipate the persuasive impact that a major prison law decision made elsewhere will have on their jurisdictions. As corrections move sharply toward a legal due process model and away from the familiar and untrammelled authority inherent in the correctional chain of command, subject only to the dictates of the governor and the legislature, most wardens and administrators find themselves in the position of reacting to and coping with court decisions." William Bennett Turner (1979, p. 639), an experienced litigator on behalf of prisoners, reaches much the same conclusion after an exhaustive nationwide study of prisoners' civil rights suits from 1973 to 1977: "Nearly everyone we interviewed believed that the cases have had great impact. Many have pointed out that even losing cases have resulted in reform." And finally, Allen Breed, former head of California's Youth Authority and the present director of the National Institute of Corrections, remarked in a recent speech that "the role of courts over the past fifteen years in acting as a catalyst for much needed change in our nation's prisons cannot be overemphasized." My own observations and interviews with prisoners and prison officials around the country lead me to the same conclusion. Perhaps the discrepancy between those who think the prisoners' rights movement has been ineffective and those who see it as the crucial influence on prison reform may be explained by the absence of a methodology for identifying impacts and the absence of criteria for judging their importance.

A. The Problem of Identifying Impacts

I argued earlier that two decades of effort to transform the legal status of prisoners should be viewed as a sociopolitical movement. It will not do to describe or analyze the prisoners' rights movement in terms of the breadth or narrowness of particular court holdings, or even in terms of administrative com-

454   James B. Jacobs

pliance with court orders. Some of the most important effects of the prisoners' rights movement include the organization of prisoners, citizen and interest group mobilization, legislative and administrative budget-making decisions and law-making, professional standard-setting, and the redistribution of power inside the prisons (see Jacobs 1977). Narrow impact studies do not deal with these secondary effects. They focus, almost always, on the ability of courts to achieve compliance with their decrees. But even this subject is fraught with conceptual and methodological difficulties, as I hope to show.

B. The Problem of the Worst Case

Almost all critics of the propriety or effectiveness of judicial activism in reform of complex institutions have based their conclusions on a few "worst cases," such as South Boston High School (school desegregation), Partlow Hospital in Alabama (institutions for the mentally ill and retarded), and Cummings and Tucker Prison Farms in Arkansas (prisons). Critics point out that, in cases like these, litigation dragged on for years, "communities" became polarized, and the courts were never entirely successful in achieving their goals; sometimes, unintended secondary effects like "white flight" defeated the goals of reform.

It is difficult, as I will argue later on, to know what "success" is in cases like these. Surely it would be naïve to imagine that the worst, most neglected, prisons in America could be renovated overnight to resemble the best facilities anywhere. At this point, however, I want to emphasize that for every instance of protracted institutional litigation like that involving the Arkansas prisons, there exist a dozen run-of-the-mill cases and consent decrees in which constitutional violations are remedied without such high drama.

To be fair, I must admit that the preceding assertion is only my impression. To be systematic we should examine as comprehensively as possible the responses over time to prisoner demands for greater rights and entitlements in a representative sample of jails and prisons throughout the country. While no such comprehensive survey has yet been carried out, it would likely find enormous variations in almost everything having to do with jails and prisons. Some prisons and jails have been the focus of a great deal more legal activity than others. This may be accounted for by such factors as particularly bad conditions, the presence of politicized prisoners, the existence of outside legal resources, the fortuity of a "liberal" federal district judge, or some combination of these. In a real sense, there is no "typical" American jail or prison. Enormous variation exists across regions, and even among states in the same region, and jurisdictions within the same state. Thus, fully to evaluate the impact of the prisoners' rights movement requires a more precise understanding of the extent of variance among federal district courts and among penal facilities.

Some prison officials welcome judicial intervention and have used the courts to obtain resources which otherwise would have been unobtainable (Schwartz 1972, p. 791). Shrewd reform-oriented administrators can sign consent decrees and blame change on the courts—as a tactic for overcoming anticipated staff opposition. In some prisons, top officials cannot implement changes even when they desire to do so, because of administrative ineffectiveness, poor morale, and incomplete bureaucratization. Of course, compliance often depends upon the cooperation of other state officials, including the governor and legislature. We need to follow a cohort of cases through the federal courts to see how the "typical case" is resolved (see Turner 1979). Short of that, we must rely on impressions drawn from a few extraordinary cases which receive disproportionate attention and surely distort our perception of the amount of conflict produced by legal change and the amount of institutional resistance to change.

C. The Difficulty of Defining Success

How can one tell whether the judicial resolution of a particular controversy has been successfully implemented? If the mark of success is a restructured institution where all interests have been harmonized, and where the original intent of the court has not only been followed to the letter but has produced no dysfunctions, even years later, no institutional litigation will ever succeed. A perceptive student comment in the *Harvard Law Review* (1977, p. 434) puts the matter bluntly, and in my view correctly:

> Yet failure is a function of expectations: we tend to expect complete protection of all legal rights by someone—either legislator, administrator, or judge. However, given intense conflicts of interest, lack of cooperation among necessary parties, shortage of resources, and the complexities of control and unresponsiveness that characterize organizations, the probability of full implementation of reform policies is likely to be quite low.

Prison and mental health bureaucracies are large and complicated. They are frequently racked by conflicting goals and competing staff factions. Needless to say, prisons rarely function "smoothly." Perhaps the question should not be whether a particular court intervention on behalf of prisoners was "successful," but whether it made a positive contribution to prisoners' lives or to prison administration. Even to answer this question, however, will be difficult, particularly when there will be disagreement about which organizational changes—for example, improved programs, freer correspondence policy, a better warden, lower guard morale—can be attributed to a particular court intervention, to the more active role of courts generally, or to the prisoners' rights movement broadly defined. And how will we judge the net effect of changes that point in opposite directions—for example, less severe and arbitrary punishments, but more inmate-on-inmate aggressions? I do not pretend to have a methodology for evaluating impacts; in this essay I will be content to point out the complexity of the problem. (Recent writing on the impact of prisoners' rights litigation includes Champagne and Haas 1976; Calhoun 1978; Glick 1973; Hawkins 1976; Rubin 1974; on the general subject of legal impact studies, see Brown and Crowley 1979.)

D. The Problem of Assessing Compliance

Simply to measure the extent to which a particular prison administration complies with a particular court decision is not a satisfactory way to assess the impacts of the prisoners' rights movement on institutions; the most important impacts may operate indirectly. But even in measuring compliance with court decrees we encounter substantial conceptual difficulty. How can one tell whether an injunction has been complied with? Initially one needs to know what the decision required. But many declaratory judgments, consent decrees, and injunctions in prison cases are ambiguous. Many details are deliberately left to the parties to resolve. The court may retain jurisdiction for several years. What is required is often not apparent for some time after the initial decision. Reasonable men may differ sharply on what a decree "really means."

Nor is it clear when compliance should be measured. Immediately following a decree there may be confusion, limited resources, and lack of organizational skill. Considerable time must pass before we can know whether inactivity is merely the temporary product of inefficiency and turmoil or is instead a "failure of compliance." However, as time passes, intervening variables emerge to confound evaluation. Initial compliance may quickly be eradicated by new events. No directed social change can be expected to persist in perpetuity. That more lawsuits are later necessary to vindicate previously declared rights or to establish new ones need not mean that the original court intervention "failed."

E. Hypotheses on the Impacts of the Prisoners' Rights Movement

One way to think about the impacts of the prisoners' rights movement is to determine the extent to which changing legal norms have been implemented. Another way is to consider how the changing legal status of prisoners is reflected in social, political, and organizational change. This second approach requires a good deal of speculation and imagination, even intuition, but in the end it may provide a more profound understanding of the prisoners' rights movement. Based on my own reading and research, the following hypotheses suggest the kinds of empirical research and theory building which need to go on if we are to increase our understanding of the impact of legal change on prisons.

1. *The prisoners' rights movement has contributed to the bureaucratization of the prison.* As Max Weber (1954) pointed out, there is a close relationship between law and bureaucracy. Until recently, prisons operated as traditional, nonbureaucratic institutions (Jacobs 1977). There were no written rules and regulations, and daily operating procedures were passed down from one generation to the next. Wardens spoke of prison administration as an "art"; they operated by intuition. The ability of the administration to act as it pleased reinforced its almost total dominance of the inmates.

Early lawsuits revealed the inability of prison officials to justify or even to explain their procedures. The courts increasingly demanded rational decision-making processes and written rules and regulations; sometimes they even demanded better security procedures. The prisons required more support staff to meet the increasing demand for "documentation." New bureaucratic offices and practices began to appear. Lawrence Bershad (1977, p. 58) notes, "Court-imposed due process requirements have made extensive and time consuming documentation a necessity." Harris and Spiller (1977, p. 24) draw the following conclusion from their comprehensive study of four cases of protracted jail and prison litigation: "By focusing attention on the severe deficiencies of the correctional system, the litigation created pressure for management reforms. Contemporaneously with the litigation, or soon thereafter, a broad range of important changes occurred. Those changes assumed different forms—new organizational structure, increased funding, new administrators, changes in personnel policies, new facilities, additional personnel, improved management procedures, etc. These changes were generally considered beneficial" (see also Jacobs 1977, chaps. 5 and 6).

2. *The prisoners' rights movement has produced a new gen-*

eration of administrators. Litigation created pressures to establish rational operating procedures, to clarify lines of authority, and to focus responsibility. Wardens were required to testify in court. Their rules and practices were subject to blistering cross-examination. The despotic wardens of the old regime were neither temperamentally nor administratively suited to operate in the more complex environment fostered by court judgments and gradually have been replaced by a new administrative elite, which is better educated and more bureaucratically minded (Alexander 1978).

3. *The prisoners' rights movement expanded the procedural protections available to prisoners.* The Supreme Court, in *Wolff v. McDonnell,* 418 U.S. 539 (1974), ruled that prisoners were entitled to rudimentary procedural protections when faced with forfeiture of good time or with special punitive confinement. The extension of procedural due process to prisoners continues, despite setbacks (see e.g. *Meacham v. Fano,* 427 U.S. 215 [1976]). *Vitek v. Jones,* 48 U.S.L.W. 4317 (1980), affirms the prisoner's right to a hearing before transfer to a mental hospital.

Many legislatures and administrative agencies responsible for operating prisons also mandated more procedures in a variety of decision-making contexts. Many corrections departments have instituted prison grievance procedures which provide a formal and orderly mechanism for dispute resolution; some provide for final step arbitration by a neutral outsider (Breed 1976; Breed and Voss 1978; Singer and Keating 1973; Keating 1975, 1976). Recent federal legislation requires the attorney general to promulgate "minimum standards" for inmate grievance proceedings and to certify whether the states are in substantial compliance.

4. *The prisoners' rights movement has heightened public awareness of prison conditions.* Prison cases are increasingly brought to the attention of the public through the mass media. In 1976, the *New York Times* reported on prisoners' rights litigation on seventy-eight different occasions, accounting for 16 percent of its total prison coverage. Prisoners' rights cases made the CBS national news on eight separate occasions (Brooks and Jacobs 1980). Prison litigation may be the peaceful equivalent of

a riot, in bringing prisoners' grievances to public attention and in mobilizing political support for change. On this point the observations of Harris and Spiller (1977, p. 26) are instructive:

> The litigation sensitized public officials and public servants to correctional deficiencies and increased responsiveness to correctional needs. Legislative, regulatory, and supervisory bodies adopted rules, provided funds, and took other actions that facilitated correctional improvements. Changes were initiated that had not been ordered by the courts. In each jurisdiction, progressive administrators were able to take advantage of the general climate change that accompanied the litigation. In a sense, the court was used as a "scapegoat" and the court orders as a tool for improving correctional programs.

5. *The prisoners' rights movement has politicized prisoners and heightened their expectations.* The availability of judicial forums encouraged prisoners to believe that their grievances would be redressed. But it is not clear that the movement has assuaged prisoners' discontent; to the contrary, it may have intensified it. Indeed, it would be surprising in light of historical experience if rising expectations did not outpace the realities of reform. This may increase frustration and fuel prison tensions, but at the same time maintain a high level of prisoner pressures for continued improvements in prison conditions. Fred Cohen (1972, p. 864) provides the following insight on the prisoners' rights movement's psychological impact on prisoners:

> In my own experience in visiting and talking with numerous inmates (adult and juvenile) and parolees, there can be no doubt that their self-image has been dramatically altered. Where two or three years ago the questions asked of me would be almost exclusively concerned with defects in the conviction or, with regard to prison conditions, loss of good time and the vagaries of detainers, now the discussion focuses on *rights. . . . Advances that are not attributed to prison rebellions seem most closely linked to successful litigation.* That this may prove to be dangerously

romantic and disillusioning is the one point that I hope
remains with the reader. [My emphasis.]

6. *The prisoners' right movement has demoralized prison staff.*
There is some basis to believe that today's correctional officers
are more insecure, both morally and legally, about their position
vis-à-vis inmates (Jacobs and Crotty 1978) than were their
predecessors. Staff resent the inmates' access to the courts
(*U.C.L.A. Law Review* 1973, p. 494). They resent even more
the impression that courts believe the prisoners, and "favor them"
over the guards. Leo Carroll's (1974, p. 54) research at Rhode
Island's maximum security prison led him to observe:

> The result of these [judicial] intrusions upon the coercive
> powers of the custodians has not only been normlessness in
> the area of job performance, but also a deterioration of
> the working relationships among the custodians. Like the
> police in the case of the Miranda decision, the officers
> view the court decisions as placing the law and the courts
> on the side of the inmate and in opposition to them. By
> extending legal rights to inmates, restricting the power
> of the officers and placing the institution on eighteen
> months probation, the decision makes the prisoners the
> "good guys." In short, the officers feel themselves
> betrayed and "sold out" by agencies that should support
> their authority. These agencies are not only the courts but
> the Department of Corrections itself. The nature of the
> court ruling was in the form of a consent decree, a
> compromise agreement between counsel for the plaintiffs
> and the Department of Corrections. The officers interpret
> this action as a betrayal by their own superiors.

Not only the officers but the top administrators also may
resent being "second guessed" by the courts. It takes a high
degree of professionalism to accept that courts have their job
to do and must test administrative practice against statutory
and constitutional requirements. Thus, Lawrence Bershad (1977,
p. 61) notes:

Courts define correctional staff consistently as defendants —a startling role change for people who entered prison work ostensibly for a combination of law enforcement and social work reasons. Correctional administrators no longer live in obscurity; rather their thoughts are memorialized in court transcripts and their careers become the subject of debate in the media.

Added to the psychological impact of frequent publicity is the consistent failure to persuade the courts of the wisdom and 'rightness' of correctional methodology. Thus, frustration, bitterness, confusion, and demoralization inevitably result, although usually without public expression.

7. *The prisoners' rights movement has made it more difficult to maintain control over prisoners.* The prisoners' rights movement has brought about significant limitations on the punishments that can be used against prisoners. Starvation, whipping, standing at attention, and exposure to freezing temperatures have been eliminated. There are also restrictions on the reasons for which a prisoner can be punished. Guard brutality may also have been deterred (although hardly stamped out) by the threat of liability for money damages in a suit for prisoner abuse. The net result is that prisoners are harder to control. More staff may be necessary to maintain order. Less punitive but possibly more intrusive mechanisms of control are now becoming more popular—closed circuit televisions, more frequent use of tear gas, sophisticated locking systems, and unit management which seeks to limit inmate movement and contact.

8. *The prisoners' rights movement has contributed to a professional movement within corrections to establish national standards.* At least among the top correctional leadership, there is a strong desire to avoid the embarrassment of judicial scrutiny and denunciation. These officials do not want to be rebuked in federal court for poor administration and maintenance of inhumane institutions. Like workers generally, they place a high value on autonomy—they would strongly prefer to run the prisons without outside intervention. There is a growing feeling that

good administrators stay "ahead of the courts." Professional rule making and standard setting is seen as an opportunity to increase correctional resources, improve conditions, and shield the profession from scathing outside criticism. The American Correctional Association, the professional organization of American prison officials, has recently embarked upon a concerted accrediting process, based upon rigorous standards covering almost all aspects of prison management (American Correctional Association 1978). If, as appears likely, most states voluntarily agree to subject their penal facilities to accreditation review, the process could have an enormous influence on corrections in the next decade.

III. Assessing the Significance of the Prisoners' Rights Movement

Many prison observers, including lawyers, express misgivings over the benefits brought about by the prisoners' rights movement. Perhaps some prisoners' rights advocates hoped that the recognition and vindication of constitutional rights would dismantle the entire American prison system. To their disappointment, the same facilities and many traditional problems remain; even the best run, most benign prison remains an institution of punishment. They have therefore concluded that expansion of prisoners' rights and judicial reform will not significantly change the "system."

The indirect effects of the prisoners' rights movement are difficult to identify and difficult to evaluate. Is it better or worse that today's prison is more fully bureaucratized than the prison of a decade ago? Some of the autocratic wardens may have been rooted out of corrections, but excessive bureaucratization has its own dysfunctions. Prisoners may find something insensitive and inhuman about administration by the book. While bureaucratization was a response to an earlier form of organization which could not justify its decisions or focus responsibility, excessive bureaucratization may lead to the same result: a mass of offices and office holders insulated from effective outside scrutiny.

Closely related to the advent of bureaucratization is the proliferation of due process. Here too, one can legitimately question whether more and better procedures have led to higher quality and better outcomes. The Harvard Center for Criminal Justice (1972) found positive prisoner reaction to the disciplinary procedures implemented by *Morris v. Travisono*, 310 F. Supp. 857 (D.R.I. 1970), although the researchers themselves doubted the significance of the procedural changes. My Stateville study (Jacobs 1977) revealed no change in the numbers of prisoners sent to disciplinary confinement, nor in the offenses charged after the establishment of disciplinary due process. That the same personnel continued to make the decisions under the new rules undercut the value of the improved procedures. But the involvement of the central office of the Illinois Corrections Department in final-step grievance resolution has produced a credible administrative vehicle for dealing with complaints. While the "justice model" (Fogel 1975) remains to be fully elaborated and tested it remains an intriguing possibility for a new organizational model built upon the rule of law.

It is a speculation worth pursuing that the prisoners' rights movement has made the provision of welfare benefits to prisoners more logical and legitimate (see e.g. *New York University Law Review* 1976). A recent study by Abt Associates documents the large increase of noncustodial service-type personnel in American prisons since 1950, especially in the past decade. Therapists, teachers, counselors, and medical technicians have become visible members of the prison regime. Schooling has almost achieved the status of a right. The prisons constitute school districts in some states (see Miller 1978). Availability of a school education seems to be nearly universal. Tuition-free programs in which prisoners can earn college credits are also common (Seashore and Haberfeld 1976). At Attica one-sixth of the prisoners are enrolled in college or junior college programs.

In the last several years, and particularly since the Supreme Court's decision in *Estelle v. Gamble*, 429 U.S. 97 (1976), there has been substantial improvement in prison medical services (Neisser 1977). In 1975, at Stateville, there was only a handful of medical personnel. In 1979, the Illinois Department of Corrections and Prison Legal Services signed a consent decree which called for a medical staff of forty-eight persons (*Cook v. Rowe,* No. 76 C 2224, N.D. Ill. 1979). Care is to be provided around the clock and includes the services of medical technicians stationed in each cell house, fully qualified nurses, a half-dozen dentists, several doctors, a physical therapist, and an X-ray technician. The American Medical Association sponsors an influential prison medical services project and publications program to improve medical care and health services in correctional institutions. As in other prison areas, suits over medical care have spurred the development of American Correctional Association accreditation standards.

The direct effects of the prisoners' rights movement are easier to identify, if difficult to quantify. In practically every prison in the United States one could point to concrete improvements in administrative practices and living conditions directly attributable to the prisoners' rights movement. Inmates who previously were not permitted to have the Koran, religious medallions, political and sociological monographs, and law books now possess them. Inmates once afraid to complain to relatives and public officials about their treatment are now less afraid. Censorship of outgoing mail has been all but eliminated. Censorship of incoming mail is less thorough and intrusive, increasing the privacy of written communication. Prisoners in isolation, segregation, and other disciplinary confinement suffer less from brutal punishments, cold, hunger, infested and filthy cells, and boredom. In some cases, Arkansas, for example, unspeakable tortures have been stopped. In some jails and penitentiaries, prisoners are spared the misery of greater overcrowding than already exists because court decrees limit the number of inmates. In numerous institutions major advances in the quality and delivery of medical services can be directly attributed to court decisions.

None of this denies the considerable suffering still imposed upon those who are incarcerated in the United States. The question is whether the prisoners' rights movement has made things significantly better. One's answer depends upon one's definition of "significantly" and some standard of reform against which current efforts can be compared. An exploration of the legal rights of prisoners inevitably leads to philosophical questions about the nature of imprisonment in a democratic society. To what extent must it be punitive and impose suffering? In my opinion, neither the extension of the rights of citizenship to prisoners nor judicial scrutiny of prison conditions and practices will alter the punitive reality of imprisonment any more than expansion of the franchise and passage of equal employment legislation will alter the reality of the ghetto. In neither case am I ready to conclude that legal reform is not significant or important, although, to be sure, one must recognize the limits of legal reform. The prisoners' rights movement has not transformed the American prison into a utopian institution and will not.

Prisons are too often dilapidated, overcrowded, underfunded, and poorly governed. Still, the impact of prisoners' rights must be judged in light of social and political realities, and in my view, seen in that light, the movement has contributed greatly to the reduction of brutality and degradation, the enhancement of decency and dignity, and the promotion of rational governance.

REFERENCES

Alexander, Elizabeth. 1978. "New Prison Administrators and the Court: New Directions in Prison Law," *Texas Law Review* 56: 963–1008.

American Bar Association. 1977. "Tentative Draft of Standards Relating to the Legal Status of Prisoners," *American Criminal Law Review* (Special Issue).

American Bar Association, Resource Center on Correctional Law and Legal Services. 1974. "Providing Legal Services to Prisoners," *Georgia Law Review* 8:363–432.

American Bar Association, Commission on Correctional Facilities and Services. 1975. *When Society Pronounces Judgment.* Washington, D.C.: American Bar Association.

American Correctional Association. 1978. *Accreditation: Blueprint for Corrections.* Washington, D.C.: American Correctional Association.

Bershad, Lawrence. 1977. "Law and Corrections: A Management Perspective," *New England Journal of Prison Law* 4:49–82.

Bickel, Alexander M. 1962. *The Least Dangerous Branch.* Indianapolis: Bobbs-Merrill.

Breed, Allen F. 1976. "Instituting California's Ward Grievance Procedure: An Inside Perspective," *Loyola of Los Angeles Law Review* 10:113–25.

Breed, Allen F., and Paul H. Voss. 1978. "Procedural Due Process in the Discipline of Incarcerated Juveniles," *Pepperdine Law Review* 5:641–71.

Brierley, J. R. 1971. "The Legal Controversy as It Relates to Correctional Institutions—a Prison Administrator's View," *Villanova Law Review* 16:1070–76.

Bronstein, Alvin J. 1977. "Reform Without Change: The Future of Prisoners' Rights," *Civil Liberties Review* 4:27–45.

Brooks, H., and J. Jacobs. 1980. "Public Opinion and the Prison: An Analysis of the News Media's Coverage." Unpublished paper, Department of Sociology, Cornell University.

Brown, D. W., and D. W. Crowley. 1979. "The Societal Impact of Law: an Assessment of Research," *Law and Policy Quarterly* 1:253–84.

Calhoun, E. 1978. "The Supreme Court and the Constitutional Rights of Prisoners: A Reappraisal," *Hastings Constitutional Law Quarterly* 4:219–47.

Cardarelli, A. P., and M. M. Finkelstein. 1974. "Correctional Administrators Assess the Adequacy and Impact of Prison Legal Services Programs in the United States," *Journal of Criminal Law and Criminology* 65:91–102.

Carroll, Leo. 1974. *Hacks, Blacks and Cons: Race Relations in a Maximum Security Prison.* Lexington, Mass.: D. C. Heath.

Champagne, A., and K. C. Haas. 1976. "The Impact of *Johnson v. Avery* on Prison Administration," *Tennessee Law Review* 43:275–306.

Chayes, Abram. 1976. "The Role of the Judge in Public Law Litigation," *Harvard Law Review* 89:1281–1316.

Clemmer, Donald. 1940. *The Prison Community.* New York: Holt, Rinehart & Winston.

Cohen, Fred. 1972. "The Discovery of Prison Reform," *Buffalo Law Review* 21:855–87.

Eisenberg, T., and S. C. Yeazell. 1980. "The Ordinary–Extraordinary in Institutional Litigation," *Harvard Law Review* 93:465–517.

Fiss, Owen. 1978. *The Civil Rights Injunction.* Bloomington: Indiana University Press.

———. 1979. "The Forms of Justice," *Harvard Law Review* 93:1–58.

Fogel, David. 1975. *"We Are the Living Proof . . .": The Justice Model for Corrections*. Cincinnati: W. H. Anderson Co.

Frank, Jerome. 1949. *Courts on Trial: Myth and Reality in American Justice*. Princeton: Princeton University Press.

Frankel, Marvin. 1976. "The Adversary Judge," *Texas Law Review* 54:465–87.

Fuller, Lon L. 1978. "The Forms and Limits of Adjudication," *Harvard Law Review* 92:353–409. (The initial version of this paper was circulated to the members of the Legal Philosophy Discussion Group at Harvard Law School in 1957. A revised and expanded version was prepared for use in Mr. Fuller's course in jurisprudence in 1961; that version was published in the *Review*.)

Glazer, Nathan. 1975. "Towards an Imperial Judiciary," *Public Interest* 41:104–23.

Harris, M. Kay, and D. P. Spiller, Jr. 1977. *After Decision: Implementation of Judicial Decrees in Correctional Settings*. Washington, D.C.: U.S. Department of Justice, Law Enforcement Assistance Administration.

Harvard Center for Criminal Justice. 1972. "Judicial Intervention in Prison Discipline," *Journal of Criminal Law and Criminology* 63:200–28.

Harvard Law Review, Note. 1977. "Implementation Problems in Institutional Reform Litigation," *Harvard Law Review* 91:428–63.

Hawkins, Gordon. 1976. *The Prison: Policy and Practice*. Chicago: University of Chicago Press.

Hirschkop, Philip, and M. A. Millemann. 1969. "The Unconstitutionality of Prison Life," *Virginia Law Review* 55:795–839.

Horowitz, D. L. 1977. *The Courts and Social Policy*. Washington, D.C.: The Brookings Institution.

Irwin, John. 1980. *Prisons in Turmoil*. Boston: Little, Brown.

Jacobs, James B. 1976. "Stratification and Conflict among Prison Inmates," *Journal of Criminal Law and Criminology*, 66:476–82.

———. 1977. *Stateville: The Penitentiary in Mass Society*. Chicago: University of Chicago Press.

———. 1979a. *Individual Rights and Institutional Authority: Prisons, Mental Hospitals, Schools and Military*. Indianapolis: Bobbs-Merrill Co.

———. 1979b. "Race Relations and the Prisoner Subculture." In *Crime and Justice: An Annual Review of Research*, vol. 1, ed. Norval Morris and Michael Tonry. Chicago: University of Chicago Press.

Jacobs, James B., and N. Crotty. 1978. *Guard Unions and the Future of the Prisons*. Ithaca, New York: Cornell University, New York State School of Industrial and Labor Relations Press.

Keating, J. M. 1975. "Arbitration of Inmate Grievances," *Arbitration Journal* 30:177–90.

———. 1976. "The Justice Model Applied: A New Way to Handle the Complaints of California Youth Authority Awards," *Loyola of Los Angeles Law Review* 10:126–48.

Lottman, Michael. 1976. "Enforcement of Judicial Decrees: Now Comes the Hard Part," *Mental Disability Law Reporter* 1:69–76.

Mannheim, Karl. 1940. *Man and Society in an Age of Reconstruction*. New York: Harcourt Brace Jovanovich.

Miller, L. M. P. 1978. "Toward Equality of Educational Opportunity Through School Districts in State Bureaus: An Innovation in Correction Education," *Harvard Journal on Legislation* 15:221–96.

McCormack, Wayne. 1975. "The Expansion of Federal Question Jurisdiction and the Prisoner Complaint Caseload," *Wisconsin Law Review* 1975:523–51.

Nathan, V. M. 1979. "The Use of Masters in Institutional Reform Litigation," *University of Toledo Law Review* 10:419–64.

National Council on Crime and Delinquency. 1966. *Standard Act for State Correctional Services*. Paramus, N.J.: National Council on Crime and Delinquency.

———. 1972. *A Model Act for the Protection of Rights of Prisoners*. Paramus, N.J.: National Council on Crime and Delinquency.

Neisser, E. 1977. "Is there a Doctor in the Joint? The Search for Constitutional Standards for Prison Health Care," *Virginia Law Review* 63:921–73.

Orland, Leon. 1975. "Can We Establish the Rule of Law in Prisons?" *Civil Liberties Review* 2:57–67.

New York University Law Review, Note. 1976. "Workers' Compensation for Prisoners," *New York University Law Review* 51:478–92.

Rothman, D. 1973. "Decarcerating Prisoners and Patients," *Civil Liberties Review* 1:8–30.

———. 1980. *Prison Reform in the Progressive Era*. New York: Harper & Row.

Rubin, S. 1974. "The Impact of Court Decisions on the Correctional Process," *Crime and Delinquency* 20:129–34.

Scheingold, Stuart A. 1974. *The Politics of Rights*. New Haven: Yale University Press.

Schwartz, Herman. 1972. "A Comment on Sostre v. McGinnis," *Buffalo Law Review* 21:775–93.

Seashore, Marjorie, and S. Haberfeld. 1976. *Prisoner Education: Project Newgate and Other College Programs.* New York: Praeger.

Singer, Linda R., and J. M. Keating. 1973. "Prisoner Grievance Mechanisms," *Crime and Delinquency* 19:367–77.

Turner, William B. 1979. "When Prisoners Sue: A Study of Prisoner Section 1983 Suits in the Federal Courts," *Harvard Law Review* 92:610–63.

U.C.L.A. Law Review, Note. 1973. "Judicial Intervention in Corrections: the California Experience—An Empirical Study," *U.C.L.A. Law Review* 20:452–575.

U.S. Administrative Office of the United States Courts. 1979. *Annual Report of the Director.* Washington, D.C.: U.S. Administrative Office of the United States Courts.

U.S. Department of Justice. 1978. *Federal Standards for Corrections: Draft, 1978.* Washington, D.C.: U.S. Department of Justice.

Washington and Lee Law Review, Note. 1968. "The Regulated Practice of the Jailhouse Lawyer," *Washington and Lee Law Review* 25:281–86.

Weber, M. 1954. *On Law in Economy and Society.* Cambridge, Mass.: Harvard University Press.

Welch, R. 1979. "Developing Prisoner Self-Help Techniques: The Early Mississippi Experience," *Prison Law Monitor* 2:105, 118–22.

Wexler, David B. 1971. "The Jailhouse Lawyer as a Paraprofessional: Problems and Prospects," *Criminal Law Bulletin* 7:139–56.

Yale Law Journal, Note. 1975. "The Wyatt Case: Implementation of a Judicial Decree Ordering Institutional Change," *Yale Law Journal* 84:1338–79.

———. 1963. "Beyond the Ken of the Courts: A Critique of Judicial Refusal to Review the Complaints of Convicts," *Yale Law Journal* 72:506–58.